Introduction
to the Theory
of Programming Languages

Prentice Hall International Series in Computer Science

C. A. R. Hoare, Series Editor

BACKHOUSE, R. C., *Program Construction and Verification*
BACKHOUSE, R. C., *Syntax of Programming Languages: Theory and practice*
DEBAKKER, J. W., *Mathematical Theory of Program Correctness*
BARR, M. and WELLS, C., *Category Theory for Computing Science*
BEN-ARI, M., *Principles of Concurrent Programming*
BIRD, R. and WADLER, P., *Introduction to Functional Programming*
BJÖRNER, D. and JONES, C. B., *Formal Specification and Software Development*
BORNAT, R., *Programming from First Principles*
BUSTARD, D., ELDER, J. and WELSH, J., *Concurrent Program Structures*
CLARK, K. L., and McCABE, F. G., *micro-Prolog: Programming in logic*
CROOKES, D., *Introduction to Programming in Prolog*
DROMEY, R. G., *How to Solve it by Computer*
DUNCAN, F., *Microprocessor Programming and Software Development*
ELDER, J., *Construction of Data Processing Software*
ELLIOTT, R. J. and HOARE, C. A. R., (eds.), *Scientific Applications of Multiprocessors*
GOLDSCHLAGER, L. and LISTER, A., *Computer Science: A modern introduction (2nd edn)*
GORDON, M. J. C., *Programming Language Theory and its Implementation*
HAYES, I. (ed.), *Specification Case Studies*
HEHNER, E. C. R., *The Logic of Programming*
HENDERSON, P., *Functional Programming: Application and implementation*
HOARE, C. A. R., *Communicating Sequential Processes*
HOARE, C. A. R., and JONES, C. B. (ed.), *Essays in Computing Science*
HOARE, C. A. R., and SHEPHERDSON, J. C. (eds.), *Mathematical Logic and Programming Languages*
HUGHES, J. G., *Database Technology: A software engineering approach*
INMOS LTD, *occam 2 Reference Manual*
JACKSON, M. A., *System Development*
JOHNSTON, H., *Learning to Program*
JONES, C. B., *Systematic Software Development using VDM (2nd edn)*
JONES, C. B. and SHAW, R. C. F. (eds.), *Case Studies in Systematic Software Development*
JONES, G., *Programming in occam*
JONES, G. and GOLDSMITH, M., *Programming in occam 2*
JOSEPH, M., PRASAD, V. R. and NATARAJAN, N., *A Multiprocessor Operating System*
LEW, A., *Computer Science: A mathematical introduction*
MacCALLUM, I., *UCSD Pascal for the IBM PC*
MARTIN, J. J., *Data Types and Data Structures*
MEYER, B., *Introduction to the Theory of Programming Languages*
MEYER, B., *Object-oriented Software Construction*
MILNER, R., *Communication and Concurrency*
MORGAN, C., *Programming from Specifications*
PEYTON JONES, S. L., *The Implementation of Functional Programming Languages*
POMBERGER, G., *Software Engineering and Modula-2*
REYNOLDS, J. C., *The Craft of Programming*
RYDEHEARD, D. E. and BURSTALL, R. M., *Computational Category Theory*
SLOMAN, M. and KRAMER, J., *Distributed Systems and Computer Networks*
SPIVEY, J. M., *The Z Notation: A reference manual*
TENNENT, R. D., *Principles of Programming Languages*
WATT, D. A., *Programming Language Concepts and Paradigms*
WATT, D. A., WICHMANN, B. A. and FINDLAY, W., *ADA: Language and methodology*
WELSH, J. and ELDER, J., *Introduction to Modula-2*
WELSH, J. and ELDER, J., *Introduction to Pascal (3rd edn)*
WELSH, J., ELDER, J. and BUSTARD, D., *Sequential Program Structures*
WELSH, J. and HAY, A., *A Model Implementation of Standard Pascal*
WELSH, J. and McKEAG, M., *Structured System Programming*
WIKSTRÖM, Å., *Functional Programming using Standard ML*

Introduction to the Theory of Programming Languages

Bertrand Meyer

Interactive Software Engineering
Santa Barbara (California)

and

Société des Outils du Logiciel
Paris

Prentice Hall

New York   London   Toronto   Sydney   Tokyo   Singapore

First published 1990 by
Prentice Hall International (UK) Ltd,
66 Wood Lane End, Hemel Hempstead.
Hertfordshire, HP2 4RG
A dvision of
Simon & Schuster International Group

Typeset by Pentacor PLC, High Wycombe, Bucks
Printed and bound in Great Britain at
the University Press, Cambridge

Library of Congress Cataloguing-in-Publication Data

Meyer, Bertrand, 1950–
    Introduction to the theory of programming languages.

    (Prentice-Hall International series in computer science)
    Bibliography: p.
    Includes index.
    1. Programming languages (Electronic computers)
2. Programming languages (Electronic computers)—
Semantics. I. Title. II. Series.
QA76.7.M49   1988   005.13   87–25862
ISBN 0–13–498510–9

British Library Cataloguing in Publication Data

Meyer, Betrand, *1950–*
    Introduction to the theory of programming languages.–
    (Prentice Hall international series in computer sciences)
    1. Electronic digital computers. Programming
    005.13

    ISBN 0–13–498510–9
    ISBN 0–13–498502–8 pbk

---

1 2 3 4 5   94 93 92 91 90

A mes parents

Preface

To specify, design, implement, read, understand, document, appreciate, criticize, test, qualify, debug, maintain, adapt, port or improve programs, we need to master the notations which serve to express their final form: programming languages.

Despite the availability of precise, sometimes painstakingly detailed descriptions, the intricacies of general-purpose programming languages often confound experts as well as novices. Over the years, however, computer scientists have developed a number of mathematical modeling techniques which provide much insight into programming languages, and, as a consequence, into programming. This book is an effort to make some of that work accessible to, and applicable by, a broader audience than the usual readership of theoretical computer science publications.

The book is directed at two categories of readers. Practicing software engineers will enjoy it, I hope, if they wish to learn more about the theoretical basis of their discipline. It is also meant as a textbook for courses on programming language semantics or theoretical computer science at the advanced undergraduate or beginning graduate level.

This volume started out as lecture notes for a two-part university course entitled "Advanced Topics in Programming Languages". It covers the material of the first part, which I devoted to a theoretical study of programming languages. (The second part, which would undoubtedly deserve a text of its own, discussed features of modern programming languages: modularity, genericity, concurrency, support for functional, logic and object-oriented programming.)

Prerequisites

There are few formal prerequisites for this book. To appreciate it, you should have a taste for the practical problems of program construction, and not be too averse to mathematical reasoning.

Many software engineers, when hearing the word "formal", understand "formidable". If this book only succeeds in convincing some of them that the mathematical basis of programming is simple, useful, and even pleasurable, it will have fulfilled part of its aims. None of the mathematics it uses is hard; all necessary concepts are defined in the text (mostly in chapter 2), and all rely on elementary set theory.

In spite of the lack of formal requirements, it will not hurt if you are familiar on the practical side with compiling techniques, and on the theoretical side with the essential results of computation theory.

Topics

I have included the following topics under the heading "theory of programming languages":

- *Syntax*, with particular emphasis on the elegant concept of abstract syntax.
- Formal *semantics*, especially the two now most widely used approaches: the denotational and axiomatic methods.
- The *complementarity* between the two main approaches to semantics, showing axiomatic and denotational descriptions as two sides of the same coin.

Two other subjects were obvious candidates for inclusion: the theory of abstract data types, and the formal study of concurrency. In spite of their relevance and interest, they were kept out of this presentation to keep its size manageable.

Structure

The book is organized as follows.

Chapter 1 discusses the notion of formal definition; it advocates the need for such definitions, but does not fail to mention their limitations. It emphasizes the differences between programming languages and mathematical notations and, more generally, between language and metalanguage, a source of frequent misunderstandings.

Chapter 2 introduces the necessary mathematical background for the discussions that follow: relations, partial and total functions, finite functions. All the concepts involved are simple and any software engineer or undergraduate student should be able to master them quickly.

Chapter 3 is devoted to the notion of abstract syntax, used subsequently as basis for all programming language specifications. It introduces a notation for abstract grammars and abstract syntactic expressions, discusses applications of abstract syntax to software tools and language design, and gives a mathematical interpretation of abstract syntax notations.

Chapter 4 gives a first introduction to formal semantics, serving three purposes: first, by using a very simple programming language (but one with side-effects, input and output, not a purely applicative language such as lambda calculus), it familiarizes the reader with the very notion of mathematical specification – a non-obvious idea for many programmers and computer science students. Second, it contrasts the various approaches to formal semantics on a simple example. Lastly, it introduces, along with the denotational and axiomatic approaches refined in the next chapters, three that are not described any further (attribute grammars, translational, and operational).

Chapter 5 introduces the theory of lambda calculus, useful both as a tool for dealing with higher-order functions in denotational semantics and as example of applicative language. Two issues with close correspondents in programming languages, substitution and typing, are discussed in some detail.

Chapter 6, the first of three chapters devoted to denotational semantics, presents the complete description of a simple but representative programming language.

Chapter 7 shows how to cover more language features in the same framework: records, pointers, input and output, block structure, routines. It also sketches the extension to classes and multiple inheritance in object-oriented programming.

Chapter 8 explains the mathematical concepts needed to justify recursive definitions. Readers familiar with earlier publications on denotational semantics will find the approach somewhat unorthodox. The aim is to present a simpler view of fixpoint theory. The discussion relies entirely on simple properties of sets and partial functions; it does not need special "bottom" elements, complete partial orders, lattices etc. (The end of the chapter does give, as supplementary material, the connection with the more common presentations.)

Chapter 9 is a presentation of axiomatic semantics, covering both Hoare's theory and Dijkstra's weakest preconditions, and extending to records, arrays and recursive routines. The last section presents the notion of assertion-based program construction, discussing systematic strategies for designing loop algorithms.

Chapter 10 on consistent definitions brings final unity to the semantic scene by showing how the rules of axiomatic semantics may be proved as theorems in the denotational theory. The techniques of chapter 8, using partial functions rather than special elements, pay off here in terms of mathematical simplicity.

Notation

Particular attention has been devoted to the notations. One reason is that the study of abstract syntax and semantics is essentially a game played with formalisms, requiring care in the design and use of notations. Another is the constant risk of confusion between language and metalanguage; this problem is particularly serious with computer science students, many of whom nowadays know more about computer languages than about elementary mathematics.

When discussing issues of notation, the text often emphasizes analogies with related issues in the design of programming languages. It is not hard to recognize the general flavor of the notations retained: they have been strongly influenced by the syntax of the Algol line of languages, and its continuation in Pascal, Ada and Eiffel. It is a tribute to the best programming language designs that their notations so readily transpose to non-programming notations.

A word of advice to both instructors and independent readers is in order. It may at first seem reasonable to accept approximate notations whenever "the basic idea is right". But this is not an appropriate attitude in such a field, where so much depends on fine formal nuances. Rigor in thinking and rigor in writing help each other. Readers are encouraged to use a well-defined set of notations when practicing the material, and instructors to be strict in enforcing consistency.

Use as a textbook

The material covered is too extensive for a one-quarter course. With senior or beginning graduate students, the instructor may wish to cover chapters 1 to 4, the first section of 5 (lambda notation, without any attempt at explaining the theory), 6, selected specifications of individual programming language features in 7, the basic concepts of 8 (recursion theory), most of 9, and the gist of 10 which in all cases provides the ideal conclusion to the course. With more advanced students the instructor may wish to cover 1 to 3 in the first two weeks, treat 4 (review of specification techniques at an elementary level) as reading assignment, and devote the rest of the course to chapters 5 to 10.

All chapters (except the first) have an exercise section. Some exercises (in particular those of Chapter 2) are designed to help the reader practice essential mathematical skills, useful in the sequel; others (especially in chapter 7 and 9) require the reader to attempt the formal specification of programming language concepts not treated in the main text.

Several exercises (in chapters 4, 5 and 6) are programming assignments, the aim being to compute formal properties of programs. They can serve as a basis for term projects.

Acknowledgments

I hope to have been able to communicate to the reader some of the illumination that programming language theory projects on one of the central areas of computer science. Any credit should go to the pioneers of this field; a look at the bibliography suffices to show where my debts lie.

I am deeply grateful to Tony Hoare (beyond his milestone contributions to the field) for suggesting that this book be published in his Series, and then for waiting patiently for the result to materialize.

I have a particular debt to Jean-Raymond Abrial, who taught me much about the relation between theory and practice in computer science.

Alain Bossavit (whose collaboration led directly to some of the material in chapter 9) and Vincent Cazala read early drafts and their suggestions were most helpful. David Gray, Jay Misra and Robert Tennent, acting as reviewers on an early version, contributed comments and criticism going far beyond what is usually expected in such a case, prompting me to request a waiving of the customary rule of anonymity.

I am grateful to the students who suffered through my courses and pointed out errors in previous versions.

Jean-Louis Armand provided moral and material support at a time when I needed it most.

Finally, I could not have finished this book, at the expense of many other activities undoubtedly more profitable to Interactive Software Engineering, without the support of Annie Meyer, Jean-Marc Nerson, Tom McCarthy and my other colleagues.

For the undoubtedly many deficiencies I am of course the only one to blame.

B.M.

Santa Barbara
May 1990

Author's addresses

Interactive Software Engineering Inc.
270 Storke Road, Suite 7
Goleta, CA 93117 – USA
Facsimile: +1-805-685-6869
Electronic mail: bertrand@eiffel.com

Société des Outils du Logiciel
14 rue Jean Rey
75015 Paris – France
Electronic mail: bertrand@feiffel.fr
Facsimile: +33-1-40-56 05 81

Table

TABLE   xv

1

Basic concepts

The formal descriptions presented in this book are mathematical theories used to model and analyze the essential properties of programming languages and programs.

This chapter explains why it is useful to write such descriptions, what components they contain, and what precautions you must take to avoid possible confusions between the languages being modeled and the notations used to model them.

1.1 WHY FORMAL DESCRIPTIONS (AND WHY NOT)?

Formal descriptions serve several purposes:

- Help in understanding languages.
- Support for language standardization.
- Guidelines for language design.
- Aid in writing compilers and language systems.
- Support for program verification and software reliability.
- Model for software specification.

The following discussion considers these benefits in turn, then examines some of the arguments *against* formal specifications.

1.1.1 Help in understanding languages and language issues

Apart from any other benefits, the mere act of writing a formal specification provides insight into the elements being specified. Mathematical methods prompt you to raise questions that might remain unvoiced in a more informal approach; in the process, you understand the subject of the specification better.

This applies to formal specifications of software systems (discussed below), but also to formal specifications of programming languages. A good mathematical model of a programming language issue (such as data types, block structure, parallel processes, recursion etc.) gives powerful insights into that issue. Programmers who are familiar with formal specifications techniques have a better understanding of programming languages.

1.1.2 Support for language standardization

One of the most vexing problems facing programmers is portability: how can we write programs which will adapt to various operating environments (computers, terminals, operating systems) without undue effort?

The key to portability is standardization: standards are needed for operating systems, hardware interfaces, programming practices, and of course programming languages. Standardization in this last area does not suffice to solve the portability problem, but it is clearly crucial.

In practice, however, even the few languages that have been the object of a serious standardization effort (such as Fortran, Cobol, C, Pascal and Ada) are not free from portability problems. This is because the actual description of a full-size, realistic programming language involves a myriad of fine points which it is difficult to cover satisfactorily in a document written in a natural language. A formal specification can help solve this problem; again, mathematical techniques are particularly effective whenever circumstances demand precision and absence of ambiguity.

It would not be reasonable to require that formal specifications *replace* natural language descriptions of programming languages.[1] Natural language has a unique place for communication between humans, and any language standard should have for routine use a version in "plain English" (or French, the other language for standards of the International Standards Organization). Formal and informal versions play complementary roles; whenever ambiguities or conflicting interpretations come up in a natural language document, the formal specification may serve as the document of last resort.

This complementarity has another important aspect. The insights you gain through a formal specification effort will almost always enable you to produce better natural

---

[1] A case in which formal specifications turned out to have a negative practical effect was the original report on Algol 68, which used a clever but difficult new formalism. Although the language designers never intended it that way, many people thought they had to master the formalism to understand the language, which was enough to put them off.

language descriptions. In this way a formal specification can be an excellent starting point for writing or improving a non-formal language manual. The approach can be beneficial even if applied to a language subset only: if you are finding it particularly hard to explain some features of a language, it may be a good idea to try to specify them formally, using some of the techniques of this book, before you proceed with the writing of your informal description.

1.1.3 Guidelines for language design

The proper design of programming languages is an important issue: once its structure and format have been fixed, a language will impact many users. This is of interest not only to designers of full-scale programming languages, but to most software designers, who must often devise user interfaces for the systems they build; such interfaces are small languages. Whether they realize it or not, most programmers are language designers.

Language design is not a science, and the quality of the result is mostly determined by the designer's talent and experience. As with any design discipline, however, be it architecture or mechanical engineering, certain general principles apply.

Simplicity of specification is one such guideline: concepts that are hard to model mathematically often turn out, once transposed to language features, as hard to teach, hard to implement, or both. Although it must be balanced with other requirements – there is no absolute criterion in language design – mathematical simplicity usually pays off.

1.1.4 Help in writing compilers and language systems

In spite of significant progress made in recent years and the growing availability of tools, especially for the "front-end" of compilers (scanning and parsing), the construction of a well-engineered compiler remains a major effort.

Formal descriptions can provide a solid basis on which to design compilers and, more generally, language systems – where the expression "language systems" covers not only compilers but also the other tools that support the use of high-level languages on computers, such as interpreters, run-time systems, program checkers and debuggers. The formal description of a language may be viewed as the specification of an abstract language system for that language; the results of some of the language description methods, notably denotational semantics (chapters 6 to 8), may be understood as high-level descriptions of abstract compilers for the languages being studied.

1.1.5 Support for program verification and software reliability

Among the fundamental issues in software engineering are the correctness and robustness of programs. To ensure and verify these qualities, researchers have devoted considerable effort to the development of techniques for **proving** program correctness. The essential idea is to associate with the program a mathematical transform, and to use mathematical proof techniques to check that this transform achieves the program's stated purpose.

Three kinds of problem are involved in proving the correctness of programs.

- You must state precisely the purpose of each program or program element. This is the problem of **software specification**.

- You must develop the right kind of mathematical **theories** to reason about programs and prove properties of their behavior.

- Since the detailed proof of any realistic system is a tedious and error-prone process, efficient **tools** are needed to support this process.

Formal descriptions of programming languages are essential for achieving the second goal, since they provide the mathematical basis for reasoning about programs written in these languages.

1.1.6 Models for software specifications

Formal specifications of programming languages also have an indirect but important bearing on the first of the preceding three goals, software specification.

This problem plays a fundamental role in the quest for program correctness: how can we describe the purpose of a software product precisely and unambiguously, without commitment to a particular implementation (in other words, without *overspecification*)?

The formal descriptions studied in this book have a more limited ambition: specifying programming languages, not arbitrary software systems. But it turns out that the methods used for the first of these goals yield powerful insights into the second. Many of the basic issues and techniques are the same, and research efforts in these two areas have indeed been closely connected.

Many of the techniques studied in this book apply to both fields. Examples are the use of abstract syntax to describe the structure of a language or system (chapter 3) and axiomatic specification techniques (chapter 9).

1.1.7 Limitations of formal specifications

By no means should this discussion be construed to imply that formal specifications are a panacea against all the evils of programming.

The essential argument against formal specifications is their difficulty. Formal specifications, it is said, are hard to learn, hard to write, hard to read.

In spite of significant advances made over the past few years towards making formal notations more understandable and more usable, both the production and the use of formal specification continue to require a certain level of mathematical ability and a substantial effort. These investments should be weighed against the advantages mentioned above.

Another argument which used to be voiced against formal specifications was that they only applied to toy examples, and failed to describe full-size, realistic languages. To a large extent, this argument has been proved wrong by the appearance, in the past few years, of complete descriptions of existing languages, such as Algol 60, Pascal, PL/I, Ada. Some features of programming languages are still hard to model in a satisfactory way (examples include concurrency, floating-point arithmetic, complex data structures), but it may be said that the technology has now reached a point where it is applicable to practical languages. This book does not formally describe any realistic language in its entirety; but it introduces the basic techniques for doing so, and contains a number of references to published descriptions.

In summary, formal specifications of programming languages, like anything else, should be used properly. Where they fit, they can be of great help. (As a supplementary comment, technically quite irrelevant: they are also enjoyable to write and play with.)

1.2 SYNTAX AND SEMANTICS

The introduction to this chapter mentioned that the object of the study comprises the essential properties of programming languages and programs. The emphasis on "essential" features restricts the discussion to properties that characterize programs and programming languages independently of particular implementations.

A basic concept is the distinction between the **syntactic** properties of a language, which characterize the structure of well-formed programs in that language, and its **semantic** properties, which characterize the effect of programs and the values they produce. Programming language syntax is by now a well-known subject; the study of semantics remains a more challenging venture.

Most of this book is devoted to semantics. Its study of semantics, however, is "syntax-directed" in the same way modern compilers are; in other words, syntax will be used as a robust foundation on which various semantic constructions can be built. It is essential, then, to follow the proper discipline when laying out the principles of syntax description. This is the subject of chapter 3.

1.3 PROGRAMS VS. MATHEMATICS

Any language may be characterized by syntactic and semantic properties. This applies to mathematical notations as well as to programming languages. It is indeed fruitful to define formally the syntax and semantics of purely mathematical languages, such as the "lambda calculus" which will be studied in chapter 5 – although everyday mathematical practice does not need such formal analysis of its notations.

Yet there is something special about programming languages: most of them are *imperative*. This feature makes formal descriptions both more necessary and more difficult; to avoid many potential confusions, we must consider it carefully before proceeding with formal descriptions.

1.3.1 Imperative features

The imperative (or *operational*) style of programming is characterized by the presence of constructs describing commands issued to a machine. In the case of a high-level programming language this machine is not the actual physical hardware but a virtual machine providing access to this hardware through the compiler and operating system. An imperative construct expresses orders to be carried out by such a machine.

The construct that makes programming languages most prominently imperative is the **instruction**. In commonly used languages, programs are sequences of instructions, each describing a set of actions to be performed.

Terminology note: instruction, statement.

Programming language discussions often call commands "statements". But this is a misnomer: in ordinary English, a statement is the expression of some fact or idea – a description, not a prescription. For the imperative constructs of programming languages, *instruction* is more appropriate, and is the word used in this book.

Using "statement" for "command" could be particularly confusing in the discussion of axiomatic semantics (chapter 9), whose *assertions* may be described as *statements* (in the ordinary sense of the term) about *instructions*.

Besides instructions, common languages include two other highly imperative constructs: explicit sequencing and assignment.

- Programs use explicit control structures to specify precisely the order in which their instructions must be executed.
- The assignment instruction $x := e$ is a command: it does not assert a property, but orders the machine to change something in its internal state – the value associated with variable x. Assignment is the simplest of the instructions which work by **side effect** on the program state.

The central role of these two notions is specific to programming. In particular, there is no notion of side effect in ordinary mathematics: if I write $x = e$, I am asserting the equality of two objects, but I am not attempting to change anything. The very notion of variable in the programming sense (an object whose value may be changed at will) is foreign to standard mathematics.

Dictionary - project for students.

1.3.2 Referential transparency

At the root of differences between mathematical notations and programs, you will find an important notion: referential transparency. This is the property, enjoyed by mathematical notation, of substitutivity of equals for equals: it holds if, whenever $a = b$, any property obtained from a true property by substituting b for a throughout is still true. For example, if both of the following arithmetic properties are true:

$$x = 2$$
$$x + y > 5$$

then referential transparency makes it possible to infer

$$2 + y > 5$$

Standard mathematical notation is referentially transparent. Although seldom made explicit, this property plays a fundamental part in mathematical reasoning. Manipulations of formulae in algebra, arithmetic and logic, for example, constantly rely on it.

Programming languages, however, violate referential transparency if they permit side effects. Consider for example the following Pascal routine:

```
function f (x: integer): integer;
begin
        y := y + 1;
        f := y + x
end
```

Although called a "function" in Pascal terminology, f is not a function in the mathematical sense of the term, that is to say a mathematical object defining a certain value for any set of arguments in some domain. For f does not just produce a result computed from its arguments, but changes the state of the program as well, by modifying y (assumed here to be a global integer variable) each time it is called.

As a consequence, expressions that rely on this "function" will not be referentially transparent. Assume that $y = z = 0$ at some point, where z is a variable of the calling program. Then $f(z) = 1$ in the sense that the call $f(z)$ will return value 1. Referential transparency would then imply equality between the two expressions

$$f(z) + f(z)$$
$$1 + f(z)$$

But this is not the case: since every call to f increments y, the first expression yields 2, whereas the second yields 3.

Aliasing may also cause violations of referential transparency. Aliasing occurs whenever a given object becomes accessible through more than one name. Argument passing by reference is one of the mechanisms that cause aliasing: in Pascal, for example, if you have declared the argument of f as

var *x*: **integer**

(implying that the subprogram has direct access to the actual argument of a call), then for a call executed when both *y* and *z* have value zero *f* (*y*) and *f* (*z*) will yield different results; the first call returns 2 and the second returns 1.

One may contend, of course, that functions performing side effects on global variables or aliasing between a global variable and a subprogram argument are just bad programming practice. But the problem in fact arises as soon as a language supports variables and assignment: for if more than one assignment is permitted on the same variable *x*, I cannot use the fact that *x* = *a* at some point of the program's execution to infer a property of *x* from a property of *a* at any other point. Aliasing and side effects on global variables only magnify the issue.

Even such apparently innocuous constructs as input functions, for example the C *getint*, evidence the same problems: the two expressions

   2 ∗ *getint* ()

   getint () + *getint* ()

are usually different; the first denotes twice the value of the next integer to be read from a given input file, whereas the second denotes the sum of the next two integers read from that file. Function *getint* produces a side effect since it modifies the global state of the computation, which includes the current read position on input files.

Imperative constructs, then, jeopardize many of the fundamental techniques for reasoning about mathematical objects. Much of the work on the theory of programming languages may be seen as an attempt to explain the "referentially opaque" features of programming languages in terms of well-defined mathematical constructs – to give them mathematical dignity, if you like.

For example, denotational semantics provides (in chapter 6) a model of instruction sequencing based on the mathematical notion of function composition; the effect of assignment is described in axiomatic semantics (chapter 9) through the mathematical notion of substitution.

By providing these descriptions of programming language features in terms of standard mathematical concepts, programming language theory makes it possible to manipulate programs and reason about them using precise and rigorous techniques, similar to those used for example in manipulating arithmetic formulae. This exercise requires the referential transparency of mathematics.

1.3.3 Non-imperative programming languages

The preceding discussion has taken it for granted that programming languages must be polluted by side effects, assignments, explicit sequencing and other repugnant features. But not everybody believes that such evil is necessary.

For the reasons mentioned above, and a few others, there has been a whole movement in favor of mathematically cleaner programming languages, free of referentially opaque features. Such languages are called **functional** or **applicative**; most of them rely on function application (hence the names), rather than assignment, as the fundamental technique for computing values.

Examples of languages in this class include FP and Miranda. Related developments include dataflow languages, such as Lucid, and logic languages such as Prolog. References on these languages may be found in the bibliographical notes to this chapter.

Programming in such languages is indeed much closer to traditional mathematics. Miranda programming, for example, has been dubbed "denotational programming" since the notation and spirit are remarkably close to the formal description techniques introduced in chapter 6.

If programming was commonly done in such languages, the need for formal descriptions would perhaps be less pressing than at present. In the current state of computer technology, however, these languages are not ready for widespread practical usage, if only for efficiency reasons. More fundamentally, one may doubt whether they will ever become common, as they tend to neglect a difficult but unavoidable feature of programming – an essential difference between software engineering and pure mathematics: the need to adapt the formulation of problem solutions so that they can be run efficiently on physical hardware.

It is interesting in this respect to study the actual usage of Lisp and Prolog. These are the only examples of less imperative languages to have achieved wide enough usage. But Lisp or Prolog programs that really do something useful (as opposed to textbook examples) seem to make frequent use of imperative features: *PROG*, *SETQ*, *RPLACA* in Lisp (these three examples correspond to explicit sequencing, assignment and side effects on data structures); the "cut" mechanism (non-regular sequencing) in Prolog. Although this phenomenon would need further investigation, we may suspect that today's performance limitations are not the sole cause of imperative constructs, and that imperative reasoning is here to stay.

Whether or not one believes that functional and logic languages will become more widely applicable in the future does not change the short-term perspective: almost all programming done today is of an imperative nature. To understand what lies at its foundation requires a mathematical analysis relying on unimpeachable, referentially transparent notations.

1.4 LANGUAGE AND METALANGUAGE

Theories of programming languages purport to explain programming languages in purely mathematical terms. As has just been seen, key conceptual differences exist between mathematics and programming languages; they might be thought to remove any potential confusion between these two worlds. But this is not the case, and strict rules are in fact essential to avert possible pitfalls.

1.4.1 To describe or be described

The danger arises from a feature that most programming languages – imperative as most of them are – share with mathematics: both are based on rather formal notations. So when you formally describe some programming language concepts you are applying a certain set of notations to the description of *other* notations. Consider for example a conditional instruction, for example in the Ada or Eiffel form

if $x > y$ **then** $x := x + 1$ **else** $x := x - 1$

Chapters 6 and 9 will show two different methods for specifying the semantics of such instructions. Given the above construct, expressed in a programming language notation, the resulting specifications express its syntax and semantics in terms of some other notations.

If you are not careful this situation may be confusing, and even dangerous. Whenever a notation is introduced or used, it should be immediately obvious which world this notation belongs to: is it an element of the language being described, for example Ada? Or is it part of the formalism used for syntactic or semantic descriptions?

From now on the word **language** will only apply to the programming languages under formal study; any formalism used for these descriptions will be called a **metalanguage**.

1.4.2 Circularity

A major consequence of potential confusions between language and metalanguage is the risk of circular descriptions.

To define a programming language, that is to say a particular notation, we use a metalanguage – another notation. So we may legitimately ask how the definition is to be defined. This is is a serious epistemological issue, which has no easy solution. But we can at least attempt to avoid defining the obviously flawed case of circular definitions, where a concept is indirectly defined in terms of itself. To this end, we should ensure that the language and the metalanguage belong to significantly different conceptual levels.

These observations restrict the usefulness of such methods as "operational" or "translational" semantics (chapter 4), which in essence express the semantic properties of a program by other programs. In contrast, the two approaches studied in depth in chapter 6 and the following chapters, "denotational" and "axiomatic", stay away from such incestuous practices by expressing the semantics of programs using **mathematical** objects:

- In denotational semantics, objects from set theory – sets and functions.
- In axiomatic semantics, objects from logic: axioms and inference rules. (It should be noted, however, that the predicates used in the axiomatic method involve program objects, for instance the values of program variables, so that further theoretical clarification is needed.)

Chapter 8 will address the general problem of circularity in detail, showing that certain kinds of *recursive* definition, suspiciously close on the surface to circular ones, enjoy in fact perfectly legitimate interpretations.

1.4.3 Similarity in notations

A practical reason to be picky about the distinction between language and metalanguage is that natural similarities of notation may cause some very real misunderstandings, which threaten to annul any benefits obtained from formal specification techniques.

The issue would not arise if metalinguistic notations were inherently different from programming notations. But in spite of the obvious differences between mathematics and programming languages, formal specification metalanguages do tend to use many of the notations originally introduced for programming purposes.

As a simple example, it is often useful, in a metalinguistic specification, to define a function (that is to say, a mathematical object, belonging to a metalanguage) through case analysis, by writing something like

$f(p) = expr_1(p)$ if p is of type 1,

$f(p) = expr_2(p)$ if p is of type 2,

...

$f(p) = expr_n(p)$ if p is of type n.

where the argument may be of n different kinds and $expr_i$ gives the value of the function in the i-th case. It is nice to be able to write such a function definition with a metalanguage notation of the form

$f(p) =$
    case p **of**
        type 1 $\Rightarrow expr_1(p)$ |
        type 2 $\Rightarrow expr_2(p)$ |
        ... |
        type n $\Rightarrow expr_n(p)$
    end

Although this notation for "case expressions" is directly borrowed from programming languages, it makes perfect sense mathematically (chapter 3 gives its formal definition). But if the metalanguage uses such kinds of expression, it is essential to avoid any confusion with the "case instructions" that may exist in the language being described: Pascal and Ada, for example, have such constructs, with a syntax similar to the one above.

The metalanguage used in the following chapters, called Metanot, indeed uses such case expressions and other constructs inspired by programming languages. You must remember that these are mathematical notations, not to be confused with their look-alikes in programming.

It is a credit to the designers of the best programming languages that so many of the notations they designed have turned out to be useful for formal specifications as well. This also says a lot about what programming languages really are, independently of any connection with automatic computers: elaborate notations for thinking and problem-solving.

The method used in this book to describe the semantics of programs should help avoid confusions. Whenever it needs to refer to some program fragment, say the Pascal instruction

> **case** p **of**
>
> > 1, 3, 5: $x := a + 1$;
> >
> > 2, 4, 6: $x := a - 1$
>
> **end**

the presentation will *not* manipulate the fragment in this standard programming language notation; it uses instead a quite different formalism, **abstract syntax**, introduced in chapter 3 and embedded in the Metanot metalanguage.

1.5 BIBLIOGRAPHICAL NOTES

For a good general introduction to the study of programming languages, you may refer to [Ghezzi 1987].

Formal specifications of programming languages are just an example of formal software specification; much work has been done in recent years on the formal specification of general software systems. Of particular interest are the Z and VDM method. Successive variants of Z are described in [Abrial 1980] and [Spivey 1985]. VDM was explicitly designed for both language and software specification; [Bjørner 1982] emphasizes the first aspect, and [Jones 1986], emphasizes the second.

If you wish to learn more about software specification, [Berg 1982] is a survey and [Gehani 1985] is a collection of important articles. An illustrated discussion of the usefulness and scope of formal specifications may be found in [Meyer 1985a].

Language design methods based on formal semantic principles have been advocated by Tennent in an article [Tennent 1976] and a book [Tennent 1981]. The design of the Euclid language [Lampson 1977] [Guttag 1978] is a notable example where a formal specification was used as a tool in the design process, as opposed to *a posteriori* specifications of existing languages.

Much attention has been devoted to languages which reduce the conceptual gap between programming and mathematics; the three principal approaches are functional (also called applicative) languages, dataflow languages and logic languages. The first widely used functional language was Lisp [McCarthy 1960] (see [Steele 1984] for a more up-to-date description); in practice, however, Lisp usage is often quite imperative. High-level approaches to functional programming are advocated in [Backus 1978] and [Turner 1983, 1985]. The dataflow language Lucid is presented in detail in [Ashcroft 1985]. The best-known logic language is Prolog, described in [Colmerauer 1983].

Finally it is appropriate to mention here some other introductory books addressing some of the topics of the present one. [Manna 1974] is a classic, particularly invaluable for the study of program schemata and denotational semantics. [Livercy 1978] (in French) is also an excellent overview, emphasizing many of the same topics as Manna. At a more elementary level, [Pagan 1981] provides an introduction to programming language semantics, with special focus on the method of W-grammars, not covered in the present text. Surveys emphasizing specific methods will be mentioned in the bibliographical notes to subsequent chapters.

2

Mathematical background

*Mathematicians are like Frenchmen: whatever you
say to them they translate into their own language
and forthwith it is something entirely different...*

Goethe

This chapter introduces the essential mathematical concepts needed for the rest of the presentation, and some of the basic conventions used in this book to express formal specifications.

These are mostly conventions borrowed from standard mathematics, augmented by some notations specifically designed for the modeling of programming language concepts. Since it is convenient to have a name, the resulting metalanguage will be called **Metanot**.

2.1 CONVENTIONS AND NOTATIONS

2.1.1 Typographical and naming conventions

Any notation which belongs to either a programming language or the Metanot metalanguage will be in *italics*, with some keywords in **boldface**.

Names of sets (for example syntactic domains, as introduced in the next chapter) will normally start with a capital letter; names of members of these sets are in lower-case. Function names will also be in lower case (although functions are formally defined as sets below).

When set names are words borrowed from ordinary English, they will as a rule be in the singular; that is, when a set of "states" is needed (chapters 4, 6, 7, 10), it will be called *State* rather than *States*; this is in part because it is appropriate to introduce a member of this set, say *s*, by writing

$s: State$

which reads naturally as "s is a *State*".

2.1.2 Meta-comments

In a formal definition expressed in Metanot, any sequence of characters beginning with two dashes (--) and extending to the end of the line is a comment, which is not part of the definition (this is another notation borrowed from programming languages, in this case Ada).

Comments may need to refer to identifiers (from Metanot or from programming languages) which, as indicated above, are written in italics. The names used as identifiers may be words of everyday language. To avoid any confusion, plain comment text is in roman font, as in the following (somewhat extreme) example:

-- The value of *value* is equal to the value of *equal*

value = *equal*

2.1.3 Definition *vs.* equality

The equal sign = is commonly used with two different meanings. Consider the following quotation:

Let a, b, c be real numbers. Let $D = b^2 - 4ac$. If $D = 0$, then the second-degree polynomial $ax^2 + bx + c$ has two equal roots.

The two equal signs in this extract play quite different roles. The first denotes a definition: it introduces a new object, D, in terms of previously introduced ones. The second is a relational operator, applied to two operands D and 0, and yielding a result that may be true or false depending on the value of D.

In precise formal specifications, we cannot afford the confusion and should use distinct symbols for distinct operators. In Metanot the equality symbol = will serve exclusively as relational operator (the second case); for the operator "is defined as", Metanot uses the symbol $\triangleq$. This symbol applies in particular to function definitions (such as the definition of $f(p)$, using a **case** expression, in 1.4.3).

If you have any hesitation as to which of the two symbols should be used in a particular case, remember the following guidelines.

- If the symbol may be replaced by some other relational operator (such as $\leq$ on numbers, $\wedge$ on booleans, $\subseteq$ on sets) and still yield a formula that makes sense (perhaps a *wrong* formula, but one that means something), then the relational operator $=$ is needed; otherwise you should use the definition operator $\triangleq$. For example, the first equal sign above is used to define D, so replacing it by $>$ or $\leq$ would be absurd; but the second expresses a condition that could be replaced with $D > 0$ and still yield a meaningful sentence.

- If reversing the order of the two operands yields a meaningless sentence (as is the case with D and $b^2 - 4ac$), then we have a definition, not an equality.

- Expressions such as "if...", "such that..." and the like call for the relational operator; immediately after "let x...", the definition operator is the proper one.

The distinction between the $=$ and $\triangleq$ operators is not unlike that between equality and assignment in programming languages. The Algol-Pascal line of languages reserves $=$ for equality and uses $:=$ for assignment; this is closer to standard mathematical practice than the Fortran and C convention of writing $=$ for assignment and having some special symbol (.EQ. and $==$, respectively) for equality. The designers of PL/I thought they would satisfy everybody by using $=$ in both cases and succeeded at least in providing generations of instructors with ready-made quizzes (guess what the instruction $A = B = C$ does).

Although such decisions only affect the "concrete syntax" of a language (contrasted in the next chapter with the deeper properties captured by "abstract syntax"), they contribute significantly to its elegance, or lack thereof.

2.1.4 Auxiliary variables in expressions

We can make a complex expression more readable by introducing local names to denote sub-expressions. In Metanot, the notation **given** ... **then** ... **end** allows this. Following **given** are the definitions of one or more local names introduced as abbreviations for subexpressions; following the **then** is some expression e which may involve the local names. The value of the expression as a whole is the value of e, determined after substitution of the sub-expressions for each of the corresponding local names. For example, the expression

> **given**
>> $D \triangleq b^2 - 4*a*c\,;$
>>
>> $denom \triangleq 2*a$
>
> **then**
>> $\dfrac{-b + \sqrt{D}}{denom}$
>
> **end**

is equivalent to

$$\frac{-b + \sqrt{b^2 - 4*a*c}}{2*a}$$

The $\triangleq$ symbol is the appropriate one in the **given** clause, which says "let ... be defined as ...".

The **given** ... construct is a mere notational device that adds nothing to the intrinsic power of the metalanguage. The "local names" are not variables in the sense in which this word is used in programming; a "definition" such as $x \triangleq x + 1$ would be just as meaningless in a **given** ... clause as it is in mathematics. More generally, if the clause contains a definition

$x \triangleq e$

then expression e may only involve independently defined objects, or objects introduced by a previous definition of the same clause. This is the principle of **non-creativity** of definitions: a definition introduces new names for existing objects or properties; it does not introduce new objects or properties. Chapter 8 will examine this principle in more detail.

2.2 PROPOSITIONAL AND PREDICATE CALCULUS

Metanot uses standard boolean operators. If a and b have boolean values (true or false), then:

- $a \wedge b$, read as "a and b", is true if and only if both a and b are true.
- $a \vee b$, read as "a or b", is false if and only if both a and b are false.
- $\neg a$, read as "not a", is true if and only if a is false.
- Boolean implication uses the symbol $\supset$; the implication $a \supset b$, read as "a implies b", is defined as $\neg a \vee b$.

The symbol $\supset$, standard for implication in logic texts, is preferred here over $\Rightarrow$, reserved in this book for other purposes.

The quantifiers of predicate calculus will also be needed: $\forall$ (For all) and $\exists$ (There exists). If E is a set and P is a boolean-valued property (true or false), then:

- $\forall x : E \bullet P(x)$ means "All members of E, if any, satisfy P".
- $\exists x : E \bullet P(x)$ means "There exists at least one member of E which satisfies P".

These definitions of the quantifiers are informal. Here are more precise definitions:

- $\forall x : E \bullet P(x)$ is false if and only if there is a member x of E such that $P(x)$ is false.
- $\exists x : E \bullet P(x)$ is true if and only if there is a member x of E such that $P(x)$ is true.

As an important consequence, any $\forall$ expression for which the set E is empty is true – regardless of what the property P is. In this case, any $\exists$ expression is false.

The notations introduced above for quantified expressions reflects an important constraint, enforced by Metanot to avoid certain theoretical difficulties, The dummy identifier, x in the above examples, is always constrained to range over a specific set, here E. In other words: you cannot express a property of the form "All x satisfy P" or "Some x satisfies P"; you must be more precise and express that all members x of a clearly specified set E, or some x in this set, satisfy P.

2.3 SETS

Elementary set theory provides much of the basis for formal semantic specifications. This section introduces the basic concepts and notations.

2.3.1 Basic sets

The specifications will use a few predefined sets.

The set of integers (positive, zero or negative) is written **Z**. The subset of **Z** containing only natural (non-negative) integers is written **N**. **R** denotes the set of real numbers.

The set of boolean values is written **B**; this is a set with only two members, *true* and *false*.

The set of character strings is written **S**; character strings are written in double quotes, as in "*A CHARACTER STRING*".

2.3.2 Defining sets

You may define a finite set by enumerating its members in braces, as in

     B $\triangleq$ {*true, false*}

As a special case, { } is the empty set, more commonly written $\varnothing$.

A set definition of the above form is known as a definition by **extension**. Another way of defining a set (finite or infinite) is by **comprehension**, that is to say, by a characteristic property. For example, the set of even integers may be defined as

     Even $\triangleq$ {n: **Z** | $\exists\, k$: **Z** $\bullet$ $n = 2*k$}

As with quantifiers, the domain of the dummy variable (here n) is always restricted to a set assumed to be well-defined, such as a basic set (**Z** in the case of *Even*) or a set previously defined by extension or comprehension. So the notation actually applies to the definition of subsets of known sets.

Metanot borrows from Pascal its notation for subsets of $\mathbf{Z}$ which are contiguous intervals: for a, b in $\mathbf{Z}$, $a..b$ is the set of integers (if any) between a and b included. Formally:

$$a..b \triangleq \{i: \mathbf{Z} \mid a \leq i \land i \leq b\}$$

As implied by this definition, $a..b$ is an empty set if $b < a$.

For any set E, $\mathbf{P}(E)$ denotes the powerset of E, that is to say the set whose members are all subsets of E. For example, $\mathbf{P}(\mathbf{Z})$ is the set of all sets of integers; any interval $a..b$ as defined above is a member of that set.

2.3.3 Operators on sets and subsets

If E is a set and x is some mathematical object, x may or may not be a member of E. The boolean expression

$$x \in E$$

has value true if and only if x is a member of E. For example, $-2 \in \mathbf{Z}$ is true but $-2 \in \mathbf{N}$ is false. The notation $x \notin E$ is a synonym for $\neg (x \in E)$.

The only information that a set E carries about a certain object x is whether or not x is a member of E. In particular, "how many times" x appears in E and the "order" of E's members are both meaningless notions. The situation is different with sequences, as will be seen below.

If A and B are two subsets of a given set E, then their union and intersection are defined respectively as

$$A \cup B \triangleq \{x: E \mid x \in A \lor x \in B\}$$

$$A \cap B \triangleq \{x: E \mid x \in A \land x \in B\}$$

We will also need the generalization to infinite unions and intersections. If a subset E_i of a certain set E is given for every $i \in \mathbf{N}$, then we can define

$$\bigcup_{i:\mathbf{N}} E_i \triangleq \{x: E \mid \exists i \in \mathbf{N} \bullet x \in E_i\}$$

$$\bigcap_{i:\mathbf{N}} E_i \triangleq \{x: E \mid \forall i \in \mathbf{N} \bullet x \in E_i\}$$

The operator $\subseteq$ (subset) takes two subsets as arguments and yields a boolean value. It may be defined by

$$A \subseteq B \triangleq \{\forall x : A \bullet x \in B\}$$

Its variant $\subset$ (proper subset) may be defined by

$$A \subset B \triangleq (A \subseteq B) \ \wedge \ (\exists x : B \bullet x \notin A)$$

To avoid any confusion, all set inclusion properties will be expressed as subset properties of the form $A \subseteq B$ or $A \subset B$, rather than the inverse "superset" properties, since the symbol $\supset$ is reserved (page 18) for boolean implication. [1]

In line with the conventions introduced above, the operators $\cup$, $\cap$, $\subseteq$ and $\subset$ may not be applied to pairs of arbitrary set operands: in each case, both operands A and B must be subsets of a common set E.

A set may be finite or infinite. The expression **finite** E is true if and only if set A is finite set; for example, **finite B** is true but **finite Z** is false. If E is finite, then **card** E (the cardinal of E) is the number of its members; for example, **card B** is 2.

2.4 SEQUENCES, PAIRS, CARTESIAN PRODUCT

Let X be a set. A sequence over X is an ordered list of members of X. Sequences are written in angle brackets, as in

<monday, tuesday, wednesday, thursday, friday, saturday, sunday, monday>

In particular, <> is the empty sequence. The terms "sequence" and "list" will be used interchangeably.

The value appearing at the i-th position in the sequence for some i is called the i-th **element** of the sequence. [2]

Sequences, unlike sets, are ordered: the sequence *<a, b>* is distinct from the sequence *<b, a>*. As the above example indicates, the same object can appear more than once; *<a, a>* is distinct from *<a>*.

The set of finite sequences over X is written X^*. The next chapter introduces a few operators on sequences.

A generalization of the notion of sequence is that of tuple. Let $X_1, X_2, \ldots X_n$ be sets ($n \geq 0$) and X be their union. A tuple built from the X_i is a member of X^* – a sequence

---

[1] This convention, although regrettable since implication is naturally interpreted as a *sub*set property, follows established mathematical practice.

[2] To avoid confusions, this book is careful in its use of a few words often employed interchangeably when less precision is required: a set has *members* and a sequence has *elements*; the word *object* is more general and applies to any well defined mathematical entity such as a set, a relation, a function or a member of some set. The next chapter will add the concept of the *specimens* of a syntactic type.

of elements in X – of length n, such that the i-th element of the sequence belongs to X_i ($1 \leq i \leq n$). For example, possible tuples built from **N**, **S** and **N** are

> <3, 'Text', 2>
> <7, 'Other text', 0>

The set of all tuples built from given sets is called the **cartesian product** of these sets and written

$$X_1 \times X_2 \times \ldots \times X_n$$

A tuple with two elements is called a **pair**. Being sequences, tuples and pairs are ordered.

If we use the same set X for all the X_i, then the resulting tuples are just sequences. In other words, there is a one-to-one correspondence between X^* and the set

$$\bigcup_{i\,:\,\mathbf{N}} X^i$$

where X^0 is $\{<>\}$ (the set with one element, the empty sequence), X^1 is X, and X^{i+1} is $X \times X^i$ (for $i \geq 1$).

2.5 RELATIONS

Relations describe associations between objects. As used in this book, the word "relation" is a shorthand for "binary relation"; more general multiary relations (used for example for relational databases) will not be needed.

2.5.1 Definition

Consider two sets X and Y. A relation r between X and Y is a set of pairs

> $\{<a_1, b_1>, <a_2, b_2>, \cdots \}$

where every a_i is a member of X and every b_i is a member of Y. X is called the source set of r and Y its target set.

The figure below illustrates the finite relation

> $finrel \triangleq \{<x_1, y_1>, <x_1, y_2>, <x_3, y_2>, <x_4, y_2>, <x_4, y_5>\}$

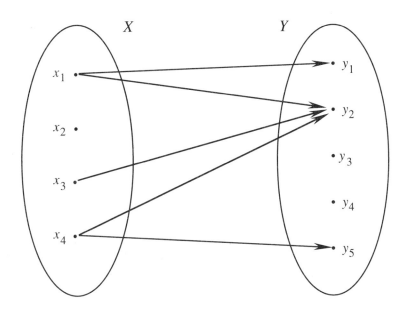

Figure 2.1: A relation

Relation *finrel* was defined by extension. A relation may also be defined by comprehension, as with the following relation between integers:

$$pm\_double \triangleq \{<m, n>: \mathbf{Z} \times \mathbf{N} \mid (m = 2 * n) \lor (m = -2 * n)\}$$

Members of relation *pm_double*, so named because the first element of each pair is "plus or minus the double" of the second, include <0, 0>, <–6, 3>, <6, 3> etc. Unlike *finrel*, relation *pm_double* is infinite.

The set of binary relations between X and Y is written $X \leftrightarrow Y$ and defined as

$$X \leftrightarrow Y \triangleq \mathbf{P}(X \times Y)$$

In other words, $X \leftrightarrow Y$ is the set whose members are all subsets of $X \times Y$, that is to say all sets of pairs whose first element is in X and whose second element is in Y.

2.5.2 Domain and range

The **domain** and **range** of a relation r, written **dom** r and **ran** r, are the sets of objects which appear as first and second elements, respectively, of at least one pair which is a member of r:

dom r $\triangleq$ $\{x: X \mid \exists\ y: Y \bullet <x, y> \in r\}$

ran r $\triangleq$ $\{y: Y \mid \exists\ x: X \bullet <x, y> \in r\}$

The domain of a relation is a subset of its source set and its range is a subset of its target set. For the two above relations:

dom *finrel* = $\{x_1, x_3, x_4\}$

ran *finrel* = $\{y_1, y_2, y_5\}$

dom *pm_double* = *Even* -- The set *Even* was defined on page 19

ran *pm_double* = **N**

2.5.3 Inverse and image

Let r be a relation in $X \leftrightarrow Y$. Its inverse, written r^{-1}, is another relation, a member of $Y \leftrightarrow X$, defined as follows:

$$r^{-1} \triangleq \{<y, x>: Y \times X \mid <x, y> \in r\}$$

In other words, r^{-1} contains a pair <y, x> if and only if r contains the pair <x, y>. In the first example above, *finrel*$^{-1}$ is

$$\{<y_1, x_1>, <y_2, x_1>, <y_2, x_3>, <y_2, x_4>, <y_5, x_4>\}$$

The inverse of relation *pm_double* is *abs_half*, whose definition is left to the reader.

Let A be a subset of X, that is to say $A \in \mathbf{P}(X)$. The image of A through r is the subset of Y containing the objects related by r to at least one member of A. This image will be written $r\ (\!A\!)$; its precise definition is:

$$r\ (\!A\!) \triangleq \{y: Y \mid \exists\ x: A \bullet <x, y> \in r\}$$

Taking the above relations as examples:

finrel $(\!\{x_1, x_2, x_3\}\!)$ = $\{y_1, y_2\}$

pm_double $(\!\{1, -1, 6, -6, 0, 14\}\!)$ = $\{0, 3, 7\}$
          -- Here 1 and −1 are not in the domain of the relation
          -- and so do not contribute to the image. Both 6 and −6
          -- contribute the same object, −3.

abs_half $(\!\mathbf{N}\!)$ = *Even*

The figure illustrates the first of these examples.

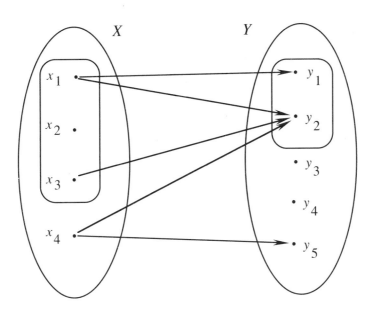

Figure 2.2: Image of a subset by a relation

Exercise 2.6 includes important properties of the image operator, which will be useful in the proof of consistency between axiomatic and denotational semantics (chapter 10).

2.6 FUNCTIONS

2.6.1 Definition

In general, given a relation r and an object $x \in X$, there may be zero, one or more objects $y \in Y$ such that the pair $<x, y>$ belongs to r (there may even be infinitely many such y). In relation *finrel*, for example, x_1 has two "buddies", x_3 has one and x_2 has none.

A relation such that there is **at most one** such y for every x is said to be **functional**. Relation *finrel* is not functional; it would be if $<x_1, y_2>$ and $<x_4, y_2>$ were removed. Relation *pm_double* is functional, but its inverse *abs_half* is not (since it associates for example both −6 and 6 to the value 3).

The set of functional relations between X and Y is written

$$X \nrightarrow Y$$

This set is a subset of $X \leftrightarrow Y$ and may be defined precisely as

$X \nrightarrow Y \quad \triangleq$
$$\{r \; : \; X \leftrightarrow Y \; | \; \forall x : X \; \bullet$$

      given
$$image\_of\_x \; \triangleq \; r \; (\!| \{x\} |\!)$$
      then
$$\textbf{finite} \; image\_of\_x \; \wedge \; (\textbf{card} \; image\_of\_x \leq 1)$$
      end$\}$

A functional relation is called a **function**.

2.6.2 Partial and total functions

If f is a function ($f \in X \nrightarrow Y$) and x is a member of X, there may be zero or one y such that the pair $<x, y>$ belongs to f. If there is one, that is to say if

$x \in \textbf{dom} \; f,$

then you may refer to y as $f(x)$. A function $f \in X \nrightarrow Y$ defined for all $x \in X$, in other words such that

$\textbf{dom} \; f = X,$

is said to be a **total** function. The set of total functions from X to Y will be written

$X \rightarrow Y$

A function which is not total is said to be **partial**. Note that whenever the discussion uses the word "function" without further qualification, it refers to both total and partial functions. The bar across the arrow in the symbol $\nrightarrow$ serves as a reminder that f may be partial, in which case $f(x)$ is not defined for some members x of X.

2.6.3 Finite functions

A special role is played by functions having a finite domain. Such functions will be called finite functions. (Some authors prefer the term "finite mapping".) The set of finite functions from X to Y will be written $X \xrightarrow{f} Y$, defined as

$X \xrightarrow{f} Y \quad \triangleq \quad \{f : X \nrightarrow Y \; | \; \textbf{finite dom} \; f\}$

Finite functions are particularly important for the modeling of programming concepts because they are the only functions that can be entirely represented in the memory of a computer: if a function has an infinite domain, there is no way you can ever hope to see the result of a complete computation of the function.

2.6.4 Defining functions by extension

One way to define a finite function is to indicate the value it takes for every possible argument in its domain. This is similar to defining a finite set by extension (page 19). Here you may define a function as a list of pairs, as illustrated by the following two examples of functions in $\{a, b, c, d, e\} \;\xrightarrow{f}\; \mathbf{N}$:

$f_1 \triangleq \{<a, 1>, <b, \; 2>, <c, 3>, <d, 4>\}$

$f_2 \triangleq \{<b, 2>, <c, 4>, <e, 4>\}$

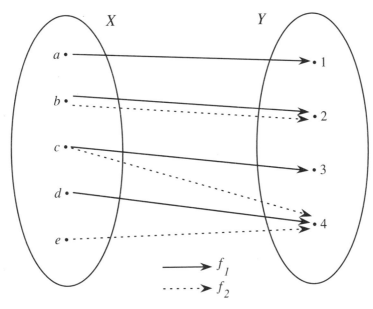

Figure 2.3: Two functions

The order of the *<argument, result>* pairs is not meaningful, but all the *arguments* must be different if the definition is to yield a function rather than just a relation.

2.6.5 Defining functions by expressions

For sets, definition by comprehension, that is to say by a characteristic property rather than enumeration, was also possible (page 19). The equivalent mechanism for functions is well known: it defines a function by an expression on formal arguments; the function's value for any actual argument values is obtained by substituting these values for the formal arguments in the expression, as in

[2.1]

  square: $\mathbf{R} \rightarrow \mathbf{R}$

  square $(x) \triangleq x * x$

  This definition means that to get the value of *square* (a) for any real number a, you substitute a for x in the right-hand side of the $\triangleq$ sign, getting $a * a$. In contrast with definition by extension, such a definition by comprehension applies to infinite as well as finite functions.

  The formal basis for this technique is known as **lambda calculus** and will be introduced in chapter 5. For the time being, definitions of the above form [2.1] will be considered clear enough. To make it absolutely obvious what the source and target sets and the domain of any function are, every function definition will consist of the following two or three steps. First you must give the source and target sets of the function under one of the two forms

   $f: X \nrightarrow Y$ -- For a possibly partial function

   $f: X \rightarrow Y$ -- For a total function

Then (in the first case only) you must specify the domain:

   dom $f \triangleq \{x \in X \mid \ \ldots$ Some boolean-valued expression on $x \ \ldots \}$

These two indications (one for a total function) constitute the function's **signature**.

  Finally, you must in both cases specify the value that the function yields for an arbitrary member of its domain, as was done above for *square*:

   $f(x) \triangleq \ \ldots$ Some value in $Y \ \ldots$

  Here the "is defined as" symbol must be used. In this last notation, it is often helpful to repeat for clarity the sets to which the arguments belong, as in

   $f(x: X) \triangleq \ \ldots$ Some value in $Y \ \ldots$

which imitates argument type declarations in the routine headings of programming languages (such as Pascal, Ada, Eiffel).

  Be careful not to confuse

   $f: X \rightarrow Y$

which gives the signature of f, declaring f to be some total function from X to Y, with

   $S \triangleq X \rightarrow Y$

which defines S as the set of all total functions from X to Y.

2.7 OPERATIONS ON FUNCTIONS

Several operations on functions will prove useful.

2.7.1 Intersection

Functions have been defined above as a special case of relations, which are themselves sets of a particular kind. This makes it possible to define the intersection of two functions, itself a function, as the set of *<argument, result>* pairs which belong to both functions. For example, the intersection $f_1 \cap f_2$ of the above two functions is the function pictured below, whose domain has only one member:

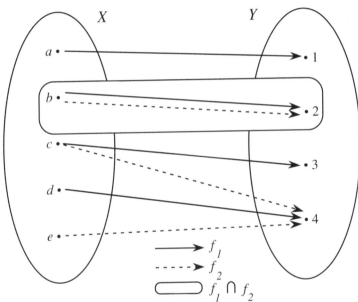

Figure 2.4: Function intersection

More precisely, the intersection of two functions is defined as follows:

Let $f, g : X \nrightarrow Y$;

Let $h \triangleq f \cap g$; then:

- **dom** $h = \{x : \textbf{dom } f \cap \textbf{dom } g \mid f(x) = g(x)\}$
- $h(x) = f(x) = g(x)$ for $x \in \textbf{dom } h$

2.7.2 Overriding union

Along with intersection, it seems natural to define the union of functions. Here, however, we must be careful: the union of two functions may well be a non-functional relation. This is the case whenever the domains of the functions are not disjoint, and the functions disagree on at least one possible argument. For example, f_1 and f_2 above have conflicting values for c, so that $f_1 \cup f_2$ is not a function. (The values for b do not cause a problem since the two functions coincide on that element.)

So if we want a union-like operation on functions function, this operation cannot be commutative (in other words, it cannot treat its operands in a symmetric way) if it is always to yield a function as result. Such a non-commutative operation is the **overriding union**, for which Metanot uses the symbol $\cup\!\!\!\!\!-$. The convention in the functional expression $f \cup\!\!\!\!\!- g$ is that g overrides f wherever they conflict. As a reminder of this convention, the bar in the symbol $\cup\!\!\!\!\!-$ makes the union "lean" towards the second operand.

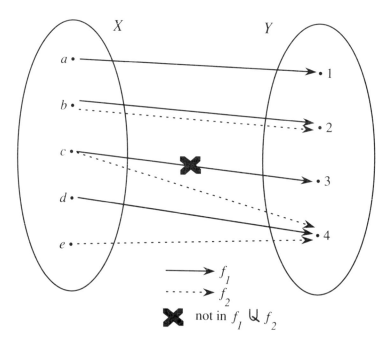

Figure 2.5: Overriding union

The operator " $\cup\!\!\!\!\!-$ " is defined more precisely as follows for f, g in $X \nrightarrow Y$. Calling

$$h \triangleq f \cup\!\!\!\!\!- g$$

then:

$$\mathbf{dom}\ h = \mathbf{dom}\ f \cup \mathbf{dom}\ g\ ;$$

$$h\ (x) = f\ (x) \text{ if } x \in \mathbf{dom}\ f \text{ and } x \notin \mathbf{dom}\ g\ ;$$

$$h\ (x) = g\ (x) \text{ if } x \in \mathbf{dom}\ g\ .$$

As an illustration of this operator, consider the two example functions given above. Then, as shown on the figure:

$$f_1 \cup\!\!\!\!\cup f_2 = \{<a,\ 1>,\ <b,\ 2>,\ <c,\ 4>,\ <d,\ 4>,\ <e,\ 4>\}$$

2.7.3 Restriction

Another important operator on functions is restriction. The restriction of a function f to a subset A of its source set, written $f \setminus A$, is defined as follows:

Let $f : X \twoheadrightarrow Y$.

Let $A : \mathbf{P}\ (X)$ (in other words, A is a subset of X).

Then $h \triangleq f \setminus A$, the restriction of f to A, is the function

$$h : A \twoheadrightarrow Y$$

such that

$$\mathbf{dom}\ h = A \cap \mathbf{dom}\ f$$

$$\text{and } h\ (a) = f\ (a) \text{ for } a \in \mathbf{dom}\ h$$

In other words, $f \setminus A$ is the same function as f, but with its domain restricted to A. Taking one of the above functions as an example again:

$$f_1 \setminus \{a,\ b,\ e\} = \{<a,\ 1>,\ <b,\ 2>\}$$

Remembering that functions, being relations, are sets of pairs, we may also define $f \setminus A$ more concisely as

$$f \cap (A \times Y)$$

The restriction operation may be defined for arbitrary relations, not just functions. However this book uses it for functions only.

2.7.4 Composition

Yet another operation on functions (which you may also generalize to relations), is composition, illustrated by the following figure.

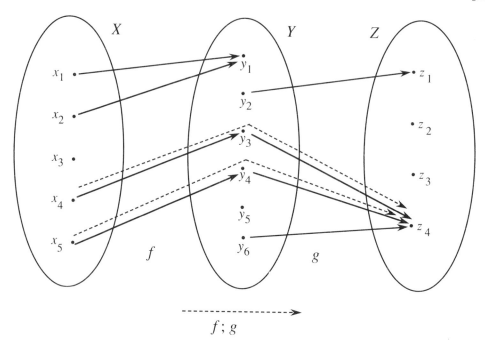

$$f ; g$$

Figure 2.6: Function composition

For any two functions f and g of signatures

$f: X \nrightarrow Y$

$g: Y \nrightarrow Z$

their composition, written $f ; g$ (a notation borrowed from VDM), is the function

$h: X \nrightarrow Z$

such that

dom h = $\{x:$ **dom** f | $f(x) \in$ **dom** $g\}$

and, wherever h is defined, then

$h(x) = g(f(x))$

Rather than $f ; g$, the more common notation for composition is $g \circ f$. The semicolon suggests (in accordance with its use in ordinary written language) that f and g are applied in the order in which they are listed.

This use of the semicolon may be seen as an homage to the concrete syntax of the Algol family of languages: as will be seen in the next chapters, composition is the mathematical equivalent of statement sequencing. No confusion will result since programs extracts, when embodied in a Metanot description, are always written with abstract, not concrete syntax.

2.7.5 Infix operators as functions

One more convention will be useful for handling functions. In common mathematical (and programming) practice, many binary functions, that is to say functions of two arguments, use a so-called **infix** notation, that is to say, with an operator between the two arguments rather than in front, as in $a + b$ rather than $plus\ (a, b)$. Examples of such infix operators are $+, -, *, /$, or the just introduced operator ";".

It is often convenient to be able to talk about the functions associated with these operators without having to introduce special names and definitions (as in "let $plus$ be the function such that, for any a and b, $plus\ (a, b) \triangleq a + b$").

The Metanot convention is borrowed from the Eiffel and Ada programming languages. If $\S$ is an infix binary operator, the notation

infix "§"

may be used to refer to the associated function. It may be abbreviated to just "§" in expressions involving the function. Applications of the function to actual arguments will use the usual infix notation.

For example, the function

infix "+": $\mathbf{N} \times \mathbf{N} \rightarrow \mathbf{N}$

is the addition on natural numbers, and for any sets X, Y, Z:

infix ";": $((X \nrightarrow Y) \times (Y \nrightarrow Z)) \rightarrow (X \nrightarrow Z)$

is function composition over X, Y, Z. As the definition indicates, **infix** ";" is a function of two arguments, one a function from X to Y and the other a function from Y to Z; its result is a function from X to Z.

Defined in this way, function composition is a typical example of a **functional**, or function which admits other functions as arguments or results. Functionals are discussed further below.

2.7.6 Predicates and the quotient operator

A predicate defined on a set X is a total function

$pred: X \rightarrow \mathbf{B}$

from X to the set $\mathbf{B}$ of boolean values (*true* and *false*).

There is a natural connection between predicates on X and subsets of X. If A is a subset of X, then we may associate with A the predicate

$characteristic_A : X \rightarrow \mathbf{B}$

such that

> $characteristic_A (x) = true$ if $x \in A$, and
>
> $characteristic_A (x) = false$ if $x \notin A$.

Function $characteristic_A$ is called the **characteristic function** of set A and is illustrated in the following figure.

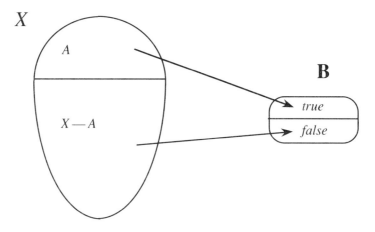

Figure 2.7: Characteristic function

Conversely, if *pred* is a predicate on X, we may define the **quotient** of X by *pred*, written X / *pred*, as the subset of X containing only those objects which satisfy *pred*:

> X / *pred* $\triangleq \{x: X \mid pred (x)\}$

For example, if X is a set of persons and *female* (x) is *true* if and only if x is a female, then X / *female* is the set of female members of X.

2.7.7 Inverse and image

The inverse and image operators (page 24) are defined for functions, since they are special cases of relations. If f is a function of signature $X \nrightarrow Y$ and A is a subset of X, then

- $f (\!(A)\!)$ is a subset of Y;
- f^{-1} is a relation (a member of $Y \leftrightarrow X$). It is not necessarily a function.

Exercise 2.6 covers several properties of images of subsets through functions.

2.8 FUNCTIONALS

As illustrated above by the composition operator, a functional, also called a higher-order function, is a function which admits functions among its arguments, results, or both. The word "functional" as used in this book only applies to **total** higher-order functions.[3]

It is important to familiarize yourself with the use of functionals, which play a major role in denotational semantics. Exercises 2.1 to 2.4 will help you master them.

2.8.1 Dispatching and parallel application

Two typical functionals are used in discussing recursion in chapter 8. They are **generic**, meaning that they may be applied to arbitrary sets U, V, X and Y (only three sets are needed for the first functional), and are expressed in infix notation. They may be called "dispatching" and "parallel application".

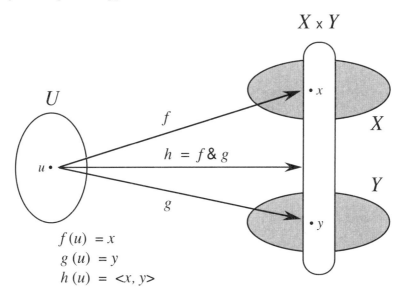

$$f(u) = x$$
$$g(u) = y$$
$$h(u) = <x, y>$$

Figure 2.8: Dispatching

Dispatching, illustrated by the above figure, is the functional of signature

infix "&": $((U \nrightarrow X) \times (U \nrightarrow Y)) \rightarrow (U \nrightarrow (X \times Y))$

which is such that for any functions

---

[3] Do not confuse "a functional", used here as a noun, with the adjective "functional" as used to characterize a relation (page 25).

$$f: U \nrightarrow X$$
$$g: U \nrightarrow Y$$

$f \,\&\, g$ is the function

$$h: U \nrightarrow X \times Y$$
$$\textbf{dom } h = \textbf{dom } f \cap \textbf{dom } g$$
$$h\,(u) \triangleq <f\,(u),\ g\,(u)>$$

In other words, as shown on the figure on the previous page, $f \,\&\, g$ "dispatches" an argument u to X through f and at the same time to Y through g.

The figure below illustrates parallel application.

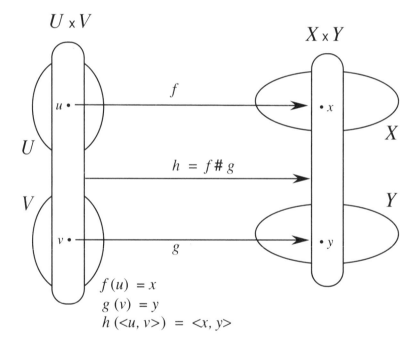

Figure 2.9: Parallel application

Parallel application is the functional of signature

infix "#": $((U \nrightarrow X) \times (V \nrightarrow Y)) \rightarrow ((U \times X) \nrightarrow (V \times Y))$

which is such that for any functions

$$f: U \nrightarrow X$$

$$g: V \nrightarrow Y$$

$f \# g$ is the function

$$h: U \times V \nrightarrow X \times Y$$

dom $h =$ **dom** $f \times$ **dom** g

$$h(u, v) \triangleq <f(u), g(v)>$$

In other words, as shown on the figure, $f \# g$ applies f and g "in parallel" to an argument from U and an argument from V, yielding a pair in $X \times Y$.

2.8.2 Currying

Another important functional is *curry* (named after the mathematician H.B. Curry, one of the major contributors to combinatory logic). This functional transforms any two-argument function into a one-argument function, whose results are themselves one-argument functions.

For total functions, *curry* may be defined as follows. For any sets X, Y, Z, if f is a total function of signature

$$f: X \times Y \rightarrow Z$$

then *curry* (f) is a total function g of signature

$$g: X \rightarrow (Y \rightarrow Z)$$

such that for any $x: X$ and $y: Y$

$$g(x)(y) = f(x, y)$$

In other words, *curry* (f) is a total function g such that, for any x, $g(x)$ is a total function from Y to Z, whose result, for any y, is precisely $f(x, y)$. The signature of *curry* itself is

$$curry: ((X \times Y) \rightarrow Z) \rightarrow (X \rightarrow (Y \rightarrow Z))$$

Exercise 2.4 explores properties of the *curry* functional and its generalization to arguments which are not necessarily total. Exercise 2.5 introduces an application of this operator to the understanding of programming language processing tools.

2.9 STRUCTURAL INDUCTION

The last mathematical technique at which we need to take a look in this chapter serves to define sets of complex objects and to prove properties of such objects. Known as structural induction, it is particularly useful for defining the concrete structure of languages.

2.9.1 An example: S-expressions in Lisp

The S-expressions of Lisp (serving as the basis for data and program structures in that language) provide a typical example of objects obtained by structural induction.

The definition may be given as follows. It assumes a separately specified notion of *atom*; to keep the discussion simple, atoms will be identifiers built as sequences of letters and digits, beginning with a letter. (Actual Lisp atoms also include numbers etc.) We may then define an S-expression by structural induction as being one of the following:

- An atom.
- Of the form $(s_1 . s_2)$, where s_1 and s_2 are S-expressions.

The intuitive meaning of such a definition is clear: S-expressions cover atoms such as *atom1*, and more complex expressions written with parentheses and a dot, such as

(*atom1* . *atom2*)

((*atom1* . *atom2*) . ((*atom3* . (*atom4* . *atom5*) . *atom6*) . (*atom7* . *atom8*) . *atom9*))

2.9.2 General form of definitions by structural induction

More generally, a definition by structural induction defines a certain set S as being made of members which are either:

A • Members of one or more predefined sets (such as the set of atoms above).

B • Deduced from previous elements of S through one or more well defined mechanisms (such as the above form with parentheses and a dot).

Such a definition has a clear mathematical interpretation: it means defining the set S as the union of an infinite family of sets

$$S \triangleq \bigcup_{i\,:\,N} S_i$$

where the S_i are defined by ordinary induction: S_0 is the set of all objects obtainable under A, and each S_{i+1} is the set of all objects obtainable from one or more members of S_j, for one or more $j \in 1..i$, through the mechanisms introduced under B.

In the case of S-expressions, for example, S_0 is the set of atoms; S_1 is the set of objects of the form $(a \cdot b)$, where a and b are atoms; S_2 is the set of objects of the form $(a \cdot b)$, where a and b are either atoms or in S_1; and so on.

Some objects may be in S_i for more than one i (actually, in the S-expression example, every S_i is a subset of S_{i+1} for positive i); this is fine since S is defined as the union of all S_i, so that it does not matter which S_i a member of S "comes from".

Viewed in this way, structural induction is a straightforward application of the usual induction on integers. What is being defined inductively is the sequence of sets S_i.

2.9.3 Proofs by structural induction

Sets defined by structural induction lend themselves to proofs organized along the same line. To prove by structural induction that all members of S satisfy a certain property p, you may successively prove that:

A • All members of the base sets satisfy p. (Base step.)

B • If a set of objects in various S_j satisfy p, any object built from them by any of the construction mechanisms used to define S_{i+1} also satisfies p. (Induction step.)

The validity of this technique follows immediately from the validity of proofs by ordinary integer induction: a proof by structural induction simply amounts to proving by integer induction the property

$$p\,(i \colon \mathbf{N}) \triangleq \text{"All elements of } S_i \text{ satisfy } p \text{ "}$$

As an example, let us prove by structural induction that every S-expression has an equal number of opening and closing parentheses. The proof contains two parts:

A • An atom has no parentheses, and so satisfies the property.

B • Consider two S-expressions e_1 and e_2, each satisfying the property. Let p_1 and p_2 be their respective numbers of opening parentheses; by assumption, these are also their numbers of closing parentheses. The construction mechanism given yields only one new S-expression from e_1 and e_2:

$$n \triangleq (e_1 \cdot e_2)$$

Counting parentheses in n, we find $p_1 + p_2 + 1$ of each kind.   □

Definitions by structural induction are a simple case of *recursive* definitions, whose significance and mathematical properties will be explored in a much more general context in chapter 8. Structural induction proofs will also find a generalization there through the notion of *stable predicate*. Justifying structural induction within the more general theory is the subject of exercise 8.4.

2.10 BIBLIOGRAPHICAL NOTES

Many of the notations introduced in this chapter have their equivalents in the work on the VDM denotational specification method [Bjørner 1982] [Jones 1986]. Some come from an early version of Z [Abrial 1980].

The article by John Backus on functional programming [Backus 1978] describes high-level functional operators not unlike some of those used in this chapter and in the exercises below. However Backus' language, FP, includes only a fixed set of higher-level functional operators; new ones may not be defined in the language proper, but in a supporting notation called FFP. A language that does permit definition of functions of an arbitrary level is Miranda [Turner 1985].

EXERCISES

Lambda notation (chapter 5) may be used to simplify some of the answers, but is not indispensable.

Exercises 2.1 to 2.4 use **R**, the set of real numbers, and some also need the set **R** $^{\bullet}$ of non-zero real numbers.

2.1 Properties of simple functions

Consider the following functions on real numbers :

> *square*, the square function
>
> *inverse*, the inverse function (*inverse* $(x) \triangleq 1/x$)
>
> "+", "−", "∗", "/" (addition, subtraction, multiplication, division)
>
> *Id* (the identity function)
>
> *add1*, such that *add1* $(x) \triangleq x+1$ for all x in **R**.

1   What are the signatures of these functions?
2   What function is *inverse* ; *inverse*?
3   What function is "+" ; *square*?

2.2 Dispatching

For arbitrary sets U, X, Y, the "dispatching" functional **infix** "&" was introduced in 2.8.1. Take U, X and Y to be all **R** $^{\bullet}$. Prove the following (referring to the functions of the previous exercise):

1   *(square & Id)* ; "/" = *Id*

2   *(square & inverse)* ; "∗" = *Id*

3   *addl* ; *square* = *(square & ((Id & Id)* ; "+")) ; "+" ; *addl*

2.3 Parallel application

For arbitrary sets *U, V, X, Y*, the "parallel application" functional **infix** "#" was introduced in 2.8.1. Let *projl* and *proj2*, be defined as the two projections from *U* × *V*:

    projl (<u, v>) ≜ *u*

    proj2 (<u, v>) ≜ *v*

1   What are the signatures of functions *projl* and *proj2*?

2   Take *U, V, X* and *Y* to be all **R·** . Prove the following:

    2.1   "/" = *(Id # inverse)* ; "∗"

    2.2   "∗" ; *square* = *(square # square)* ; "∗"

    2.3   "/" ; *square* = *(square # square)* ; "/"

    2.4   "+" ; *square* = *(((square # square)* ; "+")   &   (("∗" ; "+")) ; "+"

3   Express the following properties in the style of the equalities 2.1 to 2.4, that is to say without any reference to members of **R**, using only the functions and functionals defined so far.

    3.1 $(a - b) * (a + b) = a^2 - b^2$ for all *a, b* in **R**

    3.2 $b * (a/b) = a$ for all *a* in **R**, *b* in **R·**

    3.3 $a * (a + b) = a^2 + a * b$

    3.4   *f* is commutative
        (where *f* is a total function of signature **R** × **R** → **R**).

2.4 Iterate, apply and curry

All the functions considered in this exercise are total except in question 5.

Let *A, X, Y, Z* be arbitrary sets. For any function

    f: A → *A*

and any non-negative integer n, define *iterate* (f, n) to be the n-th iterate of f, in other words the function h such that

$$h = f ; f ; f \dots ; f \quad (n \text{ times})$$

Also, define *apply* to be the function such that, for any member a of A,

$$apply\ (f, a) \triangleq f\ (a).$$

In other words, *apply* takes two arguments, the first of which is a function. Its result is the application of its first argument to its second.

Finally, *curry* is the function defined on page 37, which takes any two-argument function as argument and yields a one-argument function as result. Its signature (if it is applied to sets X, Y and Z) is

$$((X \times Y) \rightarrow Z) \rightarrow (X \rightarrow (Y \rightarrow Z))$$

1   What are the signatures of *iterate* and *apply*?

2   Show that if set A is given, it is possible to choose sets X, Y, Z so that *curry* (*apply*) is a valid expression, denoting a function. What then is the signature of this function? What is the function itself?

3   For a given set A, can sets X, Y, Z be chosen so that *curry* (*iterate*) is a valid expression, denoting a function. If so, what is its signature? Explain informally what this function "does".

4   For each of the following functional expressions, give set assignments for A, X, Y, Z such that the expression has a value. Then give that value.

    4.1   *curry* ("/") (1)

    4.2   *curry* ("+")

    4.3   *curry* (*iterate*) (*add1*) (1)

    4.4   (*curry* ("+") # *Id*) ; *iterate*

5   As defined on page 37, *curry* applies to arguments which are total functions. Extend the definition so that its arguments and result are possibly partial functions. (**Hint**: the new definition must specify precisely the domain of the functional's result, and of its result's result, as was done for "#" and "&" in 2.8.1.)

2.5 Compilers and interpreters

Let M be a simple computer whose machine programs are assumed to compute functions of signature

$$I \rightarrow O$$

where I is the set of possible inputs and O the set of possible outputs. Machine programs for M may thus be viewed as implementations of functions from I to O.

Let L be a high-level language; let *COMP* be a compiler for L, generating M machine code and *INT* be an interpreter for L running on M.

Let *fcomp* and *fint* be the functions performed by *COMP* and *INT*, respectively.

1   What are the signatures of *fcomp* and *fint*?

2   Express a mathematical relationship between *fcomp* and *fint*? (**Hint**: look at *curry*.)

2.6 Properties of images

Let X and Y be two arbitrary sets, r and s relations in $X \leftrightarrow Y$, f and g functions in $X \nrightarrow Y$ with disjoint domains, A and A' subsets of X, B a subset of Y. Prove the following properties of the image operation $r \, (\!A\!)$ introduced page 24:

1    $r \, (\!A \cup A'\!) = r \, (\!A\!) \cap r \, (\!A'\!)$

2    $f^{-1} \, (\!B \cap B'\!) = f^{-1} \, (\!B\!) \cap f^{-1} \, (\!B'\!)$

3    $(r\,;\,s) \, (\!A\!) = s \, (\!r \, (\!A\!)\!)$

4    $(r \cup s) \, (\!A\!) = r \, (\!A\!) \cup s \, (\!A\!)$

5    $(r \cap s) \, (\!A\!) \subseteq r \, (\!A\!) \cap s \, (\!A\!)$

6    $(A \subseteq A') \supset (r \, (\!A\!) \subseteq r \, (\!A'\!))$

7    $(f \setminus A') \, (\!A\!) = f \, (\!A \cap A'\!)$

8    $(f \uplus g) \, (\!A\!) = f \, (\!A\!) \cup g \, (\!A\!)$

9    $(f \uplus g)^{-1} \, (\!B\!) = f^{-1} \, (\!B\!) \cup g^{-1} \, (\!A\!)$

10    $(f \setminus A)^{-1} \, (\!B\!) = f^{-1} \, (\!B\!) \cap A$

Dropping the hypothesis that f and g have disjoint domains, update properties 8 and 9 accordingly.

2.7 Expressing properties of relations and functions

The aim of this exercise is to learn to characterize various properties of relations and functions by higher-level functional predicates.

The generic identity function *Id*, written *Id* $[X]$ when the set X to which it applies must be made specific before the relation may· be used in practice, is such that *id* $(x) = x$ for any $x : X$.

1   Prove that a relation $r \in X \leftrightarrow Y$ is functional if and only if $r^{-1} ; r \subseteq Id \, [Y]$.

The next question uses the notion of total relation. A relation $r \in X \leftrightarrow Y$ is said to be total if and only if

$$\forall x : X \bullet \exists \, y : Y \bullet <x, y> \in r$$

In other words, r is total if and only if it associates at least one member of the target set with every member of the source set. (This is compatible with the definition of "total" when applied to functions.)

2   Prove that a relation $r : X \leftrightarrow Y$ is total if and only if $Id \, [X] \subseteq r ; r^{-1}$.

The next questions require that you express formally various properties of relations and functions in the same style as in questions 1 and 2, that is to say using relational operators such as composition (";") and inverse, with no explicit references to members of the source or target sets (such as x and y above).

3   Express that r is a surjective (or "onto") relation, that is to say such that

$$\forall y : Y \bullet \exists \, x : X \bullet <x, y> \in r$$

4   Express that r is an injective relation, that is to say such that

$$\forall x : X, y_1, y_2 : Y \bullet \quad (<x, y_1> \in r \; \wedge <x, y_2> \in r) \supset (y_1 = y_2)$$

5   Express that r is a one-to-one function (injective, surjective, total).

6   A relation $r \in X \leftrightarrow X$ is said to be

- Reflexive   iff $\forall x : X \bullet <x, x> \in r$
- Irreflexive   iff $\forall x : X \bullet <x, x> \notin r$
- Symmetric   iff $\forall x, y : X \bullet (<x, y> \in r) \supset (<y, x> \in r)$
- Asymmetric   iff $\forall x, y : X \bullet (<x, y> \in r) \supset (<y, x> \notin r)$
- Antisymmetric iff $\forall x, y : X \bullet (<x, y> \in r \; \wedge \; <y, x> \in r) \supset (x = y)$
- Transitive   iff $\forall x, y, z : X \bullet (<x, y> \in r \; \wedge \; <y, z> \in r) \supset (<x, z> \in r)$

Express each of these properties in the above style.

3

Syntax

Syntax describes the structure of well-formed programs.

This chapter shows how to specify the syntax of a programming language, beginning with the important distinction between "abstract" and "concrete" syntax. The rest of the book mostly relies on abstract syntax, which gives a bird's eye view of program structure, free of representation concerns.

3.1 THE NEED FOR ABSTRACT SYNTAX

3.1.1 Concrete syntax

The customary method of specifying the syntax of programming languages is known as the Backus-Naur Form or BNF. Using BNF, you may describe the syntax of a language by a **grammar** consisting of a set of **productions**; each production describes the form of a certain class of language elements such as instructions, expressions, routines etc.

For example, the following production, in standard BNF notation, defines the syntax of conditional instructions in some programming language:

> *<conditional>* ::= **if** *<boolean_expression>* **then** *<instruction>*
> **else** *<instruction>* **end**

This production describes how a conditional instruction may be formed in this language: write the keyword **if**, followed by some *boolean_expression*, followed by the keyword **then** and so`on.

Names of syntactic constructs such as *<conditional>*, *<boolean_expression>* or *<instruction>* are written in angle brackets. A construct appearing on the left-hand side of at least one production in the grammar is called a non-terminal construct (if more than one, they give alternative forms for constructs of the class). A construct which does not appear on the left-hand side of a production is called a terminal construct and is assumed to be defined separately; an example may be a construct *<identifier>* representing identifiers. Keywords such as **then** stand for themselves and are also considered to be terminal constructs.

3.1.2 Limitations of BNF

BNF and its variants (in particular the diagrammatic form introduced by Niklaus Wirth for the definition of the Pascal language) provide an elegant and universally accepted syntax description mechanism. They are not, however, the best basis for deeper studies of programming languages. What a BNF specification really describes is the external appearance of programs as they are seen by programmers, not their structure. BNF productions include much irrelevant detail such as keywords and other external syntactic conventions. The above production, for example, would be invalid for a PL/I-like syntax of the form

> IF *<boolean_expression>* THEN BEGIN; *<instruction>*;
> ELSE; *<instruction>*;

even though the two forms of conditional instruction correspond to the same structure.

To describe the deep structure of programs (rather than their external form), **abstract syntax** descriptions are preferable. The abstract syntax simply gives the components of each language construct, leaving out the representation details.

For example, the abstract syntax description of conditional instructions will simply state that a conditional instruction has three components: two instructions and a boolean expression. Other properties of conditional instructions are concrete icing on the abstract cake – sometimes called "syntactic sugar". They affect the way people write and read programs but are less appropriate for formal manipulations of the programs' structure.

> The use of abstract rather than concrete syntax as a basis for studies of programming languages is representative of an important trend in software engineering: the move towards a higher-level view of software objects, emphasizing deep structure rather than surface properties. Concepts such as abstract data types are another example of this trend.

The next section introduces a simple notation for describing the abstract syntax of languages.

3.2 ABSTRACT GRAMMARS

3.2.1 Definitions

An abstract syntax description of a language will be called an "abstract grammar" for that language. The word "grammar", without qualifier, will denote the abstract grammar.

A Metanot abstract grammar consists of the following ingredients:

- A finite set of names of **constructs**. By convention, construct names begin with an upper-case letter, as in *Instruction* or *Variable*.
- A finite set of **productions**, each associated with a construct.

Each construct describes the structure of a set of objects, called the **specimens** of the construct. For example a specific Pascal conditional instruction is a specimen of construct *Conditional* from the Pascal grammar. The construct is the **syntactic type** of its specimens; for example, the syntactic type of a conditional instruction is *Conditional*.

The language defined by a grammar is the set of specimens of all the grammar's constructs. These will be called the "specimens of the language".

A production has the form

$T \triangleq right\text{-}hand\text{-}side$

where T is a construct and the possible forms of *right-hand-side* are given below. Such a production is said to define T; it uses the $\triangleq$ sign since it is a definition rather than the assertion of an equality.

A construct may be defined by at most one production. (In contrast, BNF constructs may appear as left-hand side of several productions.) If there is such a production, the construct is **non-terminal**; otherwise it is a **terminal** construct.

There are three kinds of productions, called **aggregate, choice** and **list**, distinguished by their right-hand sides. This means that there are four kinds of constructs: terminal, aggregate, choice and list.

We may view a construct as a set: the set of all language objects of a certain form, for example all Pascal conditional instructions, all C variables etc. As a consequence, construct names start with a capital letter. The mathematical nature of constructs will be made more precise in 3.9.

One of the constructs is usually singled out as the **top construct** of the grammar. This construct represents the objects of highest level in the language: programs in Pascal, packages in Ada, classes in Eiffel, program units in Fortran, compilable files in C etc.

The following sections describe the three kinds of production.

3.2.2 Aggregate productions

An aggregate production defines a construct whose specimens are made of a fixed number of components. For example, you may define an abstract construct representing conditional instructions through the following Metanot aggregate production:

> *Conditional* ≙
>
> > *thenbranch*: *Instruction*;
> >
> > *elsebranch*: *Instruction*;
> >
> > *test*: *Boolean_expression*

This production defines the construct on the left-hand side, *Conditional*, as an aggregate construct. The components are separated by semicolons, each preceded by a tag indicating its role in the structure. Here a conditional instruction has three components: two instructions and a boolean expression, distinguished by the tags *thenbranch, elsebranch* and *test*.

When two or more components have the same construct, you may group their declarations for conciseness; for example, *Conditional* may be redefined as:

> *Conditional* ≙
>
> > *thenbranch, elsebranch*: *Instruction*;
> >
> > *test*: *Boolean_expression*

The order in which the various components are listed is irrelevant; this is indeed one of the differences between abstract and concrete syntax.

The definition of a construct in terms of a single other one will be considered as a special case of aggregate production, as in

> *Variable* ≙ *name*: *Identifier*

Aggregate construct definitions closely resemble definitions of *record types* in programming languages that support this notion (Algol W, Pascal, Ada, C, object-oriented languages etc.). The idea is the same: describing composite elements in terms of their components. This analogy is carried further in the "attribute grammar" method of semantic description in chapter 4. (The mathematical interpretations are indeed the same; see 3.9.1 and 7.2.)

3.2.3 Choice productions

A choice production defines a construct through a set of alternatives. The possibilities for instructions in a certain language might be defined by the production

$$Instruction \triangleq Skip \mid Assignment \mid Compound \mid Conditional \mid Loop$$

listing the various kinds of instructions in that language: a specimen of *Instruction* is a specimen of one of the constructs given in the right-hand side.

3.2.4 List productions

A construct may be defined as having specimens made of a sequence of zero, one or more specimens of another, fixed construct. List productions correspond to this case; for example, compound instructions such as they exist in Pascal, parenthesized in the concrete syntax by **begin** and **end**, may be defined by the following production:

$$Compound \triangleq Instruction^*$$

Here the asterisk has its standard language theory meaning ("Kleene star") and conforms to the convention for sequences (chapter 2). A specimen of *Compound*, as defined above, is a sequence of zero, one or more instructions.

For constructs whose specimens are lists of at least one element, the asterisk is replaced by a plus sign, as in

$$Number \triangleq Digit^+$$

3.2.5 Predefined constructs

If grammars are to define actual languages, all their constructs must ultimately be defined in terms of basic, well-defined sets – the terminal constructs.

Four predefined terminal constructs will be used in Metanot, corresponding to standard mathematical sets: **N**, the set of non-negative integers; **Z**, the set of all integers; **B**, the set of boolean values; and **S**, the set of character strings.

3.2.6 A complete abstract grammar

Below is an abstract grammar for a small but representative language, with constructs similar to those found in the common "core" of current languages, such as Pascal, Ada, C or Eiffel. This language will be used again in chapters 6 to 10. The computer field has a well-established tradition of using strange acronyms; accordingly we call the language Graal, for "Great Relief After Ada Lessons".

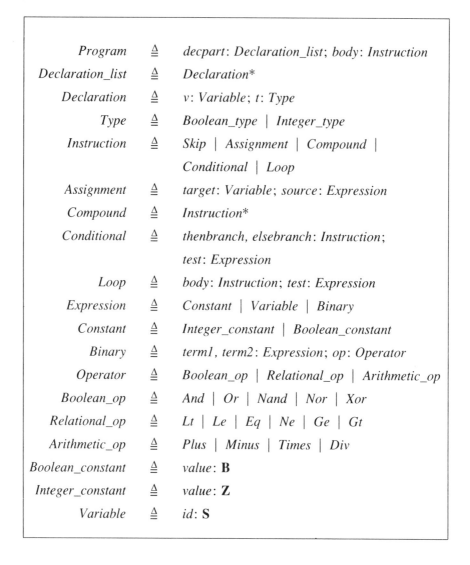

Program	≜	decpart: Declaration_list; body: Instruction
Declaration_list	≜	Declaration*
Declaration	≜	v: Variable; t: Type
Type	≜	Boolean_type | Integer_type
Instruction	≜	Skip | Assignment | Compound |
		Conditional | Loop
Assignment	≜	target: Variable; source: Expression
Compound	≜	Instruction*
Conditional	≜	thenbranch, elsebranch: Instruction;
		test: Expression
Loop	≜	body: Instruction; test: Expression
Expression	≜	Constant | Variable | Binary
Constant	≜	Integer_constant | Boolean_constant
Binary	≜	term1, term2: Expression; op: Operator
Operator	≜	Boolean_op | Relational_op | Arithmetic_op
Boolean_op	≜	And | Or | Nand | Nor | Xor
Relational_op	≜	Lt | Le | Eq | Ne | Ge | Gt
Arithmetic_op	≜	Plus | Minus | Times | Div
Boolean_constant	≜	value: **B**
Integer_constant	≜	value: **Z**
Variable	≜	id: **S**

Figure 3.1: An abstract grammar

The top construct of Graal is *Program*.

This grammar is defined recursively: for instance, one of the choices for *Instruction* is *Conditional*, itself an aggregate with two *Instruction* components. The meaningfulness of such apparently circular definitions is subject to doubt. Is it correct to use the definition sign ≜ here? Does it make any sense to define a construct indirectly in terms of itself? We shall only be able to answer these questions in chapter 8; until then, we must live with the uncertainty.

3.3 THE NEED FOR STATIC SEMANTICS

The productions for *Conditional* and *Loop* in the above Graal grammar highlight a common problem of language description.

In Graal as well as in ordinary languages, the *test* component of a loop or conditional must be a boolean expression. Yet you may have noted that the corresponding productions declare *test* merely as an *Expression*, and that the production for *Expression* covers both integer and boolean expressions. This means that a loop with an integer *test* component conforms to the grammar, even though it is clearly not acceptable.

You may correct this deficiency by modifying the grammar: simply replace *Expression* by two distinct constructs, *Boolean_expression* and *Integer_expression*, to be used respectively in the productions for conditional and loop instructions. Such a modification will make the grammar significantly longer; much of the production for *Boolean_expression* will simply repeat what is in the production for *Integer_expression*.

Here another solution as been retained. Being more permissive, the grammar can be kept simpler. This means, however, that we need a non-syntactic mechanism to cover typing rules and other constraints.

For the typing rule on *test* expressions, keeping the constraints separate is a matter of convenience and simplicity; they could in principle be expressed as part of the grammar. But other kinds of constraint simply cannot be described by purely syntactic notations. An example in Graal is the obvious requirement that no variable should be declared twice in a program, a condition that cannot be expressed in purely syntactical formalisms such as the Metanot abstract syntax notation or BNF.

Any practical language specification will have to include constraints of this kind; they constitute the **static semantics** of a language. When there is a need to distinguish, the expression **dynamic semantics** will refer to semantics proper, that is to say, the description of the effects of program execution.

> **Definition:** Static semantics is the description of the structural constraints that cannot be adequately captured by syntax descriptions.

This definition may seem contradictory, since syntax itself was introduced as describing the structural properties of programs. But the definition uses the word "syntax" in a pragmatic and more restricted sense, to denote the structural properties which may be described through abstract productions of the form discussed in the previous section. This should ideally cover all structural constraints, but unfortunately this is not possible with formalisms such as abstract syntax and BNF which only address context-free properties.

Static semantics covers the gap between these formalisms and the structural description needs of actual programming languages. Whenever we do not know how to express a structural property in abstract syntax productions, we label it static semantics and ignore it in the grammar.

Static semantics falls halfway between syntax and dynamic semantics. One reason for the name "static semantics" is that in practice the techniques for specifying static constraints resemble those used in dynamic semantics, especially under the denotational approach (chapters 6 to 8).

All language descriptions (except for the trivial language of the next chapter) will contain static semantic sections. For Graal as defined by the above grammar, the static semantic constraints on expressions and instructions are given in chapter 6.

At this point, you may want to check your understanding of the notion of abstract syntax by trying to solve exercises 3.1, 3.2 and 3.5. The last one is particularly useful because it requires defining a metalanguage (the abstract syntax formalism) in itself.

3.4 ABSTRACT SYNTACTIC EXPRESSIONS

Given a certain abstract grammar, we need ways to describe and manipulate programs that conform to this grammar. To this end, Metanot provides *abstract syntactic expressions*, used to describe abstract programs or program elements.

The various kinds of abstract expressions correspond to the classes of abstract syntax productions seen above.

3.4.1 Expressions for specimens of aggregate constructs

Consider an aggregate production, for example the first one in the grammar of Graal:

   Program $\triangleq$ *decpart*: *Declaration_list*; *body*: *Instruction*

It describes a class of objects, programs, each of which has two components, a declaration list and an instruction. Assume a declaration list *dl* and an instruction *inst* are given. Then we may define a program *p* having *dl* and *inst* as its components by

   p $\triangleq$ *Program* (*decpart*: *dl*; *body*: *inst*)

More generally, whenever you are dealing with a construct defined by an aggregate production, you may describe specimens of this construct through expressions involving the construct name (here *Program*), followed by a parenthesized list of its components; you must precede each component by its tag as given in the corresponding production (here the tags are *decpart* and *body*), separating it from its tag by a colon and from the next component by a semicolon.

As another analogy between language and metalanguage notations, this form resembles routine calls. Rather than to the more common "positional" notation, which identifies arguments by their positions in the list, it is similar to routine calls in "keyword" notation, where each argument is preceded by a unique tag (keyword). Keyword notation is used in command languages such as IBM's JCL and programming languages such as Smalltalk; Ada also offers it along with positional notation, with a syntax similar to the above. The next chapter takes advantage of this analogy to develop the "routine view" of attribute grammars (4.2.2).

Now consider a specimen of an aggregate construct, for example p of syntactic type *Program*. The components of such an object, identified by their tags, are expressed in Metanot through dot notation, again directly borrowed from programming languages (such as Pascal, C, Simula, Ada or Eiffel). For example, the components of p may be written

   p *.decpart*

   p *.body*

These components are of types *Declaration_list* and *Instruction*, respectively; for p, as defined above, the corresponding objects are *dl* and *inst*.

3.4.2 Expressions for specimens of choice constructs; case expressions

Consider a choice production, for example

   Instruction ≜ *Skip* | *Assignment* | *Compound* | *Conditional* | *Loop*

To construct a specimen of *Instruction*:
- First we must have a specimen b of *Skip*, or of *Assignment* etc.
- Then we must lift b to the status of instruction.

This lifted version of b will be written *Instruction* (b).

Assume for example that v is a variable and e is an expression. Then the following expression describes an instruction:

   Instruction (*Assignment* (*target*: v ; *source*: e))

The expression in the outermost parentheses defines a specimen of *Assignment* (an aggregate construct), of target variable v and source expression v. The overall expression represents the same assignment instruction, viewed as a specimen of *Instruction*.

This resembles a common operation of object-oriented programming: assignment involving a change of type, constrained by inheritance. In Eiffel, assuming class *VEHICLE* inherits from class *CAR*, then if v and c are declared of the corresponding types you may write the assignment $v := c$, which lifts a *CAR* object to the status of *VEHICLE*. Many non-object-oriented languages also offer type conversions, such as the "casts" of C, subject to looser constraints. The notation used above is similar to techniques used in Ada where, if N has been declared as an integer, *REAL* (N) denotes its floating-point equivalent.

Now consider a specimen of a choice construct, for example *i* of type *Instruction*. Almost all expressions defined on such an object depend on the "subtype" of the object – that is to say, in the *Instruction* case, on whether it is a Skip, an assignment etc.

Case expressions are used in Metanot to distinguish between subtypes. A case expression on a Metanot variable *i* will have the form:

> **case** *i* **of**
>> *Skip* $\Rightarrow$ *skip_exp* |
>>
>> *Assignment* $\Rightarrow$ *assign_exp* |
>>
>> *Compound* $\Rightarrow$ *comp_exp* |
>>
>> *Conditional* $\Rightarrow$ *cond_exp* |
>>
>> *Loop* $\Rightarrow$ *loop_exp*
>
> **end**

The right-hand sides expressions (*skip_exp*, *assign_exp* etc.) may be called "branch expressions". The branch expressions usually refer to *i*, the case variable; for example, *assign_exp* may refer to *i*.*target* and *i*.*source*, the target and source of an expression. For such notations to be meaningful, we must consider any occurrence of *i* in *assign_exp* to be of type *Assignment*, not *Instruction*.

This is a general convention, necessary if we want to manipulate specimens of subtypes of choice constructs. To understand it, note that in the right-hand side of a branch (such as *assign_exp*) the syntactic type of the **case** variable is constrained by the left-hand side (such as *Assignment*). The rule may be more precisely expressed as follows:

Branch typing rule for case expressions.

Let *A* be a non-terminal defined by a choice production and *K* be one of the alternatives for *A*:

$$A \triangleq \dots \mid K \mid \dots$$

Let *a* denote a specimen of *A*. For a case expression on *a*, of the form

> **case** *a* **of**
>> ... |
>>
>> *K* $\Rightarrow$ *k_exp* |
>>
>> ...
>
> **end**

any occurrence of *a* in the expression *k_exp* denotes an object of syntactic type *K*.

Some very simple right-hand side expressions k_exp may be common to more than one branch. Then the branches may be grouped for simplicity, as in

> **case** a **of**
>
> $\quad$ ... |
>
> $\quad K, L \Rightarrow kl\_exp \mid$
>
> $\quad$ ...
>
> **end**

The right-hand side here kl_exp, must be defined whenever a is of type K or L; because of the branch typing rule, this means that kl_exp must not involve a at all.

Sometimes what we need instead of a case expression is a simple boolean expression which has value true if and only if a specimen of a choice construct belongs to one of the subtypes. Metanot uses the operator **is** for this purpose, as in

> **if** i **is** *Loop* **then** ...

3.4.3 Expressions for specimens of list constructs

Consider a list production such as

> *Compound* $\triangleq$ *Instruction**

The most obvious way to construct a specimen of construct *Compound* is to list a certain number of objects of the base construct, here *Instruction*. If $i_1, i_2, \dots i_n$ are instructions, the following abstract syntactic expression defines a compound:

> *Compound* $(<i_1, i_2, \dots, i_n>)$

(Recall that angle brackets serve to write sequences or lists.) As with specimens of choice constructs, the type of the resulting object (here *Compound*) is specified explicitly. A list object specified in this way may be empty, as in *Compound* $(<>)$.

A number of operators may be applied to a list c:

- $c.EMPTY$ is a boolean value, *true* if and only if c has no specimens.
- $c.LENGTH$ is a non-negative integer value, the number of elements in c.
- c (i) is the i-th element of c (for $i \in 1 \mathinner{..} c.LENGTH$).

- If c and d are lists then $c \mathbin{+\kern-0.5em+} d$ is their concatenation. For example $<u, v> \mathbin{+\kern-0.5em+} <v, w, u>$ is the list $<u, v, v, w, v>$. To apply this operator to a list and a single element x, apply it to the one-element list $<x>$, as in $<v> \mathbin{+\kern-0.5em+} <u, v, w>$ (prepend) or $<u, v, w> \mathbin{+\kern-0.5em+} <v>$ (append).

The next four primitives are only defined if $c.EMPTY$ is false, or, equivalently $c.LENGTH > 0$:

- $c.FIRST$ is a synonym for c (1), the first element of c.
- $c.LAST$ is a synonym for c ($c.LENGTH$), the last element of c.
- $c.HEAD$ is c deprived of its last element.
- $c.TAIL$ is c deprived of its first element.

All the above operators are applicable to any list, although they will mostly be used for specimens of list constructs. For example if c is a *Compound*, then $c.FIRST$ or c (1) is its first element; similarly, *Compound* ($<u, v>$) $++$ *Compound* ($<v, w, u>$) is *Compound* ($<u, v, v, w, u>$).

Let f be a function with an argument c of list type. Often, in defining such a function, we will need **conditional expressions** of the following form:

> **if** $c.EMPTY$ **then**
>   "Value of the function for empty lists"
> **else**
>   "Value for non-empty lists, often expressed recursively
>   in terms of $c.FIRST$ and the value of the function for $c.TAIL$ "
> **end**

This notation is similar to the conditional expressions found in such programming languages as Lisp, Algol W, Algol 68, C – and should not be confused with conditional *instructions*, for which there would be no role in Metanot. Since the expression must always define a value, the **else** part is required. (In programming languages, the **else** clause of conditional instructions is usually optional.)

Conditional expressions with more than two cases avoid unnecessary nesting by using the form (present in Algol 68, Ada, Eiffel) **if** ... **then** ... **elsif** ... **then** ... **else** ... **end**.

Section 3.9.3 will introduce a notation for defining functions on lists without explicit use of recursion and conditional expressions.

3.4.4 Expressions of terminal type

Since terminal constructs are by definition not described in any further detail, the construct name will stand for a specimen of the construct not specified further. For example, a Graal *Skip* instruction will be written just *Skip*.

3.4.5 Complex syntactic expressions

An abstract syntactic structure may be represented by a syntactic expression built by repeated application of the above mechanisms. For complex expressions, it is usually clearer to use auxiliary expressions.

Consider for example the following Graal program, given here in an ad hoc concrete notation:

program

declare

x: INTEGER;

begin

x := 0;

x := x + 1

end

An abstract syntactic expression *prog* representing this program may be defined as follows, with the help of auxiliary expressions.

var1 ≜ Variable (id: 'x')

exp1 ≜ Expression (Integer_constant (value: 0))

exp2 ≜ Expression (var1)

exp3 ≜ Expression (Integer_constant (value: 1))

exp4 ≜ Expression (Binary
                 (term1: exp2; term2: exp3; op: Operator (Arithmetic_op (Plus))))

decl1 ≜ Declaration_list (<Declaration (v: var1; t: Type (Integer_type))>)

inst1 ≜ Instruction (Assignment (target: var1; source: exp1))

inst2 ≜ Instruction (Assignment (target: var1; source: exp4))

inst3 ≜ Instruction (Compound (<inst1, inst2>))

prog ≜ Program (decpart: decl1; body: inst3)

As evidenced by this example, the abstract syntax notation is unwieldy for complex syntactic expressions. Fortunately, there is no need to write really large ones: abstract syntax is a formal tool for *reasoning* about programs, not a notation for *writing* programs. For this latter application, standard concrete syntax is the obvious choice.

3.4.6 Abstract syntax trees

When a clear picture of the abstract syntax of a program is desired, a useful representation is provided by abstract syntax **trees**. An example abstract syntax tree, corresponding to the above syntactic expression, is given in the figure below, which should be self-explanatory.

An abstract syntax tree is close to the parse trees used in syntactical analysis. Our trees are abstract, however: they do not include any purely concrete information such as keywords.

Because of the way abstract grammars are defined, there are three possible kinds of node in an abstract syntax tree:

- Terminal nodes, appearing as leaves only.
- Aggregate nodes, corresponding to aggregate productions, with a fixed number of children.
- List nodes, corresponding to list productions, with a variable number of children.

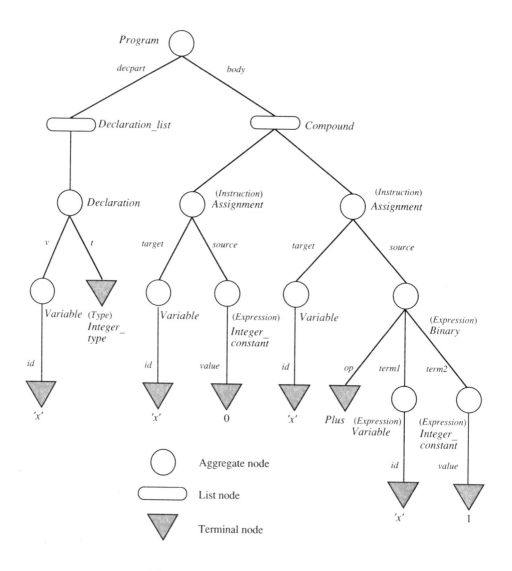

Figure 3.2: An abstract syntax tree

There is no special kind of node for choice productions: nodes resulting from one or more successive choices simply have one or more supplementary labels, giving the names of the corresponding choice constructs, in parentheses. For example, the nodes representing instructions on figure 3.2 have the extra label "(*Instruction*)".

The abstract syntax tree provides a convenient graphical view of program structure. Some important program manipulation systems use abstract syntax trees as their central data structure (see "structural editors" in 3.7.1 below).

3.5 ADDING CONCRETE SYNTAX

A first application of the above notations is the addition of concrete syntax to the abstract grammar of a language.

As a simple example, consider a language describing non-negative integers, expressed in decimal notation. The following abstract grammar describes this language:

$Number \triangleq Digit^+$

$Digit \triangleq Zero \mid One \mid Two \mid Three \mid Four \mid$

$\qquad Five \mid Six \mid Seven \mid Eight \mid Nine$

Given this abstract grammar, we may describe the concrete syntax by two functions which yield the external, concrete form of any decimal number from its abstract structure:

$concrete_{Number}: Number \rightarrow \mathbf{S}$

$concrete_{Digit}: Digit \rightarrow \mathbf{S}$

where $\mathbf{S}$ is the set of character strings. (This example illustrates a naming convention which later discussions will regularly use to deal with a set of related functions, applying to various constructs: select a common name, such as *concrete*, subscripted by the construct names, such as *Number* or *Digit*.)

Here are possible definitions for the above two functions:

$concrete_{Digit} (d: Digit) \triangleq$

   case d **of**

   $Zero \Rightarrow "0" \mid One \Rightarrow "1" \mid Two \Rightarrow "2" \mid Three \Rightarrow "3" \mid$

   $Four \Rightarrow "4" \mid Five \Rightarrow "5" \mid Six \Rightarrow "6" \mid$

   $Seven \Rightarrow "7" \mid Eight \Rightarrow "8" \mid Nine \Rightarrow "9"$

   end

$$concrete_{Number} \ (n: Number) \ \triangleq$$

> **if** $n.EMPTY$ **then** <>   -- The empty list
>
> **else**
>
>> $$concrete_{Digit} \ (n.FIRST) \ // \ concrete_{Number} \ (n.TAIL)$$
>
> **end**

where //, a notation borrowed from the PL/I programming language, indicates string concatenation (as in "FORMAL " // "SEMANTICS"). This should be distinguished from the ++ notation for list concatenation (page 55).

> The order of the two operands to the concatenation in the definition of $concrete_{Number}$ may appear wrong. Think twice, however, before you decide there is an error. Then look at 3.10 at the end of this chapter.

It is interesting to consider the role of the *concrete* functions in comparison with the role of parsers. A parser for a language analyzes the concrete form of programs in that language, and produces an equivalent but more abstract representation, such as a parse tree. The *concrete* functions do exactly the reverse: generate a concrete form from an abstract description.

Some programming tools, appropriately called **unparsers**, perform the task of the *concrete* functions. They are an important component of structural editors, discussed later in this chapter (3.7.1).

3.6 ADDING SEMANTICS, STATIC AND DYNAMIC

Abstract syntax may also serve as a basis for defining another important category of functions: functions describing the static and dynamic **semantics** of the language. One of the main advantages of using abstract syntax is precisely the possibility of grafting semantics onto a syntactic stem pruned of any detail that characterizes the external form of programs only.

As a simple example, consider again the language of decimal numbers. Only one semantic property is relevant for an element of that language: the associated numerical value. As a consequence, we may define the dynamic semantics of the language through a function

$$value_{Number}: Number \ \rightarrow N$$

which associates an integer with any specimen of the construct *Number*, in other words with any non-empty sequence of decimal digits. To define $value_{Number}$, we need an auxiliary function, giving the value associated with a single digit:

$value_{Digit}: Digit \rightarrow \mathbf{N}$

Although very simple, $value_{Number}$ and $value_{Digit}$ are typical of the semantic functions used in the **denotational** specification of more advanced languages, studied in chapters 6 to 8. The source sets of semantic functions (here *Number* and *Digit*) are constructs, also called **syntactic domains**; in contrast, their target sets (here **N** in both cases), whose specimens denote possible "meanings", are called **semantic domains**[1].

The two functions may be defined as follows:

$value_{Digit} (d: Digit) \triangleq$

> **case** d **of**
>
> > $Zero \Rightarrow 0 \mid One \Rightarrow 1 \mid Two \Rightarrow 2 \mid Three \Rightarrow 3 \mid Four \Rightarrow 4 \mid$
> >
> > $Five \Rightarrow 5 \mid Six \Rightarrow 6 \mid Seven \Rightarrow 7 \mid Eight \Rightarrow 8 \mid Nine \Rightarrow 9$
>
> **end**

$value_{Number} (n: Number) \triangleq$

> **if** $n.EMPTY$ **then** 0
>
> **else**
>
> > $value_{Digit} (n.FIRST) + 10 * value_{Number} (n.TAIL)$
>
> **end**

(If you still think there is something wrong with this definition, be sure to check 3.10 below.)

Be sure to distinguish the definitions of the *value* functions from their *concrete* counterparts seen above: the results of the *concrete* functions are strings (hence the quotes around 0, 1, etc.), whereas the *value* functions yield numbers.

As mentioned previously, abstract syntax may also be used as a basis for the specification of static semantics, that is to say well-formedness conditions that cannot be captured by syntax alone. Such a condition is expressed through a **validity function**, which is a predicate on a construct, such as

$V_{Number}: Number \rightarrow \mathbf{B}$

An object which satisfies the validity function on its type is said to be **valid**. Here a specimen n of *Number* is valid if and only if $V_{Number} (n)$ has value *true*.

---

[1] For the time being you may understand the word "domain" as a synonym for "set"; it does not have the more common meaning of domain of a relation of function, as introduced in 2.5.2. Chapter 8 will explain the more precise nature of syntactic and semantic domains.

It is an absolute rule that dynamic semantics specifications only apply to valid specimens of a construct. (As a consequence, the static part will normally be given before the dynamic semantics, although in the present example the dynamic semantics was introduced first.)

For the decimal number language, a possible constraint may be that decimal numbers have no leading zeroes. This may be expressed by the following validity function (see also 3.10 and exercise 3.4):

$$C_{Number}\ (n: Number)\ \triangleq$$

   case $n.LAST$ **of**

   $Zero\ \Rightarrow false\ |$

   $One, Two, Three, Four, Five, Six, Seven, Eight, Nine\ \Rightarrow true$

   end

3.7 APPLICATIONS OF ABSTRACT SYNTAX

Two important applications of abstract syntax deserve a mention here: structural editors and language design.

3.7.1 Structural editors

Structural editors are software engineering tools. A structural editor (also known by the more restrictive names "syntax-directed editor" and "language-sensitive editor") is a system for constructing and manipulating structured documents such as programs, program designs or formal specifications. As opposed to standard text editors, which treat any text as an amorphous sequence of characters, structural editors know the structure of the documents they manipulate; for example, a structural editor for Pascal will know about the syntax of Pascal and will be able to maintain the syntactic validity of programs.

Structural editors relieve users of many syntax-related chores; for example, a Pascal structural editor will be able to come up with an **end** for every **begin** entered by the user. They facilitate automatic program manipulation and systematic transformations. They can also be used as a sound basis for complete **software engineering environments**.

Examples of structural editors developed in recent years are given in the bibliographical notes. All these tools rely on language descriptions based on abstract syntax; the internal data structure used for representing documents is, accordingly, the abstract syntax tree.

3.7.2 Language and system design

As discussed in chapter 1, software designers often have to invent languages to allow users to communicate with their systems. A typical mistake in this activity is to concentrate too early on the concrete form of the interaction; the result is to obscure the issues and to freeze details prematurely.

This mistake is all the more damaging that many systems actually need at least three interfaces, offering the same functions but in a different form:

- A *batch* interface making the system available through packaged sequences of commands (this is the meaning of the word "language" that for most people comes to mind first).

- A purely *interactive* interface whereby the user gives commands at a terminal (possibly using graphical techniques) and sees the results immediately.

- A *routine* interface that makes the system's functions available to other programs, usually through a routine library.

The "languages" used by these various interfaces differ widely in their external appearance, even though they are functionally equivalent. Abstract syntax provides a convenient way of designing a language by concentrating first on the important aspects (the functions) and postponing the representation details. The following section illustrates the idea.

3.8 AN EXERCISE IN LANGUAGE DESIGN

[You may wish to skip this section on first reading, continuing with 3.9.]

An example will illustrate the use of abstract syntax for language and system design, outlining a general method. The example is small but representative of what goes on in the design of a new language.

3.8.1 A mini-language for genealogy

The example is a small language for performing genealogical work – perhaps for historical research, for demographic studies, or just to reconstruct one's lineage. The acronym for this language will be Cargo ("Computer-Aided Research into Grandma's Origins"). Cargo will allow the recording and exploitation of genealogical information relative to births, marriages, deaths, location of a certain person at a certain date etc.

Defining Cargo as a language in the traditional sense, that is to say starting with a BNF, would be too restrictive. The three types of interface mentioned above may be needed here:

- A classical language interface ("batch") in which commands and queries are expressed using a certain concrete syntax and submitted to the system.
- A routine interface in which the Cargo primitives are made available to other programs: for example, a program that automatically analyses certain data bases or historical records for statistical or demographic research could directly execute Cargo operations like recording a marriage, a birth etc.
- An interactive, menu-driven, graphical interface through which commands and queries are sent one by one for immediate response.

Because of the considerable differences that may be expected to exist between these interfaces, it is preferable to concentrate at first on the abstract syntax.

3.8.2 The abstract syntax

Let us look at the language constructs in a bottom-up order, from basic constructs to more elaborate ones.

Persons

> *Identifier* $\triangleq$ *name*: **S**
>
> *Person* $\triangleq$ *first_name, last_name*: **S**; *short_name: Identifier*

The basic entities are "persons". The example assumes a simplified world in which every person is characterized by a first name and a last name. (Of course, this is not necessarily true in genealogical research, even in the Western world.) A *short_name* is associated with every person for easy reference; for example the researcher may want to identify Modeste Mussorgsky as just Muss for later reference. All these attributes are strings; recall that **S** is the predefined construct string.

Places

> *Place* $\triangleq$ *p*: **S**

A place (such as a town) is simply identified by a name.

Dates

> *Date* $\triangleq$ *day, month, year*: **N**

Recall that **N** is the predefined construct whose specimens are non-negative integers. In a more complete design, some of the components would be optional: we may have only partial information (for example the year only) about a certain date. The notation for abstract syntax may be extended to allow optional elements in aggregates: see exercise 3.6.

Declarations

> *Declaration* ≜ *Person | Place | Date*

The above primitive constructs may be called "declarations". The next few correspond to "commands", which record some information.

Spottings

> *Spotting* ≜ *who: Identifier; where: Place; when: Date*

A "spotting" expresses the information that a certain person (denoted by his short name) is known to have been at a certain place on a certain date. This might result from the analysis of some document such as a contract.

Marriages

> *Marriage* ≜ *groom, bride: Identifier; where: Place; when: Date*

Births

> *Birth* ≜ *mother, child: Identifier; where: Place; when: Date*

(Recall that **B** is the construct boolean.) Again, some of the components should be optional in a realistic system since historical records do not always identify the mother and the birth date unambiguously.

Deaths

> *Death* ≜ *who: Identifier; where: Place; when: Date*

Operations

> *Operation* ≜ *Birth | Marriage | Spotting | Death*

Operations are used to enter information about persons.

The last set of constructs contains queries about the information entered. What follows is only a few examples, with no attempt at completeness.

Who_is

> *Who_is* ≜ *first_name, last_name:* **S**; *short_name: Identifier*

A *Who_is* query returns the first and last name of the person associated with a given short name. If there is no such person, the first name will be an empty string and the last name will be *UNKNOWN*.

Where_born

> *Where_born* ≜ *where*: **S**; *short_name*: *Identifier*

A *Where_born* query returns the birthplace of a person.

Further possible queries are listed below. Details of their individual syntax are left to the reader.

Queries

> *Query* ≜ *Who_is* | *Where_born* | *Where_died* | *Husband* | *Wife* |
> *Father* | *Mother* | *Number_of_children* | *Children* | ...

Clauses and units

Here finally is the structure of a Cargo "unit". A unit is a list of "clauses", each of which may be either a declaration, an operation or a query.

> *Clause* ≜ *Declaration* | *Operation* | *Query*
>
> *Clause_list* ≜ *Clause**
>
> *Unit* ≜ *unitname*: **S**; *body*: *Clause_list*

3.8.3 Introducing explicit interfaces

Once an abstract syntax has been fixed, the language design may be completed. The next obvious step would be to work on the semantics; this, however, would require the techniques introduced in the next chapters. For the purpose of this example, we content ourselves with the intuitive semantics suggested by the name of each construct, and examine the possible interfaces.

Some static semantic constraints and three possible versions of the concrete syntax are given by the table below. The first two columns repeat the above abstract syntax; however, as befits a systematic summary presentation, a top-down order is used this time: from global constructs to specific ones. The third column gives some informal static semantic constraints. The last three columns explain how each construct is entered in each of the three interfaces introduced above: programming language, routine library, interactive usage.

Construct	Abstract	Static	Concrete	Routine	Interactive
Unit	*unitname : S;* *body:* *Clause_list*	All short names of persons in a unit must be different.	**cargo** *unitname* **begin** *body* **end**	To open new unit: *start (unit_name)* To close unit: *close* Clauses in-between will be part of unit *unit_name*	To open new unit: Push left mouse button; select "new unit" on menu; enter unit name; push left again. To close unit: Push left; select "end unit" on menu.
Clause_list	*Clause**		*clause;* *clause;* *...*	Include successive routine calls, one per clause.	Enter successive clauses; after each clause, push left.
Clause	*Declaration |* *Operation |* *Query*				Select type of clause on menu.
Declaration	*Person |* *Place |* *Date*				Select type of declaration on menu.
Person	*first_name : S;* *last_name : S;* *short_name : Identifier*	*short_name* must not have been previously used in the same unit	**for** *first_name* *last_name* **say** *short_name*	*person (first_name, last_name, short_name)*	Enter three components in spaces provided.
Identifier	*name : S*		*name*	*'name'*	Enter *name*.
Place	*p : S*		*p*	*'p'*	Enter *p* in space provided.
Date	*day : N;* *month : N;* *year : N*	must be legal date (1 ≤ *month* ≤ 12, etc.)	*<day, month, year>*	*date (day, month, year)*	Enter *day, month, year* in spaces provided.
Operation	*Birth |* *Marriage |* *Spotting |* *Death*				Select operation on menu.

Construct	Abstract	Static	Concrete	Routine	Interactive
Birth	*child : Identifier;* *mother : Identifier;* *where : Place;* *when : Date;*		**born** *child* **of** *mother* **at** *where* **on** *when*	*Birth (child,* *mother, where,* *when)*	Enter components in spaces provided.
Marriage	*groom : Identifier;* *bride : Identifier;* *where : Place;* *when : Date*		**man** *groom* **married** *bride* **at** *where* **on** *when*	*married* *(groom, bride,* *where, when)*	Enter components in spaces provided.
Spotting	*who : Identifier;* *where : Place;* *when : Date*		**spotted** *who* **at** *where* **on** *when*	*spotted (who,* *where, when)*	Enter components in spaces provided.
Death	*who : Identifier;* *where : Place;* *when : Date*		**died** *who* at *where* **on** *when*	*died (who,* *where, when)*	Enter components in spaces provided.
Query	*Who_is |* *Where_born |* *Where_died |* *Husband |* *Wife |* *Father |* *Mother |* *Number_of_children |* *Children | ...*				Select query on menu.
Who_is	*first_name : S;* *last_name : S;* *short_name : Identifier*		**who is** *short_name*	*whois* *(first_name,* *last_name,* *short_name)*	Enter *short_name* in space provided.
Where_born	*where : S;* *short_name : Identifier*		**where born** *short_name*	*whborn (where,* *short_name)*	Enter *shortname* in space provided.

The concrete interface uses a programming-language-like syntax in the Pascal-Ada tradition; for example, a *Person* declaration will be expressed as, say

for *Nikolai Rimsky-Korsakov* **say** *Nick*

The routine interface offers access to the same primitives in the form of routines in a library; the routine call for the same example will be

person ("Nikolai", "Rimsky-Korsakov", "Nick")

The interactive interface allows entering the same declarations, commands and queries in a conversational manner. Assume a mouse and a keyboard; under this interface (which is only a rough first design), a user will enter the same declaration by pushing the left button of the mouse; a menu appears, listing the available types of clauses:

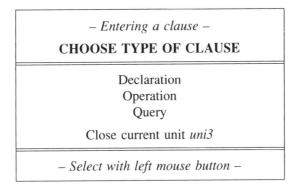

Assuming the user has chosen the first alternative (using the left mouse button), a new menu appears:

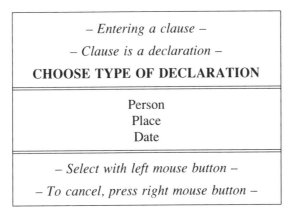

If the user takes the first choice again, he will now see the following entry form:

```
┌─────────────────────────────────────────────┐
│                                               │
│    – Entering a clause: person declaration –  │
│                                               │
│       ENTER PERSON DECLARATION                │
├─────────────────────────────────────────────┤
│                                               │
│       First name: _____                   │
│       Last name: _____                   │
│   To be known as: _____                   │
├─────────────────────────────────────────────┤
│                                               │
│   – Type in names, then press left mouse button –  │
│                                               │
│      – To cancel, press right mouse button –  │
│                                               │
└─────────────────────────────────────────────┘
```

To achieve the same effect as above, the user will type *Nikolai*, *Rimsky-Korsakov* and *Nick* in the fields provided, then press the left button of the mouse.

For some of the non-terminals defined by choice productions (*Clause, Declaration, Operation, Query*) the "concrete" and "routine" entries are blank in the above table; this is because the choice may be determined unambiguously from the construct chosen by the user. For example, in the *Clause* case, the form of the clause entered determines whether it is a *Declaration*, an *Operation* or a *Query*. This is frequently the case with choice productions.

3.8.4 Assessment

Abstract syntax only captures part of a language; the hard part, studied in the next chapters, is semantics. But abstract syntax provides a clean basis on which to build the rest. (A technique which goes one step further towards abstraction, and includes semantics, is that of *abstract data types*; see the bibliographical notes.)

The general approach to language description outlined above does provide significant help in clarifying the basic structure of a language. It favors consistency and regularity; it separates external representation from deeper issues.

The example also emphasizes a principle of wide applicability: when designing a software system of some ambition, **plan two interfaces** – or more.

Having more than one interface will help you understand which aspects of the system are essential and which ones are circumstantial. Most systems will need several interfaces anyway: how good is a system whose commands are available to interactive users, but not to other programs, or conversely? So you might just as well plan them together. This avoids inconsistent conventions and other frequent deficiencies. For example, reliance on abstract syntax naturally led us to using the same order in each of the three concrete interfaces for components in aggregate constructs (for example *first_name*, *last_name*, *short_name* for the *Person* construct), making it easier for users to switch between interfaces.

3.9 MATHEMATICAL BASIS FOR ABSTRACT SYNTAX

The above presentation of abstract syntax used informal definitions to introduce concepts such as constructs and abstract syntactic expressions, and the associated Metanot notations. It is time to explore their mathematical meaning.

For each of the three categories of productions, we must provide not only a mathematical model for the right-hand sides of the corresponding productions, but also an adequate interpretation of the operations defined on specimens of the corresponding constructs.

The models will rely on elementary set theory: they interpret every construct as defining a set, whose members are the construct's specimens, and every operation on specimens as an operation on the corresponding set members.

3.9.1 Aggregates

Assume that *Variable* and *Type* are previously defined constructs. Consider the following definition of an aggregate construct:

$Declaration \triangleq v: Variable; t: Type$

Assuming we know how to interpret *Declaration* and *Variable* as sets, this definition may be viewed as introducing a new set called *Declaration*. Any specimen d of *Declaration* has two components: one, written $d.v$, belongs to *Variable*, and the other, written $d.t$, belongs to set *Type*.

The first mathematical model that comes to mind for such constructs is cartesian product: as a set, *Declaration* might be understood as the *Variable* $\times$ *Type*, that is to say the set of pairs of the form $<x, y>$ such that x belongs to *Variable* and y to *Type*.

There is more to aggregates than cartesian product, however, since the definition of an aggregate also introduces "tags" to distinguish the components – v and t in the example above. It is legitimate to consider that these tags are part of the definition. For example, we probably want to consider that the following two definitions

$Book \triangleq title: \mathbf{S}; publication\_date: \mathbf{N}$

$Person \triangleq name: \mathbf{S}; age: \mathbf{N}$

define two distinct constructs even though the right-hand sides are identical as cartesian products. To account for such differences, the mathematical model must take the tags into account[2].

---

[2] A similar problem occurs with record types in programming languages such as Pascal: should specimens of two different record types with the same structure be considered compatible (for instance with respect to assignment)? For an in-depth discussion of the various kinds of type equivalence in Pascal see [Welsh 77].

To satisfy this requirement we may instead model each member of an aggregate construct as a **function**, more precisely a finite function from tags to values. Consider for example the following specimens of the above two types:

> *novel_1* ≜ *Book* (*title*: "Mansfield Park"; *publication_date*: 1811)
>
> *author_1* ≜ *Person* (*person*: "Jane Austen"; *age*: 35)

Each may be understood as representing a finite function, as follows:

> *novel_1* = {<*title*, "Mansfield Park">, <*publication_date*, 1811>}
>
> *author_1* = {<*name*, "Jane Austen">, <*age*, 35>}

In other words, we are defining *Book* and *Person* formally as sets of finite functions:

> *Book* ≜ {*title, publication_date*} $\underset{f}{\rightarrow}$ **N** ∪ **S**
>
> *Person* ≜ {*name, age*} $\underset{f}{\rightarrow}$ **N** ∪ **S**

Both cases assume a constraint expressing that each function must map the first argument to a member of **N** and the second to a member of **S**.

This model generalizes to arbitrary aggregate productions. Consider some sets $V_1, V_2, \ldots, V_n$, to be used as components of an aggregate type; assume that they have been previously defined. Let V be the union of all the V_i sets: $V \triangleq V_1 \cup V_2 \cup \ldots \cup V_n$. Let T be the set of possible tags.

An aggregate production defining X from $V_1, V_2, \ldots, V_n$, tagged respectively by $t_1, t_2, \ldots, t_n$, all members of T, is written in Metanot as

> $X \triangleq t_1: V_1 ; t_2: V_2 ; \ldots ; t_n: V_n$

From now on we understand this definition as defining the set

> $X \triangleq \{x : S \rightarrow V \mid \forall i : 1 .. n \bullet x\ (t_i) \in V_i\}$

where S is the subset of T containing only the tags of interest:

> $S \triangleq \{t_1, t_2, \ldots, t_n\}$

In other words, any specimen of X is considered as a finite function which associates with every tag t_i a member of the corresponding component set V_i.

This model is preferable to the cartesian product model since any aggregate object now includes its tags. The cartesian product model becomes a special case: if the tags $t_1, t_2, \ldots, t_n$ are chosen to be the integers 1, 2, ... n, then X is a set of functions from the interval $1 .. n$ to V, easily shown to be in one-to-one correspondence with the cartesian product $V_1 \times V_2 \times \ldots \times V_n$.

The two kinds of abstract syntactic expression associated with aggregate productions (3.4.1) are not hard to interpret in this model. The first was used to describe specimens of an aggregate construct:

$$x \triangleq X(t_1: v_1; t_2: v_2; \ldots ; t_n: v_n)$$

where each v_i is a member of the corresponding set V_i. In light of the above discussion, this defines x as being the function

$$x \triangleq \{<t_1, v_1>, <t_2, v_2>, \ldots , <t_n, v_n>\}$$

The other Metanot notation associated with aggregate productions is dot notation for accessing components of aggregates: if x is a specimen of X, then its component corresponding to the tag t (where t is a valid tag for objects of X, in other words one of the t_i) is written $x.t$ in abstract syntax notation. In the above mathematical model this denotes

$$x(t)$$

that is to say, the result of applying function x to t – which, by assumption, belongs to the function's domain.

For example, *novel_1.title* is understood as a Metanot notation for *novel_1* (*title*), that is to say application of function *novel_1* to argument *title*, the result here being the string "*Mansfield Park*".

The aggregate mechanism may be described as a "tagged cartesian product". The notation is convenient for dealing with tuples because individual components of the tuples are named, enhancing readability. This makes it applicable beyond abstract syntax; in fact, subsequent chapters will use the notation for dealing with various sets of tuples arising in purely semantic specifications.

As already mentioned, a programming language notion conceptually similar to the aggregate constructs of abstract syntax is the notion of record type. Existing languages variously express access to a component of an instance of a record type as

$x.t$ -- Pascal, Ada, PL/I, C, Eiffel.

$x\ t$ -- Smalltalk.

t **of** x -- Algol 68, Cobol.

$t(x)$ -- Algol W.

The last convention seems to treat a component tag, such as t, as a function defined on aggregate objects such as x. This view is a natural one. But the above mathematical model implies the opposite interpretation: it treats not the tags but the object itself, x, as a function; the domain of this function is the set of component tags.

This discussion has assumed that the component sets V_i were available. In many examples, however, syntactic domains are defined on top of each other and, as pointed out in 3.1, an abstract grammar for a realistic language will involve mutual recursion, X being defined in terms of Y which itself involves X directly or indirectly. The model above does not extend to such cases. Not until chapter 8 shall we be able to provide a reasonable interpretation for such complex systems of aggregate definitions.

3.9.2 Choice

The second type of abstract syntax productions includes productions of the form

> *Fruit* ≜ *Apple* | *Orange*

How can we interpret the | sign mathematically? If you are thinking ∪ (union), you are not far off, but not quite right either. The problem with set union here is that there is no way to tell whether a member of a union "came from" – whether a fruit is an apple or an orange.

In practice the distinction is necessary since we must often reason by case analysis. This was the reason for introducing case expressions (page 53), as in the following, assuming *f* is of type *Fruit:*

> *calories_per_100_grams* (*f*) ≜
>
> > **case** *f* **of**
> > > *Apple* ⟹ *58* |
> > >
> > > *Orange* ⟹ *35*
> >
> > **end**

To support this kind of discrimination, we need a variant of the union operation such that every member of the resulting set carries an indication of its set of origin. Such an operation is called **disjoint union**. In a set defined by disjoint union, every member is a pair of the form *<value, tag>*. The first component is the actual value from the set of origin; the second is a tag identifying that set.

For tags, it is simplest to use integers. For example a specimen of construct *Fruit* will have one of the following two forms:

- *<a, 1>*
- *<o, 2>*

for *a* of type *Apple* or *o* of construct *Orange*. The first component of such a pair is either an apple or an orange, and the second is 1 or 2 to indicate which of the two is the case.

This technique can be used for arbitrary disjoint unions. We may formally define the disjoint union

> $A_1 \mid A_2 \mid \ldots \mid A_n$

as

> $(A_1 \times \{1\}) \cup (A_2 \times \{2\}) \cup \ldots \cup (A_n \times \{n\})$

Below is an illustration of $A \mid B \mid C$ in this model. The result is a subset of $(A \cup B \cup C) \times \{1, 2, 3\}$ in which the second component of each pair is 1 if the first component is in A, 2 if it is in B, 3 if it is in C.

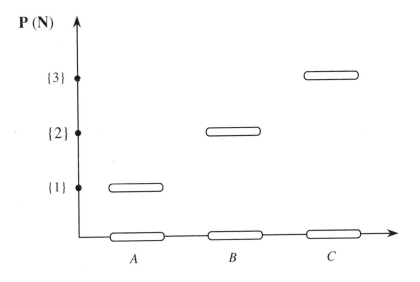

Figure 3.3: Disjoint union

More generally, a specimen a of $A_1 \mid A_2 \mid \ldots \mid A_n$ is a pair $<x, tag>$ in which x is a specimen of one of the A_i for some i in $1 .. n$ and tag is precisely that i. This way we can distinguish apples from oranges, and the world is a safe place again.

You may now understand a case expression on a, of the form

    case a **of**

            $A_1 \;\Rightarrow\; expression_1\,(a)$ -- Defined when a is a member of A_1 $\mid$

            $A_2 \;\Rightarrow\; expression_2\,(a)$ -- Defined when a is a member of A_2 $\mid$

            $\ldots$

            $A_n \;\Rightarrow\; expression_n\,(a)$ -- Defined when a is a member of A_n

    end

as denoting

    given

        $<x, tag> \;\triangleq\; a$

    then

        if $tag = 1$ **then** $expression_1\,(x)$

        elsif $tag = 2$ **then** $expression_2\,(x)$

        $\ldots$

        elsif $tag = n$ **then** $expression_n\,(x)$

    end

In the expression appearing on the right-hand side of each branch, x has lost its tag: it is no longer a member of the disjoint union, as a was, but a member of A_1 in the first branch, of A_2 in the second branch etc. This is exactly the meaning of the **branch typing rule** (page 54): in each right-hand side expression $expression_i$, any occurrence of the case variable a denotes an specimen of the construct A_i given by the corresponding left-hand side.

The disjointness of the "union" denoted by the $|$ symbol is important in practice. It ensures in particular that abstract grammars are never ambiguous, because abstract syntactic expressions always explicitly state the syntactic type of every sub-expression. For example, a BNF grammar containing the productions

$$Expression ::= <Variable> \mid Expression + Expression \mid$$
$$Expression * Expression$$

is ambiguous, as $a * b + c$ may be parsed in two different ways. But the corresponding abstract productions

Expression	$\triangleq$ *Variable* $\mid$ *Addition* $\mid$ *Multiplication*
Addition	$\triangleq$ *term1, term2: Expression*
Multiplication	$\triangleq$ *term1, term2: Expression*

are not ambiguous; every abstract expression will carry its type, as in

$e_1 \triangleq Expression$
    (Plus (term1: Expression (Times (term1: a; term2: b)); term2: c))
$e_1 \triangleq Expression$
    (Times (term1: a; term2: Expression (Plus (term1: b; term2: c))))

The price to pay for the removal of ambiguity is a heavier notation, making abstract syntax suitable for mathematical reasoning but not for writing or reading programs.

3.9.3 Lists

An abstract syntax production of the form

   Compound $\triangleq$ *Instruction**

describes finite sequences of objects, all of which belong to the same base set (here *Instruction*).

Although sequences are well-known objects, we need a mathematical model to associate a precise meaning with the list expressions introduced in 3.4.3.

> **Definition**: Let X be a set. $X*$, the set of finite sequences of elements of X, is the set of finite functions from N to X whose domains are intervals of the form $1..n$ for some natural number n.

In symbols:

$$X* \triangleq \{s \in N \underset{f}{\rightarrow} X \mid \exists\, n \in N \bullet \mathbf{dom}\ s = 1..n$$

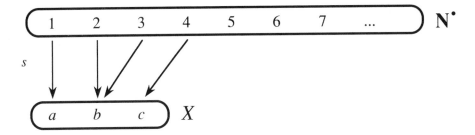

Figure 3.4: A sequence as function

So a sequence, or list, is defined as a partial function. The above figure illustrates the sequence $s \triangleq$ <a, b, b, c> as the function defined for arguments 1, 2, 3 and 4 only, and whose value is a for 1, b for 2 and 3, and c for 4. ($N^\bullet$ is the set of positive integers.)

The definition allows $n = 0$: empty interval, hence empty function, that is to say empty list. Also, it justifies the notation s (i) for the i-th element of list s, which is the result of applying function s to the value i.

The length $s.LENGTH$ of a list s is defined as the largest integer for which the associated partial function is defined (n in the above definition). The other notations introduced for lists in 3.4.3 have a straightforward definition:

- $s.EMPTY$ is true of list s if and only if $s.LENGTH = 0$.
- $s.FIRST$, the first element of s, is s (1). This expression, like the ones that follow, is defined if and only if $s.EMPTY$ is **false.**
- $s.LAST$ is s ($s.LENGTH$).
- $s.HEAD$, or s deprived of its last element, may be defined as a restriction of function s:

  $$s.HEAD \triangleq s \setminus 1..(s.LENGTH - 1)$$

- Finally, $s.TAIL$, or s deprived of its first element, may be defined as

  $$s.TAIL \triangleq succ\ ;\ s$$

  where $succ$ denotes the "successor" function on integers ($succ$ $(x) \triangleq x+1$). The figure illustrates this definition: starting for example from 3, the composition of $succ$ and s yields s (4), indeed the third element of $s.TAIL$, whose value is c.

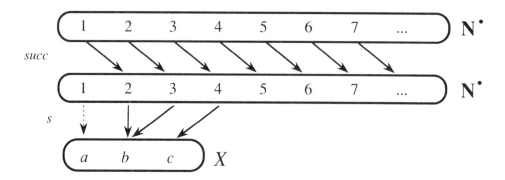

Figure 3.5: List tail as composition

One more list notation will be useful. As noted on page 56, many functions on lists are defined recursively in terms of the first element and the tail; more precisely, such functions are of the form

F (*s: Some_list_construct*) $\triangleq$

   if $s.EMPTY$ **then** val_0 **else** g ($s.FIRST$) § F ($s.TAIL$) **end**

where g is a function defined on list elements and "§" is a function of two arguments, used to combine the values obtained for the first element and the rest of the list. Here this function has been assumed to be of the form **infix** § for some operator § to be used in infix form; the above scheme is of course useful for non-infix functions as well.

Let n be the length of the list and let $g_i \triangleq g$ ($s(i)$) for $i = 1, 2, \ldots, n$. Seen globally, the function F, when applied to a list s of n elements, yields the value

g_1 § (g_2 § (… § (g_n § val_0)…))

and the definition normally assumes that val_0 is a neutral element (a zero) for "§".

This pattern is frequent enough to warrant a special Metanot notation, avoiding explicit recursion. The right-hand side of a definition of the above form may be written:

   over s **apply** g **combine** op **empty** val_0 **end**

where op is the function used to be applied to adjacent elements, usually of the form **infix** "§". (The word **infix** may be omitted.)

For example, if s is a list of n integers, then the sum of the squares of these numbers, $s(1)^2 + s(2)^2 + \ldots + s(n)^2$, may be written:

   over s **apply** *square* **combine** "+" **empty** 0 **end**

where *square* is the square function (*square* $(x) \triangleq x^2$).

The **over**... notation is reminiscent of loops in programming languages, but of course what it defines through iteration is an expression, not an instruction.

In defining the function applied to the successive elements of the list (g above, *square* in the example), it is sometimes necessary to refer to the index of the current element; the symbol # will denote this index, beginning at 1 for the first element.

3.10 A NOTE ON ORDER IN ABSTRACT SYNTAX

It is time now to clear a little mystery introduced earlier in this chapter. The definition of $concrete_{Number}$ on page 60 may seem erroneous since it expresses the concrete syntax of a number with the abstract syntax

$$<d_1, d_2, ... , d_n>$$

as being the string of digits

$$"d_n \ ... \ d_2 d_1"$$

with units first, then tens etc. The definitions of $concrete_{number}$ on page 60, $value_{Number}$ on page 61 and V_{number} on page 61 appear to suffer from the same oversight.

But this is an error only if we assume that the order of elements must be the same in the abstract and concrete grammars. As stated at the beginning of this chapter, nothing prevents the designer of an abstract grammar from listing the components of abstract objects in an order different from that of the concrete components in the external representation.

So the given function definitions are not wrong; they simply mean that low-order digits appear first in the abstract syntax given for numbers in this chapter, whereas usual decimal notation lists them last.[3]

Of course, it is often a good idea to list abstract components in the same order as their concrete counterparts. But this requirement is not absolute. In fact, it does not even always make sense: some languages require the same abstract component to appear more than once in the concrete form. A standard convention of Ada and Eiffel provides an example: in these languages, programmers are invited to repeat the name of each routine in a comment appearing after the routine's **end**. In such a case, the notion of order of concrete components simply does not exist.

---

[3] For a discussion on which digits should come first, rendered as a modern version of the Swiftian fight between "big-enders" and "little-enders", see Danny Cohen, "On Holy Wars and a Plea for Peace", *IEEE Computer*, 14, 10, October 1981, pp. 48-54.

3.11 BIBLIOGRAPHICAL NOTES

There is a wealth of literature on programming language syntax, mostly concerned with concrete syntax. Two surveys are [Backhouse 1979] and [Cleaveland 1977]. For applications to syntax analysis, see [Aho 1977] or [Waite 1984].

The notion of abstract syntax was introduced by John McCarthy in connection with the development of the Lisp language and its application to the theory of computation [McCarthy 1963a, 1963b].

The VDM method for language specification [Bjørner 1982] [Jones 1986] relies systematically on abstract syntax (with a different notation from the one used in this book) and expresses static semantics through "context conditions" similar to the validity functions of this book.

As mentioned in 3.7.1, abstract syntax plays an essential role in structural editors. Structural editors whose authors have defined abstract syntactic formalisms include Mentor [Donzeau-Gouge 1984] with the meta-language Metal [Kahn 1983], Gandalf [Habermann 1982] with ALOE [Medina-Mora 1982], and Cépage [Meyer 1985a, 1986a] with LDL (Language Description Language) [Meyer 1986b].

An abstract syntax production gives an exhaustive set of components (aggregate productions) or alternatives (choice productions). Any addition of components or alternatives will affect existing productions. To support a more incremental specification style – a goal which is particularly relevant to language and system design (3.8) – you may move on to an even more abstract notion, which also covers semantics: abstract data types. See [Guttag 1977] for an introduction to abstract data types and [Meyer 1988] for their application to software construction (object-oriented design).

EXERCISES

3.1 Abstract syntax for a subset of Pascal

Consider the following Pascal program (from the original Pascal report, [Jensen 1974], page 61):

        program *insert* (*input, output*); **var** *ch*: *char*; **begin**
            while not *eof* **do begin**
                write (' ');
                while not *eoln* **do begin**
                    read (*ch*); *write* (*ch*)
                end;
                writeln; readln
        end.   **end**

Give an abstract grammar for a subset of Pascal which makes it possible to describe the above program.

3.2 Abstract syntactic expressions

Write an abstract syntactic expression describing the program of exercise 3.1, using the grammar obtained in that exercise. In order to keep the expression simple, you should define intermediate expressions corresponding to the various components of the program.

Draw the corresponding abstract syntax tree.

3.3 Commented Pascal procedure declarations

The BNF rule below, adapted from [Jensen 1974], gives a simplified syntax of procedure declarations in Pascal:

> <procedure_declaration> ::=
>
> **procedure** <identifier> (<formal_argument_list>);
>
> <declaration_list> **begin** <compound_instruction> **end**

1 - Give a corresponding abstract syntax production defining the construct *Procedure_declaration*. You may assume that all the necessary supporting constructs (*Identifier*, *Formal_argument_list* etc.) have been defined separately.

2 - Express the concrete syntax of Pascal procedure declarations as a function $concrete_{Procedure\_declaration}$, defined on specimens of the construct *Procedure_declaration*, extending the Pascal language so that the final **end** of a procedure is always followed by a comment (in braces { }) repeating the name of the procedure, as in

> **procedure** *somename* (...);
>
>   ...
>
> **begin**
>
>   ...
>
> **end** {*somename*}

You may assume that the concrete functions for the other constructs ($concrete_{Identifier}$, $concrete_{Formal\_argument\_list}$ etc.) have been defined separately.

3.4 Leading zeroes

Modify the abstract grammar for the decimal number language (page 59) so that it precludes leading zeroes in decimal numbers (avoiding the need for the static semantic constraint given on page 62).

3.5 Abstract and concrete syntax of abstract syntax

This chapter has introduced (3.2.1) the Metanot notation for describing the abstract syntax of a language. Use this notation to specify the abstract syntax of the notation itself, using *Grammar* as the top construct.

Using the techniques introduced in 3.5, define the *concrete* syntax of that notation.

3.6 Aggregate constructs with optional components

It is often useful to be able to reason about aggregate constructs with optional components. For example, in most languages, the "else" part of conditional instructions may be absent.

Extend the Metanot notation for abstract syntax introduced in this chapter so that aggregate productions may specify optional components. Introduce associated extensions to the notation for abstract syntactic expressions, and to the mathematical model introduced in 3.9.1.

3.7 Not in Graal

The Graal language (3.2.6) does not include unary operators, so it has no built-in "not" expressions. Define a function

$$Not : Expression \nrightarrow Expression$$

such that *Not* (e) is an expression whose intuitive semantics is the negation of e; the function should be applicable to any boolean expression. **Hint**: Express negation in terms of other boolean operators and constants.

3.8 Concrete syntax of lists

Consider a construct L defined by a list production:

$$L \triangleq X^*$$

The aim of this exercise is to define a generic function yielding the associated concrete syntax; such a function was given in 3.5 for the mini-language of decimal integers.

In most cases, the concrete syntax of specimens of L may be characterized by three character strings: a header, a terminator and a separator. For example, in Pascal compound instructions (defined abstractly by the production $Compound \triangleq Instruction*$), the header is **begin**, the terminator is **end**, and the separator is the semicolon.

Define a function

$$concrete_L : L \times S \times S \times S \rightarrow S$$

such that *concrete* (*object_L, header, terminator, separator*) is the concrete form of the abstract syntactic object *object_L* of type L. **Hint**: Use the **over** ... notation introduced on page 78.

3.9 Membership test for specimens of choice constructs

Give a mathematical interpretation for the **is** operator (page 55).

3.10 Modeling choice productions

Devise an alternative model for constructs defined by choice productions (page 74), based on functions. **Hint**: Get some inspiration from the models used for aggregate and list constructs.

3.11 List concatenation

Within the mathematical model defining lists as partial functions (page 77), define the **concatenation** of lists in the same style as the other operations. **Hint**: Use the *iterate* function defined in exercise 2.4.

3.12 Matrices

Devise a specification of two-dimensional integer matrices and associated operations, based on the same approach as the specification of lists given in 3.9.3.

3.13 Infinite lists

The lists over a certain set, as discussed in chapter 2 and 3.9.3, are finite lists. Devise a specification of infinite lists based on a similar approach. Define the major operations on infinite lists in the context of this specification.

4

Semantics:
the main approaches

This chapter introduces and contrasts the main approaches to the description of programming language semantics.

Because our focus for the time being is on the description methods rather than the language features they describe, the discussion uses as example an extremely small programming language which (although it may not be the most useless ever invented) certainly makes no claim to realism. In a limited sense, however, it is representative of common languages: it has output, a very simple form of input, and the imperative notions of instruction and variable. While assuredly a toy language, then, it is a toy *programming* language.

The following chapters address the specification of more advanced features from actual programming languages.

4.1 A TOY LANGUAGE

The example language goes by the acronym Lullaby, for Little-Used Lilliputian Language Appropriate for Beginners and the Young.

Lullaby is a language for a machine that has a single word of memory, also used as register and accumulator, a single sequential output device, and a numeric keyboard used only when the machine is started. It only manipulates non-negative integers.

When switched on, the machine clears its output and prompts its user to type in a value, which it copies into the register. There will be no further input.

The instruction set has operations for doubling the value in the register, doubling it and adding one, halving it, and outputting it.

Here is the abstract syntax of Lullaby:

Program	≜	*body: Instruction*
Instruction	≜	*Double_to_even* | *Double_to_odd* | *Halve* | *Print* | *Compound*
Compound	≜	*Instruction**

Figure 4.1: Abstract syntax of Lullaby

The following abstract syntactic expression, called *example*, describes a Lullaby program and will serve to illustrate the various description methods studied in this chapter.

example ≜

    Program (body: Compound

        (<Instruction (Double_to_even), Instruction (Double_to_odd),

        Instruction (Print), Instruction (Double_to_odd),

        Instruction (Double_to_odd), Instruction (Halve),

        Instruction (Double_to_even), Instruction (Print)>))

A more readable form of program *example*, using an ad hoc concrete syntax, is:

program

    compound

        Double_to_even; Double_to_odd; Print; Double_to_odd;

        Double_to_odd; Halve; Double_to_even; Print

    end

  end

The following abstract syntax tree is a representation of this program.

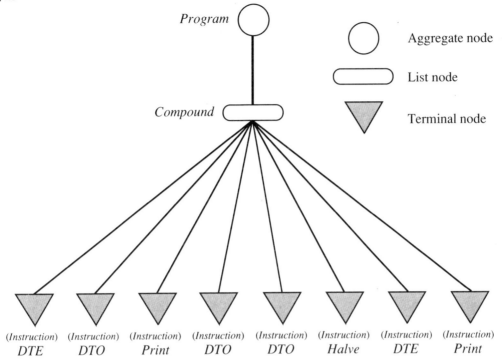

Figure 4.2: A Lullaby abstract syntax tree

The intuitive semantics of this program is straightforward. Assuming we exercise it with an input value of 0, *example* will end its execution in a state where the variable has value 6 and the machine has written values 1 and 6, in that order, on the output medium. In the rest of this chapter, the result of a program will be considered simply to be the contents of the output file when the program terminates.

The rest of this chapter describes the semantics of Lullaby under five fundamental approaches:

- Attribute grammars, which extends the grammar by a set of rules for computing properties of language constructs (4.2).
- Translational semantics, where the semantics is expressed by a translation scheme to a simpler language (4.3).
- Operational semantics, which specifies the semantics by providing an abstract interpreter (4.4).
- Denotational semantics, with associates with every programming construct a set of mathematical functions defining its meaning (4.5).
- Axiomatic semantics, which for every programming language defines a mathematical theory for proving properties of programs written in this language (4.6).

4.2 ATTRIBUTE (AFFIX) GRAMMARS

Of all the methods listed, attribute grammars, also called affix grammars, remain closest to syntax, and for this reason deserve to be studied first.

4.2.1 Decoration

Attribute specifications describe a language by extending syntactic descriptions – grammars – with supplementary elements covering the semantics. Although concrete syntax may be chosen as basis for these extensions, abstract syntax is clearly more appropriate.

The process of adding semantics to a syntactic description, abstract or concrete, is often called **decoration**.

A grammar, as defined in the previous chapter, defines the syntax of a language as a set of productions. Each production specifies one construct by describing the structure of specimens of the construct. You may turn the grammar into a full specification of both syntax and semantics by decorating both constructs and productions:

- To decorate a construct, you define **attributes** which describe the semantic properties of specimens of this construct.

- To decorate a production, you define one or more **rules** expressing the relationship between the attributes of the specimens of its left-hand side construct and the attributes of the right-hand side's construct specimens.

There are two ways to to describe the details of the attribute approach: a *procedural* (or "routine-oriented") way, where the emphasis is on the rules; and an *object-oriented* way, where the emphasis is on the constructs. These viewpoints are complementary rather than contradictory and will be introduced in turn.

4.2.2 The procedural view

Consider the production for *Program* in Lullaby:

> *Program* ≜ *body*: *Instruction*

This production defines the structure of objects of syntactic type *Program*: any such object has a single component of type *Instruction*, called its *body*. To add attribute semantics to this syntactic definition, you specify how the properties – attributes – of a specimen of *Program* relate to those of its *body*.

The only properties of a specimen of *Program* that matter for the semantic definition of Lullaby are the initial input value entered by a user and the final contents of the output file. So *Program*, as it appears in the left-hand side of this production, will be decorated by two attributes:

Program (**in** *input*: **N**; **out** *file*: **N***)

Recall that **N** is the set of non-negative integers and **N*** the set of possibly empty sequences of non-negative integers.

This notation for decorated left-hand sides distinguishes between **in** attributes, whose values are obtained by any specimen of the construct from its environment, and **out** attributes, which are returned by the specimen to its environment. Here *input* is **in** and *file* is **out**: a program obtains its initial *input* from the context (user's input); in return, it produces its final *file*. The relation between these two attributes will define the semantics of programs.

This example shows the connection between decorated syntax productions, in their "procedural" interpretation, and the programming notion of **routine** (or "procedure"). One way to look at the undecorated syntax production

Program $\triangleq$ *body*: *Instruction*

is to view it as the definition of a routine such as they exist in programming languages. The left-hand side is the routine heading; the right-hand side is the routine body; the routine declaration says: "To build a specimen of construct *Program*, you must build its *body*, a specimen of construct *Instruction* ".

To capture the semantics of the language, we must extend this building process by specifying the correspondence between the semantic properties of the two specimens. This is done, as above, by adding "arguments" to the "routine" describing the construct *Program*. These arguments are the attributes; adding them is the purpose of the decoration process.

> Not surprisingly, the Metanot notation resembles the conventions used in programming languages for declaring formal arguments of routines. The **in** and **out** qualifiers play a role similar to that of their Ada or Algol W counterparts.

These similarities justify the use of routine terminology. In particular, the names of a construct's attributes appear in two different roles:

- In the left-hand side of the production, we may call them **formal arguments**.
- Any occurrence of a construct's attribute in the right-hand side of a production, as part of a "call" to the construct, may be called an **actual argument** to the call.

The same concepts apply readily to choice, list and terminal constructs. For example, a specimen of *Instruction* in Lullaby has four attributes of interest: the values of the register and of the file before and after execution of the instruction. The "before" values are **in** attributes and the "after" values are **out** attributes. So the left-hand side of the production for *Instruction* will be:

Instruction (**in** *initial_register*: **N**, *initial_file*: **N***;

      out *final_register*: **N**, *final_file*: **N***)

The full attributed abstract grammar of Lullaby may be expressed as follows.

Program (**in** *input:* **N**; **out** *file:* **N***) ≜

  body: Instruction (*input*, <>, , *file*←)

Instruction (**in** *initial_register:* **N**, *initial_file:* **N***;

      out *final_register:* **N**, *final_file:* **N***) ≜

  Double_to_even (*initial_register*, *final_register*←) |

  Double_to_odd (*initial_register*, *final_register*←) |

  Halve (*initial_register*, *final_register*←) |

  Print (*initial_register*, *initial_file*, *final_file*←) |

  Compound (*initial_register*, *initial_file*,

        final_register←, *final_file*←)

Double_to_even (**in** *initial_register:* **N**; **out** *final_register:* **N**) ≜

  action: Assign ($2 * initial\_register$, *final_register*←)

Double_to_odd (**in** *initial_register:* **N**; **out** *final_register:* **N**) ≜

  action: Assign ($2 * initial\_register + 1$, *final_register*←)

Halve (**in** *initial_register:* **N**; **out** *final_register:* **N**) ≜

  action: Assign (*initial_register* **div** 2, *final_register*←)

Print (**in** *register:* **N**, *initial_file:* **N***; **out** *final_file:* **N***) ≜

  action: Assign (*initial_file* ++ <*register*>, *final_file*←)

Compound (**in** *initial_register:* **N**, *initial_file:* **N***;

      out *final_register:* **N**, *final_file:* **N***) ≜

  *Instruction** (*initial_register*, *initial_file*,

        final_register←, *final_file*←)

Figure 4.3: An attribute grammar for Lullaby (procedural view)

The preceding specification uses the following conventions:

- Each left-hand side is treated as a routine header, and each right-hand side as the corresponding routine body. A construct name occurring on the right (for example *Instruction* in the right-hand side for *Program*) is treated as a call to the associated routine, with actual arguments as given. For clarity, a ← sign, suggesting assignment, follows any actual argument whose value must be computed by the routine.

- *Instruction* has an **out** argument (attribute), *final_register*, whose final value is not needed by *Program* because the result of a program is given by the final file contents alone. The corresponding actual argument is absent from the call; hence the two consecutive commas in the right-hand side of the production for *Program*.

- The basic instructions of Lullaby (*Double_to_even* etc.) are terminal constructs in the abstract syntax, and so had no production in the original grammar. But they must have productions in the attribute grammar since they affect the semantics (the attributes). The right-hand sides of these productions use a special construct *Assign* (*source, target*). There is no production in the grammar for such special constructs, which have a predefined semantics. For *Assign*, the semantics is to assign the value of the *source* attribute to the *target* attribute. As is the rule with aggregates, the productions using *Assign* identify the corresponding component through a tag, here *action*.

- All values involved are non-negative integers; **div** denotes integer division.

- Notations (reminder): <> is the empty sequence, ++ is sequence concatenation.

The techniques illustrated by this example may be used to write attribute grammar specifications for actual programming languages. The specifications will need other purely semantic constructs, in the spirit of *Assign*, to describe operations on attributes.

4.2.3 The object-oriented view

The above discussion modeled constructs as routines. As it is so often the case in software, this "function-oriented" (procedural) view is not sufficient and we should complement it with an "object-oriented" (data) view, which will help us grasp the full extent of the attribute concept.

In this approach, constructs will be viewed as abstractly defined **data types**, such as they exist in modern programming languages, or, even more appropriately, as **classes** in the sense that object-oriented programming has given to this term.

In an object-oriented language such as Simula, Smalltalk or Eiffel, a class describes a number of possible run-time **objects** with the same structure; these objects are the **instances** of the class. A class is similar to a record type of Pascal or Ada, but with one important addition: a class specification describes not just the data fields of the class's instances, but also all the operations, applicable to these instances. As in Eiffel, the terms **attribute** and **routine** will refer respectively to data fields and operations. (The Smalltalk terminology is "instance variable" and "method".)

For example, a system for navigation control or simulation may include a class *SHIP*; instances of the class are objects representing individual ships. The class declaration will include not just data fields such as registry, name, tonnage and so on, but also routines applicable to ships, such as *sail* or *turn*.

The object-oriented interpretation of attribute grammars natural for a programmer:

- If you visualize a program's syntax in terms of its abstract syntax tree, then the decoration process amounts to adding semantic information to the nodes of this tree; these nodes are the "objects" of interest.

- The "classes" of which these objects are instances are simply the grammar's constructs, extended with the proper attributes. (Here the use of "attribute" to describe the data fields in object-oriented programming coincides with the meaning of this term for attribute grammars.)

- The "class declarations" are the grammar's productions.

- The "routines" are the rules for computing the value of the attributes for each node of the tree.

Below is the decorated version of the tree of figure 4.2, corresponding to the Lullaby *example* program.

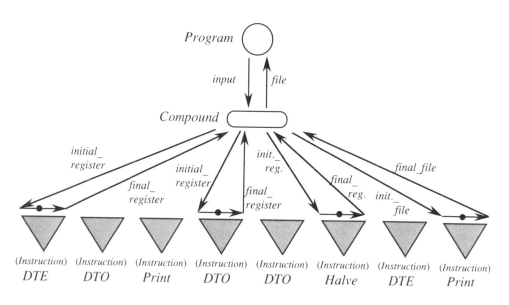

Figure 4.4: A decorated Lullaby abstract syntax tree

Semantics is represented by attribute propagation between nodes. To avoid cluttering the figure, this information has been pictured for only one specimen of each construct, and the branches between nodes, shown on figure 4.2, have been omitted. Simple arrows ($\rightarrow$), labeled by attribute names, show attributes being passed to objects or returned from them;

bulleted arrows (•→) show attribute computations. The source and target of each arrow indicate which attributes are "in" and which are "out".

The flow of attribute values shown on the figure explains the standard terminology for the two kinds of attributes: "in" attributes are called **inherited** since their values are passed to a node from its parent; "out" attributes, whose values are obtained from the node's children, are called **synthesized** attributes.[1]

For a Pascal or C programmer, the decorated tree nodes are just records which, on top of the syntactic fields representing the tree structure (children, parent...), have semantic fields representing the attributes. For example, construct *Program* may be described as a Pascal record type:

> **type** *Program* =
> > **record**
> > > -- Field representing the syntax:
> > >
> > > *body*: *Instruction*;
> > >
> > > > -- Fields representing the attributes:
> > > >
> > > > *input*: **integer**;
> > > > *output*: *Integer_list*
> >
> > **end**

where types *Instruction* and *Integer_list* must be defined separately (see "note on the exercises" at the end of this chapter); the program uses *output* in lieu of *file*, a Pascal keyword.

Beyond records, however, we should see these constructs as classes which contain not just attributes but also routines – the rules for calculating inherited and synthesized attributes. The notation imitates Eiffel, as illustrated by the following class definitions for the Lullaby constructs *Print* and *Program*.

> **class** *Print* **syntax**
> **attributes**
> > *register:* **N**;
> > *initial_file, final_file:* **N***;
>
> **rules**
> > *final_file* := *initial_file* ++ *<register>*
>
> **end** -- class *Print*

Figure 4.5: From an attribute grammar for Lullaby (O-O view): *Program*

---

[1] The notion of inherited attribute should not be confused with the notion of class inheritance, a central idea of object-oriented programming.

```
class Program syntax
    body: Instruction
attributes
    input: N; file: N*
rules
    body.initial_register := input,
    body.initial_file := <>,
    file := body.final_file
end -- class Program;
```

Figure 4.6: From an attribute grammar for Lullaby (O-O view): *Print*

The definition of a construct, now called a class and covering both syntax and semantics, includes three parts:

- The **syntax** part is identical to the right-hand side of the original production defining the construct. It is empty for terminal constructs such as *Print*.
- The **attributes** part gives extra semantic fields.
- The **rules** part describes the attribute computations to be performed during the life of an object of the construct.

It is a good exercise at this point to write the whole attributed Lullaby grammar in this new style (exercise 4.2).

4.2.4 Computing the attributes

In the attribute grammar approach, you obtain the semantics of any particular object – specimen of a given construct – by computing the value of the object's attributes. The object-oriented form makes it easier to understand these attribute computations.

The attribute computations on an object may involve the attributes of the object itself as well and attributes of its components.

- Attributes of of the object itself may be called **local** attributes. For example, *input* in class *Program* and *final_file* in class *Print* are local.
- Attributes of the fields are written with a dot notation and may be called **remote** attributes. Examples in class *Program* include *body.initial_register* and *body.final_file* .

The "local" or "remote" qualification only makes sense with respect to a given class: an attribute which is local to a class may be used as remote in other classes.

Let us say that an attribute a used as the target of an assignment in the **rules** part of a class is a **local target** if it is a local attribute of the class, and a **remote target** if it is a remote attribute. In class *Program*, *file* is a local target and *initial_register* is a remote target.

There is a simple connection between these notions and the distinction introduced above between inherited and synthesized (**in** and **out**) attributes:

> In an attribute grammar, an attribute is inherited if it appears as remote target in a class, and synthesized if it appears as local target in a class.

An obvious requirement for usable attribute grammars is that any attribute (of some construct, say T) should appear as the target of **at most one** assignment over the whole grammar – either local, in the class for T, or remote, in another class. This implies in particular that **no attribute may be both inherited and synthesized**.

The order in which the rules part lists the attribute computations is not meaningful. (This is why they are separated by commas, rather than semicolons which carry a connotation of order.) But it does not mean that these computations may be performed in *any* order. If an attribute appears both as the target of one assignment and in the right-hand side of another assignment, then the former assignment must be performed first. Two assignments that have no such connection may be performed in an arbitrary order, or in parallel.

So the order of the computations is governed by the attributes that they involve, not by the order in which they are listed in the class. An active area of research in attribute grammars is the design of algorithms to analyze attribute grammars and produce acceptable orderings, minimizing attribute computation time.

4.2.5 Attribute grammars: summary and perspective

The attribute grammar technique is a simple and productive idea, based on an incremental approach that uses syntax as the basis for specifying semantics. It has proved to be well adapted to compiler design: many of the current "compiler-compiler" efforts, aimed at producing compilers automatically from language descriptions, are based on attribute grammars for their semantic part. So are semantic extensions to the structural editors mentioned in the previous chapters.

The rest of this book does not discuss attribute grammars any further for two reasons:

- The method is in a sense too "algorithmic" vis-à-vis the general goal of providing mathematically unimpeachable specifications of programming languages. Even though the concepts could be introduced in a more mathematical spirit than above, notions that bear a strong procedural scent, such as assignment to a component of a data structure, must play an important part.

- Paradoxically, the attribute approach may also be considered as not complete enough, since so much depends on the choice of attributes and rules. What you get is a framework for semantic specification methods rather than a fully defined method. The above specifications of Lullaby were representative of one particular style, which may be called "interpreter-oriented" since they include the input and output of a given program as part of the attributes; in this respect, they are close to the *operational* specification given below in 4.4. "Compiler-oriented" attribute grammar specifications, of the kind used in compiler-compilers, are also possible; they rely on attributes characterizing the programs alone (excluding their data), and so can be used for code generation.

We might almost say that any semantic specification method is a variant of the attribute grammar as long as it defines semantics on top of the abstract syntax, since it may then be viewed as adding semantic properties of some kind to the nodes of abstract syntax trees. Such a broad definition would cover all the methods described in this book.

These observations on attribute grammars do not detract from the importance of the concepts, which you may further explore through exercises 4.1 and 4.2.

4.3 TRANSLATIONAL SEMANTICS

The idea of translational semantics is to express the meaning of a language by a translation schema which, for any program in the language, yields a program in a simpler and, it is hoped, better understood language.

The figure at the top of the adjacent page illustrates the idea. The bottom half of the figure ("Execution") is outside of the semantic specification proper; it shows how the semantic function, applied to a source program, yields a target program which, if run on input data, will yield results.

4.3.1 Translating Lullaby into Oulala

In the case at hand, we may choose as target language an assembly language well adapted to the postulated machine and to Lullaby. Consider the low-level language Oulala ("Outrageously Useless Lilliputian Assembly Language for Analphabets") with the instructions shown next. Oulala is so small that we do not bother to distinguish between its abstract and concrete grammars.

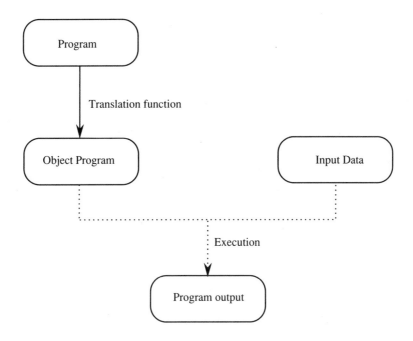

Figure 4.7: The translational approach

Instruction	Argument	Effect
STOP	no argument	Switch machine off.
READ	no argument	Read non-negative integer value *val* from keyboard and store it into register.
WRITE	no argument	Print out value of register.
OR	*val*	Perform boolean "or" of value *val* with value of register.
SHIFT	*val*	Shift binary value of register by |*val*| positions (left or right shift depending on whether *val* is positive or negative); fill emptied positions with zeroes.

The translational semantics of Lullaby will consist of two functions, mapping Lullaby instructions and programs to their Oulala equivalents:

$T_{Program}$: *Program* $\rightarrow$ *Sequence of Oulala instructions*

$T_{Instruction}$: *Instruction* $\rightarrow$ *Sequence of Oulala instructions*

These functions are defined as follows:

$T_{Program}$ (*p*: *Program*) $\triangleq$ *<READ> ++ T (p.body) ++ <STOP>*

$T_{Instruction}$ (*i*: *Instruction*) $\triangleq$
>   **case** *i* **of**
>>   *Double_to_even* $\Rightarrow$ *<SHIFT* 1*>* $|$
>>   *Double_to_odd* $\Rightarrow$ *<SHIFT* 1, *OR* 1*>* $|$
>>   *Halve* $\Rightarrow$ *<SHIFT* –1*>* $|$
>>   *Print* $\Rightarrow$ *<WRITE>* $|$
>>   *Compound* $\Rightarrow$
>>>   **if** *i.EMPTY* **then** *<>*
>>>   **else** *T* (*i.FIRST*) *++ T* (*i.TAIL*) **end**
>   **end**

With this definition, the following translation into a sequence of Oulala instructions gives the translational semantics of the *example* program:

<READ, SHIFT 1, *SHIFT* 1, *OR* 1, *WRITE, SHIFT* 1,

   OR 1, *SHIFT* 1, *OR* 1, *SHIFT* –1, *SHIFT* 1, *WRITE, STOP>*

4.3.2 Discussion

Despite the simplicity of Lullaby, the above specification shows well enough the advantages and limitations of the translational method. Once popular, this method has not been much pursued in recent years.

On the positive side, a translation scheme gives insight into the language, and may help compiler writers. But the method lacks abstraction and generality. A translational specification is too dependent on the choice of a particular target machine to satisfy the other goals of formal specifications, such as language standardization or program verification.

On closer look, even applicability to compiler writing is questionable since you may need to rework a translational definition completely for a different target machine.

The method also suffers from a more fundamental limitation. It amounts to defining a programming language in terms of another – undoubtedly simpler, but still a programming language. This leads to the natural question, "How is the target language itself defined?". An acceptable answer would require a target language whose semantics is defined beyond doubt. This will be achieved by the denotational method (4.5): there too we will encounter a translation scheme, but the target of the translation is a set of mathematical objects, not a programming language.

As a result of these limitations, the translational method does not appear adequate as a general method for programming language specification. But it retains its use in two important respects, one practical and the other more theoretical.

4.3.3 Specifying compilers

The first application uses the translational method as a formal tool for the design of compilers: by writing a set of translation functions, you specify the precise transformations that a compiler must perform.

In spite of the above reservations, this remains useful in connection with the growing practice of writing compilers for higher-level languages that produce code in a low-level but relatively portable programming language such as Fortran or C.

4.3.4 Two-tier specifications

The other important application of translational semantics is to simplify language specifications based on some other method.

Most programming languages contain conceptually redundant constructs, which can be defined in terms of others. For example, the **repeat** ... **until** .. and **for** ... loops of Pascal, C, Ada and other languages are among the notational conveniences (sometimes called "bells and whistles") which do not contribute any new concept, since both can be expressed in terms of a **while** loop. In such a case you may divide the language into two parts for the purpose of semantic specification: a *core* to be specified using an advanced method, and *extensions* whose semantics will be expressed in terms of the core constructs, using the translational method. The resulting two-tier specifications are more easily understood than a specification lumping all features together.

Assuming for example that we want to extend Graal (3.2.6) with a **repeat** ... loop, with the abstract syntax

Repeat ≜ *rbody*: *Instruction*; *exit*: *Expression*

then for any *Repeat* construct *r* you may define an equivalent construct in the Graal core:

Compound (<r.body,
            Loop (body: r.rbody, test: Expression (Binary
                    (term1 : r.exit,

                    term2: Expression (Constant (Boolean_constant (false))),

                    op: Operator (Relational_op (Eq))))) >)

This definition accounts for the two features that distinguish a *Repeat* instruction from a while *Loop*: the *Repeat* always executes its body at least once, and its boolean expression is an exit condition, not a continuation condition.

If you are given a specification of any flavor for the rest of the language, including *Compound* and *Loop*, you may use the above translation scheme as an excuse for not writing a specification of the semantics of *Repeat* from scratch. Chapter 7 uses this technique to extend the specification of core Graal; for example, 7.7 will "implement" routines, in a formal sense, using a specification developed earlier for blocks (7.6)

4.4 OPERATIONAL SEMANTICS

4.4.1 Overview

If a translational semantic definition amounts to a compiler for the language, an operational semantic definition is like an interpreter. The idea is to express the semantics of a language by giving a mechanism that makes it possible to determine the effect of any program in the language. Such a mechanism is an "interpreting automaton": a formal device capable of formally executing a program.

The following figure illustrates the approach; it should be contrasted with its translational equivalent in figure 4.7 (page 97). The semantic description is seen here as an abstract mechanism that yields the result of executing an arbitrary program on an arbitrary input.

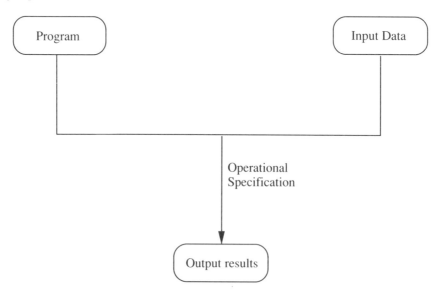

Figure 4.8: The operational approach

What characterizes operational semantics is the use of an interpreting automaton to
define the semantics of constructs. But this defines a class of methods rather than a single
method; there is room for much variation in the choice of interpreting automaton. In
particular, some automata may be quite concrete – close to executable programming
languages – whereas others are much more mathematical.

Two such variants are sketched below.

4.4.2 Operational semantics with a concrete automaton

In the first variant, the interpreting automaton is assumed to be a computer which can
execute programs written in a simple programming notation similar to what is found in
common programming languages. This automaton is equivalent to what is often called a
"virtual machine", that is to say the combination of an actual computer and a compiler for
a language, here Eiffel-like, running on that computer.[2]

The description consists of two routines, one for programs and one for instructions.
In programming terminology these are "function" routines, that is to say routines which
return a result, not to be confused with mathematical functions. (Following the Eiffel
convention, each function routine has access to a special variable *Result*, local to each call,
whose final value is what the routine returns to its caller.)

The routine describing the semantics of Lullaby programs returns the final contents of
the output file:

program_effect (*p* : *Program*; *input*: **N**): **N* is**

        -- Returns the file resulting from an execution of *p*
        -- when a user types in the initial value *input*.

  do

        Result := instruction_effect (*p*.*body*, *input*, <>) (2)
          -- Routine *instruction_effect* is given below

  end -- *program_effect*

The symmetric treatment of arguments *p*, representing the program, and *input*,
representing the input, is typical of interpretive approaches, as illustrated in figure 4.8.

Routine *program_effect* relies on a routine *instruction_effect*, which returns a two-
element sequence, containing the final values of the register and the file; *program_effect*
only uses the second element of that result. Here is *instruction_effect*:

---

[2] Apart from the use of a simplified loop syntax in one of the routines, the only difference
between this notation and actual Eiffel is the use of three Metanot conventions: **N** rather than Eiffel's
INTEGER; pairs of the form <*a, b*>; and sequences. It is in fact easy to manipulate pairs and
sequences in Eiffel through different notations, using library classes.

instruction_effect (*i*: *Instruction*, *r*: **N**, *f*: **N***): **N** × **N*** **is**

        -- Returns the register and file resulting from an execution of *i*
        -- starting with *r* as initial register and *f* as initial file.

  do
     inspect
       i
     when *Double_to_even* **then** *Result* := <2∗*r*, *f*>
     when *Double_to_odd* **then** *Result* := <2∗*r* + 1, *f*>
     when *Halve* **then** *Result* := <*r* **div** 2, *f*>
     when *Print* **then** *Result* := <*r*, *file* ++ <*r*>>
     when *Compound* **then**
         Result := <*r*, *f*>;
         for *i*: 1 .. *i*.*LENGTH* **loop**
            Result := *instruction_effect* (*s* (*i*), *Result* (1), *Result* (2))
         end
     end;
  end -- *instruction_effect*

Like the **case** instructions of Pascal and Ada, the **inspect** instruction describes multi-branch choices.

The branch corresponding to the *Compound* case may also be written, replacing the **for** loop with further recursion, as *Result* := *compound_effect* (*i*, *Result* (1), *Result* (2)), with the following routine definition:

compound_effect (*c*: *Compound*, *r*: **N**, *f*: **N***): **N** × **N*** **is**

        -- The register and file resulting from an execution of *c*
        -- starting with *x* and *f* as initial register and file.

  do
     if not *c*.*empty* **then**
        Result := *instruction_effect* (*c*.*FIRST*, *r*, *f*);
        Result := *compound_effect* (*c*.*TAIL*, *Result* (1), *Result* (2))
     end
  end -- *compound_effect*

You may translate the operational definition given by the above routines into an actual program that will compute the result of any Lullaby program (see exercise 4.4).

4.4.3 A more abstract specification

The preceding specification is very concrete and almost directly executable. A way to make operational specifications more abstract while keeping the same structure is to repudiate routines, which are a programming concept, and to replace them with mathematical objects: functions. (Here of course the word "function" is used in its mathematical sense, not in its programming sense of routine which returns a result.)

For example we may define a mathematical function *instruction_effect* by removing all explicit imperative constructs. The function will look as follows.

$$instruction\_effect\text{: } Instruction \times \mathbf{N} \times \mathbf{N}^* \rightarrow \mathbf{N} \times \mathbf{N}^*$$

instruction_effect (*i*: *Instruction*, *register*: **N**, *file*: **N***) $\triangleq$

    case *i* **of**

        Double_to_even $\Rightarrow$ *<2*register, file>* |

        ...

        Print $\Rightarrow$ *<register, file* ++ *<register>>* |

        ...

    end

The function takes as arguments an instruction, an integer representing the initial register value, and an integer sequence representing the initial file contents. Its result is the pair *<final register value, final file contents>*. The two cases given are self-explanatory; you may easily complete the others, which will resemble clauses of the denotational specification given later in this chapter. (The *Compound* case may use an auxiliary function *compound_effect*.)

The following function, readily adapted from the corresponding routine in the first form, gives the semantics of an entire program:

$$program\_effect : Program \times \mathbf{N} \rightarrow \mathbf{N}^*$$

program_effect (*p*: *Program*, *register*: **N**) $\triangleq$

    instruction_effect (*p.body*, *register*, *output*) (2)

(As before, *program_effect* drops the register component of *instruction_effect*'s result by selecting the pair's second element, the file.)

The *<register, file>* pairs (members of $\mathbf{N} \times \mathbf{N}^*$) which appear in these definitions describe **states** that may exist during the execution of a program. Operational specifications describe the semantics of a computation as a sequence of transitions from state to state. We will encounter the notion of state again in denotational semantics.

4.4.4 Discussion and assessment

The operational approach presents some definite advantages. It gives a concrete, intuitive description of the programming language being studied; it appeals to programmers because the descriptions given are so close to real programs. Also, it is fairly easy to devise a mechanism (interpreter) to execute such a description on example programs; this makes operational semantics attractive as a tool for testing new languages or language features, whose effect can be simulated through actual execution of semantic descriptions, long before any compiler has been written.

Operational semantics may thus be viewed as the application to language design and implementation of ideas that have attracted much attention in software engineering: the notions of **rapid prototyping** and **executable specifications**.

Using these methods, one tries to build a working system early in the life-cycle of a software project. This system, usually inefficient (as is an interpreted language implementation compared to a compiled one) is not the final product, nor even a preliminary version of it; indeed, it is designed to be discarded later. Being made available early and at much less expense than the final product, it may provide the designers with insights into the problem, and help them avoid costly mistakes in areas such as user interfaces, data structures and algorithms.

The very qualities of the operational method, however, also speak of its limitations. Striving to be executable, operational descriptions lose one of the essential qualities of specifications: independence from the implementation. What an operational description specifies is one particular way to execute programs.

Even the functional form of operational description (the second given), although more abstract than the first, still specifies a precise sequence of states through which a computation must go. (If the first form looks like a program in an imperative programming language, the second is close to a Lisp implementation.)

Like its translational counterpart, then, an operational description runs the risk of being over-constraining, and consequently of offering little help for several of the applications of semantics mentioned in chapter 1: program proving, understanding languages at a high level of abstraction, compiler writing, language standardization.

4.5 DENOTATIONAL SEMANTICS

4.5.1 Overview

The approach considered next, denotational semantics, may be viewed as a variant of translational semantic: using this method, we will express the semantics of a programming language by a translation schema that associates a meaning (**denotation**) with each program in the language. Indeed, the following illustration of the method resembles the top half of the corresponding figure for the translational method (figure 4.7, page 97).

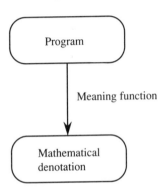

Figure 4.9: The denotational approach

The difference is in the result of the translation. In translational semantics the meaning of a program is another program; in denotational semantics it is a mathematical object. This avoids the circularity problem.

The denotational description of a programming language is given by a set of **meaning functions** M associated with constructs of the grammar; each of these functions is of the form

$$M_T : T \to D_T$$

where T is a construct such as *Instruction*, *Program* etc. Such functions will consistently have names of the form M (for "meaning"), subscripted by the name of a construct.

Most of the M functions will turn out to be "higher-order" functions, yielding functions as results. To highlight the specific nature of these functions, Metanot encloses their arguments in brackets rather than ordinary parentheses, as in $M_T [t]$.

The sets D_T of denotations may be different for the various constructs T; they are called **semantic domains**. In contrast, constructs are called **syntactic domains**.

In the context of this book, syntactic and semantic domains are simply sets; the term "domain" does not bring anything new. It has been kept for consistency with the rest of the denotational literature. Be careful to avoid any confusion with the domain of a partial function (2.5.2).

A denotational description has already been encountered in chapter 3: the semantics of the "language" of decimal integers. In that case, both semantic domains were **N**, the set of integers. In general, however, denotations will be objects more complex than just integers – usually functions.

4.5.2 Semantic domains and state

What semantic domains are needed for Lullaby?

The input to any Lullaby program is the value initially typed by the user; so the set of possible inputs is **N**, the set of non-negative integers. The result of a Lullaby program is the content of the output file on termination, that is to say a member of the set **N*** of sequences of non-negative integers. So we may view an arbitrary Lullaby program p as a mechanism which for any member of **N** will compute a member of **N***.

This transformation from input value to output file may be taken as the **meaning**, or **denotation** $M_{Program}\ [p]$ of the program (the target of the arrow on figure 4.9). Mathematically, such a transformation may be modeled as a function from **N** to **N***. So for a given p the function $M_{Program}\ [p]$ has signature

$$M_{Program}\ [p]: \mathbf{N}\ \rightarrow\ \mathbf{N*}$$

The meaning function $M_{Program}$ associates such a denotation (a function from **N** to **N***) with any program p. $M_{Program}$ itself is a functional (a higher-order function, whose result is itself a function), with signature

$$M_{Program}: Program\ \rightarrow\ (\mathbf{N}\ \rightarrow\ \mathbf{N*})$$

Many such functionals will be encountered in chapters 6 to 9. The exercises of chapters 2 and 5 will help you become an expert juggler with functionals.

The set **N** → **N*** of input-to-output functions is the first semantic domain needed for the denotational description of Lullaby.

Besides $M_{Program}$, we will need to define $M_{Instruction}$, the meaning function for instructions. This will require that we model the effect of executing an instruction. This effect may only be determined if we know the conditions, or **state**, under which the instruction is executed.

In Lullaby, we may define the state of a computation entirely by providing two pieces of information:

- The value of the register.
- The current contents of the output file.

We may describe the effect of an instruction executed in such a state by giving the new state that will result from that execution.

You may picture a state as a snapshot (a symbolic "memory dump") taken at some step during program execution. The notion of state (already encountered in the operational method) plays a key role in denotational semantics. Finding the proper mathematical model for the state and other semantic domains is an essential step in writing a denotational description.

To specify formally the notion of state in Lullaby, we may introduce the following semantic domain, defined as a cartesian product:

$$State \triangleq \mathbf{N} \times \mathbf{N}^*$$

This is the second and last semantic domain needed for Lullaby.

4.5.3 Meaning functions

Equipped with the semantic domains, including the state, we can specify the denotation of an arbitrary instruction i: it is a function which, for any state in which the instruction is executed, yields the state that will result from this execution. So for given i this function is of the form

$$M_{Instruction} [i]: State \rightarrow State$$

This means that $M_{Instruction}$ itself is a second-order functional:

$$M_{Instruction} : Instruction \rightarrow (State \rightarrow State)$$

It is easy to express the value of $M_{Instruction}$ by case analysis. For any i, $M_{Instruction} [i]$ is a function from $State$ to $State$, so its value $M_{Instruction} [i] (\sigma)$ must be defined for any state σ. From the way states have been defined, σ may be expressed as a pair $<register, file>$, where $register$ is an integer and $file$ is a sequence of integers.

$$M_{Instruction} [i: Instruction] (<register, file>: State) \triangleq$$

    case i **of**

        $Double\_to\_even \Rightarrow <2*register, file> \mid$

        $Double\_to\_odd \Rightarrow <2*register + 1, file> \mid$

        $Halve \Rightarrow <register$ **div** $2, file> \mid$

        $Print \Rightarrow <register, file \mathbin{+\!\!+} <register>> \mid$

        $Compound \Rightarrow M_{Compound} [i] (<register, file>)$

    end

where the auxiliary function

$$M_{Compound} : Compound \rightarrow (State \rightarrow State)$$

is defined as:

$M_{Compound}$ [c: Compound] (<register, file>: State) $\triangleq$

    if c.empty **then**

        <register, file>

           -- Execution of an empty compound leaves the state unchanged

    else

        $M_{Compound}$ [i.TAIL] ($M_{Instruction}$ [i.FIRST] (<register, file>))

    end

The **else** branch defines the effect of executing a non-empty compound c, starting in state $\sigma \triangleq$ <register, file>, as the effect of executing the tail of c (that is to say c deprived of its first instruction) starting in the state

$\sigma' \triangleq M_{Instruction}$ [c.FIRST] (σ)

which results from the execution of the first instruction of c, starting in state σ.

If c is a non-empty compound, then $c.FIRST$ is an instruction but $c.TAIL$ is a (possibly empty) compound; this is why the specification uses a separate function $M_{Compound}$ for the Compound branch. An alternative, avoiding explicit recursion, is to use the the **over** ... **apply** ... notation (3.9.3).

The Compound branch defines function $M_{Instruction}$ [i], when i is a compound instruction, as the composition of two other functions: $M_{Instruction}$ [i.FIRST] and $M_{Compound}$ [i.TAIL]. That functional composition is an appropriate model for the notion of instruction sequencing, in other words a mathematical equivalent of the semicolon as used in Algol-like languages, is an important property to remember.

With this definition of the $M_{Instruction}$ function, expressing the meaning function $M_{Program}$ for programs is easy: the meaning of a program is the function that associates with any input value *input* the result of executing the program body starting in a state where the register has value *input* and the output file is empty. So:

$M_{Program}$ [p: Program] (input: **N**) $\triangleq$

    given

        <register, file> $\triangleq M_{Instruction}$ [p.body] (<input, <>>)

    then

        file

    end

This completes the denotational specification of Lullaby.

4.5.4 Discussion: denotational versus operational definitions

You will certainly have noted the similarity between the definitions of $M_{Instruction}$ and $M_{Program}$, on the one hand, and those of the functions *instruction_effect* and *program_effect* in the more abstract form of operational specification – the functional form given on page 103.

The relation is more than a similarity: if we make the notion of state explicit in the operational functions, the denotational functions become, quite precisely, their curried counterparts. Recall (2.8.2) that the curried version of a two-argument function, obtained by specialization on the first argument, is a one-argument function that produces a function as result.

Since currying is a one-to-one correspondence, the difference between denotational and (functional) operational specifications may seem rather feeble.

In Lullaby and in many other cases the distinction is indeed subtle. An operational specification treats program elements (objects such as programs, instructions etc.) on a par with the data (the input and the state). In contrast, the meaning functions of denotational semantics have program elements as their sole arguments, independently of any data; handling the data is not their business, but that of the functions which they yield as output when applied to individual program elements (for example $M_{Instruction}$ $[i]$ for a given i).

This distinction is the mathematical equivalent of the difference between compilers and interpreters (see exercise 2.5). More profoundly, the denotational method's exclusive focus on the programs, to the exclusion of the state and other data elements, enables it to reach a level of abstraction which cannot be obtained in the operational approach, however abstract you choose your interpreting automata. This means in particular that the state will be less visible in denotational specifications, and will often be a more abstract state, further removed conceptually from the concrete states of the computation on an actual computer.

More generally, denotational specifications provide an elegant mechanism to define the semantics of programs in terms of classical mathematical notions such as functions. By using standard mathematics as its reference base, the method avoids the circularity problems encountered previously. It achieves this elegance through abstractness, especially for non-trivial languages which will require high-order functionals in their specifications.

Denotational semantics will be studied in more detail in chapters 6 to 8.

4.6 AXIOMATIC SEMANTICS

The axiomatic method views the definition of programming languages from yet another perspective: a language's semantics as a *theory* of the programs written in that language.

Paradoxically, this approach may be viewed as both more abstract (still) and more practical than the denotational method. It is more abstract since it does not try to ascertain what a program "means", but only what may be proved about it. But this also makes it more practical from a software engineering viewpoint, since for actual software construction we are usually less interested in having a formal model of our programs than in learning important facts about these programs, such as whether they will terminate properly and what kind of values they will compute.

4.6.1 Overview

The axiomatic specification of a programming language will be a mathematical theory for that language, that is to say a system in which you can express interesting statements about programs written in this language, and prove or disprove such statements.

> Recall that this book uses the word "statement" in its usual English sense of a property being expressed (*stated*), not in the common programming sense of command, covered by the word **instruction**.

The statements of interest are formal expressions called **formulae**. A formula may be true or false; a true formula is called a **theorem**. The aim of a theory is to define which formulae are theorems.

A mathematical theory is made up of three kinds of component:

- **Syntactic rules** which determine what the well-formed formulae, expressing the statements of interest (true or false), are.
- **Axioms**: basic theorems, which are accepted without proof.
- **Inference rules**: mechanisms for deducing new theorems from previously established ones.

These components will make it possible to prove that certain formulae are theorems. A proof consists of zero or more applications of the inference rules, starting from the axioms.

The formulae of interest in axiomatic semantics are relative to programs and the effect they have on the objects they manipulate. More precisely, the well-formed formulae will be **pre-post formulae**[3] of the form

$$\{P\} \ a \ \{Q\}$$

---

[3] Chapter 9 will also introduce another kind, "wp-formulae".

where a is an instruction of the language and P and Q are **assertions**, that is to say properties of the program objects, which may be true or false. For Lullaby, assertions will serve to express such properties as "the register has a value greater than 5" or "the file contains three elements".

The meaning of a pre-post formula $\{P\}\ a\ \{Q\}$ is the following:[4]

If a is executed in a state in which assertion P is satisfied, then it will result in a state in which assertion Q is satisfied.

P is called the **precondition** in such a rule; Q is the **postcondition** (hence the name "pre-post formula").

Both the axioms and inference rules, collectively called rules, will deal with pre-post formulae; to give an axiomatic semantic specification of a programming language, you need to associate at least one rule with every construct of the language.

4.6.2 An axiomatic specification of Lullaby

The following is such an axiomatic theory for Lullaby. In this language, the only assertions of interest are relative to the values of the single register and of the output file. They may be expressed as predicates (boolean total functions) of two arguments, called *register* and *file*. Here is an example of such an assertion:

$$register \neq 7 \ \wedge\ file.LENGTH < 10 \ \wedge\ file.LAST = register + 3$$

It is not hard to see how axioms may be associated with the simple instructions of the language. Consider the *Double_to_even* instruction. Let P *(register, file)* be an assertion and assume it holds before a certain execution of this instruction. Then after the execution, the new state of the computation may be characterized by the following assertion (where *even* (x) is true if and only if x is an even integer):

$$even\ (register) \ \wedge\ P\ (register\ \textbf{div}\ 2, file)$$

In other words, the new value of the register is even, and its old value, which was half the current one, satisfied P together with the contents of the file (which have not changed).

You should be careful here to avoid a trivial but classical mistake: using $2 * register$ instead of *register* **div** 2 in the postcondition. If P was true of the value of the register before execution of the instruction, say x, then the new value is $y \triangleq 2 * x$, so P holds for y **div** 2.

---

[4] The reader who has encountered pre-post rules before will note that there is no termination problem in Lullaby. See 9.7.7 for a general treatment of termination in axiomatic semantics.

These observations yield the axiom for the *Double_to_even* instruction and, in similar fashion, for *Double_to_odd* and *Halve*. For ease of reference, each axiom will receive a name, of the form $A_{Double\_to\_even}$ etc.

$A_{Double\_to\_even}$

  {*P* (*register*, *file*)}   *Double_to_even*   {*even* (*register*) ∧ *P* (*register* **div** 2, *file*)}

$A_{Double\_to\_odd}$

  {*P* (*register*, *file*)}   *Double_to_odd*   {*odd* (*register*) ∧ *P* ((*register* − 1) **div** 2, *file*)}

A_{Halve}

  {*P* (*register*, *file*)}   *Halve*   {*P* (2∗*register*, *file*) ∨ *P* (2∗*register* + 1, *file*)}

These axioms apply to an arbitrary assertion *P* involving the register and the file; *odd* (*x*) is true if an only iff *x* is odd. Note the last axiom: since it is not known whether the previous value of *register* was odd or even, all that can be said is that *file* (which has not changed) satisfies *P* with either twice the new value or twice the new value plus one.

Next comes the axiom for the *Print* instruction:

A_{Print}

  {*P* (*register*, *file*)}

  Print

  {*P* (*register*, *file*.*HEAD*) ∧ *file*.*LENGTH* > 0 ∧ *file*.*LAST* = *register*}

The postcondition expresses that the *register* has been appended to the output *file* and everything else is unchanged; so whatever was true of *register* and *file* is now true of *register* and the head of *file*, that is to say *file* deprived of its last element.

There remains to give a rule for the *Compound* instruction. Here, however, an axiom will not suffice: even in the simple case of a compound instruction *c* consisting of just two instructions, *c* (1) and *c* (2), no general rule of the form

  {*P*} *c* {*Q*}

may be given without some assumptions on the nature of *c* (1) and *c* (2). What is needed here is an **inference rule** making it possible to deduce properties of *c* from properties of *c* (1) and *c* (2).

The inference rule, written in the general case in which *c* may consist of an arbitrary number of instructions, is as follows (for arbitrary predicates *P*, *Q* and *R* involving *register* and/or *file*):

$I_{Compound}$

$$\frac{\{P\}\ c1\ \{Q\},\ \{Q\}\ c2\ \{R\}}{\{P\}\ c1 + \!\!+ c2\ \{R\}}$$

The meaning of such an inference rule is that if the formulae above the horizontal line, called the **premises** of the rule, are theorems, then the formula below the line, called the **conclusion** of the rule, may be inferred as a new theorem. To apply the rule, you must be able to deduce every premise from the axioms by zero or more applications of inference rules.

Two more rules are needed to make $I_{Compound}$ usable in practice: one for the empty compound, and one for compounds containing just one instruction. An axiom and an inference rule will do the job. (See also exercise 4.6.)

An empty compound maintains the truth of any assertion that held before its execution, hence the axiom:

$A0_{Compound}$

$$\{P\ (register,\ file)\}\ Compound\ (<>)\ \{P\ (register,\ file)\}$$

A compound with just one instruction has the same effect as that instruction, hence the inference rule:

$I1_{Compound}$

$$\frac{\{P\}\ i\ \{Q\}}{\{P\}\ Compound\ (<i>)\ \{Q\}}$$

Finally, we need a rule for the top construct of the language, *Program*. The only preconditions that may affect a program are of the form P *(input)*, where *input* refers to the integer initially typed by the user. The effect of a program is that of its body, executed with the register initialized to the value of this initial input and the file initially empty. Hence the inference rule for programs:

$I_{Program}$

$$\frac{\{P\ (register)\ \wedge\ file.LENGTH = 0\}\ pr.body\ \{Q\ (file)\}}{\{P\ (input)\}\ pr\ \{Q\ (file)\}}$$

If *pr* is a program, *pr.body* is an instruction; so the premise must be proved using the rules which apply to instructions. In accordance with the convention that the result of a program is entirely characterized by the final state of the file, the postcondition Q only involves the output, not the register. If *pr.body* has a postcondition involving *register*, then any reference to *register* must be dropped to obtain a viable postcondition for *pr* (see exercise 4.8).

Getting a workable Lullaby semantics requires one more inference rule. The rules above are in a sense too strong in that they cannot be used to prove an obviously correct theorem such as

F
> {*register* = 3} *Double_to_even* {*register* > 2}

since axiom $A_{Double\_to\_even}$ will only yield "stronger" theorems such as

F1
> {*register* = 3} *Double_to_even* {*even* (*register*) $\wedge$ *register* **div** 2 = 3}

or

F2
> {*register* > 1} *Double_to_even* {*even* (*register*) $\wedge$ *register* **div** 2 > 1}

both of which are direct applications of the axiom. Being able to prove F1 and F2 but not the (intuitively weaker) theorem F is an anomaly. To remedy it, a general inference rule, called the **rule of consequence**, is needed. This rule, which is not specific to Lullaby, may be written (for any instruction *a*):

CONS

$$\frac{\{P\}\ a\ \{Q\},\ P' \supset P,\ Q \supset Q'}{\{P'\}\ a\ \{Q'\}}$$

Recall that $R1 \supset R2$ ($R1$ implies $R2$) means that $R2$ is true whenever $R1$ is true.

For the above example, the following are trivial theorems of ordinary mathematics:

> (*even* (*register*) $\wedge$ *register* **div** 2 > 1) $\supset$ *register* > 2
>
> *register* = 3 $\supset$ *register* > 1

so that theorem F may be deduced from either F1 or F2 using the rule of consequence.

4.6.3 A complete proof

This completes the axiomatic semantics specification of Lullaby. As an example of how proofs may be performed using such a specification, consider the program *example* introduced on page 86. Let us prove that this program, if started with input value 0, yields a file containing the values 1 and 6. The theorem to prove may be expressed as a pre-post formula:

> {*input* = 0} *example* {*file.LENGTH* = 2 $\wedge$ *file* (1) = 1 $\wedge$ *file* (2) = 6}

The program was as follows:

example $\triangleq$

   Program (body: Compound

      (<Instruction (Double_to_even), Instruction (Double_to_odd),

      Instruction (Print), Instruction (Double_to_odd),

      Instruction (Double_to_odd), Instruction (Halve),

      Instruction (Double_to_even), Instruction (Print)>)

The proof is a sequence of lines, each of which states that a certain pre-post formula is a theorem. Like a conscientious BASIC programmer, we number lines consecutively. Each has five fields:

- A line number.
- A pre-post formula stated to be a theorem, with its three components – precondition, construct, postcondition – each on a separate field.
- A justification of the theorem, showing it as either the direct application of an axiom or a consequence of previous theorems by one or more inference rules.

A justification consists of as one or more "arguments". An argument may be the name of an axiom, the name of an inference rule, a previous line number (referring to the theorem on that line), or EM ("Elementary Mathematics") for theorems that follow directly from simple mathematics. Examples of theorems that will be deemed to follow from EM without further ado are, for an integer *register*,

$$(odd\ (register)\ \wedge\ (register - 1)\ \textbf{div}\ 2 = 0)\ \supset\ register = 1$$

and for a finite sequence *file*:

$$(file.LENGTH > 0\ \wedge\ file.HEAD = <>\ \wedge\ file.LAST = x)\ \supset\ file = <x>$$

The names of the axioms or inference rules used on each line, such as A_{Print}, serve a reminder of what the corresponding instruction is. To keep the proof reasonably compact, a few abbreviations are in order:

- *EVEN* means *even (register)* and *ODD* means *odd (register)*.
- *R* means *register*, *F* means *file*.
- *FL* means *file.LENGTH*.
- *FH* means *file.HEAD*, *FLA* means *file.LAST*.
- *EB* means *example.body*, the body of program *example*.
- / means **div**, integer division.
- Finally, *EB* $(i .. j)$ denotes the compound instruction consisting of the i-th to j-th instructions of program *example*:

   $$EB\ (i..j)\ \triangleq\ Compound\ (<EB\ (i),\ EB\ (i+1),\ ...\ EB\ (j)>)$$

The complete proof runs on the adjacent page. It hardly reads like a thriller, but is worth studying.

Lines 1 and 2 refer to the first instruction of the program, *EB* (1), a *Double_to_even*. Line 1 is a direct application of the corresponding axiom. Since the aim is to prove a property of the program *example* relative to the precondition *input* = 0, the precondition needed for the body *EB* is *register* = 0 ∧ *file.LENGTH* = 0; this is readily seen by looking at the inference rule for programs, I$_{Program}$, which will eventually crown the proof (line 23). In line 2, the postcondition of line 1 is restated more simply by using the obvious mathematical simplifications; this is permitted by the rule of consequence CONS, and by EM, which makes it possible to infer $R = 0$ from $R / 2 = 0$.

Lines 3 and 4 similarly express a property of the second instruction, *EB* (2). Line 3 is the direct application of the axiom and line 4 is the simplification.

Lines 5 to 8 combine the first two results (lines 2 and 4) to give a property of the compound <*EB* (1), *EB* (2)>. First rule I1$_{Compound}$ makes it possible to deduce properties of one-instruction compounds (<*EB* (1)> and <*EB* (2)> respectively) from those of the corresponding single instructions; this is not very interesting but technically necessary because of the way the rules deal with compounds. This allows line 7 to obtain the combined property for *EB* (1..2) by applying the really significant compound rule, I$_{compound}$. Line 8 uses the EM theorem that *file.LENGTH* = 0 is the same as *file* = <> to rewrite the postcondition in a form more convenient for the next step.

Lines 9 and 10 apply to the third instruction, a *Print*. Again, line 9 is a direct application of the axiom and line 10 has a simpler postcondition obtained from the theorem that if *file.HEAD* is empty and *file.LAST* is 1, then *file* must be the one-element file <1>.

Line 11 applies to the fourth instruction, a *Double_to_odd*. Starting here, the proof is written in a more condensed form, merging several rules to do in one step what was previously written as two separate lines (as 1 and 2, 3 and 4).

Line 12 combines the effect of the third and fourth instructions. Line 13 uses 8 and 12 to yield the combined effect of the first four instructions.

Line 14 applies the *Double_to_odd* axiom to the fifth instruction, and line 15 the *Halve* axiom to the sixth instruction. In the latter case, the postcondition given may be obtained from the one in the axiom through the rule of consequence applied to the following theorem from EM:

$$(2*R = 7) \lor (2*R + 1 = 7) \supset R = 3$$

Line 16 combines the results for the fifth and sixth instructions, showing that they cancel each other's effect. Line 17 applies to the seventh, a *Double_to_even*, and line 18 to the eighth and last, a *Print* instruction. The latter results from the EM theorem

$$file.LAST = 6 \land file.HEAD = <1> \supset file = <1, 6>$$

The effect of the whole compound is obtained by merging the last two instructions (line 19), the last four (line 20), and the whole pack (21).

Line	Precondition	Construct	Postcondition	Justification
1	$\{R = 0 \wedge FL = 0\}$	EB (1)	$\{EVEN \wedge R/2 = 0$ $\wedge FL = 0\}$	$A_{Double\_to\_even}$
2	$\{R = 0 \wedge FL = 0\}$	EB (1)	$\{R = 0 \wedge FL = 0\}$	1, CONS, EM
3	$\{R = 0 \wedge FL = 0\}$	EB (2)	$\{ODD \wedge (R{-}1)/2 = 0$ $\wedge FL = 0\}$	$A_{Double\_to\_odd}$
4	$\{R = 0 \wedge FL = 0\}$	EB (2)	$\{R = 1 \wedge FL = 0\}$	3, CONS, EM
5	$\{R = 0 \wedge FL = 0\}$	$<EB$ (1)$>$	$\{R = 0 \wedge FL = 0\}$	2, $\amalg_{Compound}$
6	$\{R = 0 \wedge FL = 0\}$	$<EB$ (2)$>$	$\{R = 1 \wedge FL = 0\}$	4, $\amalg_{Compound}$
7	$\{R = 0 \wedge FL = 0\}$	EB (1..2)	$\{R = 1 \wedge FL = 0\}$	5, 6, $I_{Compound}$
8	$\{R = 0 \wedge FL = 0\}$	EB (1..2)	$\{R = 1 \wedge F = <>\}$	7, EM, CONS
9	$\{R = 1 \wedge F = <>\}$	EB (3)	$\{R = 1 \wedge FL > 0$ $\wedge FH = <>$ $\wedge FLA = R\}$	A_{Print}
10	$\{R = 1 \wedge F = <>\}$	EB (3)	$\{R = 1 \wedge F = <1>\}$	9, EM, CONS
11	$\{R = 1 \wedge F = <1>\}$	EB (4)	$\{R = 3 \wedge F = <1>\}$	$A_{Double\_to\_odd}$, EM, CONS
12	$\{R = 1 \wedge F = <>\}$	EB (3..4)	$\{R = 3 \wedge F = <1>\}$	10, 11, $I_{Compound}$, $\amalg_{Compound}$
13	$\{R = 0 \wedge FL = 0\}$	EB (1..4)	$\{R = 3 \wedge F = <1>\}$	8, 12, $I_{Compound}$
14	$\{R = 3 \wedge F = <1>\}$	EB (5)	$\{R = 7 \wedge F = <1>\}$	$A_{Double\_to\_odd}$, EM, CONS
15	$\{R = 7 \wedge F = <1>\}$	EB (6)	$\{R = 3 \wedge F = <1>\}$	A_{Halve}, EM, CONS
16	$\{R = 3 \wedge F = <1>\}$	EB (5..6)	$\{R = 3 \wedge F = <1>\}$	14, 15, $I_{Compound}$, $\amalg_{Compound}$
17	$\{R = 3 \wedge F = <1>\}$	EB (7)	$\{R = 6 \wedge F = <1>\}$	$A_{Double\_to\_even}$, EM, CONS
18	$\{R = 6 \wedge F = <1>\}$	EB (8)	$\{R = 6 \wedge F = <1, 6>\}$	A_{Print}, EM, CONS
19	$\{R = 3 \wedge F = <1>\}$	EB (7..8)	$\{R = 6 \wedge F = <1, 6>\}$	17, 18, $I_{Compound}$, $\amalg_{Compound}$
20	$\{R = 3 \wedge F = <1>\}$	EB (5..8)	$\{R = 6 \wedge F = <1, 6>\}$	16, 19, $I_{Compound}$
21	$\{R = 0 \wedge FL = 0\}$	EB (1..8)	$\{R = 6 \wedge F = <1, 6>\}$	13, 20, $I_{Compound}$
22	$\{R = 0 \wedge FL = 0\}$	EB	$\{F = <1, 6>\}$	21, CONS
23	$\{input = 0\}$	*example*	$\{F = <1, 6>\}$	22, $I_{Program}$

Figure 4.10: A proof in axiomatic semantics

     It remains to translate this property of the compound instruction *example .body* (or *EB*) into a property of the whole program *example*. To this effect, line 23 uses the rule of consequence to drop the unnecessary mention of the register in the postcondition found for *EB*; one application of $I_{Program}$ and we are through.

4.6.4 Discussion

The axiomatic method provides a firm basis on which to establish not only semantic definitions of programming languages but also such important applications as program proofs and systematic program construction, as will be seen in chapter 9.

Chapter 10 will show that an axiomatic theory may be deduced from a denotational model of the same language, making the denotational method appear theoretically more fundamental.

The Lullaby example and the proof carried out in the previous section may give the impression that proofs, although tedious, are conceptually easy: many steps and minute details are involved, but each step is a straightforward application of the axioms and inference rules. Indeed, it would seem that the proofs could be handled by a not unreasonably complicated program.

This impression is not confirmed by the practice of axiomatic semantics. The tediousness is there, although some of it may be removed by judicious use of software tools; but proofs are not as easy as the Lullaby example would tend to suggest.

In Lullaby, the axioms and inference rules make it possible to "compute" postconditions directly from preconditions (or the opposite, which is the object of exercise 4.7). Once the precondition to a program is known, no invention is needed to obtain the postcondition by working step by step through the instructions of the program, as in the above proof. (The backwards process also works without particular difficulty.) But with more realistic programming languages, in particular if they involve loop instructions, this will not be possible any more. Some of the intermediate assertions will have to be provided by the person doing the proof; unlike with Lullaby, no simple algorithm may generate these intermediate assertions.

So with real languages, human invention is still required in the proof of a program – as in the proof of a mathematical theorem. Given the theoretical power of programming languages, this should not be a surprise. More on this and related issues in chapter 9.

4.7 BIBLIOGRAPHICAL NOTES

The denotational and axiomatic methods are studied in detail in the next chapters; here references will only given on the other methods seen in this chapter.

Attribute grammars were introduced by [Knuth 1968] and have been extensively studied in connection with compiling techniques. From the considerable literature on the application of attribute grammars to compiling, chapter 8 of [Waite 1984] may be singled out. Attribute grammars have also been applied to the inclusion of semantic facilities into structure editors (3.7.1): see in particular [Reps 1984]. A closely related notion is affix grammars, introduced by [Koster 1971]; affix grammars have proved to be an effective basis not only for compiler writing but also for software development in the CDL 2 language and environment [Bayer 1981].

There are no recent publications on translational semantics; some early papers referring to this method may be found in [Steel 1966].

A variant of the translational approach not studied in this book is "two-level" or "van Wijngaarden" grammars, also known as W-grammars. This method, introduced in [van Wijngaarden 1966] and applied to the definition of Algol 68 in [van Wijngaarden 1975], uses a two-level BNF-like formalism to catch semantic information. An introduction may be found in [Pagan 1981]; see also [Marcotty 1976].

Operational methods received much attention as a result of the work of the IBM Vienna laboratory in the nineteen-sixties and seventies. The approach developed by this group, known as VDL (Vienna Definition Language), was applied to the formal definition of PL/I. A survey of VDL may be found in [Wegner 1972]; several books have been published on this approach, in particular [Ollongren 1974] and [Lee 1972]. (The VDM method, although it evolved originally from VDL, is denotational, not operational; references to it are given in chapter 6.)

EXERCISES

Note on the exercises

Exercises 4.1 to 4.5 require that you write a program to compute the semantics of Lullaby programs according to one of the methods of this chapter.

To write these programs, you may use the language of your choice; since symbolic manipulation is involved, reasonable choices include Lisp, Pascal and derivatives, Eiffel, Smalltalk, Prolog. To experiment with your solutions, you may use the Lullaby *example* program (page 86).

The program will have to operate on data structures representing Lullaby abstract syntax trees. The following type definitions (given here in Pascal) should help[5].

type

    Instruction_kind = (*double_to_even, double_to_odd, halve, print, compound*);

    Instruction_list = ↑*Instruction_list_element*;

---

[5] The definitions are expressed in "quasi-Pascal"; many actual Pascal systems will not accept the underscore _ in identifiers, and will reject *Program* as a procedure identifier.

Instruction_list_element =

    record

        current: *Instruction*;

        rest: *Instruction_list*

    end;

Instruction =

    record

    case *ik*: *Instruction_kind* **of**

        double_to_even, double_to_odd, halve, print: ();

        compound: (*elements*: *Instruction_list*)

    end

Program =

    record

        body: *Instruction*

    end;

Integer_list = ↑*Integer_list_element*

Integer_list_element =

    record

        current: **integer**;

        rest: *Integer_list*

    end

4.1 An attribute-based interpreter (programming exercise)

Rewrite the attribute grammar specification for Lullaby, procedural version (figure 4.3, page 90), as an interpreter for the Lullaby language, built as a set of routines following closely the structure of the attribute grammar. The topmost routine (*Program*) will accept two arguments, an input value (of type **integer** and mode **in**) and an output file (of type *Integer_list* and mode **out**).

4.2 A Lullaby decorator-interpreter (programming exercise)

1 - Write a complete attribute grammar for Lullaby using the object-oriented notation (pages 93-94).

2 - Based on this grammar, write a "decorator-interpreter" for Lullaby, that is to say a program that will operate on a Lullaby syntax tree and add complete semantic information to the nodes. The design of the decorator-interpreter involves two aspects:

- Defining data structures to represent attributed syntax tree elements; they should be based on the above type definitions (or their equivalent in a language other than Pascal), extended to account for the attributes.

- Writing a set of routines that will decorate a tree, based on the *input* value transmitted by the environment. If you are programming in a classical language, these routines will be independent from the data structure definitions, and will have to be called from outside; if you have access to an object-oriented language such as Eiffel or Smalltalk, the routines will be attached to the data structures and executed automatically as a result of object creation and evolution.

4.3 A Lullaby compiler (programming exercise)

Write a Lullaby to Oulala compiler based on the transformational specification of 4.3 (pages 96-100). Write an Oulala interpreter and combine the two programs to obtain a system for executing Lullaby programs.

4.4 A Lullaby interpreter (programming exercise)

Write a Lullaby interpreter based on the operational specification of 4.4 (pages 100-104).

4.5 A denotation compiler (programming exercise)

Write a Lullaby "denotation compiler" based on the denotational specification of 4.5 (pages 105-109). This program should accept as input a Lullaby abstract syntax tree, and produce as output either a diagnostic if the program is not well-formed (based on the C functions) or a denotation corresponding to the program (based on the M functions).

As seen in 4.5, the denotations of programs and instructions are functions, so the question arises of how to represent the denotation compiler's output in the normal case. One way to represent a function $f: X \rightarrow Y$ is to tabulate it, in other words implement it as **array** [X] **of** Y (Pascal notation). Of course, this is only possible if X has a finite (and reasonably small) number of specimens and if the specimens of Y are representable. So for the purpose of this exercise the range of initial input values permissible for Lullaby programs is restricted to the interval $0..9$, and the number of *Print* instructions that a

Lullaby program may contain to 20. This way, the denotation of a Lullaby *Program*, defined mathematically (page 106) as a function in $\mathbf{N} \rightarrow \mathbf{N}^*$, may be represented as an array of 10 integers, and an output file may be represented as an array and an index. (You should determine an adequate implementation for the specimens of construct *State* and for the $M_{Instruction}$ function.)

These representations having been established, your program should "compile" Lullaby programs, given as abstract syntax trees and containing no more than 20 *Print* instructions, into arrays of the above form. To experiment with your denotation compiler, write a "denotation interpreter" that will execute the resulting data structure on any input value between 0 and 9 – thus completing your "Denotational Language System".

Be careful to avoid the typical pitfall of writing an interpreter (in other words, an answer to the previous exercise) rather than a denotation compiler. The output of the compiler must **not** be the output of a Lullaby program; instead, it must be an abstract representation of the program's semantics, which the denotation interpreter may then apply to an input value, only then producing Lullaby program output.

4.6 Other rules for compounds

The aim of this exercise is to obtain a different set of axioms and inference rules for the Lullaby *Compound* instruction. The rules given in 4.6.2 (pages 112-113) include an axiom for the empty compound ($A0_{Compound}$), an inference rule for one-instruction compounds ($I1_{Compound}$), and a general inference rule ($I_{Compound}$).

1   Let c be a non-empty compound instruction. Devise an inference rule, called $I'_{Compound}$, that allows proving properties of c from properties of c.*FIRST* and c.*TAIL*.

2   Prove the following pre-post theorem using only $A0_{Compound}$ and $I'_{Compound}$ for compound instructions:

$\{input = 1\}$ *short_example* $\{file\ (2) \neq 4\}$

where *short_example* is the program

> *short_example* $\triangleq$
>> *Program (body: Compound*
>>> *(<Instruction (Double_to_odd), Instruction (Print),*
>>> *Instruction (Print), Instruction (Print)>)*

4.7 Going the other way

The axioms for the basic instructions of Lullaby (*Double_to_even, Double_to_odd, Halve, Print*) work from precondition to postcondition: they apply to the case where a precondition *P* (*register, file*) is known, and yield the corresponding postcondition for each kind of instruction.

Devise a set of alternative axioms that will work in the opposite way: in other words, assuming the postcondition *Q* (*register, file*) is known, each axiom should yield a precondition deduced from *Q* .

4.8 Dropping the register

It was mentioned on page 113 that to prove a property of a program *pr* , of the form

$$\{P \ (input)\} \ pr \ \{Q \ (file)\}$$

one must prove the corresponding property of the program body, namely:

$$\{P \ (register) \ \wedge \ file = <>\} \ pr.body \ \{Q \ (file)\}$$

However, the body of a program is an instruction and all the properties of instructions are of the form

$$\{P' \ (register, file) \ \ inst \ \{Q' \ (register, file)\}$$

so that you must drop any reference to *file* from the postcondition *Q'* of *pr.body* to obtain the postcondition *Q* on *pr*. Give a general method for "dropping" the register from postconditions. (**Hint**: Use the rule of consequence and a quantifier.)

5

Lambda calculus

Functions play a central part in the mathematical modeling of computing processes, and especially in the semantic specification of programming language constructs. Although built from simple parts, some of the functions used may be quite complex.

To define and manipulate such functions, we need clear notations and a sound theory.

5.1 FUNCTIONS AS FIRST-CLASS CITIZENS

How can we define a function?

One method, introduced in chapter 2, is definition by **extension**, which expresses a function as an explicit set of pairs, as in

$$f_1 \triangleq \{<a, 1>, <b, 2>, <c, 3>, <d, 4>\}$$

This works for simple finite functions.

In less trivial cases, however, we may need to define a function more abstractly, by giving its properties rather than listing its member pairs exhaustively. The same need arose for sets, for which definition by **comprehension** is available to specify a set through a characteristic property of its members.

Functions may also be defined by comprehension through a powerful notation known as lambda notation, which is the object of this chapter. The underlying theory (which will only be sketched) is known as lambda calculus.

The main advantage of lambda notation is that it treats functions as mathematical objects in their own right, obviating the need to refer constantly to their arguments. For example you can manipulate an object such as *sqrt*, the square root function, without having to name the numbers of which the square root is being taken. This will be of particular interest for the meaning functions of denotational semantics, such as $M_{Instruction}$, which usually are higher-order functionals.

The phrase often used to describe this approach is that it treats functions as **first-class citizens**, meaning that they acquire all the rights and privileges of mathematical objects, such as the right to be used as operands in expressions. An example of an expression having functions as operands is f ; g (composition), where f and g are functions. This is different from an expression that simply involves functions (applied to arguments), such as f (1) + g (2). In the latter example, the operator acts on function values, not on the functions themselves.

> A closely related issue in programming language design is whether to treat *routines* and "functions" (in the programming language sense) as first-class citizens. The Ada answer is no: routines cannot be passed as arguments to routines, so they do not enjoy the status of ordinary objects. PL/I answers yes (as it does to most questions) by going so far as to allow assignment to routine variables. In functional languages such as Miranda, FFP and to some extent Lisp, functions are actually "upper-class" citizens enjoying the most favorable treatment. The solutions adopted by most current languages lie somewhere in-between these extremes.

5.2 DEFINITION AND EXAMPLES

The general form of a **lambda expression** is:

$$\lambda \ id_1, id_2, \ ... \ id_n \bullet expr$$

where the id_i are identifiers and *expr* is some expression which may involve these identifiers. The external form of a lambda expression resembles that of a quantified expression in predicate calculus, the λ playing a role syntactically similar to that of a quantifier such as $\forall$ or $\exists$.

In contrast to an ordinary expression, say $a + b$, whose possible values are members of some basic mathematical set (integers, booleans, reals and the like), the value of a lambda expression is a **function**.

This function has n arguments, where n is the number of identifiers between λ and the dot. The value it yields when applied to arguments $a_1, a_2, \ ... \ a_n$ is given by *expr*, with a_1 substituted for all occurrences of id_1, a_2 substituted for all occurrences of id_2 etc.

In this chapter lambda expressions denote total functions. Chapter 8 will show how to generalize them for specifying arbitrary functions (8.7).

Here are a few function definitions in this notation, *expr* being taken from various application domains:

$$plus \quad\quad \triangleq \lambda\, a, b \bullet a + b$$

$$square \quad\quad \triangleq \lambda\, x \bullet x^2$$

$$successor \quad \triangleq \lambda\, n \bullet n + 1$$

$$predecessor \triangleq \lambda\, n \bullet n - 1$$

$$even \quad\quad \triangleq \lambda\, n \bullet divides\ (2,\, n)$$

$$max \quad\quad \triangleq \lambda\, x, y \bullet \text{ if } x \geq y \text{ then } x \text{ else } y \text{ end}$$

$$Id \quad\quad\quad \triangleq \lambda\, x \bullet x \quad \text{-- The identity function}$$

The identifiers between λ and the dot are dummy variables, playing the same role as quantified variables in mathematics, as in

$$\forall\, id_1\, id_2 \dots id_n \bullet P$$

or, in programming languages, as the formal arguments appearing in the header of a routine declaration. The choice of names is not meaningful: *max*, as defined above, is the same function as

$$\lambda\, p, q \bullet \text{ if } p \geq q \text{ then } p \text{ else } q \text{ end}$$

It is often useful to spell out the sets to which the function arguments must belong, as in the following more precise definition of *successor* on the natural numbers:

$$successor \ \triangleq \lambda\, n : \mathbf{N} \bullet n + 1$$

Then you may group arguments belonging to the same set, as in

$$plus \triangleq \lambda\, a, b : \mathbf{N} \bullet a+b$$

This version of the notation is called **typed lambda notation**; section 5.10 will present the underlying theory.

A function such as *Id* may be applied to arguments of any set and is said to be **generic**. Generic features play an important role in some modern programming languages, such as Ada and Eiffel; they are also used in formal specification languages such as Z or Clear. This book makes very little use of genericity, relying only on a small number of generic functions such as *Id* .

What do we gain from lambda notation? So far, not very much. You may have noticed that the examples seen so far may be defined without lambda notation; for example, you can fully specify the function *max* by the following property:

$$\forall x, y : \mathbf{N} \bullet max\ (x,\ y) = \textbf{if}\ x \geq y\ \textbf{then}\ x\ \textbf{else}\ y\ \textbf{end}$$

There is an important difference, however, between stating this property and writing the above definition of *max* using a lambda expression:

- By writing the "$\forall$ ..." property, you do not introduce *max* as an independent object, but merely assert a certain requirement on the value of *max* when applied to arbitrary arguments *x* and *y*.

- In contrast, the definition of *max* by a lambda expression introduces a functional object, to which functional operations such as function composition may be applied.

In other words, the "$\forall$..." property expresses a certain statement **about** the function, whereas the lambda expression **defines** the function entirely.

One benefit of such a definition is that it makes it possible to express properties of the function without reference to members of the base sets on which the function operates. A property involving integers, such as

$$\forall\ x : \mathbf{N} \bullet\ (x + 1) - 1 = x$$

may be restated in terms of functions only as

$$successor\ ;\ predecessor\ =\ Id$$

5.3 HIGHER-ORDER FUNCTIONS

The major benefit comes with higher-order functions. Lambda notation proves particularly powerful here because in the general form

$$\lambda\ id_1,\ id_2,\ ...\ id_n \bullet expr$$

the expression *expr* may be itself a lambda expression, and the arguments for which $id_1, id_2, ... id_n$ stand may be functions. As a simple example, consider the composition of one-argument functions on integers such as *successor* and *predecessor*. For any two such functions *f* and *g*, setting $h \triangleq f\ ;\ g$, the following holds:

$$\forall\ x : \mathbf{N} \bullet\ h\ (x) = g\ (f\ (x))$$

Another form of this property is:

$$\forall\ f, g : (\mathbf{N} \rightarrow \mathbf{N}) \bullet\ h = \lambda\ x : \mathbf{N} \bullet g\ (f\ (x))$$

but going up one more level you can define the composition of integer functions, **infix** ";", as a function in its own right, of signature

infix ";": $((N \rightarrow N) \times (N \rightarrow N)) \rightarrow (N \rightarrow N)$

and value

infix ";" $\triangleq \lambda f, g: (N \rightarrow N) \bullet \lambda x: N \bullet g (f (x))$

This expresses that function ";", when applied to two integer functions f and g, yields a new function (previously called h but now anonymous) which, when applied to an integer x, yields $g (f (x))$. Through this definition (which may be made generic by taking an arbitrary set instead of **N**) composition becomes itself an object worth talking about, and the game could go on.

These facilities are important for denotational semantics and are used extensively in the next chapter.

As a simple example of the application of lambda notation to express higher-order functions, consider the notion of characteristic function introduced in 2.7.6. Formally, the connection between subsets of X and predicates on X, for an arbitrary set X, is given by the function

characteristic: $\mathbf{P} (X) \rightarrow (X \rightarrow \mathbf{B})$

such that

characteristic $\triangleq \lambda s \bullet \lambda x \bullet x \in s$

Function *characteristic* is one-to-one; the inverse function may be written

associated_subset $\triangleq \lambda p: (X \rightarrow \mathbf{B}) \bullet \{x: X \mid p (x)\}$

Note that lambda notation is really what lies behind the Metanot conventions for defining functions, as introduced in 2.6.5. From now on the notation

$f (x) \triangleq expression$

will be taken as a synonym for

$f \triangleq \lambda x \bullet expression$

5.4 A FORMAL DEFINITION OF LAMBDA NOTATION

[This section and the remainder of chapter 5 may be skipped on first reading].

The above presentation of lambda notation has been mostly intuitive. Lambda notation is actually part of a formal theory – **lambda calculus** –, with well-defined syntax and semantics. Although an in-depth presentation of this theory falls beyond the scope of this discussion, familiarity with its basic concepts is useful for understanding some key programming language issues.

A more formal definition of lambda notation follows. For the rest of this chapter, "expression" is a shorthand for "lambda expression". An expression has one of the following three forms:

1 • An identifier, or **atom**.

2 • λ *x* • *e*, where *x* is an identifier and *e* a lambda expression; this form is called an **abstraction**.

3 • *f* (*e*), where *f* and *e* are lambda expressions; this form is called an **application**.

The informal meaning of expressions in each case is the following.

1 • Atoms represent constants or functions; in fact it is convenient to consider all objects of lambda calculus as functions, by treating constants as functions that yield a constant result. In practical uses of lambda calculus, certain atoms would be set aside with a predefined meaning: for example, if we are dealing with integers, we might consider atoms such as *one*, *two*, *three*, ..., *successor*, *plus* and *less_than* as predefined. However for the time being we do not need any predefined atoms.

2 • An abstraction represents a one-argument function: informally, λ *x* • *e* is the function which, when applied to an argument *a*, yields *e* with *a* substituted for *x*. (A more precise definition of substitution is given below.) The name comes from the observation that λ *x* • *e* represents *e* "abstracted" from the particular choice of identifier *x*, called the **dummy identifier** of the abstraction.

3 • An expression of the form *f* (*e*) represents the result of applying the function denoted by *f* to the value denoted by *e*, which must be a suitable argument for *f*.

All this assumes that every non-atomic function has one argument. Such a convention simplifies the discussion. It does not limit the scope of the theory: through currying (2.8.2), you can associate a unique one-argument function (yielding a one-argument function as a result) with any two-argument function, and this is easily generalized to functions of more than two arguments. For example, two steps of currying will transform the function

   λ *x*, *y*, *z* • *x* + *y* + *z*

into

   λ *x* • λ*y* • λ*z* • *x* + *y* + *z*

In practice, it may be convenient to deal directly with functions with more than one argument; such a generalization is the object of exercise 5.2.

The above definition of lambda expressions (which is easy to translate into BNF) defines a concrete grammar for the language of lambda expressions. You may have noted that this grammar is ambiguous: the expression

   λ *x* • λ*y* • *f* (*g*)

admits three possible interpretations, shown here by using braces to group sub-expressions:

1    $\bullet \; \lambda \, x \bullet \, \{\lambda y \bullet \, \{f \, (g)\}\}$

2    $\bullet \; \lambda \, x \bullet \, \{\{\lambda y \bullet f\} \, (g)\}$

3    $\bullet \; \{\lambda \, x \bullet \lambda y \bullet f\} \, (g)$

The ambiguity could be removed by complicating the grammar (to account for precedence rules) or the language (by requiring compulsory parenthesization). It is preferable to leave the grammar as it is and add to Metanot the convention that function application has the highest precedence, so that by default the interpretation of the above expression is number 1. Braces will be used (rather than parentheses, reserved for function application) to override this precedence when needed.

An abstract syntax may be defined for lambda expressions (avoiding any problem of syntactic ambiguity):

Lambda	$\triangleq$	*Identifier* | *Abstraction* | *Application*
Abstraction	$\triangleq$	*dummy*: *Identifier*; *body*: *Lambda*
Application	$\triangleq$	*operation, argument*: *Lambda*

Figure 5.1: Abstract syntax of lambda notation

5.5 FREE AND BOUND OCCURRENCES

An important notion arises in the description of lambda expressions, and has close correspondents on the programming language side: the notion of freedom and bondage.

5.5.1 Definitions

Informally, an occurrence of an identifier *id* in an expression is bound if it is within the scope of an abstraction whose dummy identifier is *id*, and free otherwise. For example, in

$$\lambda \, y \bullet x^* \, (\, \{\lambda x \bullet y \, (x^+)\})$$

the occurrence of x marked with an asterisk is free and the occurrence marked with a plus is bound. As this example shows, an identifier may have both free and bound occurrences in the same lambda expression.

The following predicate definitions, based on the above abstract syntax, express these notions formally.

occurs, occurs_bound, occurs_free: *Identifier* × *Lambda* → **B**

occurs (*x*: *Identifier*, *l*: *Lambda*) ≜

    case *l* **of**

        Identifier ⟹ *x* = *l* |

        Abstraction ⟹ *occurs* (*x*, *l*.*body*) |

        Application ⟹ *occurs* (*x*, *l*.*operation*) ∨ *occurs* (*x*, *l*.*argument*)

    end

occurs_bound (*x*: *Identifier*, *l*: *Lambda*) ≜

    case *l* **of**

        Identifier ⟹ *false* |

        Abstraction ⟹

            (*x* = *l*.*dummy* ∧ *occurs_free* (*x*, *l*.*body*))

             ∨ *occurs_bound* (*x*, *l*.*body*) |

        Application ⟹

            occurs_bound (*x*, *l*.*operation*) ∨

            occurs_bound (*x*, *l dot argument*)

    end

occurs_free (*x*: *Identifier*, *l*: *Lambda*) ≜

    case *l* **of**

        Identifier ⟹ *x* = *l* |

        Abstraction ⟹ *occurs_free* (*x*, *l dot body*) ∧ *x* ≠ *l*.*dummy* |

        Application ⟹

            occurs_free (*x*, *l*.*operation*) ∨

            occurs_free (*x*, *l dot argument*)

    end

The following property holds for any identifier *x* and lambda expression *l*:

occurs (*x*, *l*) = *occurs_free* (*x*, *l*) ∨ *occurs_bound* (*x*, *l*)

Here "occurrence" means actual usage, not just textual presence as dummy identifier in an abstraction. For example *x* occurs (bound) in λ *x* • *x* (*y*), but not in λ *x* • *y*.

5.5.2 Freedom, bondage and programming languages

To a programmer, the notions of free and bound occurrence are not difficult to understand, as they have a direct equivalent in block-structured languages such as Algol 60 and Pascal.

Call "entity" any program element such as a variable, constant, attribute, routine etc. Call "scope" a unit in which declarations may be entered. A routine is a scope; in a block-structured language where blocks may have local declarations, such as Algol 60 or Algol 68, a block is also a scope; in Eiffel a class (which may have its own attributes and routines) is a scope. If scopes may be nested hierarchically, as with Pascal routines or Algol blocks, identifiers defined in an outer scope may be redeclared with a different meaning in an inner scope. Here a declaration plays the role of a lambda binding.

An occurrence of an identifier in a certain scope is bound if the identifier denotes a local entity and free if it denotes a global entity, to be provided by any outer scope in which the scope is embedded. In a valid complete program, all identifier occurrences must be bound.

5.6 CHANGE OF DUMMY IDENTIFIER

Informally, the meaning that should be attached to an abstraction of the form

$$\lambda x \bullet e$$

is "the function that for any argument a yields e applied to a rather than x".

Clearly this function exists independently of the choice of the dummy identifier x, although it seems hard to express it without any such choice. (A companion theory of lambda calculus, called **combinatory logic**, does permit the definition of functions without explicit reference to any dummy arguments, but falls beyond the scope of this discussion.) It is necessary, however, to know when x may be replaced by another identifier without changing the mathematical object defined by the abstraction. Such an operation is called α–**conversion**, or change of dummy identifier, and needs to be defined formally.

When changing the dummy identifier x of an abstraction, you must perform the same substitution, throughout the body e of the abstraction. For example replacing the dummy identifier x by y in the expression

$$original \triangleq \lambda x \bullet \lambda z \bullet a \ (x \ (z))$$

will yield

$$new_1 \triangleq \lambda y \bullet \lambda z \bullet a \ (y \ (z))$$

You must be careful, however, when performing the substitutions in the body. Assume for example that the chosen replacement for the dummy identifier, instead of y, was a. Then you would obtain:

$$new_2 \triangleq \lambda\, a \bullet \lambda\, z \bullet a\ (a\ (z))$$

This is obviously not a lambda expression equivalent to *original*. The problem is that the identifier a occurred free in *original*, but its first occurrence in *new*$_2$ is now bound: a has been accidentally confused with the newly chosen dummy identifier. This is incorrect: we must exclude any change of dummy identifier for which the new dummy candidate occurs **free** in the body of the abstraction.

A similar problem occurs when the candidate replacement occurs **bound** in the body of the original. Assume for example that you attempt to choose z as the replacement for x in *original*. Then you would get

$$new_3 \triangleq \lambda\, z \bullet \lambda\, z \bullet a\ (z\ (z))$$

The innermost application sub-expression $z\ (z)$ now denotes the application of a function to itself, whereas the corresponding sub-expression of *original* involved two functions x and z, which in the general case may be different. Again this change of dummy identifier is invalid; we must exclude any change of dummy identifier for which the new dummy candidate occurs bound in the body of the abstraction.

With these observations in mind, we may give a formal definition of change of bound identifier. Because of the limitations just seen, the corresponding function *change_dummy*, defined with respect to the above abstract syntax, is partial:

change_dummy: Abstraction $\times$ *Identifier* $\nrightarrow$ *Abstraction*

dom *change_dummy* $\triangleq$ $\{<l, x>: \text{Abstraction} \times \text{Identifier} \mid \neg \text{ occurs } (x, l)\}$

change_dummy (l: *Abstraction*, x: *Identifier*) $\triangleq$
        Abstraction (*dummy*: x ; *body*: *substitute_free* ($l.body$, $l.dummy$, x))

In this definition, *substitute_free* (*expr, repl, id*), read "*expr* with *expr* for *id*", denotes expression *expr* with every free occurrence of identifier *id* replaced by expression *repl*. A precise definition of *substitute_free* is given below.

To understand the definition of *change_dummy*, remember that x "occurs" in l if it occurs either free or bound in l. These cases correspond to the two counter-examples seen above.

The second condition may be relaxed a little: bound occurrences of the replacing identifier are all right if there is no free occurrence of the original dummy identifier within the scope of their binding, such as the occurrence of y here. A correspondingly more liberal rule is the object of exercise 5.3.

In practice, you may need to change the dummy identifier of a sub-expression l appearing in a larger expression; in such a case, you will need to avoid clashes with names of identifiers bound in the context of l. To adapt the definition of *change_dummy* accordingly, we may add an argument f representing a set of forbidden identifiers (those which are expected to be bound in l's context); the expression giving the value of function *change_dummy* does not change, but there is a further restriction on the domain:

> *change_dummy: Abstraction* × *Identifier* × **P** (*Identifier*) $\nrightarrow$ *Abstraction*
>
> **dom** *change_dummy* $\triangleq$
>
> > $\{<l, x, forbidden>: Abstraction × Identifier ×$ **P** (*Identifier*) $|$
> >
> > $\neg\ occurs\ (x, l) \wedge x \notin forbidden\ \}$

This version of *change_dummy* is the one used in the rest of this chapter.

5.7 SUBSTITUTION

To complete the definition of *change_dummy*, there remains to express the function *substitute_free*. More generally, the notion of substituting an expression for an identifier in an expression plays an important part in manipulations of lambda expressions.

The general idea should be intuitively clear: for example, defining

> $source_1 \triangleq \lambda z \bullet z\ (y)$
>
> $replacement \triangleq \lambda x \bullet x\ (a)$

then the substitution of *replacement* for y in $source_1$ is

> $substituted_1 \triangleq \lambda z \bullet z\ (\lambda x \bullet x\ (a))$

To provide a valid definition of substitution, however, we must be careful to avoid unwanted name clashes, which may result from two different causes.

The first rule is to substitute only for **free** occurrences of y. In substituting *replacement* for y in

> $source_2 \triangleq y\ (u\ (\lambda y \bullet u\ (y)))$

we clearly want to replace the first instance of y but not the next two, in which y simply represents a dummy identifier. The confusion with the outermost y, which is free, would change the (informal) semantics of the expression.

> The problem results from the "pun" on y in $source_2$, which may be seen as the result of poor
> taste or bad luck in choosing identifiers. A similar situation arises in block-structured languages:
> the same name may be used for a global entity and an entity of an inner scope.

The second risk of confusion results from a free occurrence of an identifier in the replacement expression becoming incorrectly bound in the substituted expression, because the identifier has the same name as an identifier bound in the original. For example in substituting *replacement* for y in

$$source_3 \triangleq \lambda \, a \bullet a \; (y)$$

mere textual substitution would yield

$$substituted_3 \triangleq \lambda \, a \bullet a \; (\lambda x \bullet x \; (a))$$

where the innermost occurrence of a, which was free in *replacement*, is now bound. What is wrong here is that this occurrence became bound by mere chance; if a different name, such as b, is used for the dummy identifier in $source_3$, not affecting the intuitive meaning of $source_3$, the resulting substituted expression

$$substituted'_3 \triangleq \lambda \, b \bullet b \; (\lambda x \bullet x \; (a))$$

is clearly not equivalent to $substituted_3$.

To avoid this second risk, you may have to perform changes of dummy identifiers. Identifiers have not yet been precisely specified; all that is required is that the set of possible identifiers be infinite. This will be satisfied is valid identifiers are taken to be all finite strings constructed from a fixed alphabet (for example letters and digits). Then since the set of identifiers occurring in any lambda expression is finite, it is always possible to find a "fresh" identifier not occurring in a given lambda expression and use it as new dummy identifier. This makes it possible to postulate a function

> *sfresh*: **P** (*Identifier*) $\twoheadrightarrow$ *Identifier*
>
> **dom** *sfresh* $\triangleq$ {*id_set*: **P** (*Identifier*) | **finite** *id_set*}

such that, for any finite set *id_set* of identifiers, *sfresh* (*id_set*) $\notin$ *id_set*.

Rather than using *sfresh* directly, the definition of substitution will rely on a total function of two lambda expression arguments:

> *fresh*: *Lambda* $\times$ *Lambda* $\rightarrow$ *Identifier*

such that *fresh* (e, f) is an identifier occurring (in the precise sense of function *occurs*) neither in e nor in f. The formal definition of *fresh* in terms of *sfresh* is immediate.

Using these conventions, we may now define function *substitute_free*, which yields the result of systematic replacement of all free occurrences of an identifier. The definition is shown on the adjacent page.

Care has been taken to perform a change of bound identifiers (through *fresh*) only when strictly needed, which requires both of the following conditions:

- The identifier to be substituted for, *id*, appears free in the body of the original lambda expression *source*.
- The dummy identifier of that expression appears free in the replacement *repl*.

---

substitute_free: *Lambda* × *Lambda* × *Identifier* → *Lambda*

substitute_free (*source* , *repl* : *Lambda* , *id* : *Identifier*) ≜
    case *source* **of**
        Identifier ⟹ **if** *source* = *id* **then** *repl* **else** *Lambda* (*source*) **end** |
        Abstraction ⟹
            if *source.dummy* = *id* **then** *source*
                -- Here any occurrence of *id* in *source* is bound
                -- and so should not be replaced
        else
            given
                clean_source ≜
                        -- Remove any potential name clash
                  if
                      occurs_free (*id* , *source* .*body*) ∧
                      occurs_free (*source* .*dummy* , *repl*)
                  then
                      -- Choose new dummy identifier
                    change_dummy (*source* , *fresh* (*repl* , *source* .*body*))
                  else
                    -- No problem
                    Lambda (*source*)
                end
            then
                Lambda (*Abstraction* (
                  dummy : *clean_source.dummy* ;
                  body : *substitute_free* (*clean_source.body*, *repl*, *id*)))
            end
        end |
        Application ⟹
            Lambda (*Application* (
                function : *substitute_free* (*source* .*operation* , *repl* , *id*),
                argument : *substitute_free* (*source* .*argument* , *repl* , *id*)))
    end

Figure 5.2: Substituting an expression for the free occurrences of an identifier

This is the case exemplified above with *source*₃. The solution in such a case is to perform the substitution not on the original expression *source* but on a new version *clean_source* obtained from *source* by using a fresh dummy identifier, which averts potential clashes.

To make sure you understand the mechanics of substitution, you are invited to apply the function definition by computing *subst* (*replacement*, *y*, *original*$_2$).

The definitions of *change_dummy* and *substitute_free* are mutually recursive. Although recursive definitions have not been studied formally yet (see chapter 8), these definitions seem intuitively safe since (as you should check for all cases above) every recursive application uses as actual argument a sub-expression of the corresponding actual argument; this means that the size of the argument decreases at each step, and hence that the process is grounded.

5.8 CONTRACTION

The operation of α–conversion replaces a lambda expression by a mathematically equivalent one, but does not simplify or complicate it. The other fundamental operation on lambda expressions is meant to simplify expressions through function application. It is called contraction (or β-conversion).

Contraction corresponds to the informal semantics of abstraction and application, as given above: when λ *x* • *e* is applied to any argument *b*, the result is *e* with *b* substituted for free occurrences of *x*. This removes one abstraction (one λ) from the expression.

The basic contraction operation, called *contract1*, acts on applications; more precisely, this operation can produce a new lambda expression, with one abstraction removed, from a **redex**. A redex, for "reducible expression", is an expression of the form

{λ *x* • *e* } (*b*)

which *contract1* will reduce to *substitute_free* (*e, b, x*). The function may be defined as:

> *contract1*: *Application* → *Lambda*

> *contract1* (*a*: *Application*) ≜
>> **given**
>>> *f* ≜ *a.operation*
>> **then**
>>> **case** *f* **of**
>>>> *Identifier, Application* ⟹ *Lambda* (*a*) |
>>>>> -- Nothing interesting can be done in these cases
>>>> *Abstraction* ⟹
>>>>> -- This is the redex case
>>>>> *substitute_free* (*f*.*body*, *f*.*dummy*, *a*.*argument*)
>>> **end**
>> **end**

For example contraction may be applied to reduce

$\{\lambda\, x \bullet x\ (three\,)\}\ (successor\,)$

to

successor (*three*)

This definition of contraction may seem to provide enough basis for defining the formal **semantics** of lambda calculus. Since every contraction removes one λ, it appears that if you repeatedly apply this operation all unnecessary λs will eventually disappear and you will get a **normal form**. Here a λ is said to be "unnecessary" if it is the λ of a redex, and an expression is said to be in normal form if it contains no redexes.

An expression in normal form has a straightforward mathematical interpretation as a function; so if every lambda expression may be reduced, through a finite sequence of contractions, to an expression in normal form, this expression seems to be a good enough candidate to describe the meaning (denotation, as defined in chapter 4) of the original expression. In the example above, *successor* (*three*) is the normal form.

A function that appears to do the job of reducing a lambda expression to its normal form may be written as follows:

contract: *Lambda* $\rightarrow$ *Lambda*

contract (*l*: *Lambda*) $\triangleq$

    case *l* **of**

        Identifier $\Rightarrow$ *Lambda* (*l*) | -- Leave it as it is!

        Abstraction $\Rightarrow$
            Lambda (*Abstraction*
                (*dummy*: *l*.*dummy*, *body*: *contract* (*l*.*body*))) |

        Application $\Rightarrow$
            contract1 (*Application* (*function*: *contract* (*l*.*operation*);
                            argument: *contract* (*l*.*argument*))

    end

The figure on the next page shows an example sequence of contractions, leading to a normal form. At each step, the redex chosen for contraction is underlined. One of the steps, marked $\ast\ast\ast$, is actually not a contraction but an α–conversion; as you are invited to check, a change of dummy identifier is required there to avoid a name clash.

In this example there is only one redex at each step. If there were more than one, the question would naturally arise of which one to contract first and, even more importantly, of whether this decision may affect the final result. The answer to the latter question is unfortunately yes; however this question is beyond the scope of the present discussion. The problem will not arise in the examples studied.

{ {λ u • λ v •   {λ w • w (λ x • x (u))} (v)   } (y)} (λ z • λ y • z (y))

{   {λ u • λ v • v (λ x • x (u))} (y)}   (λ z • λ y • z (y))

{λ v • v (λ x • x (y))}   (λ z • λ y • z (y))

{λ z • λ y • z (y)} (λ x • x (y))

{λ z • λ y' • z (y')} (λ x • x (y))   ∗ ∗ ∗

λ y' • {   {λ x • x (y)} (y')   }

λ y' • y' (y)

Figure 5.3: Contraction to normal form

5.9 DIVERGENCE AND SELF-APPLICATION

The idea of defining the semantics of lambda calculus by reducing first every expression to normal form (for which a simple mathematical denotation exists) by a sequence of contractions is attractive but, unfortunately, does not work as simply as suggested by the preceding example.

The problem is that, since every contraction step (*contract1*) removes a λ, we have deduced a bit hastily that it decreases the overall number of λs. We have neglected the possibility for a contraction step actually to *add* one λ, or even more, while it removes another.

This unpleasant possibility may indeed arise, as shown by the following example of application expression, which will be called SELFSELF:

$$\{\lambda x • \{x (x)\}\}(\lambda x • \{x (x)\})$$

SELFSELF is a slightly pathological case of self-application. Call SELF the function to be applied: λ x • {x (x)}. SELF takes an argument x and applies it to itself. This argument must be a function, which is no surprise since the ability to describe functions that take functions as arguments is one of the prime goals of lambda notation. SELFSELF may seem to be overdoing it a little, since it is itself the application of function SELF to argument SELF; yet nothing in the definition of lambda expressions excludes such expressions, which are readily expressed in the abstract syntax introduced at the beginning of this chapter.

If you try to contract SELFSELF, you will replace every occurrence of x in the body of SELF by the argument SELF. However as this body is x (x) you will get as a result SELF (SELF) which is nothing else than the original expression SELFSELF. Seen from an operational viewpoint, the "computation" of the recursively defined function *contract* would never terminate.

With SELFSELF, all contractions yield back the original expression, keeping the number of λs constant. In other cases, an (ill-named) contraction may actually increase this number, making the expression grow indefinitely. (You are invited to devise an example.)

What went wrong? The problem is recursion. In all previous cases, recursion was grounded: every time a function was applied recursively, the actual argument was a sub-expression of the original argument; so, intuitively at least, the recursive definitions made sense. But for *contract* this is not the case: for an *Application* expression e the definition recursively applies *contract*, and hence *contract1*, to an expression which is not necessarily "smaller" than e. Hence the potential undefinedness.

This is but one instance of a more general issue – how to interpret and handle recursive definitions – which will be discussed in chapter 8. We may address the immediate problem by associating **types** with the objects of lambda calculus.

5.10 TYPED LAMBDA CALCULUS

In practice, even if higher-order functions are used, the aberrant behavior of lambda expressions such as SELFSELF should not occur in common uses of lambda notation.

This is because the set of expressions defined by the grammar of lambda calculus (5.4) is broader than what we need in practice. Some lambda expressions definable in this formalism may not enjoy an interpretation as functions on some well-defined mathematical sets – even though defining functions is the very purpose of lambda notation. SELFSELF provided an example: what concretely useful function could this expression represent?

We may therefore seek to restrict the class of acceptable lambda expressions.

One way to do this is to associate type information with lambda expressions. The resulting variant of the theory – typed lambda calculus – will include rules for determining the type of a lambda expression, and type constraints which a valid expression must meet. As a result of these constraints, the set of valid typed lambda expressions is a proper subset of the class of untyped lambda expressions. The following discussion introduces the rules and constraints.

> The path followed here is similar to the introduction of **static semantic** constraints in the formal specification of programming languages (see 3.3 and 6.2). In both cases we start from a grammar defining a set of potential construct specimens, and impose additional requirements (called "validity functions" in denotational semantics) for the specimens to be valid.

5.10.1 A type hierarchy

First we need an appropriate notion of type. The type system of lambda calculus will be defined by structural induction. A type is of either of two forms:

- A basic type, taken from a number of predefined types such as **N**, **B** etc.
- A function type, written ($\alpha \rightarrow \beta$), where α and β are types. This describes the type whose instances are functions taking arguments of type α and yielding results of type β.

We may drop redundant parentheses with the convention that the arrow associates to the right, that is to say

$$\alpha \rightarrow \beta \rightarrow \gamma$$

means

$$\alpha \rightarrow (\beta \rightarrow \gamma)$$

It is easy to introduce an abstract grammar defining a construct *Ltype* representing this structure; this would remove any potential ambiguity and the need for a convention on parentheses. The language of types is simple enough that we can keep the concrete notation, with arrows, for this discussion.

This makes it possible to assign a type to every valid lambda expression. Let us look at this process first for identifiers, then for other expressions.

5.10.2 Typing identifiers

For every occurrence of an identifier in an expression, the identifier must be given a type. Here there is a difference between typed and bound occurrences. For bound occurrences, the type will result from an explicit declaration. For free occurrences, however, there is no information in the expression itself that specifies the type.

To assign a type to free occurrences, we must assume that every identifier x has a default type *default* (x). This will be used as the type of the identifier when it occurs free in an expression.

Typing bound occurrences requires the presence of a type declaration at the point where the dummy identifier is introduced in an abstraction. This means that we must change the abstract syntax for abstractions to

   Abstraction $\triangleq$ *dummy*: *Identifier* ; *btype*: *Ltype* ; *body*: *Lambda*

The *btype* thus attached to a bound identifier may be called its **bound type**. In the concrete Metanot notation used above for typed lambda expressions, such as

   $\lambda\, n : \mathbf{N} \bullet \ldots$

the bound type of the dummy identifier was written after the colon in the λ-binding.

This suggests how to assign a type to every identifier occurrence in an expression:

- If the occurrence is bound, its type is the bound type of the identifier in the innermost enclosing binding.
- If the occurrence is free, its type is the default type of the identifier.

This convention corresponds to the intuitive typing of lambda expressions. For example in

$$\lambda\ n: \mathbf{N} \bullet successor\ (successor\ (n))$$

the type of the (bound) occurrence of n is its bound type, $\mathbf{N}$; on the other hand, the occurrences of *successor* are free, so that their types are the default type *default* (*successor*), which we may assume to have been defined as $\mathbf{N} \rightarrow \mathbf{N}$ if *successor* denotes the predefined successor function.

This suggests a correct interpretation of lambda expressions which bind predefined identifiers in some sub-expression (assuming one indulges in such a practice, similar to redefining library primitives in a programming language). Consider for example

$$\lambda\ n: \mathbf{N} \bullet successor\ ($$
$$\lambda\ successor: (\mathbf{N} \rightarrow \mathbf{N}) \rightarrow (\mathbf{N} \rightarrow \mathbf{N}) \bullet\ \ \{successor\ (predecessor\,)\}\ (n))$$

The first occurrence of *successor* is free and so has the default type. The second is bound, and has its bound type: it denotes a new dummy identifier with no connection to the original. Although bizarre, such a redefinition is permitted by the above conventions.

5.10.3 Typing rules

We can now proceed to defining the type of general lambda expressions:

1. - The type of an atom occurrence is as just explained: for a free occurrence, the default type, for a bound occurrence, the bound type.
2. - The type of an abstraction $\lambda\ x: \alpha \bullet e$ is $\alpha \rightarrow \beta$, where β is the type of e.
3. - The type of an application $f\ (e)$ is β, where the type of f is $\alpha \rightarrow \beta$ and the type of e is α.

Rather than resorting to words, it would be preferable to introduce a function

$$exp\_type: Lambda \rightarrow Ltype$$

defining precisely the type of any lambda expression. This is the topic of exercise 6.1. Although such a definition does not require any new mathematical concept, it will benefit from the techniques of denotational semantics (type maps, or static environments), introduced in the next chapter. You may want to try your hand at *exp_type* without waiting for the presentation of these techniques.

Chapter 9 will introduce yet another formal definition of typing in lambda notation, using the axiomatic approach (see 9.3).

As announced above, introducing typing into lambda calculus implies adding validity constraints ("static semantics"). Here the single constraint appears in case 3: for any application f (e), the expression f must be of type $\alpha \rightarrow \beta$ and e of type α, for some types α and β. This is a reasonable rule if application has the intuitive semantics of applying a function to an argument. To say that f is of type $\alpha \rightarrow \beta$ is to express that it expects an argument of type α and will yield a result of type β. An expression applying f to an argument of another type would not be valid.

5.10.4 An example

To see how to apply the typing mechanism to determine the type of a valid expression, consider the expression

$$\lambda \, x : \mathbf{N} \rightarrow \mathbf{N} \bullet \lambda y : \mathbf{N} \rightarrow \mathbf{N} \bullet \lambda z : \mathbf{N} \bullet x \; (\; \{\lambda x : \mathbf{N} \bullet y \; (x)\} \; (z\,))$$

The application of the above rule is pictured below; the process is self-explanatory. The type of the whole expression appears on the last line.

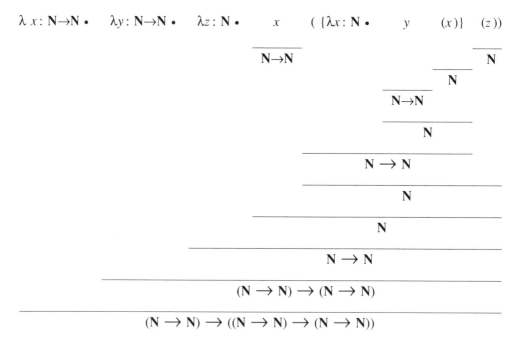

Figure 5.4: Typing a lambda expression

You will see this example again in 9.3, where it will be treated as the proof of a property in an axiomatic theory.

5.10.5 Consequences of the typing constraints

The semantic constraint imposed on applications has important consequences. In contrast with untyped lambda calculus, not all syntactically correct lambda expressions are now acceptable; the class of valid expressions has been restricted. For example, the troublesome SELFSELF is no longer valid. This expression was written

$$\{\lambda x \bullet \{x \ (x)\}\} \ \{\lambda x \bullet \{x \ (x)\}\}$$

which cannot be made into a typewise valid expression: if you choose a type α for x, then x would also need to have type $\alpha \longrightarrow \alpha$, which is a contradiction.

The typing constraints introduced still allow higher-order functionals to an unlimited level, but they prohibit self-application. Types, and correspondingly lambda expressions, have implicitly been classified into levels: at level 0 are basic types; at level i ($i > 0$) are types

$$\alpha \longrightarrow \beta$$

where one of α and β is at level $i-1$, and the other at level $i-1$ or less. So no function may take itself as argument. Note that a type of level i has at most $2^{i-1} - 1$ arrows.

In typed lambda calculus, the normal form property holds:

> **Theorem**: Any expression of typed lambda calculus may be reduced into normal form through a finite number of contractions.

To prove this result, note that the application of *contract1* to any redex removes one arrow from the expression's type.   □

5.11 BIBLIOGRAPHICAL NOTES

Lambda notation was introduced in [Church 1951]. The reference work on this theory and more generally on "combinatory logic", which goes even further towards permitting manipulation of higher-level functions without reference to the base elements is [Curry 1958, 1971]. A very readable introduction may be found in [Hindley 1972].

One of the first authors to study the formal connections between lambda calculus and programming languages was Peter Landin [Landin 65], although the Lisp language [McCarthy 1960], explicitly based on lambda calculus, had been available as early as 1959.

EXERCISES

5.1 Higher-order functional operators

Consider the operations on functions defined in chapter 2: intersection, overriding union, restriction, image, quotient. Call X and Y the base sets. Express each of these operations as a higher-order function defined by a lambda expression, as was done on page 129 for composition.

5.2 Functions with multiple arguments

Modify the abstract syntax of lambda expressions (page 131) to account for functions with an arbitrary number of arguments. Discuss how the rest of the presentation, in particular the discussion of typing, must be adapted.

5.3 Change of dummy identifier

Redefine the domain of the function *change_dummy* to account for the more liberal constraint mentioned after the definition of that function on page 134.

5.4 List operators as lambda expressions

Using lambda expressions, define formally the functions corresponding to the operators on lists (*TAIL*, *EMPTY* etc.), introduced in chapter 3.

5.5 Computing the type of a lambda expression

(**Programming assignment**) Write a program that, given an expression in typed lambda calculus (as defined in 5.10), will determine if the expression is valid and, if so, compute its type.

You may either start from a concrete form of the calculus (in which case you will need to write a simple parser) or from data structures representing the abstract form, along the lines of the "Note on the exercises" for chapter 4. Any programming language supporting recursion and composite data types may be used.

(Prolog programmers may investigate how the resolution mechanism makes it possible to define a single Prolog predicate that will both determine the type validity of an expression and, if it is indeed valid, its type.)

5.6 The paradoxical combinator

In untyped lambda calculus, define a lambda expression Y such that, for any f, if $u_f \triangleq Y\ (f)$, then the expression $f\ (u_f)$ contracts to u_f; in other words, u_f may be viewed as a fixpoint of f (see chapter 8 for a more general treatment of fixpoints). **Hint**: Y (often called the "paradoxical combinator") is a variation on the expression SELFSELF introduced in 5.9.

Would Y be possible in typed lambda calculus?

6

Denotational semantics: fundamentals

This chapter presents the method of denotational semantics on an simple programming language.

The language is Graal, introduced in chapter 3 for the discussion of syntax. In contrast to Lullaby (the toy example of chapter 4), Graal embodies some of the essential features of common programming languages. Since the discussion will frequently refer to details of Graal, the abstract grammar has been reproduced on the inside back cover for ease of reference.

We may occasionally need to look at program fragments in a more user-friendly form than abstract syntax. In such a case the discussion will use an "Ada-hoc" (ad hoc Ada-like) concrete syntax.[1]

Since the constructs of Graal – instructions, loops, conditionals, blocks, expressions and others – are present in some for or other in all major imperative languages, the discussion will assume that you informally understand their intended effect, and will devote itself entirely to the formal specification of that effect.

Graal will be extended in the exercises and in the following chapter, allowing us to study the formal semantics of more advanced constructs.

---

[1] Ada-hoc may or may not be a trademark of the US Department of Defense (Ada Joint Program Office).

6.1 OVERVIEW

The denotational method expresses the meaning of a programming language by associating with each construct T two functions:

$$V_T : T \rightarrow \mathbf{B}$$
$$M_T : T \nrightarrow D_T$$

The validity function V_T defines the construct's static semantics; validity functions are also called "context conditions" or "constraints". The meaning function M_T gives the construct's dynamic semantics, or **denotation**. The name of each validity or meaning function will be subscripted by the corresponding construct T. Recall that constructs are also called **syntactic domains**; the sets of denotations D_T are called **semantic domains**.

The V and M functions serve different purposes:

- A validity function is a predicate, that is to say a boolean-valued function. It yields the value *true* if and only if its argument is a valid specimen of the corresponding program construct. Chapter 3 explained the reason why we need validity functions: To complement syntactic descriptions with the context-sensitive constraints that they cannot handle, such as typing constraints.

- The M functions describe the effect of each valid construct by specifying its mathematical denotation.

By distinguishing between the V and M functions, we can obtain more modular language descriptions than if we lumped static and dynamic semantics into a single mechanism. In particular, the definition of the meaning functions will always assume that the argument a to the function is valid from the point of view of static semantics, in other words that $V_T\ [a]$ is true. This is essential to keep the M function definitions simple.

> The convention that M functions are only applied to statically valid elements corresponds to normal programming practice, as enforced by all reasonable language systems: one does not attempt to execute a program which has a compilation error (such as a type incompatibility). In typed languages, compilers can perform significant static analysis and catch many errors which, if undetected until run time, could cause considerable damage.

Because M functions are only applied to statically valid arguments, they will need to be specified as possibly partial functions. There is also another, deeper reason that prevents these functions from being total; it has to do with the possibility of non-terminating computations and will be explained later in this chapter (6.5.7).

The denotational descriptions below will use a variety of functions; in particular, the denotations returned by M will usually be functions. A convention will help us distinguish the fundamental functions V and M, whose source sets are syntactic domains, from others whose source sets are semantic domains: enclosing the arguments to these functions, and to them only, in square brackets. For example:

$$V_T \; [pe]$$

$$M_T \; [pe]$$

where *pe* is some program or program element. Other functions will use ordinary parentheses.

6.2 STATIC SEMANTICS

Static semantic constraints will affect four syntactic categories in Graal: programs, instructions, expressions and declaration lists. So we need four validity functions:

$$V_{Program} : Program \; \rightarrow \mathbf{B}$$

$$V_{Instruction} : Instruction \; \rightarrow \mathbf{B}$$

$$V_{Expression} : Expression \; \rightarrow \mathbf{B}$$

$$V_{Declaration\_list} : Declaration\_list \; \rightarrow \mathbf{B}$$

The signatures given for the last three functions are provisional; the actual forms, given below, need more arguments.

It is convenient to examine these four predicates in bottom-up order, from declaration lists to programs.

6.2.1 Validity of declaration lists

The abstract syntax for declarations is:

$$
\begin{array}{rcl}
Declaration\_list & \triangleq & Declaration^* \\
Declaration & \triangleq & v\text{: } Variable;\ t\text{: } Type \\
Variable & \triangleq & id\text{: } \mathbf{S}
\end{array}
$$

Here only possible cause for non-validity would be for the same variable to be declared twice. Hence the first validity function:

$$V_{Declaration\_list} \; [dl\text{: } Declaration\_list] \; \triangleq$$
$$(\forall i, j \in 1..\, dl\,.LENGTH \; \bullet \; i \; \neq \; j \; \supset \; dl(i).v \neq dl(j).v)$$

This may also be expressed as the requirement that the function $\lambda \, i \bullet dl \, (i) \bullet v$ be an injection (a "one-to-one into" function).

A more tolerant form would have permitted multiple occurrences of the same variable provided it has the same type each time. But this is only because Graal's type system is so simple: as soon as we extend the language with constructed types (such as arrays, records etc.), we would need to define what it means for two types to be equal, a non-trivial question. Declaring the same variable twice is silly anyway in a language without block structure, so the definition should just exclude this case. Such complications in the formal definition are early warnings of trouble which would eventually plague the compiler writer.

6.2.2 Type maps

To define the V functions on the other constructs of Graal requires a little more work. There is no such thing as an intrinsically "valid" or "invalid" expression or instruction: these notions are only meaningful with respect to a particular set of declarations. For example, the expression $a + b$ or the assignment $a := b$ are valid if a and b have been declared with compatible types, and invalid otherwise.

The notion of type map addresses this problem. A type map (also called a static environment) is a function from variables to "type values", where a type value represents a Graal type: bt for boolean and it for integer. For example the following declarations (in concrete notation)

$$x, y: INTEGER; z: \textbf{boolean}$$

yield the type map

$$t \triangleq \{<x, it>, <y, it>, <z, bt>\}$$

Formally, the set of possible type maps (a **static semantic domain**) is defined as:

$$Type\_map \triangleq Variable \xrightarrow{f} Type\_value$$

with

$$Type\_value \triangleq \{bt, it, ut\}$$

The type value ut will be needed later for variables used but not declared.

A type map must be a finite function since a program may only declare a finite number of variables. Only those variables that appear in declaration list belong to the domain of the corresponding type map.

> From the compiler writer's viewpoint, a type map is the mathematical representation of a **symbol table**, that is to say a data structure which serves to record the type of each variable (and other properties if necessary).

The target set defined for type maps is not the syntactic domain *Type*, but the static semantic domain *Type_value* introduced specially for this purpose. One reason for not identifying the two is the need for the "undefined type" value *ut*. For languages more complex than Graal, another reason would be the desire to treat certain type definitions as defining the same type even if they are syntactically different. For example, an implementation of Pascal may consider that the following type definitions, syntactically different, denote the same type:

record *a, b*: **integer end**;

record *a*: **integer**; *b*: **integer end**;

For Graal the following simple function serves to translate a type (viewed as a syntactic object) into a type value:

> *typeval*: *Type* $\longrightarrow$ *Type_value*

> *typeval* (*t*: *Type*) $\triangleq$
> > **case** *t* **of**
> > > *Boolean_type* $\Rightarrow$ *bt* |
> > > *Integer_type* $\Rightarrow$ *it*
> > **end**

We now have all the elements needed to define the function that associates a type map with any list of declarations. Let us call it *typing*:

> *typing*: *Declaration_list* $\longrightarrow$ *Type_map*

Then *typing* (*dl*), for a declaration list *dl*, will give the set of variable-to-type bindings implied by *dl*:

> *typing* (*dl*) $\triangleq$ {<v_1, t_1>, <v_2, t_2>, ... <v_n, t_n>}

where *n* is *dl.LENGTH* and for *i* $\in$ 1.. *n*:

- v_i is *dl*(*i*)dotv, the variable of the *i*-th declaration.
- t_i is *typeval* (*dl*(*i*).*t*), the associated type.

The value of *typing* may be expressed as follows (using the **over**... notation introduced in 3.9.3):

typing (*dl: Declaration_list*) $\triangleq$
> **given**
>
> > *associate_type* $\triangleq$ λ *d: Declaration* • {<*d*.*v*, *typeval* (*d*.*t*)>}
>
> **then**
>
> > **over** *dl* **apply** *associate_type* **combine** "$\cup$" **empty** $\varnothing$ **end**
>
> **end**

Function *associate_type*, when applied to a declaration *d* involving variable *x* and type *y*, yields the one-member-domain function {<*x*, *typeval* (*y*)>}. The **over...** operator yields the union of all these functions when *d* ranges over the declaration list *dl*, which is precisely the type map that should result from applying *typing* to *dl*.

Function *typing* is total: it is defined for erroneous declaration lists that include two declarations for the same variable. In such a case, the last declaration takes precedence: from the definition of the overriding union operator, {<*v*, *t*>} $\cup$ {<*v*, *t'*>} is equal to the second operand, {<*v*, *t'*>}. If, on the other hand, *dl* satisfies the constraint expressed by the validity function $V_{Declaration\_list}$, then the overriding union used in the definition is equivalent to a standard union.

If you studied the section on typed lambda calculus (5.10) you will have noted that the notion of type map may fruitfully be applied to that language as well. It was noted there that the type of an atom occurrence in a lambda expression depends on the context; for example the two occurrences of *x* in

$$\lambda x : \mathbf{N} \rightarrow \mathbf{N} \bullet \lambda y : \mathbf{N} \rightarrow \mathbf{N} \bullet \lambda z : \mathbf{N} \bullet x \ (\ \{\lambda x : \mathbf{N} \bullet y \ (x)\} \ (z))$$

have different types. The type of an atom occurrence depends on the types that may have been assigned to the atom in the enclosing bindings; the notion of type map conveniently captures this property. Defining properly the function that determines the type of a lambda expression is the object of exercise 6.1; similar ideas will apply to type declarations in block-structured languages in the next chapter.

6.2.3 Valid expressions

A validity function is needed to express the type constraints for expressions.

First we need the notion of type of an expression, given by the following auxiliary static semantic function:

> *expression_type*: *Expression* × *Type_map* $\rightarrow$ *Type_value*

which is defined below.

Here the special type value *ut* accounts for the possible presence of an undefined variable in the type map. Function *expression_type* is total and so assigns a type to any expression, even an invalid one.

The abstract syntax of expressions is:

$$
\begin{array}{rcl}
\textit{Expression} & \triangleq & \textit{Constant} \mid \textit{Variable} \mid \textit{Binary} \\
\textit{Constant} & \triangleq & \textit{Integer\_constant} \mid \textit{Boolean\_constant} \\
\textit{Binary} & \triangleq & \textit{term1, term2}: \textit{Expression}; \; \textit{op}: \textit{Operator}
\end{array}
$$

The following function serves to determine the type of an expression.

expression_type (*e*: *Expression, tm*: *Type_map*) $\triangleq$

> **case** *e* **of**
>> *Constant* $\Rightarrow$
>>> **case** *e* **of**
>>>> *Integer_constant* $\Rightarrow$ *it* $\mid$
>>>> *Boolean_constant* $\Rightarrow$ *bt*
>>> **end** $\mid$
>>
>> *Variable* $\Rightarrow$
>>> **if** *e* $\notin$ **dom** *tm* **then** *ut*
>>> **else** *tm* (*e*) **end** $\mid$
>>
>> *Binary* $\Rightarrow$
>>> **case** *e.op* **of**
>>>> *Relational_op, Boolean_op* $\Rightarrow$ *bt* $\mid$
>>>> *Arithmetic_op* $\Rightarrow$ *it*
>>> **end**
>
> **end**

Constants have an innate type; for declared variables, the type map *tm* gives the type (which otherwise is *ut*); for binary expressions, *expression_type* just looks at the operator. This method of assigning types to binary expressions is rather coarse, but it is adequate for our present purposes.

The advance work being completed, we can now express the validity condition for expressions. The validity of an expression is only meaningful with respect to a certain type map, so that the signature of the validity function will be

$$
V_{\textit{Expression}} : \textit{Expression} \times \textit{Type\_map} \rightarrow \mathbf{B}
$$

The function is defined as follows:

$V_{Expression}$ [e: Expression, tm: Type_map] ≜

    case e **of**

        Constant ⟹ true |

        Variable ⟹ e ∈ **dom** tm |

        Binary ⟹

            given

                typ1 ≜ expression_type (e.term1, tm);

                typ2 ≜ expression_type (e.term2, tm);

                oper ≜ e.op

            then

                $V_{Expression}$ [e.term1, tm] ∧

                $V_{Expression}$ [e.term2, tm] ∧

                case oper **of**

                    Boolean_op ⟹ typ1 = bt ∧ typ2 = bt |

                    Relational_op, Arithmetic_op ⟹

                        typ1 = it ∧ typ2 = it

                end

        end

    end

Note the interplay between functions *expression_type* and $V_{Expression}$. The former gives what may be termed the "candidate type" of an expression, which coincides with its actual type if the expression is valid; however *expression_type* is total and will always return a result. Based on the candidate types supplied by this function, $V_{Expression}$ determines whether the expression is valid or not. Having two separate functions in charge of finding the candidate type of a (possibly invalid) expression and of ascertaining its validity keeps the specification simple. (See also exercise 6.2.)

6.2.4 Valid instructions

Instructions are syntactically defined as:

    Instruction ≜ Skip | Assignment | Compound | Conditional | Loop

As with expressions, we may only define the validity of an instruction with respect to a certain type map; this suggests a validity function of signature

$$V_{Instruction} : Instruction \times Type\_map \to \mathbf{B}$$

defined by case analysis on the syntactic type of an instruction:

$V_{Instruction}$ [*i*: *Instruction*; *tm*: *Type_map*] $\triangleq$

    case *i* **of**

        Skip $\Rightarrow$ **true** |

        Assignment $\Rightarrow$

            $V_{Expression}$ [*i.source*, *tm*] $\wedge$

            i.target $\in$ **dom** *tm* $\wedge$

            tm (*i.target*) = *expression_type* (*i.source*, *tm*) |

        Conditional $\Rightarrow$

            $V_{Expression}$ [*i.test*, *tm*] $\wedge$

            $V_{Instruction}$ [*i.thenbranch*, *tm*] $\wedge$

            $V_{Instruction}$ [*i.elsebranch*, *tm*] $\wedge$

            expression_type (*i.test*, *tm*) = *bt* |

        Loop $\Rightarrow$

            $V_{Expression}$ [*i.test*, *tm*] $\wedge$

            $V_{Instruction}$ [*i.body*, *tm*] $\wedge$

            expression_type (*i.test*, *tm*) = *bt* |

        Compound $\Rightarrow$

            over *i* **apply**

                λ *inst* $\bullet$ $V_{Instruction}$ [*inst*, *tm*]

            combine " $\wedge$ " **empty** *true* **end**

    end

This definition is straightforward. There is no way a *Skip* instruction can be invalid. An assignment instruction must have a declared target variable, a valid source expression, with the same type for both. A conditional or loop instruction must be made of a valid boolean expression and of one or two (respectively) valid instructions. Finally, a compound instruction is valid if and only if all the instructions it contains, if any, are valid.

The lambda expression in the *Compound* branch is necessary because $V_{instruction}$ is a function of two arguments, an instruction and a type map, but the **over** operator needs a function of just one argument (a list element).

The condition in the *Compound* branch could have been written without the **over...** notation, using recursion:

if $i.EMPTY$ **then** *true* **else**

$$V_{Instruction} \; [i.FIRST, tm] \; \wedge \; V_{Instruction} \; [Instruction \; (i.TAIL), tm]$$

end

This form obviates the need for a lambda expression. The argument to the second recursive application of $V_{Instruction}$ cannot be just $i.TAIL$, which is syntactically a *Compound*, not an *Instruction*; the notation *Instruction* $(i.TAIL)$ elevates $i.TAIL$ to the status of instruction.

6.2.5 Valid programs

It is now an easy task to define the validity function for programs:

$$V_{Program} : Program \rightarrow \mathbf{B}$$

The Graal grammar gives:

$$Program \triangleq decpart: Declaration\_list; \; body: Instruction$$

A program has two components, a declaration list and an instruction; it will be valid if and only if the declaration list is valid and the instruction is valid under the type map induced by the declaration list:

$$V_{Program} \; [p: program] \; \triangleq$$

$$V_{Declaration\_list} \; [p.decpart] \; \wedge \; V_{Instruction} \; [p.body, \; typing \; (p.decpart)]$$

This concludes the static semantics of Graal.

Although such a static semantic specification does not exhibit the really salient features of the denotational method, and could in fact be used as a prologue to a specification of the dynamic semantics based on another method, it combines particularly well with a denotational description of the dynamic semantics: the structure of the M function definitions, to be studied now, closely parallels that of the V functions.

6.3 DYNAMIC SEMANTICS: BASICS

6.3.1 Dynamic semantic domains

The meaning functions will need the following domains:

- **Z**, the set of integers (positive, zero or negative);
- **B**, the set of boolean values, with two members *true* and *false*
- *Value*, the set of values: *Value* $\triangleq$ **N** $\cup$ **B** $\cup$ $\{unknown\}$

The special value *unknown* will be discussed below.

An essential ingredient in defining the semantics of a language is the choice of an appropriate mathematical domain to model the notion of program **state**. A state represents an instantaneous snapshot taken during program execution, which includes all useful information about what the program has computed so far.

In the case of the simple Graal language, the only relevant information is the value of program variables. The set of possible states may simply be defined, then, as the set of functions from variables to values; more precisely, since any program may only have a finite number of variables, only finite functions need to be considered. Hence the semantic domain representing the set of possible program states:

$$State \triangleq Variable \xrightarrow{f} Value$$

In other words, the state of a program at some instant of its execution is defined mathematically as the finite function which, to each of the program's variables, associates the value of the variable at that instant.

Assume for example that a program has the declaration part used above as example:

x, y: *INTEGER*; z: **boolean**

Then one possible state σ of this program is the function

$\sigma = \{<x, 3>, <z, false>\}$

This represents a state in which variable x has value 3 and variable z has value *false*; variable y has not yet been assigned a value.

A state such as σ is a function which, for every variable in its domain, yields the value of the variable in the state. In the example, $\sigma(x)$ is 3, the value of x in the computational state that σ represents.

The structure of states will become more complex in the next chapter as we add such features as input and output, pointers and others.

A programmer may view a state as a snapshot of the computer's **memory**, given by all the values it contains. This is not, however, the memory of an actual computer, which, if modeled by a function, would have domains of the form

$$0..memory\_size - 1 \; \xrightarrow[f]{} \; Value$$

but a more abstract notion of memory, whose states are functions from variables to values. The intermediate functions from variables to memory locations are implicit. In other words, the states considered here are more like symbolic dumps as produced by debuggers for high-level languages.

To model the state for a language with block structure, where the same variable name may refer to several run-time objects, an intermediate domain representing memory locations will be needed, as discussed in 7.6.4.

6.3.2 Dynamic semantic functions

The specification needs the following meaning functions:

$$M_{Program}: \; Program \nrightarrow State$$

$$M_{Instruction}: \; Instruction \nrightarrow State \nrightarrow State$$

$$M_{Expression}: \; Expression \rightarrow State \rightarrow Value$$

The signatures of these functions have been determined as follows:

- The denotation of a program is the state in which its execution terminates, as given by the final values of all the program's variables. This is the only way the program's effect can be determined since Graal has neither input nor output instructions.

- Any instruction, when executed in a certain state, will yield a new state upon termination. In other words, an instruction's denotation is a state-to-state transformation, modeled by a function in $State \nrightarrow State$.

- The computation of an expression yields a value; this value depends on the state. As a result, the denotation of an expression is a function from states to values.

Why some of the above arrows indicate total functions and others indicate possibly partial functions is the subject of exercise 6.3; this question is examined briefly later in this chapter (6.5.7) and in more detail in chapter 8.

The next sections give the values of the three meaning functions in bottom-up order, from expressions to programs.

6.4 THE MEANING OF EXPRESSIONS

6.4.1 Definition

Case analysis gives the denotation of expressions:

[6.1]

$$M_{Expression} \ [e: Expression] \ \triangleq$$

   $\lambda \ \sigma: State \ \bullet$

      case e **of**

         $Constant \ \Rightarrow$

            case e **of**

               $Integer\_constant \Rightarrow e \ . value \ \ |$

               $Boolean\_constant \Rightarrow e \ . value$

            end $|$

         $Variable \ \Rightarrow$

            if $e \notin \mathbf{dom} \ \sigma$ **then** $unknown$

            else$\sigma \ (e) \ $ **end** $\ \ |$

         $Binary \ \Rightarrow$

            $apply\_binary \ (e \ . op \ ,$

                              $M_{Expression} \ [e. term1] \ (\sigma),$

                              $M_{Expression} \ [e. term2] \ (\sigma))$

                     -- $apply\_binary$ is defined below.

      end

Here are a few explanations.

- $M_{Expression} \ [e]$ is a function from states to values: hence the initial $\lambda \ \sigma$.
- If e is a constant, $M_{Expression} \ [e]$ is the associated boolean or numeric value. The state is not involved in the result for this case, as is appropriate for a constant.
- Assume now that e is a variable; then for any state σ, by the definition of the notion of state, $\sigma \ (e)$ is the value of the variable e in state σ. This is only meaningful, however, if the variable belongs to the domain of σ. When this is not the case, the function yields the special value $unknown$, included in set $Value$ (page 159) for this purpose. More on unknown values below.
- If e is a binary expression with operands $e. term1$ and $e. term2$ and operator $e.op$, then its value in an arbitrary state σ is the result of applying the operator to the values of the two operands, as evaluated in that same state σ; to know the values of the two operands, we must apply $M_{Expression}$ recursively.

6.4.2 Applying mathematical operators

The as yet undefined function *apply_binary* should apply a binary operation to two integer operands. A sketch of its definition is:

[6.2]

$$apply\_binary: Operator \times Value \times Value \nrightarrow Value$$

$apply\_binary \triangleq$

    $\lambda\ op,\ v_1,\ v_2\ \bullet$

        case *op* **of**

            Arithmetic $\Rightarrow$

                case *op* **of**

                    Plus $\Rightarrow v_1 + v_2$ |

                    Times $\Rightarrow v_1 * v_2$ |

                    etc.

                end |

            Relational $\Rightarrow$

                case *op* **of**

                    Lt $\Rightarrow v_1 < v_2$ |

                    Le $\Rightarrow v_1 \leq v_2$ |

                    Eq $\Rightarrow v_1 = v_2$ |

                    etc.

                end |

            Boolean $\Rightarrow$ etc.

        end

Function *apply_binary* establishes the relationship between the programming language descriptions of computations and their mathematical counterparts. In a more complete programming language, it would be complemented by other similar functions (such as *apply_unary*).

6.4.3 Unknown values and a first view of strictness

You may have noted that the above partial definition of *apply_binary* does not specify how to handle *unknown* values. This is representative of the more general problem of undefined values.

Special values such as *unknown* are a constant source of trouble in formal descriptions (as the events they represent are in actual programming), and it would be nice if one could avoid them altogether. Unfortunately, this is usually impossible.

Among the events of program execution considered so far, only one may yield an *unknown* value: a reference to an uninitialized variable (in [6.1], page 161). As every programmer knows, however, this is not an uncommon occurrence, and the specification must take it into account.

There are three approaches to the problem of uninitialized variables.

1 • The most common solution (or rather lack thereof) is mirrored in the above specification: it delays the problem until run-time; if a variable is accessed without having been assigned a value, the value returned is "whatever happens to be there" (in the memory cell assigned to the variable).

2 • Another solution is to prevent the problem from occurring by defining rules ensuring that no variable may be accessed at run-time before it has been properly initialized. It is best to define these rules as *static* semantic constraints; sufficient rules are indeed not hard to find for a language such as Graal which has only simple variables and no arrays, records etc. (General rules may be more restrictive than is strictly necessary in some cases: for example a program *inst* ; $y := x$ will be treated as invalid if *inst* is a **while** loop whose body assigns to x, because the loop may have zero iterations, although no error will occur if it has one or more.) One of the principal tasks of the software engineering tools known as **static analyzers** is precisely to check program texts for the possibility of a variable being accessed before it has been assigned a value.

3 • Yet another solution is to make initialization rules part of the official language definition, by specifying an initial value for each type, such as 0 for numbers, *true* for booleans etc.

The author definitely prefers solution 3 which has the advantage of simplicity and clarity, and simplifies the programmers' task if the initialization values are well-chosen. Of course, these values should be part of the official language definition, not implementation-dependent. Examples of languages which use this approach are the object-oriented languages Simula and Eiffel.

Adapting the definition of Graal to conventions 2 and 3 is the object of exercises 6.4 and 6.5.

However, most current languages rely on solution 1, so the specification of Graal should reflect this convention for realism. This is achieved by having $M_{Expression}$ return *unknown* for a variable which is not part of the state's domain. To be consistent, we must also make sure that any unknown value appearing in an expression makes the whole expression unknown. It would be a very strange situation indeed if you were not able to compute an operand of an expression (say a in $a + b$), but could still determine, through some magical mechanism, the value of the expression as a whole!

Since the only non-simple expressions in Graal are binary expressions, this requirement is easy to express in the definition of *apply_binary*:

apply_binary $\triangleq$

   λ *op* : *Operator* , v_1: *Value* , v_2: *Value* •

     if v_1 = *unknown* $\lor$ v_2 = *unknown* **then**

       unknown

    else

       ... As above ([6.2], page 162) ...

    end

This requirement that *apply_binary* yield *unknown* whenever one or more of its arguments is *unknown* is a special case of a general property called **strictness**. Here *apply_binary* is said to be strict on both its arguments. If the language included other kinds of complex expression (such as unary expressions), the associated semantic functions would similarly be specified as strict on all their arguments.

Strictness will be studied in a more general context in chapter 8 (8.5.2 and 8.7). Although strictness is a natural idea, it sometimes contradicts standard mathematical properties: for example *apply_binary* (*Operator* (*Eq*), *unknown, unknown*) is *unknown* according to the above definition, even though it would seem to be a universal rule that $a = a$ is *true* for any value a .

Value *unknown* may be used to denote the result of other erroneous operations – for example, the result of a division by zero, which has been left unspecified in the definition of *apply_binary*. Alternatively, you could define different unknown values corresponding to various abnormal situations (such as arithmetic overflow etc.). Then you should clearly state their strictness priority (that is to say, the result of *apply_binary* when applied to different error values). A single *unknown* will suffice for this presentation.

6.4.4 Towards a more abstract approach to handling errors

[This section may be skipped on first reading. It assumes that you are familiar with the notion of abstract data type].

The above approach to errors may be criticized as overspecifying: in particular, as just noted, there is only one "unknown" value, which seems to imply that the value returned for an uninitialized variable is always the same, even though a program which tests for the equality of two unknown values returns *unknown* rather than *true* .

The fault may be seen to lie with the explicit definition given for the semantic domain *Value* , through a list of its members. A more implicit definition, in the spirit of the theory of abstract data types, would just assert that there is a set *Value* , characterized by a certain number of functions such as:

$is\_boolean$: $Value \rightarrow \mathbf{B}$

$is\_integer$: $Value \rightarrow \mathbf{B}$

$is\_unknown$: $Value \rightarrow \mathbf{B}$

$boolean\_value$: $Value \rightarrow \mathbf{B}$

$integer\_value$: $Value \rightarrow \mathbf{N}$

The idea is that a member of *Value* carries with it a certain number of boolean attributes (*is_integer*, *is_boolean*, *is_unknown*) which express what information is known about it. Clearly a value may not (in a typed language) be both a valid boolean and a valid integer, so that the following property holds:

$$\forall v: Value \bullet \neg\ is\_boolean\ (v)\ \vee\ \neg\ is\_integer\ (v)$$

(This property is a of "state invariant", which will be satisfied in every possible state; the next chapter will introduce other examples of state invariants.)

The above property may also be expressed more simply, using the quotient operator of chapter 2:

$$(Value\ /\ is\_boolean)\ \cap\ (Value\ /\ is\_integer) = \varnothing$$

We do not need, however, to prohibit a value from being both unknown and boolean, or both unknown and integer; the understanding is that the *value* functions will only be applied if the value is not unknown. They may also be defined as total functions, if they are only applied to values such that *is_boolean* and *is_integer*, respectively, are true.

> This is very much like the situation that prevails with the implementation of typed languages on most common computers: although the hardware permits interpreting the same memory cell (bit string) as either a boolean or an integer, the static checking performed by the compiler ensures that no bad-taste combination ever occurs at run-time.

With this approach we cannot completely specify the $M_{Expression}$ function since its result is not known exactly in some cases, for example when an expression includes an uninitialized variable; but the above definition ([6.1], page 161) may be adapted to express the relevant properties of this function, in the following style:

$\forall e: Expression, \sigma: State \bullet$

   given

       $val \triangleq M_{Expression} [e] (\sigma)$

   then

      case e **of**

         Constant $\Rightarrow$

              $\neg$ *is_unknown* (*val*) $\wedge$ *val* = ... See [6.1] ... |

         Variable $\Rightarrow$

              if $e \in$ **dom** σ **then** $\neg$ *is_unknown* (*val*) $\wedge$ *val* = σ (*e*)

              else *is_unknown* (*val*) **end** |

         Binary $\Rightarrow$

              characterize_binary (*e .op* ,

                           $M_{Expression}$ [*e.term1*] (σ),

                           $M_{Expression}$ [*e.term2*] (σ),

                           val)

        end

   end

Function *characterize_binary* yields a boolean result from four arguments rather than three and is otherwise similar to *apply_binary*:

characterize_binary $\triangleq$

     λ *op* : *Operator* , v_1: *Value* , v_2: *Value* , *val* : *Value* $\bullet$

        if *is_unknown* (v_1) $\vee$ *is_unknown* (v_2) **then**

            is_unknown (*val*)

      else

          case *op* **of**

             Arithmetic $\Rightarrow$

                case *op* **of**

                    Plus $\Rightarrow$ *val* = $v_1 + v_2$ |

                    Times $\Rightarrow$ *val* = $v_1 * v_2$ |

                  etc. (see [6.2], page 162)

Such implicit characterizations of semantic functions, which do not completely define these functions but only express their relevant properties, are useful whenever you wish to leave certain aspects of a language specification open.

Leaving the result of a computation undefined in the formal specification is not the same as requiring this result to be some special "undefined" value. In fact, the result may be perfectly defined in some implementations. For example, some operating systems initialize the contents of memory to a fixed value (often corresponding to zero for integers) before a program is loaded; on such a system, the result of a computation involving uninitialized variables is well defined. By specifying the result to be unknown in the formal specification, however, you prevent programmers from relying on any implementation-dependent property of uninitialized variables.

In general, an axiomatic specification (chapter 9) may be preferable to a denotational one when you wish to leave certain aspects of a language unspecified. By writing axioms or inference rules which are only applicable under certain conditions, you can avoid the need to specify explicit erroneous results for programs which do not satisfy these conditions: you simply make it impossible to prove anything of interest about them.

6.5 THE MEANING OF INSTRUCTIONS

6.5.1 Overview

The meaning function for instructions has signature

$$M_{Instruction}: \; Instruction \nrightarrow State \nrightarrow State$$

So if i is an instruction, $M_{Instruction} [i]$ is a function which takes a state as argument and yield as a result a new state, the one in which execution of the instruction, starting in the original state, will terminate – if it does terminate at all, of course, but let's not anticipate.

The value of $M_{Instruction}$ depends on what kind of instruction i is, so a definition by case analysis is once again appropriate. For convenience of exposition, and also for ease of modification in the next chapter and in the exercises, the function definition uses auxiliary functions (M_{Skip}, $M_{xm} SkipAssignment$ etc.) corresponding to the various kinds of instruction and detailed in the next paragraphs.

[6.3]

$$M_{Instruction} \; [i: Instruction] \; \triangleq$$

     case i **of**

            $Skip \; \Rightarrow \; M_{Skip} \; [i] \quad |$

            $Assignment \; \Rightarrow \; M_{Assignment} \; [i] \quad |$

            $Compound \; \Rightarrow \; M_{Compound} \; [i] \quad |$

            $Conditional \; \Rightarrow \; M_{Conditional} \; [i] \quad |$

            $Loop \; \Rightarrow \; M_{Loop} \; [i]$

     end

The auxiliary functions have signatures

$M_{Skip}: Skip \rightarrow State \rightarrow State$

$M_{Assignment}: Assignment \nrightarrow State \rightarrow State$

$M_{Compound}: Compound \nrightarrow State \nrightarrow State$

$M_{Conditional}: Conditional \nrightarrow State \nrightarrow State$

$M_{Loop}: Loop \nrightarrow State \nrightarrow State$

The question of why some of the functions considered may be partial and some are total arises again and will be discussed later.

6.5.2 Skip instructions

The semantic function for *Skip* instructions is trivial:

$M_{Skip} \ [s: Skip] \ \triangleq \ Id$

Id is the identity function $\lambda \sigma \bullet \sigma$, applied here to set *State*. Execution of a *Skip* instruction leaves the state unchanged, so $M_{Skip} \ [s](\sigma) = \sigma$ for any state σ if s is a *Skip* instruction.

6.5.3 Assignment

The following function gives the denotation of an an assignment instruction a, acting on variable $a.target$ and expression $a.source$:

$M_{Assignment} \ [a: Assignment] \ \triangleq$

$\qquad \lambda \sigma \bullet (\sigma \ \leftY \ \{<a.target, M_{Expression} \ [a.source] \ (\sigma)>\})$

In other words, the state σ' resulting from execution of a in an arbitrary state σ is identical to σ except for the value of variable $a.target$, which is now the value of expression $a.source$, as evaluated in state σ.

Remember that the states σ and σ' are finite functions from variables to values. The definition shows function σ' to be σ "overridden" by the single-member finite function $\{<a.target, v>\}$ where v is the value of the source expression in state σ. This means that the value of a variable x in state σ' is

$\sigma' (x) =$

> **if** $x \neq a.target$ **then** $\sigma (x)$ -- Same value as before the assignment
>
> **else** $M_{Expression}$ $[a.source]$ (σ) **end**

6.5.4 Compound

The effect of a compound instruction (syntactically a list of instructions) is the composed effect of its components:

> $M_{Compound}$ $[cp : Compound]$ $\triangleq$
>
> > **over** cp **apply** $M_{Instruction}$ **combine** ";" **empty** Id **end**

The function composition operator ";" serves to describe the combination of the effects of the successive elements of the list: the result of executing a compound made of instructions $i_1, i_2, ..., i_{n-1}, i_n$, starting in a state σ, is the state

> $M_n (M_{n-1} (... (M_2 (M_1 (\sigma)))...))$

where for each $j \in 1.. n$, M_j is the denotation $M_{Instruction}$ $[cp(j)]$ of the compound's j-th instruction. Function composition is the mathematical equivalent of the intuitive notion of executing cp_1, then cp_2, ..., then cp_{n-1}, then cp_n.

As in the corresponding branch of the V function (6.2.4), a recursive definition could have been used instead of the **over...** notation, as follows:

> $M_{Compound}$ $[cp : Compound]$ $\triangleq$
>
> > **if** $cp.EMPTY$ **then** Id
> >
> > **else** $M_{Instruction}$ $[cp.FIRST]$; $M_{Compound}$ $[cp.TAIL]$ **end**

6.5.5 Conditional

If cd is a conditional instruction, its effect depends on the value of the boolean expression $i.test$, as evaluated in the state in which the conditional instruction is executed:

$M_{Conditional}$ [cd: Conditional] $\triangleq$

    given

                 Where_true $\triangleq$ *State* / $M_{Expression}$ [cd.test];

                 Where_false $\triangleq$ *State* – *Where_true*

    then

                   $(M_{Instruction}$ [cd.thenbranch] \ *Where_true*) $\uplus$

                   $(M_{Instruction}$ [cd.elsebranch] \ *Where_false*)

    end

This definition uses a partition of *State* into two subsets *Where_true* and *Where_false*: *Where_true* is the set of states such that $M_{Expression}$ [cd.test] (σ) has value true, and *Where_false* is its complement. The minus sign in *State* – *Where_true* denotes set difference.

The quotient notation used to define *Where_true* was introduced in 2.7.6; it is appropriate here since $M_{Expression}$ [cd.test] is a function from *State* to **.xm**expressionB , the set of boolean values, thus a predicate on *State*. Recall that *State* / *pred* is the subset of *State* containing all the members for which predicate *pred* (here the denotation of *cd*.test) takes value true.

An equivalent definition for *Where_true*, written without the quotient notation, is

    $\{\sigma \in$ *State* | $M_{Expression}$ [cd.test] (σ) = *true*$\}$

that is to say, the set of states in which the boolean expression of the conditional instruction evaluates to *true*.

The effect of *cd* is that of its "then" branch on *Where_true* and of its "else" branch on *Where_false*. This is expressed with the functional operators \ (restriction of a function to a subset of its source set) and $\uplus$ (overriding union): the semantic function for *cd* is the union of the semantic function for its branches, each restricted to the set of states in which it is applicable.

Since *Where_true* and *Where_false* are by construction disjoint, the "overriding union" operator is equivalent here to a plain union; however $\cup$ is not appropriate since, as mentioned in chapter 2, simple union, when applied to two arbitrary functions, yields a relation, not necessarily a function.

Function $M_{Conditional}$ could also have been expressed without the help of the functional operators $\uplus$, / and \ by referring explicitly to the state, as follows:

$\lambda\, \sigma \bullet$

>   **if** $M_{Expression}$ $[cd.test]$ (σ) **then**
>
>   > $M_{Instruction}$ $[cd.thenbranch]$ (σ)
>
>   **else**
>
>   > $M_{Instruction}$ $[cd.elsebranch]$ (σ)
>
>   **end**

Some people prefer this style of denotational definitions, which makes the state more directly visible. The result also looks more like programs. The use of functional operators makes definitions more concise, and more abstract.

6.5.6 Loop

The last case is loops, whose semantic definition bears some resemblance to conditionals, using the same partition of the set of states.

> M_{Loop} $[l: Loop]$ $\triangleq$
>
>   >   **given**
>   >
>   >   > $Where\_true$ $\triangleq$ $State\ /\ M_{Expression}$ $[l.test]$;
>   >   >
>   >   > $Where\_false$ $\triangleq$ $State - Where\_true$
>   >
>   >   **then**
>   >
>   >   > $(Id\ \backslash\ Where\_false)$ ⩀
>   >   >
>   >   > $((M_{Instruction}$ $[l.body]$; M_{Loop} $[l]) \backslash Where\_true)$
>   >
>   >   **end**

Here the denotation of the loop depends on whether the initial state is a member of *Where_true*, the set of states that satisfy the predicate associated with the continuation condition *l.test*, or of its complement *Where_false*:

- When executed in a state belonging to *Where_false*, the loop is equivalent to a *Skip*.
- In any other state, the loop's effect is that of executing its body *l.body*, and then starting the whole process again; so its denotation is the composition of the semantic functions for *l.body* and *l* again as a whole. It is as though *l* were a compound instruction with two components: *l.body* and *l* itself.

You are urged at this point to check your understanding of M_{Loop} by writing an alternative version which does not use functional operators but refers explicitly to the state, as done above for the *Compound* and *Conditional* cases.

6.5.7 Comments on the meaning of expressions and instructions

Both M function definitions given so far – for expressions and instructions – are recursive. Before proceeding, we must try to weigh the consequences of this property.

The definition of $M_{Expression}$ ([6.1], page 161) is recursive in its branch for *binary*. This recursion intuitively seems safe because the recursive invocations refer to components of the expression e (the argument to the function), in other words to "smaller" expressions. So we may feel relatively confident that the definition, although recursive, does define a function in all cases. (Seen from an operational viewpoint, computation of $M_{Expression}$ should always "terminate".) This is of course no more than an informal argument; we are not yet in a position to prove anything rigorously about such recursive definitions.

For $M_{Instruction}$, things are far less clear. This function is recursive for compounds, conditionals and loops. The first two cases rely on a recursion pattern similar to the scheme for expressions: arguments to recursive invocations are components of the original instruction i. But the loop case is different. The definition of M_{Loop} [l] uses not only $M_{Instruction}$ [$l.body$] but also M_{Loop} [l] itself – the function applied to its original argument!

True, the recursive call restricts the domain of M_{Loop} [l] to a subdomain (*Where_true*), but, still, we may wonder whether we have defined anything at all. A detailed answer to this question – which turns out to be a deep one – will have to be deferred until chapter 8.

One observation, however, is already possible. You must realize that there can be **no** a priori guarantee that the definition of loop semantics will always yield a result. This corresponds to a fact of programming life: as every programmer knows, it is all too easy, in any realistic programming language, to write an instruction that will not terminate. Such an instruction does not compute anything; it is natural, then, that the function giving the denotation of instructions should not be defined for that particular argument.

This necessity to account for the unfortunate but inevitable prospect of non-termination is the key reason why some of the semantic functions of this chapter are partial, as pointed out at their place of introduction (page 160; see also exercise 6.3). More on this issue in chapter 8.

6.5.8 The meaning of programs

To complete the semantic definition of Graal, there remains to express the function $M_{Program}$, giving the semantics of entire programs.

This meaning function is of signature

$$M_{Program} : Program \nrightarrow State$$

that is to say, defines the semantic effect of a program as the state in which the program's execution terminates (if it does). Recall from the abstract grammar that a program consists of a list of declarations and an instruction (which of course will usually be a compound):

$$Program \triangleq decpart: Declaration\_list; \; body: Instruction$$

so that the effect of the program should be that of its "body" instruction. The body is executed in an initial state in which no variable has a value; such a state is represented by the empty function ∅. This yields the meaning function for programs in Graal:

> -- The state resulting from execution of $p.body$
> -- in an empty initial state

$$M_{Program} \; [p: Program] \; \triangleq$$

$$\qquad M_{Instruction} \; [p.body] \; (\varnothing)$$

> -- ∅ is the empty set, which is here the empty function

6.6 COMPLETE SPECIFICATION OF GRAAL

As a conclusion to this chapter, it is useful to collect the various pieces of the specification of the Graal language, as introduced in this chapter. This section reproduces them without further comment; it may serve as a reference for the successive language extensions studied in the next chapter, and as a checklist of the necessary components in the complete denotational specification of any language.

6.6.1 Abstract syntax

The abstract syntax of Graal is reproduced on the inside back cover.

6.6.2 Static semantic domains

$$Type\_value \; \triangleq \; \{bt, \, it, \, ut\}$$

$$Type\_map \; \triangleq \; Variable \; \xrightarrow[f]{} \; Type\_value$$

6.6.3 Static semantic functions

$V_{Declaration\_list}: Declaration\_list \rightarrow \mathbf{B}$

$V_{Declaration\_list} [dl: Declaration\_list] \triangleq$
   $(\forall \ i, j \in 1..dl.LENGTH \bullet i \neq j \implies dl\,(i).v \neq dl\,(j).v)$

$typeval: Type \rightarrow Type\_value$

$typeval\,(t: Type) \triangleq$
   case t **of**
         $Boolean\_type \implies bt \mid Integer\_type \implies it$
   end

$typing: Declaration\_list \rightarrow Type\_map$

$typing\,(dl: Declaration\_list) \triangleq$
   given
         $associate\_type \triangleq \lambda\,d:Declaration \bullet \{<d.v, typeval\,(d.t)>\}$
   then
         over dl **apply** $associate\_type$ **combine** " $\curlyvee$ " **empty** $\varnothing$ **end**
   end

$expression\_type: Expression \times Type\_map \rightarrow Type\_value$

$expression\_type\,(e: Expression, tm: Type\_map) \triangleq$
   case e **of**
         $Constant \implies$
               case e **of**
                     $Integer\_constant \implies it \mid Boolean\_constant \implies bt$
               end $\mid$
         $Variable \implies$ **if** $e \notin$ **dom** tm **then** ut **else** $tm\,(e)$ **end** $\mid$
         $Binary \implies$
               case $e.op$ **of**
                     $Relational\_op, Boolean\_op \implies bt \mid Arithmetic\_op \implies it$
               end
   end

$V_{Expression}$: $Expression$ × $Type\_map$ → **B**

$V_{Expression}$ [e: $Expression$, tm: $Type\_map$] $\triangleq$

    case e **of**

        $Constant \Rightarrow true$ | $Variable \Rightarrow e \in$ **dom** tm |

        $Binary \Rightarrow$

            given

                $typ1 \triangleq expression\_type \ (e.term1, tm)$;

                $typ2 \triangleq expression\_type \ (e.term2, tm)$;

                $oper \triangleq e.op$

            then

                $V_{Expression}$ [$e.term1$, tm] $\wedge$ $V_{Expression}$ [$e.term2$, tm] $\wedge$

                case $oper$ **of**

                    $Boolean\_op \Rightarrow typ1 = bt \ \wedge \ typ2 = bt$ |

                    $Relational\_op, Arithmetic\_op \Rightarrow$

                        $typ1 = it \ \wedge \ typ2 = it$

              end

            end

    end

$V_{Instruction}$ [i: $Instruction$; tm: $Type\_map$] $\triangleq$

    case i **of**

        $Skip \Rightarrow$ **true** |

        $Assignment \Rightarrow$

            $i.target \in$ **dom** $tm \wedge$

            $V_{Expression}$ [$i.source$, tm] $\wedge$

            $tm \ (i.target) = expression\_type \ (i.source, tm)$ |

        $Conditional \Rightarrow$

            $V_{Expression}$ [$i.test$, tm] $\wedge$ $expression\_type \ (i.test, tm) = bt \ \wedge$

            $V_{Instruction}$ [$i.thenbranch$, tm] $\wedge$ $V_{Instruction}$ [$i.elsebranch$, tm] |

        $Loop \Rightarrow$

            $V_{Expression}$ [$i.test$, tm] $\wedge$ $expression\_type \ (i.test, tm) = bt \ \wedge$

            $V_{Instruction}$ [$i.body$, tm] |

        $Compound \Rightarrow$

            over i **apply**

                $\lambda \ inst \bullet V_{Instruction}$ [$inst$, tm]

            combine " $\wedge$ " **empty** $true$ **end**

    end

$V_{Program} : Program \rightarrow \mathbf{B}$

$V_{Program}$ $[p: program]$ $\triangleq$

   $V_{Declaration\_list}$ $[p.decpart]$ $\wedge$ $V_{Instruction}$ $[p.body, typing\ (p.decpart)]$

6.6.4 Dynamic semantic domains

$Value$ $\triangleq$ $\mathbf{Z}$ $\cup$ $\mathbf{B}$ $\cup$ $\{unknown\}$

$State$ $\triangleq$ $Variable$ $\xrightarrow{f}$ $Value$

6.6.5 Dynamic semantic functions

$apply\_binary: Operator$ $\times$ $Value$ $\times$ $Value$ $\nrightarrow$ $Value$

$apply\_binary$ $\triangleq$ λ $op: Operator$, $v_1, v_2: Value$ •
   if $v_1 = unknown$ $\vee$ $v_2 = unknown$ **then** $unknown$ **else**
      case op **of**
         $Arithmetic$ $\Rightarrow$
            case op **of**
               $Plus$ $\Rightarrow v_1 + v_2$ $\mid$ $Minus$ $\Rightarrow v_1 - v_2$ $\mid$
               $Times$ $\Rightarrow v_1 * v_2$ $\mid$
               Div $\Rightarrow$ **if** $v_2 = 0$ **then** $unknown$ **else** v_1 / v_2 **end**
            end $\mid$
         $Relational$ $\Rightarrow$
            case op **of**
               $Lt \Rightarrow v_1 < v_2$ $\mid$ $Le \Rightarrow v_1 \le v_2$ $\mid$
               $Eq \Rightarrow v_1 = v_2$ $\mid$ $Ne \Rightarrow v_1 \ne v_2$ $\mid$
               $Ge \Rightarrow v_1 \ge v_2$ $\mid$ $Gt \Rightarrow v_1 > v_2$
            end $\mid$
         $Boolean$ $\Rightarrow$
            case op **of**
               $And \Rightarrow v_1 \wedge v_2$ $\mid$ $Or \Rightarrow v_1 \vee v_2$ $\mid$
               $Nand \Rightarrow \neg (v_1 \wedge v_2)$ $\mid$ $Nor \Rightarrow \neg (v_1 \vee v_2)$ $\mid$
               $Xor \Rightarrow (v_1 \vee v_2) \wedge \neg (v_1 \wedge v_2)$
            end
      end
   end

$M_{Expression}: Expression \rightarrow State \rightarrow Value$

$M_{Expression} [e: Expression] \triangleq$

    $\lambda\ \sigma: State \bullet$

        case e **of**

            $Constant \Rightarrow$

                case e **of**

                    $Integer\_constant \Rightarrow e.value\ |$

                    $Boolean\_constant \Rightarrow e.value$

              end $|$

            $Variable \Rightarrow$ **if** $e \notin$ **dom** σ **then** $unknown$ **else** $\sigma\ (e)$ **end**

            $Binary \Rightarrow$

                $apply\_binary\ (e.op,$

                              $M_{Expression}\ [e.term1]\ (\sigma),$

                              $M_{Expression}\ [e.term2]\ (\sigma))$

        end

$M_{Instruction}: Instruction \nrightarrow State \nrightarrow State$

$M_{Skip}: Skip \rightarrow State \rightarrow State$

$M_{Assignment}: Assignment \rightarrow State \rightarrow State$

$M_{Compound}: Compound \rightarrow State \nrightarrow State$

$M_{Conditional}: Conditional \rightarrow State \nrightarrow State$

$M_{Loop}: Loop \rightarrow State \nrightarrow State$

$M_{Instruction} [i: Instruction] \triangleq$

      case i **of**

            $Skip \Rightarrow M_{Skip}\ [i]\ |$

            $Assignment \Rightarrow M_{Assignment}\ [i]\ |$

            $Compound \Rightarrow M_{Compound}\ [i]\ |$

            $Conditional \Rightarrow M_{Conditional}\ [i]\ |$

            $Loop \Rightarrow M_{Loop}\ [i]$

      end

$M_{Skip}\ [s: Skip] \triangleq Id$

$M_{Assignment}\ [a : Assignment]\ \triangleq$

$\qquad \lambda\ \sigma\ \bullet\ (\sigma\ \underset{\curlyvee}{}\ \{<a.target,\ M_{Expression}\ [a.source]\ (\sigma)>\})$

$M_{Compound}\ [cp : Compound]\ \triangleq$

$\qquad$ **over** cp **apply** $M_{Instruction}$ **combine** ";" **empty** Id **end**

$M_{Conditional}\ [cd : Conditional]\ \triangleq$

$\qquad$ **given**

$\qquad\qquad Where\_true\ \triangleq\ State\ /\ M_{Expression}\ [cd.test];$

$\qquad\qquad Where\_false\ \triangleq\ State\ -\ Where\_true$

$\qquad$ **then**

$\qquad\qquad (M_{Instruction}\ [cd.thenbranch]\ \backslash\ Where\_true)\ \underset{\curlyvee}{}$

$\qquad\qquad (M_{Instruction}\ [cd.elsebranch]\ \backslash\ Where\_false)$

$\qquad$ **end**

$M_{Loop}\ [l : Loop]\ \triangleq$

$\qquad$ **given**

$\qquad\qquad Where\_true\ \triangleq\ State\ /\ M_{Expression}\ [l.test];$

$\qquad\qquad Where\_false\ \triangleq\ State\ -\ Where\_true$

$\qquad$ **then**

$\qquad\qquad (Id\ \backslash\ Where\_false)\ \underset{\curlyvee}{}$

$\qquad\qquad ((M_{Instruction}\ [l.body];$

$\qquad\qquad M_{Loop}\ [l])\ \backslash\ Where\_true)$

$\qquad$ **end**

$M_{Program}\ [p : Program]\ \triangleq\ M_{Instruction}\ [p.body]\ (\varnothing)$

6.7 BIBLIOGRAPHICAL NOTES

The original articles on denotational semantics, by Scott and Strachey (writing separately or together), are still recommended reading – not just for their historical interest. Particularly noteworthy are [Strachey 1966], [Scott 1970], [Scott 1971], [Scott 1972] and [Strachey 1973].

Many books deal with denotational semantics. Presentations of the theoretical aspects (addressed in part by chapter 8) may be found in [Manna 1974] and [Livercy 1978]. [Gordon 1979] is an introductory monograph and [Tennent 1976] an overview article; at the other extreme, [Milne 1976] is a complete treatise. Somewhere half-way is [Stoy 1977], a classic. [Tennent 1981] develops principles of programming language design based for a large part on the denotational theory. [Schmidt 1986], which also addresses language design, covers the denotational semantics of many language constructs.

The emphasis in the above publications is on the method and on the description of individual language features rather than on the full description of an actual programming language. VDM (the Vienna Development Method) includes a set of techniques and notations for this purpose, using the the META-IV metalanguage. The reference on this effort is [Bjørner 1982], which includes descriptions of Algol 60 and Pascal. [Bjørner 1980] gives a VDM specification of a language close to full 1979 Ada; see also [Donzeau-Gouge 1980]. It appears from [King 1989] that the official standard for Modula-2 will be its VDM specification.

Static analysis was mentioned on page 163 as a technique to detect uninitialized variables. Examples of tools which apply this technique to various programming languages are RXVP-80 [Deutsch 1982] and Lint [Johnson 1978]. A theoretical basis for static analysis is given in [Fosdick 1976].

[Barringer 1984] investigates mathematical techniques for dealing with undefined or erroneous values (6.4.3)

EXERCISES

6.1 Semantics of the typed lambda calculus

Consider typed lambda calculus, as introduced in 5.10. Define the abstract syntax and the static semantics of this language rigorously; for static semantics, some of the methods used in the present chapter, such as the concept of type map and the interplay between functions *expression_type* (page 155) and $V_{Expression}$ (page 155), will be useful.

Define the denotational semantics of this language by contraction to normal form (5.8).

6.2 Doing both jobs at once

(This exercise is for readers familiar with Prolog.) Using Prolog-like notations for defining functions with more than one unknown, write a variant of the validity function on expressions (6.2.3) which does the task of both $V_{Expression}$ and *expression_type*, determining the type of an expression and its sub-expressions as part of the process of verifying its type validity.

6.3 Definition of the meaning functions

For each of the meaning functions introduced in 6.3.2 and each function space involved, explain why a normal arrow (for total functions) or crossed arrow (for functions which may be either total or partial) is used.

6.4 Forced initialization

Augment the static semantic constraints of Graal so as to ensure that at run-time no instruction may reference a variable unless some previously executed instruction has assigned a value to the variable, as suggested by solution 2, page 163.

6.5 Default initialization

As suggested by solution 3, page 163, modify the definition of Graal to include explicit initialization for all variables (0 for integers and *false* for booleans).

6.6 Indexed loops

Most languages have an "indexed loop" instruction of the form

>   **for** j: *first, last, step* **do**
>
>   *inst*
>
>   **end**

where j is a variable, *first*, *last* and *step* are integer-valued expressions and *inst* is an instruction (which may involve j).

1 - Add this instruction to the abstract syntax and the denotational semantics of Graal given in this chapter. Rely on your intuitive understanding of the effect of this instruction.

2 - Actual languages differ in some of the features of indexed loops. For example:

- In most languages, the expressions *first*, *last* and *step* are considered to be evaluated once and for all upon loop initialization, so that the number of executions of the loop body *inst* may be determined upon loop entry from the initial values F, L and S of the expressions, even if these expressions involve one or more variables whose values may be changed by *inst*; but the Algol 60 convention is that the expressions are evaluated anew on each iteration to increment j and determine whether execution should continue.

- In some languages (Pascal, Ada, older versions of Fortran), the step can only be 1 or -1.

- In Algol 68 and Algol W, j is considered to be an integer variable declared by context through its appearance in the loop, and does not conflict with any declared variable of the same name; in other languages (such as Pascal), j must be declared as a normal variable of type **integer** (or a subrange in Pascal).

- If j is indeed treated as a normal variable, then its value upon loop exit may be considered undefined, or equal to the value of *last*, or to the last value obtained by successive incrementations (often the value of *last* + *step* if the loop body has been executed at least once).

- Versions of Fortran prior to Fortran 77 even had the strange convention of not specifying, in the language standard, the effect of an indexed loop when $F > L$ (for $S = 1$); this enabled most language implementers to gain a little efficiency by placing the test at the end of the loop in the compiler-generated code, so that the loop body was always executed at least once, even when $F > L$.

Examine your specification to see how it deals with these points. Does the existence of a formal description bring any light to the discussion of these issues in language feature design?

6.7 A denotational compiler (term project)

This project is a programming assignment. The aim is not to produce a "good" program in the standard sense, but to use the computer as a vehicle for experimenting with and gaining insight into denotational definitions.

The assignment is to write a **Graal Denotational Compiler** which will translate a Graal program into a set of **denotations**, and a **Denotation Interpreter** which will execute denotations. (These programs are referred to below as just the compiler and interpreter.)

What distinguishes this assignment from a true compiler writing effort is the nature of the "intermediate code" and the emphasis of the project. The intermediate code should consist of computer representations of the denotations used in the denotational semantics of Graal, as given in this chapter – in particular functions such as states; the emphasis is on producing a compiler which will mimick as closely as possible the denotational specification of this chapter.

Striving to make the program resemble the specification as much as possible means that you will have to implement the high-level operations of the metalanguage: composition (";"), quotient ("/"), restriction ("\\"), "**over** ... **apply** ...", **dom**, overriding union etc.

Several choices of programming language are possible for the implementation. Lisp is an obvious candidate as you will be able to represent the compiler, the interpreter and the denotations themselves in the same formalism. On the other hand, this may also result in some confusion and you may prefer to use a language such as Pascal or Eiffel in which data structures are completely distinct from programs. Whatever language you choose should support recursion and complex data structures. (*Hint*: do not use Fortran.)

The output of the compiler, which is also the input of the interpreter, consists of denotations, representing functions. You will need to find a suitable symbolic representation for these denotations. As with exercise 4.5, make sure that your representation supports higher order functions (whose arguments and/or results are functions). If you are using Lisp, do *not* treat these objects as Lisp functions, but introduce your own implementation. The interpreter will need a representation for states; remember that states are *finite* functions, for which a special representation may be found (**Hint**: look at the Lisp notion of "association list" for ideas).

Evaluation of your work should be possible even though the compiler will produce just data structures and the interpreter produces no actual result (as Graal has neither input nor output). Thus you should equip both the compiler and the interpreter with a well-designed **tracing facility** that will allow monitoring their execution. At each traced step, the tracing facility should report what the tool (compiler or interpreter) is doing and give a readable description of the data structures involved.

A final issue is the input to the compiler. Normally, the compiler should start from data structures representing abstract syntactic constructs. It is recommended that you provide a more friendly user interface by designing a simple concrete syntax for Graal and writing a parser that will produce the abstract syntactic form from it. This may be done through a standard parser generator such as the Unix yacc, or just as well by designing a special-purpose parser. However this is not a parsing project; a compiler that works on abstract constructs only will be preferable to a perfect parser accompanied by an incomplete or inadequate compiler/interpreter.

The result of the project should include the listing of the compiler and interpreter, commented trace listings of the execution of both tools, and a report on the solutions chosen.

Make sure you avoid the pitfall of writing a Graal *interpreter*. The aim is not to execute Graal programs directly (this would be a less than exciting assignment), but to compile them into data structures representing high-level mathematical denotations, and then to interpret these denotations.

7

Denotational semantics: language features

This chapter extends the denotational definition of the example language Graal, as given in the previous chapter, to account for various features of actual programming languages.

The features under study are:

- Records.
- Arrays.
- Pointers and dynamic data structures.
- Input and output (limited to sequential files as in Pascal).
- Block structure with associated scope rules.
- Routines, including recursive ones.
- Classes of object-oriented languages, with inheritance (for which the problems will only be sketched).

Other interesting extensions are considered in the exercises.

Every section describing such an extension (except for those which only outline a solution) has the same general structure: first an intuitive, informal description of the extension; then the corresponding modifications to the abstract syntax; then changes to the static semantics; then new semantic domains and/or auxiliary functions, if necessary; finally, required changes to the M meaning functions.

You will have another opportunity to look at records, arrays and routines, from an axiomatic perspective, in chapter 9.

7.1 CONVENTIONS

7.1.1 Independence of the extensions

This chapter introduces extensions independently, not cumulatively. For example the discussion of pointers assumes that there is no input or output, and conversely.

The reason is that each extension complicates some aspects of the specification; for example, it is usually necessary to add new components to the *State* semantic domain. Accumulating these additions would make the descriptions too complex. Instead, each new feature will be described as a single extension to the specification of Graal from the previous chapter.[1]

As an exception to this general convention, it will be convenient to base the specification of routines (7.7) on the mechanisms developed for block structure (7.6)

To highlight additions to the base specifications of the previous chapters, new components in aggregates or choice productions will be underlined.

7.1.2 Notations

Some notations will aid in describing this multiple extension process.

First, descriptions of objects having a fixed number of components will systematically rely on aggregates (3.2.2, 3.4.1) rather than cartesian products. In other words, instead of introducing a composite syntactic or semantic domain as

$$X \triangleq V_1 \times V_2 \times \ldots \times V_n$$

the definitions will use named components:

$$X \triangleq t_1 : V_1 ; t_2 : V_2 ; \ldots ; t_n : V_n$$

where the t_i are members of a tag set T.

With this convention we can easily refer to an individual component of a member e of X by using the component's tag, as in $e \cdot t_i$. This is particularly useful to describe states which, as we add features to our languages, will get more components.

Section 3.9.1 established the mathematical respectability of these notations and showed how to interpret cartesian product as a special case of aggregation, with natural integers as tags.

Semantic descriptions may similarly benefit from the notations and operators for disjoint union (3.2.3, 3.4.2, 3.9.2) and lists (3.2.4, 3.4.3, 3.9.3), initially introduced for syntactic domains.

---

[1] To remove this restriction, Metanot would need a mechanism similar to the classes of object-oriented programming, based on abstract data types rather than just sets, and the power of multiple inheritance to combine various extensions.

In describing the effect of various constructs we will sometimes need to define an aggregate element e' which differs from a given one, e, by the value of one or more fields. The **except** notation will be used for this purpose. If e is a member of X as defined above, the expression

e **except** $t_i : b$

denotes another member of X, identical to e except that its i-th component is b (which must be a member of V_i). This notation in an abbreviation for

$X \, (t_1 : e . t_1 ; \, t_2 : e . t_2 ; \, ... ; \, t_i : b \; ; \, ... ; \, t_n : e . t_n)$

or more simply

$e \, \cup \, \{ <t_i, \, b> \}$

if we remember (3.9.1) that an aggregate is simply a finite function, a member of $T \xrightarrow[f]{} V$ (V being the union of the V_i).

   The notation also applies to more than one field, as in

e **except** $(t_i : b; \, t_j : c; \, ...)$

provided the tags given are all different.

7.2 RECORDS

The first extension addresses the notion of record type, also called structure type. This is in fact the programming counterpart of the mathematical concept of aggregate, discussed above.

7.2.1 The feature and its purpose

Record types describe composite data structures. An instance of a record type consists of one or more fields, each of which is a value of a given type. For example, a record type describing books may be declared in Pascal as:

```
type BOOK =
        record
                author, title, isbn_code: STRING;
                publication_year: integer
        end
```

Similar declarations are permitted in such languages as ALGOL W, C, PL/I and Ada.

Object-oriented languages such as Simula, Smalltalk and Eiffel have generalized records by introducing **classes**, whose components may be not just data fields but also routines. Classes will be studied below (7.8).

If b is a variable of type $BOOK$, the value of b at execution time will be a quadruple with four fields, each with the type given. The fields of this object are denoted in Pascal, C or Ada through dot notation: $b.author$ etc. Syntactically, this notation is equivalent to a variable: you may not only access the value of $b.author$ but assign to it, as in

> $b.author := "Victor\ Hugo"$

A language implementing information hiding (usually as part of support for object-oriented programming) would not permit this direct assignment; in Eiffel, for example, you must call a procedure which sets the field to the appropriate value, as in

> $b.set\_author\ ("Victor\ Hugo")$

This discussion will, however, use the Pascal model.

Records are similar, at the programming language level, to the aggregates of Metanot. The model developed for aggregates in 3.9.1, treating them as finite functions from tags to values, will provide the inspiration for the denotational specification of records: record types will be viewed as functions of tags to types, and the values of record variables as functions of tags to values.

7.2.2 Changes to the abstract syntax

The required changes affect not only the notion of type but also variables, to account for qualified variables of the form $x.t$.

Declaration_list	$\triangleq$	*td: Type_declaration_list*; *vd: Variable_declaration_list*
Variable_declaration_list	$\triangleq$	*Variable_declaration**
Variable_declaration	$\triangleq$	*v: Variable*; *t: Type*
Type_declaration_list	$\triangleq$	*Type_declaration**
Type	$\triangleq$	*Boolean_type* | *Integer_type* | *Type_name*
Type_declaration	$\triangleq$	*name: Type_name*; *components: Record_type_description*
Type_name	$\triangleq$	*id:* **S**
Record_type_description	$\triangleq$	*Component**
Component	$\triangleq$	*ctag: Tag*; *ctype: Type*
Tag	$\triangleq$	*name:* **S**
Variable	$\triangleq$	*Simple_variable* | *Qualified_variable*
Simple_variable	$\triangleq$	*id:* **S**

$$Qualified\_variable \quad \triangleq \quad root\!: Simple\_variable\,;\ qualifier\!: Tag$$

Making the *qualifier* a list of *Tag* elements rather than just one *Tag* would allow multiply qualified variables of the form $x.t_1.t_2....t_n$ (exercise 7.1).

7.2.3 Changes to the static semantics

The constraints on declaration lists now reads

$$V_{Declaration\_list}\ [dl] \triangleq V_{Variable\_declaration\_list}\ [dl.vd] \ \wedge\ V_{Type\_declaration\_list}\ [dl.td]$$

where $V_{Variable\_declaration\_list}$ is the old $V_{Declaration\_list}$, stating that no variable is declared more than once, and $V_{Type\_declaration\_list}$, left to the reader, says the same for types. (A constraint prohibiting recursive type definitions will be added below.)

The notion of *Type_value* must now support record types in addition to *bt*, *it* and *ut* (boolean, integer and undefined types). Here is a way to include them:

$$type\_value \triangleq Simple\_type\_value \ |\ Type\_name$$
$$Simple\_type\_value \triangleq \{br, it, ut\} \qquad \text{-- This is what } Type\_value \text{ was before}$$

Function *typeval*, which associates a type value with every type, becomes:

$$typeval\ (t\!: Type)\ \triangleq$$
      case *t* **of**
                Boolean_type $\Rightarrow$ *Type_value* (*bt*) |
                Integer_type $\Rightarrow$ *Type_value* (*it*) |
                Type_name $\Rightarrow$ *Type_value* (*t*)
                              -- The type name, *t* itself in this case
      end

Taking the "type value" of a record type to be its name is an important decision: it means that the specification will treat two separately declared types as different even if they have the same structure. This policy is known as **name equivalence**; the reverse one is **structural equivalence**. Exercise 7.2 explores the differences.

Function *typing* remains applicable but it only captures the meaning of a variable declaration list. It may be replaced by

$$variable\_typing\ (vdl\!: Variable\_declaration\_list)\ \triangleq$$

      ... As *typing* before ...

It is also necessary to record the meaning of a list of type declarations. Using the same techniques as in the specification of aggregates, we may take as denotation of a record type the function from its tags to the associated type values. For example, the denotation of a type defined by

> **record**
>   *full_time*: *BOOLEAN*; *age, salary*: *INTEGER*; *birth*: *DATE*
> **end**;

will be the finite function

[7.1]

>   {*<full_time, bt>, <age, it>, <salary, it>, <birth, DATE>*}

(The second components of the pairs are abuses of language for *Type_value* (*bt*), *Type_value* (*DATE*) etc.)

Such denotations are members of the static semantic domain

$$Record\_type\_denotation \triangleq Tag \xrightarrow{f} Type\_value$$

and we may attach record types to them, as in the above examples, through the following function:

> *record_mapping: Record_type_description* $\longrightarrow$ *Record_type_denotation*

> *record_mapping* (*r: Record_type_description*) $\triangleq$

> **over** *r* **apply**

> λ *c*: *Component* • {*<c.ctag, typeval (c.ctype)>*}

> **combine** "$\cup$" **empty** $\emptyset$ **end**

The denotation of a list of record type declarations will be a function from a set of type names to the corresponding record type denotations; such functions are members of the domain

$$Record\_type\_environment \triangleq Type\_name \xrightarrow{f} Record\_type\_denotation$$

For example, the denotation of the single declaration

> **type** *EMPLOYEE* =
>   **record**
>   *full_time: BOOLEAN; age, salary: INTEGER*;
>   *birth: DATE*
>   **end**;

will be the one-element "record type environment"

>   {*<EMPLOYEE, {<full_time, bt>, <age, it>, <salary, it>, <birth, DATE>}>*}

Such a *Record_type_environment* is a second degree function, of signature

> $Type\_name \xrightarrow{f} (Tag \xrightarrow{f} Type\_value)$

A record type environment will result from processing a list of record type declarations, just as a type map results from processing a list of variable declarations. The function

$$type\_binding: Type\_declaration\_list \rightarrow Record\_type\_environment$$

serves this purpose in the same way as *typing* for variables. It is defined as follows:

$type\_binding$ (*tdl*: *Type_declaration_list*) $\triangleq$

> **given**
>> $bind\_a\_type \triangleq \lambda\ td: Type\_declaration \bullet$
>>> $\{<td.name,\ record\_mapping\ (td.components)>\}$
>
> **then**
>> **over** *tdl* **apply** *bind_a_type* **combine** "⊌" **empty** ∅ **end**
>
> **end**

The context condition $V_{Expression}$, which previously had two arguments, an expression e and a type map tm, must now include a third: a record type environment rte. The only change is the branch for *Variable*, which previously read $e \in$ **dom** tm and must be replaced by

$$V_{Variable}\ [e,\ tm,\ rte]$$

where $V_{Variable}$ takes care not only of simple variables but also of qualified variables of the form *vroot.vqualifier*:

$V_{Variable}$ [v: *Variable*, tm: *Type_map*, rte: *Record_type_environment*] $\triangleq$
> **case** v **of**
>> $Simple\_variable \implies v \in$ **dom** tm | -- Same as before
>>
>> $Qualified\_variable \implies$
>>> **if** $v.root \notin$ **dom** tm **then** *false*   -- Root is not declared
>>> **else**
>>>> **given**
>>>>> $root\_type \triangleq tm\ (v.root)$
>>>> **then**
>>>>> **if** $root\_type \notin$ **dom** rte **then**
>>>>>> *false*   -- Root type is not record
>>>>> **else**
>>>>>> $v.qualifier \in$ **dom** $rte\ (root\_type)$
>>>>>>> -- The qualifier must be a proper tag
>>>>>>> -- for the root's type
>>>>> **end**
>>>> **end**
>>> **end**
> **end**

The second case expresses that *vroot.vqualifier* is only valid if *vroot* has been declared and its type is a record type whose type denotation in the type environment *rte*, given by *rte* (*vroot*), is a function from tags to types, $\{<tag_1, type_1>, \ldots <tag_n, type_n>\}$ such that one of the tags is *v.qualifier*.

Function *exp_type* requires a similar change: in addition to the arguments *e*: *Expression* and *tm*: *Type_map*, it should now have an argument *rte*: *Record_type_environment*, and its *Variable* branch, previously

> if *e* ∉ **dom** *tm* **then** *ut* **else** *tm* (*e*) **end**

should now read *variable_type* (*e*, *tm*, *rte*), with

> *variable_type* [*v*: *Variable*, *tm*: *Type_map*, *rte*: *Record_type_environment*] $\triangleq$
> > **if** *v* ∉ **dom** *tm* **then** *ut*
> > **else**
> > > **case** *v* **of**
> > > > *Simple_variable* ⟹   -- As before:
> > > > > **if** *v* ∉ **dom** *tm* **then** *ut* **else** *tm* (*v*) **end** |
> > > > *Qualified_variable* ⟹
> > > > > **if** *v*.*root* ∉ **dom** *tm* **then** *ut*
> > > > > **else**
> > > > > > **given**
> > > > > > > *root_type* $\triangleq$ *tm* (*e*.*root*);
> > > > > > > *tag* $\triangleq$ *v*.*qualifier*
> > > > > > **then**
> > > > > > > **if** *root_type* ∉ **dom** *rte* **then** *ut* **else**
> > > > > > > > **if** *tag* ∉ **dom** *rte* (*root_type*) **then** *ut*
> > > > > > > > **else** *rte* (*root_type*) (*tag*) **end**
> > > > > > **end**   **end**   **end**
> > > > **end**
> > **end**   **end**

In the above example, this function will yield $type_i$ if *v*.*qualifier* is tag_i.

The context condition $V_{Instruction}$ must be adapted accordingly. It too needs the extra argument *rte*, and its branch for *Assignment* must be rewritten as follows:

> $V_{Variable}$ [*i*.*target*, *tm*, *rte*] ∧   -- Replaces *i*.*target* ∈ **dom** *tm*
> -- from previous version
>
> $V_{Expression}$ [*i*.*source*, *tm*, *rte*] ∧   -- Unchanged except for extra argument
>
> *variable_type* (*i*.*target*, *tm*, *rte*) = *exp_type* (*i*.*source*, *tm*, *rte*)
> -- Left-hand side replaces *tm* (*i*.*target*)

7.2.4 Changes to the dynamic semantics

The essential change to the dynamic semantics is the necessity to take into account composite values; for example, an "employee" has a composite value with four components.

We might be tempted to describe such values simply as tuples, that is to say members of cartesian products. Tuples, however, do not include the tags: viewed as tuples, both a book (with author, title, ISBN code and publication year) and a car (with make, owner, license plate and price) will be objects with three string fields and one integer field. This loses some of the intuitive semantics of records.

As announced at the beginning of this discussion, the mathematical interpretation of aggregates as finite functions (3.9.1) provides guidance here. In static semantics, the denotation of a record type was a function from tags to type values; similarly, the denotation of an instance of a record type will be a finite function from tags to values. For example, the denotation of a certain book object may be the function

$$\{<author, "MARCEL\ PROUST">,$$
$$<title, "A\ LA\ RECHERCHE\ DU\ TEMPS\ PERDU">,$$
$$<isbn\_code, "XXX">,\quad <publication\_year, 1919>\}$$

This model has the further advantage that it readily adapts to the case of records having components that are themselves of record types; in this case one or more function values will themselves be finite functions. For example, *EMPLOYEE* above had a component of type *DATE*; assuming a proper declaration for this latter type, the denotation of an instance of *EMPLOYEE* may be:

$$\{<full\_time, false>, <age, 32>, <salary, 50000>,$$
$$<birth, \{<day, 8>, <month, 8>, <year, 1964>\}>\}$$

This interpretation enables us to redefine the semantic domain *Value*, which becomes

$$Value \triangleq Simple\_value \mid \underline{Record\_value}$$

with

$$Simple\_value \triangleq \mathbf{N} \cup \mathbf{B}$$
$$Record\_value \triangleq (Tag \xrightarrow{f} Value)$$

The only other parts of the specification that need updating are those which involve the notion of variable: $M_{Expression}$ and $M_{Assignment}$, which now includes qualified variables of the form $x.t$. The changes to the abstract syntax (repeated here for ease of reference) are

$$Variable \quad \triangleq \quad Simple\_variable \mid \underline{Qualified\_variable}$$
$$Simple\_variable \quad \triangleq \quad id: \mathbf{S}$$
$$Qualified\_variable \quad \triangleq \quad root: Simple\_variable; \ qualifier: Tag$$

The definition of $M_{Assignment}$ $[a]$ (σ), which previously read

$$(\sigma \lor \{<a.target, M_{Expression} [a.source] (\sigma)>\})$$

should now account for the case in which $a.target$ is a qualified variable. It becomes:

[7.2]

> **given**   -- The value to be assigned
>> $left \triangleq a.target;$
>> $right \triangleq M_{Expression} [a.source] (\sigma)$
>
> **then**
>> **case** *left* **of**
>>
>>> $Simple\_variable \Rightarrow (\sigma \lor \{<left, right>\}) \mid$ -- This case as before
>>>
>>> $Qualified\_variable \Rightarrow$
>>>> **given**
>>>>> $initial\_mapping \triangleq$
>>>>>> **if** $left.root \notin$ **dom** σ **then** $\varnothing$ **else** σ $(left.root)$ **end**
>>>> **then**
>>>>> $(\sigma \lor \{<left.root,$
>>>>>
>>>>> $initial\_mapping \lor \{<left.qualifier, right>\}>\})$

end   **end**
                    end

For example, in the assignment $x.full\_time := true$, the *initial_mapping* represents the value of x, of type *EMPLOYEE*, in the initial state. If x or any of its component has previously been assigned a value, this will be a function whose domain is a subset of the set of tags $\{full\_time, age, salary, birth\}$; otherwise, *initial_mapping* is taken to be the empty function. The result of the assignment is to associate the value *true* to tag *full_time* in this function. So if the initial state was

$$\{<y, 3>, <z, true>, <x, \{<full\_time: false>, <age: 32>\}>\}$$

with only two variables other than x, both simple, then the state resulting from the assignment will be

$$\{<y, 3>, <z, true>, <x, \{<full\_time: true>, <age: 32>\}>\}$$

The branch for *Variable* in $M_{expression}$ $[e]$ must be similarly updated. It previously read

$$\textbf{if } e \notin \textbf{dom } \sigma \textbf{ then } unknown \textbf{ else } \sigma \ (e) \textbf{ end}$$

and should now be:

[7.3]

     case *e* **of**

          Simple_variable $\Rightarrow$ ... *As before* ... |

          Qualified_variable $\Rightarrow$

               if *e.root* $\notin$ **dom** σ **then** *unknown* **else**

                   given

                         record_val $\triangleq$ σ (*e.root*)

                   then   --∗

                       if *val.qualifier* $\notin$ **dom** *record_val* **then** *unknown*

                       else *record_val* (*e.qualifier*) **end**

                 end

             end

     end

This definition is correct only if we can be sure that the value of any record variable, *record_val*, is a *Record_value* (a function from tags to values) rather than a simple value; otherwise the notation *record_val* (*e.qualifier*) would be incorrect. This may be expressed as *Invariant* (*p*) (σ), where *Invariant* is the following boolean-valued function on states:

    Invariant : *Program* $\rightarrow$ *State* $\rightarrow$ **B**

    Invariant (*p*) (σ) $\triangleq$

        given

              typemap $\triangleq$ *typing* (*p.variables*);

              Declared_record_variables $\triangleq$

                     {*v* : **dom** *typemap* | *typemap* (*v*) **is** *Type_name* **and** *v* $\in$ **dom** σ}

        then

             $\forall$ *v* : *Declared_record_variables* •

                 σ (*v*) = *Value* (*unknown*) $\lor$ σ (*v*) **is** *Record_value*

        end

The constraint defined by this function is an example of **state invariant**; it must be guaranteed by all the operations of the semantic specification that may create a state, and maintained by all those that may transform a state.

Here it is indeed the case that the initial state of execution satisfies *Invariant* (*p*) by default, and that the new branch of $M_{Assignment}$ introduced above ([7.2]) for field assignments of the form *x.field* := *value.* preserves it. In fact, the reason for taking the empty function $\varnothing$ as the value of a record variable which has not yet been assigned a value (first case for *initial_value* in [7.2]) is precisely to maintain *Invariant*. As you can easily check, the denotation of the other relevant instruction, the assignment *x* := *y* where both *x* and *y* are record variables, also preserves the invariant.

Because of this invariant, the new definition of the *Variable* case for $M_{Expression}$ ([7.3]) treats *record_val*, that is to say σ (*e . root*), as a member of *Record_value*. This form has been used for simplicity but is not quite correct typewise. The correct (although somewhat heavy) formulation for the property on *record_val* (marked --* above) is

> **case** *record_val* **of**
>> *Simple_value* ⟹ *unknown* | -- Although this case is impossible
>>
>> *Record_value* ⟹   -- As before:
>>> **if** *val . qualifier* ∉ **dom** *record_val* **then** *unknown*
>>> **else** *record_val* (*e . qualifier*) **end**
>
> **end**

7.2.5 Avoiding recursive definitions

There remains a problem with the above definition of records. The abstract syntax as given is

> *Type_declaration* ≙ *name*: *Type_name*; *components*: *Record_type_description*
>
> *Record_type_description* ≙ *Component**
>
> *Component* ≙ *ctag*: *Tag*; *ctype*: *Type*
>
> *Type* ≙ *Boolean_type* | *Integer_type* | *Type_name*

This allows mutually recursive definitions of the form

> **type** *A* = **record** *bb*: *B*; *n*: **integer**; ... other components ... **end**;
>
> **type** *B* = **record** *aa*: *A*; *n*: **integer**; ... other components ... **end**;

or even directly recursive ones (a record type *A* with one or more components of type *A*). In fact, such definitions do not lead to any inconsistency: the above semantics gives them an interpretation, and they can be used in programs. The trick is that the evaluation of any uninitialized item will not have any bad consequences; it simply yields *unknown*.

For example, the following program fragment has the intuitively appropriate effect under the above semantics:

> *a1, a2*: *A*; *b1, b2, b3*: *B*; *i*: **integer**;
>
> *a1.n* := 5; *b1.n* := 10; *a1.bb* := *b1*;
>
> *b3* := *a1.bb*;   -- Will assign to *b3* a copy of *b1*
>
> *x* := *b3.n*   -- Will assign to *x* the value 10
>
>> -- An attempt to use *b1.aa* or *b3.a1* here would yield *unknown*.

The above recursive declarations describe conceptually infinite structures, but this raises no particular problem as long as any computation only uses a finite part. This is close to the notion of lazy evaluation, studied in the next chapter (8.7.6).

In practice, however, programming languages do not permit recursive record type definitions since actual computers do not offer any simple implementation. An object of type A above may have a component of type B, which may have a component of type A, which... As noted, a terminating program may only create a finite structure conforming to this pattern; but the compiler must generate data structures representing objects of type A in such a way that the execution can insert new bb components into such objects by repeatedly "writing smaller" as the components get expanded. There is no easy way to achieve this in the memory of a computer.

In practice, this means that programming languages only allow recursive record type definitions when the recursive components involve records indirectly, through references (pointers). Pascal, for example, does not permit recursive record type definitions unless at least one declaration in the recursion cycle "protects" the corresponding record type through pointers. The above declarations of A and B are then incorrect; you may, however, write the following:

type
$A = $ **record** bb: $\uparrow B$; ... **end**;
$B = $ **record** aa: $\uparrow A$; ... **end**;

where $\uparrow T$ means "pointer to T". This way the values of components such as aa are pointers to records rather than the records themselves. Since a pointer holds a fixed amount of memory space, the compiler can generate the proper data structure layout. (7.6 below sketches the denotational semantics of pointers.)

The precise Pascal rule is that any forward reference in a record type declaration must be protected by a $\uparrow$. A forward reference is any mention of a record type not declared previously (including the type in whose declaration the mention appears). So the above is still correct if you drop the $\uparrow$ for aa in B, but the one for bb in A is required.

An extreme solution is taken in languages such as Algol W or Simula or where all variables or record components declared of record types are understood as pointers. This way, arbitrary recursion is possible.

An intermediate solution is to allow components and variables with actual record values, but to prohibit recursion. This is the approach used in Pascal. In Eiffel, record components are either of "expanded" types, in which case no recursion is permitted, or of class types, in which case the corresponding fields are references and there is no constraint on recursion.

A simple way to implement the Pascal rule in Graal extended with records is to add a clause to the constraint $V_{Type\_declaration\_list}$ (page 187). The constraint prohibits forward references and so it avoids recursion: if the type R declared for a component of a record type S is itself a record type, then R must have been declared before S.

To express this, we may define functions *Needed* and *Previous* as follows. Each applies to a type declaration list and yields a list of sets of types. If the *i*-th element of a type declaration list *tdl* is the type declaration *td*, then:

- The *i*-th element of *Needed* (*tdl*) is the set of type names mentioned in the declaration of *td*.

- The *i*-th element of *Previous* (*tdl*) is the set of type names declared in *tdl*, up to and including *td*.

Then the constraint is simply that every element of *Needed* (*tdl*) be a subset of the corresponding element of *Previous* (*tdl*). The following predicate expresses this requirement:

> *No_forward_references* (*tdl*: *Type_declaration_list*) $\triangleq$
>
> $\forall i : 1 .. \; tdl . LENGTH \bullet Needed \; (i) \subseteq Previous \; (i)$

with

> *Previous, Needed: Type_declaration_list* $\rightarrow$ (**P** (*Type_name*))*

Previous $\triangleq$
    given
        type_name $\triangleq$ λ *td* : *Type_declaration* $\bullet$ *td . name*
    then
        λ *tdl* : *Type_declaration_list* $\bullet$
            over *tdl* **apply**
                λ *td* : *Type_declaration* $\bullet$
                      {<#, **ran** ((*tdl* ; *type_name*) \ 1 .. #)>}
            combine "$\cup$" **empty** $\varnothing$ **end**
    end

Needed $\triangleq$
    given
        Component_type_names $\triangleq$
            λ *td* : *Type_declaration* $\bullet$
                $\displaystyle \bigcup_{j : 1 .. \; \{td . components . LENGTH} \quad td . components \, (j) . ctype \}$
    then
        λ *tdl* : *Type_declaration_list* $\bullet$ (*tdl* ; *Component_type_names*)
    end

Recall from 3.9.3 that the symbol # occurring in the **over**... **apply**... expression for *Previous* denotes the index of the current list element. *Needed* uses the composition of a list and a function on list elements (see the definition of *TAIL* in 3.9.3).

7.3 ARRAYS

Arrays are in many ways similar to records; the extension is in fact simpler because all elements of an array have the same type.

As with records, the notion of variable must be extended, here to include array elements, such as t [i] in the Pascal notation. In a manner similar to the above "qualified variables", we may view these as "indexed variables".

For dynamic semantics, we may model the run-time value of an array as a list (3.9.3), extending the domain *Value* accordingly.

Arrays have bounds, and the specification should describe a mechanism for checking that an element is within the bounds.

Mathematically, it is not much more difficult to model dynamic array allocation (with a special instruction, say **allocate** a **bounds** m, n) than static allocation (where the bounds must be constant and are given in the array declaration).

The details of these extensions are left to the reader as an exercise (7.3).

7.4 POINTERS

Another important mechanism for building composite types and data structures is pointers, also known as references.

7.4.1 The feature and its purpose

In some languages such as C or PL/I, pointers simply give programmers access to the physical memory addresses of the program's entities (exercise 7.5). In others such as Pascal, Ada, Simula or Eiffel, pointers (references) are used in connection with **dynamically allocated objects**. This is the more interesting application, and the one examined here.

More precisely, assume pointer types may be defined from base types; using the Pascal concrete syntax, if T is a type, $\uparrow T$ is the type whose specimens are pointers to objects of type T. T may be a pointer type itself; also, it is essential here to permit mutual recursion, so that T may be $\uparrow S$ where S is $\uparrow T$.

In practice, the interesting pointer types $\uparrow T$ are those for which T is a record type, so that a pointer will point to an object which has some fields of non-pointer types, as on the figure below.

To introduce the formal specification techniques, however, it suffices to consider a simple model where the only base types (the possible T) are Graal's types, integer and boolean. We may allow an infinite number of possible pointer types, of the form $\uparrow\uparrow \ldots \uparrow T$, where T is integer or boolean.

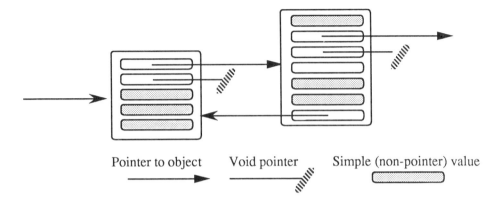

Figure 7.1: Pointers and records

At run-time, a pointer may be **attached** to an object; if attached to no object, the pointer is **void**. There are four fundamental operations on a pointer variable p:

- Creation: create a new object and attach it to p.
- Re-attachment: attach p to an existing object – de-attaching it from the object to which it was previously attached, if any.
- Forget: make p void.
- Dereferencing: access the value of the object attached to p.

In Pascal, creation uses the **new** predefined procedure; re-attachment is obtained through assignment to the pointer variable p; "forget" is assignment of the special "null" pointer value; and the expression denoting the object to which p is attached is written $p\uparrow$.

You may treat a dereferenced variable $p\uparrow$ as a standard variable; in particular, it may be the target of an assignment, denoting a change to the object to which p is attached. In contrast, the effect of an assignment to p itself is to attach p to another object.

An important property of pointers in this model is that they may only be attached to objects in the heap. Call "basic store" the memory area which hosts the values of variables; the basic store is usually either a fixed area of storage or (in the presence of block structure or routines, discussed later in this chapter) a stack. Pointers may occur as the values of either variables or heap objects. The possible relations are summarized on figure 7.2: there may be pointers from the basic store to the heap, or from the heap to the heap, but not from the heap or the basic store to the basic store. C and PL/I do not enforce these restrictions, opening up all sorts of risks at run-time, since pointers may be kept to deallocated areas of the basic store.

In their more disciplined version, pointers are both useful and dangerous. They are useful for describing linked data structures such as linked lists, trees (in many of their implementations), circular chains and the like. The danger comes from the phenomenon of **dynamic aliasing** introduced by pointers: if p and q point to the same object, a assignment to $p\uparrow$ changes $q\uparrow$ even though it does not officially name q.

In practice, dynamic data structures also raise the problem of space reclamation: after re-attachment operations, some objects may become inaccessible, wasting memory space; programmer-controlled deallocation is tedious and error-prone, requiring implementors to provide efficient automatic mechanisms for "garbage collection".

Because of their low level of abstraction and the dangers of misuse, pointers have been compared to the infamous "goto" instruction. For the goto, however, higher-level replacements exist, with the consequence that no reasonable programming language should include a goto construct (and that such a construct is not addressed in this book). No such generally agreed upon replacements exist for pointers. Whether or not we like pointers, any program that deals with non-trivial data structures will need them.

Stack   *Heap*

Figure 7.2: What a pointer may point to

7.4.2 Outline of the modification

The abstract grammar must extend the notion of type to include pointer types with an arbitrary number of ↑ signs, and the notion of variable to include dereferenced variables $x\!\uparrow$. The **new** instruction must also be added to the list of choices for *Instruction*.

For static semantics, we must express not only the context condition on pointer assignments (written in Pascal $x := y$ where both variables are of pointer types) but also the constraint on assignments to dereferenced pointers: in $x\!\uparrow := e$, x must be of type $\uparrow\! t$ where e is of type t.

For dynamic semantics, we may redefine the state as

    State $\triangleq$ *static*: *Simple_state*; *dynamic*: *Heap*

where *Simple_state* is the previous notion of state and *Heap* is

    values: $(\mathbf{N} \xrightarrow[f]{} Value)$; *top*: $\mathbf{N}$

The choice of **N** for addresses assumes a linear, "von Neuman" model of the memory. More abstract models are also possible. The one used here closely follows the standard implementation technique.

The domain *Value* of values should now include pointers, represented by integers in this model.

The *M* function for expressions must be redefined to account for dereferenced pointers. In the denotation of instructions, we must not only account for the **new** instruction (allocate a new position in the heap and make the variable point to it), but also adapt the semantics of assignment instructions to deal with targets which are pointers or dereferenced values.

You are invited to carry out the details of this construction (exercise 7.4).

7.5 INPUT AND OUTPUT

Graal supported neither input nor output. This section shows how to add Pascal-like file manipulation, generalizing simple techniques introduced for Lullaby in chapter 4.

7.5.1 The feature and its purpose

Input and output do not require justification: a program without communication with the outside world is of little use.

There are two general methods for dealing with input and output in programming languages. Some designs, such as those of Fortran, Cobol, PL/I and Pascal, expressly include input and output constructs; others keep the needed mechanisms outside of the language proper. The first among these was Algol 60, whose designers felt that input and output were too machine-dependent to be made part of the definition of a universal language; as a result, the original language definition did not include any input or output construct, which led every compiler writer to design his own – not a very pleasant situation for users concerned with portability. (Later versions of Algol 60 defined a standard mechanism.) More recent designs such as C, Ada and Eiffel keep input-output mechanisms out of the language, in the Algol tradition, but do not shirk their responsibilities since they define one or more standard input-output libraries. This, of course, still leaves compiler writers with the task of finding a language that does support at least some primitive input and output operations.

The following discussion limits itself to sequential file manipulation, similar to the Pascal model.

Bringing a Pascal-like concept of files to Graal means a few extensions:

- Two new types, "file of booleans" and "file of integers".
- A *Read* instruction, which reads an element and advances the read cursor.
- A *Reset* instruction, which moves the read cursor to the beginning of the file.
- A *Write* instruction, which writes a new element after the last written position.
- A *Rewrite* instruction, which erases all written positions.

7.5.2 Changes to the abstract syntax

Type ≜ *Simple_type* | *File_type*

Simple_type ≜ *Boolean_type* | *Integer_type*

File_type ≜ *basetype*: *Simple_type* -- The type of the elements in a file

Instruction ≜ ... As before ... | *Reset* | *Rewrite* | *Read* | *Write*

Reset ≜ *file*: *Variable*

Rewrite ≜ *file*: *Variable*

Read ≜ *target*: *Variable*; *file*: *Variable*

Write ≜ *source*: *Expression*; *file*: *Variable*

7.5.3 Changes to the static semantics

First the notion of *Type_value* (6.2.2) must now include the two file types:

Type_value ≜ {*bt, it, ut, bft, ift*}

Function *typeval* must be redefined accordingly:

    type_value (*t*) ≜

        case *t* **of**

            Simple_type ⟹ -- as before:

                case *t* **of**

                    Boolean_type ⟹ *bt* | *Integer_type* ⟹ *it*

                end |

            File_type ⟹

                case *t*.*basetype* **of**

                    Boolean_type ⟹ *bft* | *Integer_type* ⟹ *ift*

                end

        end

There is no need to change the *V* function for expressions. Instructions (6.2.4) need the following new cases:

... |

Reset, Rewrite $\Rightarrow$ *tm* (*i.file*) = *bft* $\vee$ *tm* (*i.file*) = *ift*

Read $\Rightarrow$

$\quad\quad$ *i.target* $\in$ **dom** *tm* $\wedge$

$\quad\quad\quad\quad$ ((*tm* (*i.target*) = *bt* $\wedge$ *tm* (*i.file*) = *bft*) $\vee$

$\quad\quad\quad\quad$ (*tm* (*i.target*) = *it* $\wedge$ *tm* (*i.file*) = *ift*))

$\quad\quad$ *Write* $\Rightarrow$

$\quad\quad\quad\quad$ $V_{Expression}$ [*i.source* , *tm*] $\wedge$

$\quad\quad\quad\quad\quad\quad$ ((*exp_type* (*i.source*, *tm*) = *bt* $\wedge$ *tm* (*i.file*) = *bft*) $\vee$

$\quad\quad\quad\quad\quad\quad$ (*exp_type* (*i.source*, *tm*) = *it* $\wedge$ *tm* (*i.file*) = *ift*))

7.5.4 New semantic domains

For dynamic semantics, the notion of *State* does not change but the domain *Value* of values (6.3.1) must be extended with file values:

$\quad\quad$ *Value* $\triangleq$ *Simple_value* $\cup$ *File_value*

with

$\quad\quad$ *Simple_value* $\triangleq$ **N** $\cup$ **B** $\cup$ {*unknown*}

$\quad\quad$ *File_value* $\triangleq$ *contents*: *File_contents*; *cursor*: **N**

$\quad\quad$ *File_contents* $\triangleq$ *Simple_value**

$\quad\quad$ A "file value" is a pair whose first element is a possibly empty list of simple values; the second element is an integer which indicates the position of the read "head" in the file. Writing is always done at the end.

7.5.5 New semantic functions

It is convenient to introduce the following functions to represent file manipulations:

$\quad\quad$ *past_eof*: *File_value* $\rightarrow$ **B**

$\quad\quad$ *past_eof* (*f*) $\triangleq$ *f.cursor* > *f.contents.LENGTH*

$\quad\quad$ *current*: *File_value* $\rightarrowtail$ *Simple_value*

$\quad\quad$ **dom** *current* = {*f* $\in$ *File_value* | **not** *past_eof* (*f*)}

$\quad\quad$ *current* (*f*) $\triangleq$ *f.contents* (*f.cursor*)

$advance: File\_value \xrightarrow{f} File\_value$

$\textbf{dom } advance = \{f \in File\_value \mid \textbf{not } past\_eof (f)\}$

$advance (f) \triangleq f \textbf{ except } cursor: f.cursor + 1$

$append: File\_value \times Simple\_value \rightarrow File\_value$

$append (f, v) \triangleq f \textbf{ except } contents: f.contents +\!\!+ <v>$

Function *current* returns the value of the element at cursor position, if any; *advance* moves the cursor one position ahead; *append* writes a value at the end of the file, without affecting the cursor position.

7.5.6 Changes to the meaning functions

The *M* function for instructions (6.5.1) needs new cases for *Reset*, *Rewrite*, *Read* and *Write*. Here are the corresponding functions.

$M_{Reset} [r : Reset] \triangleq$
        -- Do not change file contents; reset cursor to start of file.

    $\lambda \sigma \bullet \ \sigma \ \underset{\cdot}{\curlyvee} \ \{<r.file, \sigma (r.file) \textbf{ except } cursor: 1>\}$

$M_{Rewrite} [r : Rewrite] \triangleq$
        -- Empty file; reset cursor to position after start of file.

    $\lambda \sigma \bullet \ \ \sigma \ \underset{\cdot}{\curlyvee} \ \{<r.file, File\_value (contents: <>; cursor: 1)>\}$

$M_{Read} [r : Read] \triangleq$
        -- Assign value of current file element to variable; advance cursor.

    $\textbf{if } past\_eof (r.file) \textbf{ then } Id$
        -- Attempt to read past end of file. No effect.
    $\textbf{else}$

        $\lambda \sigma \bullet \sigma \ \underset{\cdot}{\curlyvee}$

                $\{<r.target, current (\sigma (r.file))>,$
                   $<r.file, advance (\sigma (r.file))>\}$

    $\textbf{end}$

$M_{Write} [w : Write] \triangleq$
        -- Append value of expression to the file; do not move cursor.

    $\lambda \sigma \bullet (\sigma \ \underset{\cdot}{\curlyvee} \ \{<w.file, append (\sigma (w.file), M [i.source] (\sigma))>\})$

7.6 BLOCK STRUCTURE

Block structure, introduced by Algol 60, found its way into many of its successors such as Algol W and Algol 68. Restricted forms are present in Pascal, Ada and Eiffel.

The term actually covers several related facilities for structuring programs hierarchically, and our first task will be to clarify the variants.

7.6.1 The feature and its purpose

We may distinguish three successive levels of block structure:

1   • Syntactic grouping of instructions.

2   • Static scope for local variables.

3   • Unit of dynamic storage allocation.

The first level, syntactic grouping, simply supports compound instructions, as present in Graal. They serve to make sure that a list of instructions may be used in any context where the language syntax requires one instruction. The Algol 60 concrete syntax uses the keywords **begin** and **end** as parentheses and the semicolon as separator:

>   **begin**
>   *instruction*$_1$;
>   ...;
>   *instruction*$_n$
>   **end**

A compound of this form is acceptable wherever the grammar requires an instruction, for example as a branch of a conditional or body of a loop or routine. This also permits compound instructions to be nested without ambiguity; **begin** and **end** play the same role as parentheses in mathematical expressions.

Although this method is simple and uniform, the current fashion trends in designer syntax tend to favor a different convention, first introduced by Algol 68: implicit blocks. What this means is that the grammar permits a list of instructions, without parenthesis-like delimiters, wherever it accepts a single instruction. For example, in the Ada or Eiffel syntax for conditional instructions

>   **if** *expression* **then** *instructions* **else** *instructions* **end**

one or more instructions, separated by semicolons, may appear in either branch. This is consistent with the idea of a language whose concrete grammar is an **operator grammar,** containing constructs all of the form

>   *operator operand operator operand ... operator*

where operators are keywords and special symbols (such as semicolon), and operands are user-chosen identifiers.

The second level of block structure adds the notion of static scoping. Here blocks are not only compounds but also units for the declaration of variables. Blocks may contain declarations as well as instructions; in this way they resemble the "programs" of Graal, a similarity which will be put to good use in the formal specification. The scope of every variable is the block in which it is declared.

The main consequence of static scoping is to allow disjoint blocks to use the same variable names. Furthermore, an embedded block may declare a variable with a name already used in an enclosing block; a reference to a name will always denote the innermost variable declared with that name. Consider for example the following structure, where all variables are declared of the same type:

```
begin -- Block B1
        x, y: INTEGER;

        ... Body of B1 ...

        begin -- Block B2
                x, z: INTEGER;
                ...
        end    -- Block B2

        begin -- Block B3
                y, z: INTEGER;
                ...
        end    -- Block B3

        ... Body of B1 (continued) ...

end    -- Block B1
```

There are here two variables associated with each of the names x, y and z. The two variables called z appear in disjoint blocks; on the other hand, the redeclarations of both x and y appear within the scope of their original (B1) namesakes. The name x refers to the outermost (B1) variable bearing that name when it appears in the body of B1 or B3, but to the B2 variable when it appears in B2, and similarly for y.

It is impossible to refer to the outermost x in B2, or to the outermost y in B3. Blocks B2 and B3 are said to be **holes** in the scopes of the outermost x and y, respectively.

The purpose of these conventions, as introduced by Algol 60, was to enable programmers to pick names freely for separately developed program parts without risk of conflict. While nobody would deny programmers the right to choose identical names in disjoint program units (after all, even Fortran subroutines permit this), the usefulness of overriding the declarations of enclosing blocks is more questionable. Critics have pointed out risks: a program whose author has forgotten to declare a variable may still appear valid to the compiler if the variable happens to have the same name as another declared in an enclosing block. For example, a misspelling of *y* as *x* in B3 will remain undetected by the compiler since the name matches that of a variable of the enclosing B1.

Pascal distinguishes between compound instructions and static scoping units. Normal **begin** ... **end** blocks may not include declarations; the only scoping units are main programs and routines. A similar distinction is made in such languages as Ada or Eiffel. (The latter offers only two levels: classes may contain routines; routines may not be nested.) The only disadvantage is the inability to write a block of the form

> **if** *y* > *x* **then**
> >   -- Swap the values of *x* **and** *y*
> > **local**
> > >   **var** *t*: *T*   -- *T* is the type of *x* and *y*
> > **begin**
> > >   *t* := *x*; *x* := *y*; *y* := *t*
> > **end**

which is too simple to justify a routine. In such a case, you will need to declare the local variable *t* in the enclosing program unit rather than in the more restricted scope where you really need it.

Finally, the third level of block structure concepts, dynamic binding, extends the previous static scoping rules to the dynamic (run-time) life of the program: variables declared local to a block are allocated anew every time the block is executed.

Since block inclusions form a tree hierarchy, the execution may only leave a block once it has left all its internal blocks; this means that block invocations follow a simple last-in, first-out scheme, and that implementers may use a stack to allocate the local variables.

With this last interpretation of block structure, the static scope of a variable (the portion of the program in which its name is meaningful) coincides with its dynamic scope (the portion of the program during whose execution the variable is physically allocated).

This association of static and dynamic scope was introduced by Algol 60. It is an elegant idea but suffers from a practical drawback: a block will often need *persistent* variables, whose values are kept from one activation to the next; but these may not be declared local to the block, since every execution would allocate them again. This means that the declaration of a persistent variable must be at least one scoping level higher than the block which needs it.

In Pascal, for example, this often leads to declaring all persistent variables at the highest possible level (the main program). The result is a loss of clarity, since many variables are declared in a context broader than the one in which they are actually used, simply because they must be persistent.

In C and PL/I, the dynamic scope of a variable is its static scope by default, but variables declared as "static" are persistent throughout the execution; in other words, their dynamic scope is the outermost block. A similar possibility existed in Algol 60 (**own** variables), but raised consistency problems with dynamically allocated arrays. Object-oriented languages make it possible to attach persistent values with an object; the corresponding variables (called "attributes" in Eiffel) are declared at the level of the associated class (the program structure enclosing a routine).

Graal already has compound instructions. The following discussion assumes that compound instructions are extended to represent blocks with local variables (level 2) and dynamic allocation (level 3). The latter extension only affects the dynamic semantics.

7.6.2 Changes to the abstract syntax

The changes to the abstract grammar are simple. A new construct *Block* is needed:

[7.4]

$$Block \triangleq variables: Declaration\_list; body: Instruction$$

The definition of *Instruction* must now include *Block* as one of the alternatives. The structure of blocks is identical to what the structure of programs was before, hence the redefinition

$$Program \triangleq b: Block$$

7.6.3 Changes to the static semantics

We must extend the validity function for instructions (6.2.4) with a new branch for blocks:

$$Block \implies V_{Instruction} \ [i.body, tm \ \forall \ typing \ (i.variables)]$$

In other words, if a block is checked in the context of a certain type map tm, its constituent instruction must be checked against tm overridden by the local declarations of the compound. This is nicely expressed by the overriding union operator $\forall$.

This is all there is to do for static semantics. Note how simple this modification is thanks to the $\forall$ operator and the notion of type map. They express concisely the gist of scope rules in block-structured languages – declarations of the outer block remain in effect in the inner blocks unless there is a name clash, in which case the inner name takes precedence.

7.6.4 Semantic domains

The dynamic semantics of blocks at level 3 (with dynamically allocated variables) requires some new semantic domains.

The notion of state as finite function from variables to values is not sufficient any more: variables were defined as identifiers, that is to say names; but now the same variable may refer to more than one run-time object.

One technique is to introduce explicitly a notion of location, as an intermediary between variables and values, representing the set of available addresses. "Storage maps", also called **environments**, then serve to describe the mapping from variables to their assigned locations:

$Location \triangleq \mathbf{N}$

$Environment \triangleq Variable \underset{f}{\nrightarrow} Location$

$Memory \triangleq Location \underset{f}{\nrightarrow} Value$

As with heaps (page 199), the choice of a linear memory model may be considered overspecifying, but keeps the discussion simple. See exercise 7.9 for a more abstract specification.

The next step is to redefine the state:

[7.5]

$State \triangleq addresses: Environment; content: Memory$

A state σ is now a pair; the environment component, *addresses*, gives the correspondence between variables and memory locations and *content* gives the value associated with each useful memory location.

Since $\sigma.addresses$ is a finite function for any state σ, we may define the following function:

$top: State \rightarrow \mathbf{N}$

$top\ (\sigma) \triangleq max\ (\mathbf{ran}\ \sigma.addresses)$

For any σ, $top\ (\sigma)$ is the highest memory address that has been allocated in state σ.

7.6.5 State invariant

Not every pair made of an environment and a memory, as defined above, is acceptable as state: locations must be allocated sequentially. This property may be expressed as the state invariant

$\forall \sigma: State \bullet Invariant\ (\sigma)$

with the following definition:

[7.6]

   Invariant: *State* $\rightarrow$ **B**

   Invariant (σ: *Bstate*) $\triangleq$

    given

        highest $\triangleq$ *top* (σ)

    then

        ran σ.*addresses* $= 1..\ highest$ $\wedge$ **dom** σ.*content* $\subseteq 1..\ highest$

    then

The domain of σ.*content* is constrained to be a subset of $1..\ highest$; it will cover the whole interval if all allocated variables have been assigned a value.

7.6.6 Accessing and modifying variable values

The value of a variable x in a state σ is not simply given by σ (x) any more, but by the function:

    variable_value (x) (σ) $\triangleq$

        given

            address $\triangleq$ σ.*addresses* (x)

        then

            if *address* $\notin$ **dom** σ.*content* **then** *unknown*

            else σ.*content* (*address*) **end**

        end

The invariant ensures that *address* is in the interval $1..\ highest$, but not that it is in the domain of σ.*content* (a subset of that interval); this is why the value may be *unknown*.

    Function *variable_value* (x), applicable only to declared variables, is partial:

    dom *variable_value* (x) $\triangleq$ {σ: *State* | $x \in$ **dom** σ.*addresses*}

    The following function describes the effect of changing the value of a variable:

    set_value: *Variable* $\times$ *Value* $\rightarrow$ *State* $\twoheadrightarrow$ *State*

    set_value (x, v) (σ) $\triangleq$

        σ **except** *content*: σ.*content* $\cup$ {$<\sigma$.*addresses* (x), $v>$}

    The domain of *set_value* (x, v) is the same as the domain of *variable_value* (x). Function *set_value* (x, v) preserves the state invariant: if σ satisfies the invariant and is in the domain of the function, then *set_value* (x, v) (σ) also satisfies the invariant.

7.6.7 The run-time stack

Last, we must specify the process of allocating space for a new block and deallocating space after exiting from a block. Allocation is expressed by the function

$$allocate: State \rightarrow Declaration\_list \rightarrow State$$

with:

[7.7]

$\quad$ $allocate\ (\sigma)\ (dl)\ \triangleq$

$\quad\quad$ σ **except**

$\quad\quad\quad$ $addresses:\ \sigma.addresses\ \cup$

$\quad\quad\quad\quad$ **over** dl **apply**

$\quad\quad\quad\quad\quad$ $\lambda\ d: Declaration\ \bullet\ \{<d.v,\ top\ (\sigma)\ +\ \#>\}$

$\quad\quad\quad\quad$ **combine "$\cup$" empty** $\varnothing$ **end**

The expression used for the new value of $\sigma.addresses$ represents:

$$\sigma.addresses\ \cup\ \{<dl(1).v,\ top\ +\ 1>,\ <dl(2).v,\ top\ +\ 2>,\ ...\ <dl(n).v,\ top\ +\ n>\}$$

for $n \triangleq dl.LENGTH$. Local block variables are allocated successive positions beyond the previous top of the stack.

$\quad$ Function $allocate$ preserves the state invariant since:

given

$\quad\quad$ $\sigma' \triangleq allocate\ (sigma)\ (dl\ );$

$\quad\quad$ $highest' \triangleq top\ (\sigma')$

then

$\quad\quad$ **ran** $\sigma'.addresses\ =\ $ **ran** $\sigma.addresses + n\ =\ 1.. \ highest'\quad\wedge$

$\quad\quad$ **dom** $\sigma'.content\ =\ $ **dom** $\sigma.content\ =\ 1.. \ highest' -n\ \subseteq\ 1.. \ highest'$

end

$\quad$ To express deallocation we may define a function

$$deallocate: State \rightarrow State \rightarrow State$$

with the understanding that $deallocate\ (\sigma)\ (\sigma'\ )$, read as "$\sigma'$ deallocated to the variables of σ", is the same state as σ', but restricted to the variables of state σ. This means that any variable of σ' that is not in σ is lost; any name associated with both a variable of σ' and a variable of σ only retains its σ connection. This is exactly what should happen on exit from an inner block: the variables allocated in this block are lost; any variable of the outer block whose name had been overtaken by a variable of the inner block becomes active again (the hole in its scope is closed).

Here is a definition for *deallocate*:

deallocate (σ) (σ') ≜

σ' **except** (*addresses*: σ.*addresses*; *content*: σ'.*content* \ **ran** σ.*addresses*)

The result of *deallocate* will satisfy the invariant if both σ and σ' did. The need to preserve the invariant is the reason why the second clause of the **except** modifies the state's *content* component, so as to rid its domain of any member outside the range of *addresses*.

7.6.8 Changes to the meaning functions

The above preparation yields the necessary modifications to the meaning functions.

In the definition of the *M* function for expressions (6.4.1), the *Variable* case should no longer use σ (*e*) but

variable_value (*e*) (σ)

with no more need for the test

e ∉ **dom** σ

which has been integrated into the above definition of *variable_value*.

In the *M* function for instructions (6.6), a branch must be added for blocks, with M_{Block} [i] as right-hand side; also, the $M_{Assignment}$ function must be adapted.

The modified and the new functions are:

[7.8]

$M_{Assignment}$ [*a*: *Assignment*] ≜ *set_value* (*a*.*target*, *M* [*a*.*source*])

M_{Block} [*b*: *Block*] ≜

λ σ • (*M* [*b*.*body*]; *allocate* (*b*.*variables*); *deallocate* (σ)) (σ)

and finally, to specify the semantics of a whole program, now viewed (page 207) as a block:

$M_{Program}$ [*p*: *Program*] ≜ M_{Block} [*p*.*b*] (∅)

7.7 ROUTINES

Using some of the mechanisms defined for block structure, we can now see how to add a routine construct to Graal. (Routines are also called subprograms, subroutines and procedures.)

7.7.1 The feature and its purpose

Routines are computational abstractions. A routine describes a certain computation and associates a name with that computation. Software elements can then trigger the computation through **calls**, which refer only to the routine's name, not to the details of the computation.

In the software development process, routines serve two complementary purposes:

- Once you have written a software element performing a useful computation, you may want to give it a name and existence of its own, independently of the original context for which you produced it, so that it may be reused for other purposes. This is the *bottom-up* use of routines.

- When developing a non-trivial algorithm, you may want to express it in terms of simpler computations; you know the goal (specification) of each such subcomputation, but may prefer to postpone writing its implementation until you have finalized the higher-level picture. It is appropriate then to use routine calls to capture the elements to be developed later. This is the *top-down* use of routines.

Technically, there are two categories of routines. A routine describing the computation of one or more values is a **function** (a somewhat unfortunate name since it conflicts with its use in mathematical metalanguages, but one which has stuck). If the computation only produces changes in the state, without returning a direct result, the routine is a **procedure**.

> In some contexts, as mentioned above, "procedure" is simply a synonym for "routine", but this
> book uses "procedure" in the more specific sense of a routine which does not return a result.

7.7.2 Actual arguments, actual results and calls

A routine usually describes not just one immutable computation but a set of possible computations, parameterized by values supplied by the caller and producing results to be returned to the caller. The data elements exchanged by the caller and the routine are called **arguments**. (The term "parameter" is a synonym in most contexts.)

This discussion will in fact use a more precise terminology: "arguments" will only refer to the data elements passed by the caller to the routine ("in" arguments). The values returned (sometimes called "out" arguments) will be called **results**.

Any particular call to a particular routine must include two lists of elements from the calling unit:

- A list of expressions, the **actual arguments**, whose values are passed to the routine.

- A list of variables, the **actual results**, meant to be updated to the routine's results as computed by the call.

This suggests an abstract syntax for call instructions:

[7.9]

Call $\triangleq$ *called*: *Identifier*; *input*: *Expression**; *output*: *Variable**

called is the routine name; *input* is the list of actual arguments; *output* is the list of actual results. The elements of *input* represent values to be passed to the routine, so they may be arbitrary expressions, including variables, constants or operator expressions. In contrast, the elements of *output* will receive a new value as a result of the call, so they must have a modifiable value. Besides simple variables, they may be array elements or qualified variables in languages supporting arrays or records.

A possible concrete syntax for [7.9] is:

[7.10]

call *called* (*input*) **return** *output*

The abstract and concrete versions of the syntax describe a call instruction. As noted above, function calls are commonly thought of as expressions rather than instructions. We do not lose any generality, however, by removing the distinction between procedures and functions, and treating all calls as instructions. If the *output* list is empty, the routine corresponds to a procedure. If not, the concrete syntax [7.10] stands for what many programmers would write as an assignment with a function call on the right-hand side:

[7.11]

output := *called* (*input*)

Although the notation of [7.11] is often convenient in concrete syntax, it is less appropriate for the theoretical model. The denotational specification of expressions (and consequently of assignments) in chapter 6 assumed that expression evaluation cannot change the state – produce side effects. Of course, functions producing arbitrary side effects are bad programming practice. But many practical routine calls may need to change the state in legitimate ways even if they return a result. For example, as soon as a routine performs some input, or creates a new object, it affects the state. (The next chapter will return to this question.) So even with good programming practice it is more convenient to treat all routine calls as instructions of the general abstract form [7.9].

This convention need not affect the concrete syntax; when specifying denotationally a language supporting function calls as expressions, we may first perform the conceptual transformation from [7.11] to [7.10] (or a form including more routine calls and assignments if the right-hand side is a more complex expression than in [7.11]). You may view this as an example of two-tiered specification, as described in 4.3.4.

7.7.3 Abstract syntax for routines

A routine declaration must specify the name of the routine and the numbers and types of the arguments and results. It also includes a body, which is a possibly complex instruction. Finally, the body needs its own local names for referring to the actual arguments and results of any particular call; these local names are called **formal arguments** and **formal results**. Any particular call will associate an actual argument (expression of the calling unit) to every formal argument, and an actual result (variable of the calling unit) to every formal result.

This suggests the following abstract syntax for routine declarations:

$$Routine \triangleq name: Identifier; \; body: Instruction; \; argument, result: Declaration\_list$$

7.7.4 Static semantic constraints

Some constraints must apply to routines and calls:

- All formal arguments must have different names and all formal results must have different names (this is captured by the standard constraint on *Declaration_list*, as seen in 6.2.1).

- No formal argument may have the same name as a formal result, since this would lead to ambiguity in the body.

- The actual arguments and results for any call must match their formal counterparts in number and type.

The formal specification of these constraints is left to the reader.

7.7.5 In-out arguments

Many practical programming languages support not just "in" arguments and "out" results, but also "in-out" arguments. As with an in argument, the original value of an actual in-out argument is available to the routine, but, as with a result, that value may be updated by the routine. This means that the actual argument must be a variable or other modifiable entity.

This discussion will not consider in-out arguments, however, because we can easily simulate their effect by allowing a given variable of the calling program to appear in both the actual argument list and the actual result list. This works because the mode of argument passing assumed for this discussion will be "value-result", whose conceptual effect is to have all formal arguments initialized to the corresponding actuals at the time of call, and all actual results updated to the final value of the corresponding formal results at the time of return.

7.7.6 Getting rid of arguments and results

To make the specification of routine calls simpler, and allow it to concentrate on the most original aspects of routines, it is convenient to limit our attention to routines with empty lists of arguments and results. This can be done through a theoretical device: treating argument and result passing as assignment.

The idea is to consider a call

$$Call\ (called:\ r;\ input:\ i;\ output:\ o)$$

as roughly equivalent to a call to a routine r', with no arguments or results, and the following body (expressed in concrete syntax):

[7.12]   -- Approximate equivalence only
  argument := *i* ;
  r.*body* ;
  o := *result*

where r' is a routine with no arguments or results, but with the same body as r. The assignments operate on lists i, o, *argument*, *result*; the notion of list assignment will be clarified below.

For this to make sense, we must be able to treat the arguments and results as local variables within the body of r', allocated anew for each routine call. To do this, we may simply consider that body as a block, as studied above (7.6), and use all the properties of this notion including dynamic storage allocation (level 3 of the classification on page 204).

Form [7.12] is not quite correct because it assumes that the actual arguments and results, i and o, are statically accessible to the routine. This is only the case if the routine is declared in a scope which is internal to the calling unit. To get away from this rather severe restriction, we may introduce special global list variables, *in_actual* and *out_actual*, declared in the outermost scope, and hence accessible to both the caller and the routine body. (To avoid any ambiguity, we must then prohibit programmers from using these names for any other variables.) Then a more correct equivalence for the call is

[7.13]
  in_actual := *i*;
  call *r'* ;
  o := *out_actual*

where r' itself has the body:

[7.14]
  argument := *in_actual*;
  r.*body* ;
  out_actual := *result*

Variables *in_actual* and *out_actual* are only used temporarily at the time of call and return (respectively), so that they may safely be global. You may view them as modeling techniques actually used by language implementations for routines: the result of a function is often available, on function return, through a fixed register, corresponding to *out_actual*. (The corresponding technique for arguments is less common because routines may have a variable number of arguments, whereas in most languages functions have exactly one result.)

Since the previous discussions have given us precise denotational models for assignments and compounds, we can restrict the discussion of calls to routines without arguments or results. This is again an example of two-tiered language specification.

A direct specification of routines with arguments, not going through the preceding conceptual device, is of course also possible (see the bibliographical references of chapter 6). The two-tiered approach simplifies the discussion, which will concentrate on the more original features of routines.

7.7.7 List assignments

The above technique for dealing with arguments uses assignments involving lists, such as

> *out_actual* := *result*

As specified in chapter 6, however, assignment only applies to individual variables of simple types. To clarify the techniques just introduced for getting rid of arguments and results, we need to know what a list assignment means.

If *a* is a list of variables and *e* a list of expressions of identical length and matching type, we should view the assignment

[7.15]
> *a* := *e*

as representing the sequence of assignments

[7.16]
> *a* (*i*) := *e* (*i*)

for $i : 1 .. a. LENGTH$. In terms of the denotational specification, this means replacing a state σ with

[7.17]
> $\sigma \lor$
>
> > **over** *a* **apply**
> >
> > > $\lambda \, v : Variable \bullet \{<v, M_{Expression} \, [e \, (\#)] \, (\sigma)>\}$
> >
> > **combine** "$\lor$" **empty** $\varnothing$ **end**

If, however, a variable appears twice or more in a, the effect of the sequence of assignments [7.16], as evidenced by the formal semantics [7.17], depends on the order in which variables are listed in a. Although the specification [7.17] is still meaningful in this case, it is clearly inappropriate; the order of variables in the list should be immaterial, and we should be able to interpret the assignments [7.16] as simultaneous. As a consequence, we should only accept list assignments of the form [7.15] if a contains no duplicate variable.

Let us check what this rule means for the list assignments used to model argument passing ([7.13] and [7.14]). For the assignment to *argument*, the static constraint on declaration lists covers the rule. For the assignments to *in_actual* and *out_actual* no problem will arise, since these are lists of "artificial" variables under the specifier's control. But we must take the rule into account for the assignment to o, the actual result list in a call. This yields a static semantic constraint (left for the reader to express formally): in any routine call, the elements of the actual result list must all be different variables.

It is easy to see the practical importance of this constraint: without it, the result of a call would depend on the order in which the final values of out formal arguments are copied into the corresponding actual arguments on return – a decision best left to the compiler writers and kept out of the language manual.

Many programming language specifications indeed explicitly include the above static constraint.

7.7.8 Abstract syntax of routine declarations

The rest of this discussion assumes Graal extended with routines without arguments.

We may allow every block to include declarations of such routines, with the usual rules of block structure at level 2: different routines may have the same name if they are declared in different blocks; in case of conflict with the name of a routine declared in an enclosing block, the innermost name wins.

It is convenient to separate (as in the concrete syntax of Pascal) routine declarations from declarations of variables. This means updating the syntactic specification of blocks (see [7.4], page 207) to:

$Block \triangleq routine\_part: Routine\_list; \; variables: Declaration\_list; \; body: Instruction$

with

$Routine\_list \triangleq Routine\_declaration*$

$Routine\_declaration \triangleq name: Identifier; \; body: Instruction$

7.7.9 Semantics of a call

This section and the next outline the required changes to the semantic specification, beginning with the semantics of calls.

For dynamic semantics, $M_{Instruction}$ needs a new branch for calls; because the effect of calling a routine without arguments is to execute its body, the denotation of a call to a routine of name r should be of the form

$$M_{Call} \; [c : Call] \; \triangleq \; \lambda \, \sigma \; \bullet \; routine\_denotation \; (r , \sigma) \, (\sigma)$$

This assumes a function *routine_denotation* such that *routine_denotation* (r , σ) is the denotation of the routine of name r in state σ. The denotation of a routine must be a state-to-state transformation, which the above branch applies to σ itself to yield the state resulting from the call.

To define *routine_denotation*, we must make sure that every routine declared in a block has the proper "routine denotation" attached to it as part of the state generated on block entry.

For Graal extended with block structure, the state is of the form ([7.5], page 208):

$$State \; \triangleq \; addresses : Environment; \; content : Memory$$

where the *Memory* component describes the values stored in used locations, and the *Environment* component describes the mapping from variables to locations.

Neither of these components is really appropriate for storing procedure denotations:

- Common languages do not have "routine variables" to which the execution may assign different routines at run time, the "value" of a routine being computable dynamically.

- Even in a block-structured language where different routines declared in different blocks may share the same name, a given routine name always refers to the same routine in a given block, so that we should not model routine names as being "reallocated" on each execution of their block, the way variables are.

These comments do not necessarily apply to all languages: Lisp and other functional languages effectively support routine variables and the run-time fabrication of routines; object-oriented languages with dynamic binding make it possible to have the same routine name refer to different actual routines at run-time.

For the routine mechanisms of classical languages, however, it is more appropriate to introduce a third component into the state, giving

$$State \; \triangleq \; routines : Routine\_environment; \; addresses : Environment; \; content : Memory$$

with

$$Routine\_environment \; \triangleq \; Variable \; \xrightarrow[f]{} \; (State \rightarrowtail State \,)$$

In a given state, then, the following function gives the routine denotation of a routine of name r:

$routine\_denotation$: $Identifier \times State \nrightarrow (State \nrightarrow State)$

dom $routine\_denotation \triangleq \{<r, \sigma> \mid r \in$ **dom** $\sigma.routines \}$

$routine\_denotation$ $(r : Identifier, \sigma: State) \triangleq \sigma.routines$ (r)

To complete the specification, we must see how to record routine denotations into a routine environment. This can be done at block entry. The semantics of blocks becomes:

M_{Block} $[b: Block] \triangleq \lambda \sigma \bullet$

    $(M [b.body]$; $\underline{record\_routines (b.routines)}$;

    $allocate (b.variables)$; $deallocate (\sigma)) (\sigma)$

where the underlined part is the addition to the earlier specification ([7.8], page 211). Function $record\_routines$ is easy to define:

$record\_routines$: $Routine\_list \rightarrow (State \rightarrow State)$

$record\_routines$ $(rdl: Routine\_list) \triangleq$

    given

        $record\_one \triangleq$

            λ $rd: Routine\_declaration \bullet$ λ $\sigma: State \bullet$

                σ **except** $routines$: $\sigma.routines$ $\uplus$

                                $\{<rd.name, M_{Instruction}$ $[rd.body]\}$

    then

        over rdl **apply** $record\_one$ **combine** "$\uplus$" **empty** $\varnothing$ **end**

    end

According to this specification, every execution of a block enters the denotation of the block's routines into the state. You may view this as the formal representation of the fundamental notion of "stored program computer".

In light of the above discussion, it is unpleasant to have the denotation of each routine formally "recomputed" on every execution of the block in which the routine is declared. In ordinary programming languages, you may determine the meaning of a routine once and for all through static analysis of the program text. To model this better, however, we would need to associate $record\_routines$ with the function that decodes declarations. This function is called $typing$ and produces a $Type\_map$, that is to say a finite function from variable names to types (6.2.2). We would need to complement it with a function producing a "$Routine\_map$", in other words a finite function from routine names to routine denotations.

This approach is certainly feasible and you are invited to try it. It results in a blurring of the distinction between static and dynamic semantics, since type maps must contain routine denotations, which themselves contain instruction denotations referring to the M functions (see $M_{Instruction}$ $[rd.body]$ in the definition of $record\_routines$ above).

This reflects what compilers do: to process a variable declaration, it suffices to update the symbol table (the *Type_map*); but to process a routine declaration, you must also generate the corresponding code (applying the equivalent of the *M* functions.)

The solution retained above is perhaps further from actual implementation techniques but preserves a clear-cut distinction between static and dynamic semantics.

7.7.10 Recursion

The above specification brings a considerable amount of recursion to the definitions. A routine itself may be recursive, so that its *routine_denotation* will use $M_{Instruction}$ applied to the routine's body; if that body contains a recursive call, the value of $M_{Instruction}$ depends on the *routine_denotation*. But the problem is deeper, as evidenced by a look at the semantic domain definitions: *State* is defined in terms of *Routine_environment*, itself defined in terms of *State* $\rightarrow$ *State*. This raises serious problems.

The following terminology will help clarify these problems. A set X is **smaller** than a set Y if and only if there exists a one-to-one correspondence between X and a subset of Y. For finite sets, this corresponds to the usual notion of X having fewer members than X; but the notion applies to infinite sets as well. For infinite sets, X may be smaller than Y and Y smaller than X at the same time. For example, **N** is clearly smaller than **Z**, but there is also a one-to-one correspondence between **Z** and the even subset of **N** (obtained for example by associating the value $4*i$ with every non-negative number, and the value $-4*i - 2$ with every negative number).

Set theory indicates, however, that if Y has two or more elements none of the following sets is smaller than X:

$$X \rightarrow Y$$

$$X \nrightarrow Y$$

$$X \underset{f}{\nrightarrow} Y$$

As a classical example, there is no one-to-one correspondence between the set of natural integers, **N**, and the set of functions **N** $\rightarrow$ $\{0, 1\}$, which itself is in one-to-one correspondence with the set of real numbers **R**.

Here consider the definition of *State*, which is of the form

   State $\triangleq$ *routines*: *Routine_environment*; ... other components ...

implying that *Routine_environment* is smaller than *State* (if you pick a member of *Routine_environment*, there will be one or more members of *State* with the corresponding *routines* component). *Routine_environment* itself, however, is defined as

   Variable $\underset{f}{\nrightarrow}$ (*State* $\nrightarrow$ *State*)

implying that *State* $\nrightarrow$ *State* is smaller than *Routine_environment*. Then *State* $\nrightarrow$ *State* must be smaller than *State* ("much" smaller, in fact). But this directly contradicts the above results on function spaces. We seem to be in trouble.

Fortunately, such contradictions will only arise if we consider semantic domains containing **all** the possible functions from one set to another. Here we need only consider functions which are of interest for denotational descriptions. The next chapter will rescue us by restricting the sets of relevant functions.

7.8 A PEEK AT CLASSES AND INHERITANCE

To conclude this discussion, it is interesting to take a brief look at a very important concept of modern programming methodology: the classes of object-oriented programming. This section will only introduce the concepts, making no attempt at a complete specification.

The systematic use of classes exerts a profound influence on the software design process. From the more restricted viewpoint of this discussion, classes are just a generalization of records, with two important new properties:

- A class may **inherit** from one or more others, meaning it directly obtains all of their components, adding its own specific ones if needed. The classes that inherit from a class A, directly or indirectly, are A's **descendants**. The inverse notion is **ancestor**.
- The components of a class may include not just data fields (attributes), but also routines, representing operations on the instances of the class (objects) at run-time. The term **feature** covers both attributes and routines.

Inheritance is not hard to model, at least in principle, in the framework defined above for records. Let A be a class, and T_A the set of tags (feature names) of A. The preceding specification of records models instances of A as finite functions from tags to values, with domain T_A. If we introduce inheritance, these will be called **direct instances** of A; the word "instance", unqualified, now refers to all direct instances of A or any of its descendants. Then the instances of A are simply finite functions whose domain is a superset of T_A.

This also applies to *multiple* inheritance (the case of a class inheriting from two or more parents): the tag set of the new class includes the tag sets of both parents.

Language rules are needed to resolve name clashes – identical tags in parents, which would prevent the union of two functions from yielding a function. Eiffel addresses this problem through **renaming** rules.

In some cases the clash occurs for a feature inherited from a common ancestor. This is called **repeated inheritance** in Eiffel; the language rules imply that the feature is duplicated if inherited under different names, and shared otherwise. All this is easy to model using finite functions and the $\uplus$ operator.

The second key task of the specification is to model those features of classes which are routines rather than attributes. As in the above specification of routines in a more classical context, we must then associate with a feature name not just type information but also a state-to-state transformation.

The specification must also take another important aspect into account: the role of the primary target of a routine call. If routine r is declared in class C, callers will use it under the form

[7.18]

    $x \cdot r$ (... *arguments* ...)

where x is an entity (variable) of type C, or a descendant of C. In other words, every routine has an implicit argument, the "current object", representing the primary target of the operation (x in the above call).

Furthermore, r may have different denotations in C and its descendants. The technique known as **dynamic binding** implies that the version of r to apply in a call such as [7.18] depends on the actual type of the object to which x refers at run-time – not necessarily A, but possibly a descendant of A. This fundamental software engineering technique, essential to achieve modularity and decentralization of software architectures, raises interesting specification problems.

7.9 BIBLIOGRAPHICAL NOTES

[Suzuki 1982] describes an attempt to restrict the use of pointers to avoid some of the problems of dynamic aliasing.

For a denotational description of multiple inheritance, see [Cardelli 1984]. An algebraic specification of related concepts, based on category theory, may be found in [Goguen 1978]. The Eiffel conventions for renaming and repeated inheritance are described in [Meyer 1988a].

EXERCISES

7.1 Records: multiple qualifiers

Modify the specification of the record extension (7.2) to allow multiply qualified variables of the form $x \cdot t_1 \cdot t_2 \dots t_n$.

7.2 Structural equivalence

Change the semantic specification of the record type extension (7.2.3, page 187) so that it reflects structural equivalence rather than name equivalence. Discuss the pros and cons of structural and name equivalence (see [Welsh 77]).

7.3 Arrays

Extend Graal with arrays, as outlined in 7.3. Limit yourself to one-dimensional arrays, with dynamic allocation. The axiomatic specification (9.7.3) may provide some hints.

7.4 Pointers and dynamic allocation

Complete the extension of Graal for Pascal-like pointers and heap, outlined in 7.4.

7.5 C Pointers

In C, pointers are not necessarily associated with dynamic allocation. If x is a variable, the notation $\&x$ denotes a pointer to x; if p is a pointer variable, $p*$ denotes the value pointed to by the value of p. Hence the value of $(\&x)*$ is the same as the value of x.

Specify an extension to Graal along these lines. You may first assume that only one $\&$ or $*$ operator may be applied to a variable, and then extend the specification to handle expressions of the form $\&\&\&..\&x$ and $p**...*$.

7.6 Records and pointers

Combine the specification of record and pointer types to account for a type system such as exists in Pascal, where pointers may only point to records.

7.7 Records or pointers

To handle the problem of recursively defined records (page 194), the following approach offers an alternative to the two solutions mentioned (treating as pointers all variables declared as records, and prohibiting recursive declarations). When dealing with a component c of a record type S, where c is itself declared of a record type R, implement c as a record of type R if R was declared before S, and as a pointer to a record of type R otherwise. Is this a good idea?

7.8 Properties of block structure

In the specification of block structure (7.6):
- Can a local variable be assigned different locations in different activations of its block?
- Does a local variable keep its value from one activation of its block to the next?

7.9 A more abstract specification of blocks

The specification of block structure (see page 208) associates with every state a binding between the active variables and a linear set of accessible "memory" addresses. Devise an alternative model where $\sigma(x)$, for any state σ and variable x, is a list of values for x; the list is managed as a stack, its top (first element) giving the value of x in σ, and subsequent elements giving values of x in states corresponding to enclosing blocks.

7.10 Pronouns: An exercise in language design

The article reproduced below in condensed and slightly adapted form appeared in the ACM SIGPLAN Notices, vol. 19, no. 11 November 1984, page 7. (Reproduced with permission from the author, K.L. Pentzlin, and the ACM.) Describe how to add the proposed language feature to Graal, detailing the necessary extensions to abstract syntax, static semantics and meaning functions.

An extension proposal for Pascal: The pronoun in assignments

(by Karl Ludwig Pentzlin)

Abstract

Updating a variable (assigning to it a new value which depends on the variable's previous value) requires the variable to be specified in the target part of an assignment instruction and again in the source part. Writing such instructions is tedious and error-prone.

Description

The "commercial at" character (@), called **pronoun** by analogy with natural languages, may occur in the source expression of an assignment, representing the value that the target had before the assignment. Any function call necessary to evaluate the pronoun itself, for example to compute the value of an array index, is not repeated when evaluating the pronoun in the source.

Examples

$a := @ + 1$

    -- Instead of $a := a + 1$

$b[i + 1] := @ + func1(@)$

    -- Instead of $b[i + 1] := b[i + 1] + func1(b[i + 1])$

vector $[func2(x, y)] := @ * 2$

    -- Instead of *vector* $[func2(x, y)] := vector[func2(x, y)] * 2$,

    -- but with *func2* called only once.

Comments

The proposed solution is more general than, for example, the ALGOL 68 +:= and −:= operators or the Modula-2 *INC* and *DEC* standard procedures.

8

The mathematics
of recursion

Several of the formal definitions introduced in previous chapters, both for abstract syntax and for denotational semantics, were recursive. Recursive definitions, although clearly a powerful and elegant device, sometimes venture dangerously near to circularity. The previous discussions mentioned some of the problems, but did not attempt to provide solutions.

It is time now to take a closer look at recursion and to examine under what conditions a recursive definition may be used safely. Since the aim of formal descriptions is to specify programming languages precisely and unambiguously, we cannot let our formalisms rely on a shaky theoretical basis.

You may view this chapter as exorcism: justifying the common uses of recursion – not just in formal definitions, but also in programming – and reassuring ourselves that we can go ahead with them without fear of uncovering some menacing Dybbuk.

8.1 THE TROUBLE WITH RECURSION

A recursive definition is a definition of a certain class of objects, such that the body of the definition refers to one or more objects of the class.

A definition may be **indirectly** recursive if it refers to objects whose definitions refer (directly or indirectly) to objects of the class being defined.

8.1.1 Recursion in denotational semantics

Two kinds of recursive definition were encountered in the preceding denotational specifications: definitions of **domains** and of **functions**.

Examples of the first kind include both syntactic and semantic domains. A syntactic domain defined by indirect recursion appears in the abstract syntax of Graal (3.2.6 and back cover), which includes

Instruction $\triangleq$ ... Other choices ... | Conditional

Conditional $\triangleq$ thenbranch, elsebranch: Instruction; ... Other components ...

so that *Instruction* is defined in terms of *Conditional*, itself defined in terms of *Instruction*. Two other branches of the *Instruction* definition are constructs defined in terms of *Instruction*: *Compound* (defined as list of instructions) and *Loop*. The definition of construct *Expression* is similarly recursive.

Semantic domains were also defined recursively. An example was the domain of denotations for values of record types (7.2.4): *Record_value* was boldly defined as $Tag \xrightarrow{f} Value$, where *Value* is *Simple_value* | *Value*. The discussion of routines in 7.7.9 introduced an even higher level of recursion, appearing to introduce a one-to-one correspondence between $State \xrightarrow{f} State$ and a subset of *State*

As noted in 7.7.10, this seems to contradict basic results of set theory.

Examples of functions defined recursively are the semantic functions $M_{Expression}$ (in the *Binary* case, 6.4.1) and $M_{Instruction}$ (6.5.1), several branches of which include references to $M_{Instruction}$: the branches for *Compound*, *Conditional* and *Loop*.

As pointed out in 6.5.7, the last case, loop semantics, appears more disturbing than the others. In the semantic functions for expressions, compounds and conditional expressions, the denotation of an object is defined in terms of the denotations of its constituents; this, intuitively, seems a legitimate use of recursion. But the formula for $M_{Instruction}$ [i], when i is a loop, includes a reference to $M_{Instruction}$ [i] itself – a dubious practice, one might think.

8.1.2 Recursion in programs

Recursion is a familiar tool for programmers in high-level languages. In modern languages you may declare both recursive *routines*, which contain a direct or indirect call to themselves, and recursive *data types*, which include a direct or indirect reference to specimens of the same type.

It is well known that both cases require precautions. For example, the control flow of any usable routine must contain at least one non-recursive branch; a typical form is

```
routine (x, ...) is
    do
        if simplecase then
                non-recursive actions
        else
                ...
                routine (x', ...)
                ...
        end
    end -- routine
```

since if all possible branches included a recursive call, executions of the routine would have no hope of terminating. Only one recursive call has been shown in the recursive part, but of course it may contain more than one.

Another requirement (in the absence of side effects on global objects) is that any recursive call must have at least one input actual argument, such as x' above, whose value is different from the initial value of the corresponding formal argument, here x: otherwise the internal call would result in exactly the same sequence of events as the initial one, and so would never terminate.

For data types, as noted in 7.2.5, language rules protect the recursive part using pointers. In Pascal, for example, the declaration

```
type integerlist =
    record
            first: integer; rest: integerlist
    end
```

is not permitted; *rest* must be declared of type ↑*integerlist* (pointer to *integerlist*). Although conceptually correct, the form without pointer would imply that an *integerlist* contains an integer and an *integerlist*, which itself contains an integer and an *integerlist*, which itself...: too much for a compiler to figure out an adequate computer implementation.

In Eiffel, where the types are defined as classes, the convention is different: an entity declared of a programmer-defined type is taken by default to represent references (pointers) to instances of that type – not the instances themselves. This removes the possibility of self-inclusion. An entity may also be declared as **expanded**, meaning that its value is an object, not an object reference; an entity declared of one of the basic types – integer, boolean etc. – is understood to be expanded. The language rules explicitly disallow any cycle in the relation "class A includes a expanded component of type B".

As seen in the previous chapters, these recursive programming structures yield recursive denotational definitions, and similar problems may be expected, in a more abstract form, at the semantic description level.

8.1.3 Non-creativity

In general, the use of recursive definitions may be seriously questioned. The issue is circularity: when I define h using h itself, it is not clear whether I have defined anything at all.

To understand the problem in a more general context, consider a definition of the form

$$h \triangleq D$$

Normally, the role of such a definition is clear: it allows us thereafter to use h to mean D. As opposed, for example, to an axiom, a definition should be **non-creative** in the sense that any property expressible with h may also be expressed without h, by replacing h with D throughout.

But assume D is an expression of the form $\tau(h)$, containing one or more occurrences of h: then non-creativity is not satisfied any more; if you take a text containing occurrences of h and replace them throughout with D, the resulting text will still contain occurrences of h.

It is therefore improper in this case to use the definition symbol $\triangleq$, and it is only through an abuse of language that one talks about recursive "definitions".

Because the standard, naive interpretation of such "definitions" is simply incorrect, the problem we face in this chapter is to provide a mathematically correct interpretation for them.

Before proceeding with the theory, it is useful to take a closer look at some actual uses of recursion and their intuitive meaning. In the meantime, we must refrain from using the $\triangleq$ sign whenever the right-hand side (the value used for the definition, or definiens) contains one or more occurrences of the left-hand side (the object being defined, or definiendum). We shall be content in such a case with the more modest $=$ sign, which merely expresses equality between the two sides.

8.1.4 Examples

Four recursive "definitions", expressed as equalities, will serve as working examples for the rest of this discussion. The functions considered, called f, g, u and v, are all in $\mathbf{N} \nrightarrow \mathbf{N}$.

[8.1]
$$f = \lambda\, n\, \bullet\, \textbf{if } n = 0 \textbf{ then } 1$$
$$\textbf{else } n * f\,(n-1) \textbf{ end}$$

$g = \lambda\, n \bullet$ **if** $n = 0$ **then** 1

$$\textbf{else}\ \frac{g\ (n+1)}{n+1}\ \textbf{end}$$

$d = \lambda\, n \bullet$ **if** $n = 0$ **then** 1

      elsif $n = 1$ **then** $d\ (3)$

      else $d\ (n-2)$ **end**

$e = \lambda\, n \bullet$ **if** $n = 1$ **then** 1

      elsif $even\ (n)$ **then** $e\ (\dfrac{n}{2})$

      else $e\ (3*n + 1)$ **end**

Let us first take an informal look. The equality for f seems innocent enough; it is satisfied by the factorial function. But compare it with the equality for g, which is also satisfied by the factorial function: there is an important intuitive difference, apparent if you take a more operational view of these definitions – a programmer's view. A computation of $f\ (n)$ from the formula given will yield a result for any $n \in \mathbf{N}$, whereas computation of $g\ (n)$ will fail to terminate for positive n.

If the "definition" of d actually defines a function, then this function must take on value 1 for all even integers, and yield the same value, say ov, for all odd integers. It is not possible, however, to determine the value of ov from the definition alone. Taking again the computational viewpoint, computation of $d\ (n)$ will not terminate for an even n, so that it is perhaps preferable to consider ov as undefined.

The definition of e is even more intriguing. Assuming again that it indeed defines a function, the value of that function is easily seen to be 1 for all powers of 2, for all integers n such that $3*n + 1$ is a power of 2, for all integers m such that $3*m + 1$ is such an n etc. More precisely, the function must have value 1 for any member of the set T whose members are obtained, starting with 1, by any number of applications of the two functions

$\lambda\, n \bullet 2*n$

$(\lambda\, n \bullet (n - 1) / 3) \setminus P$ with $P \triangleq \{n\colon \mathbf{N} \mid \exists\, p\colon \mathbf{N} \bullet n = 6*p + 4\}$

The second function is restricted to the set P of numbers of the form $3*q + 1$ for some odd q – and then yields that q.

The question is whether T is the whole of $\mathbf{N}^{\bullet}$ (the set of positive integers) or some proper subset. Although T does appear to cover all positive integers, the author knows no proof of this.

8.2 "GOOD" AND "BAD" RECURSIVE DEFINITIONS

8.2.1 Elementary criteria

A natural question to ask whenever you are presented with a recursive definition is whether it defines anything at all.

In some cases, the answer is clearly no: if I say "Computer science is computer science", I hardly help you understand what that profession is. Saying "Computer science is the formal study of program construction, programming languages, operating systems, theoretical computer science, algorithms and other areas of computer science" (a doubly recursive "definition") is more informative but still subject to circularity.

To be sure, many recursive definitions do seem legitimate. For example, classical recursive definitions of functions of the natural integers (such as the factorial function) in the form

[8.2]

$$h\ (0) \triangleq w_0 \ ;$$

$$h\ (i) \triangleq F\ (i, <h\ (i-1), \ldots, h\ (0)>) \qquad (i > 0)$$

where w_0 is an integer and F is a known function, are intuitively well-grounded, since they allow the computation of the value of $h\ (i)$, for any $i \geq 0$, from the initial value w_0 through a finite number of applications of F.

Such recursive definitions are an essential tool in mathematics. They may be reconciled with the principle of non-creativity: clearly, for any given i, any occurrence of $h\ (i)$ may be replaced through a finite number of substitutions by an expression not involving h.

It would be nice to have a simple characterization of recursive definitions into "safe" and "unsafe" ones, whereby safe definitions would be easy to recognize. Unfortunately, although it is possible to find conditions that are *sufficient* to ensure safety of recursive definitions (such as being of the form [8.2] above), such rules are too restrictive: in other words some perfectly valid definitions do not conform to the rules. Nor is the existence of such exceptions of theoretical interest only: neither the recursive syntactic domain definitions nor the definition of loop semantics conform to the restricted model of [8.2].

8.2.2 Undefinedness

What then is meant by a "safe" recursive definition? In the case of functions, we might require the definition to specify unambiguously a **total** function. From this standpoint, the definition of f would seem to be acceptable, but not that of d; the status of g is unclear (does any function other than factorial satisfy the definition?), and that of e awaits clarification of the underlying mathematical problem of whether T is the same as $\mathbf{N}^{\bullet}$.

But the restriction to total functions would be too restrictive, at least in the case of semantic functions. It is no accident that the most intriguing recursive definitions in our specifications arise for loops: as any programmer knows, loops are subject to the deplorable habit of not terminating at times. What is the denotation (semantic function) of a loop that may not terminate?

In general, the denotation of a loop, as of any other instruction, is a function from *State* to *State*. Termination of a loop depends not only on the loop but on the state in which it is started; for example, the following loop will terminate if and only if it is executed in a state where n, assumed to be a natural integer variable, is even:

> **while** $n \neq 0$ **do**
>> $n := n - 2$
> **end**

In general, let l be a loop and $ld \triangleq M_{Loop} [l]$ its denotation. If σ is a state in which execution of l terminates, $\sigma' \triangleq ld (\sigma)$ is the state resulting from this execution. But if the execution of l does not terminate when started in σ, no value may be found for σ'. As noted in 6.5.7, the best attitude here is to consider that ld is a partial function, whose domain does not include σ.

So the need for possibly partial functions arises naturally in connection with program constructs whose execution may not terminate. This is why the semantic functions for instructions and programs were introduced in chapter 6 as possibly partial, except for *Skip* and assignment which are guaranteed to terminate (this would not necessarily be true of assignment in a language with function calls). The only real culprit in Graal is the loop, but its presence makes other instructions potentially unsafe, since compounds and conditionals may contain loops.

8.2.3 Limitations of a theory of recursive definitions

The preceding observations remove any hope we may have entertained of finding a general method to determine whether a recursive definition is safe or not. For in the case of functions "safe" would mean "total"; and if there were such a general method, then we could use it to ascertain whether a given loop does or does not always terminate. This – the **halting problem** – is well known to be undecidable. So the best we may ever hope for is sufficient conditions, of the form seen previously.

The limits imposed by computation theory are actually harsher: even if we were only looking for a general method to determine whether a recursively defined function is defined for a *given* argument in its source set, this too would be impossible, for it would amount to a universal algorithm to find out whether a computation terminates when started in a given state – another impossible goal.

So the aims of the theory must of necessity be more modest. We shall see that what may be obtained in the general case is a sequence of **approximations** of a function which satisfies a given definition.

8.3 INTERPRETING RECURSIVE DEFINITIONS

The first step in building a theory of recursively defined functions and domains is to write recursive definitions in such a way as to dispel any doubt over their legitimacy. The circularity of such a definition – a class of objects being defined in terms of objects of that very class – must be removed.

8.3.1 Fixpoints

One solution is to interpret a recursive definition as a **fixpoint equation**. In general, a fixpoint (or fixed point) of a function $\tau: X \rightarrow\!\!\!\!\rightarrow X$ is an object $x \in$ **dom** τ such that

$$x = \tau\,(x)$$

Taking functions τ in $\mathbf{N} \rightarrow\!\!\!\!\rightarrow \mathbf{N}$ as examples:

- $\lambda\,x \bullet x^2$ has two fixpoints, 0 and 1.
- $\lambda\,x \bullet x{+}1$ has no fixpoint.
- Any member of $\mathbf{N}$ is a fixpoint of the identity function $\lambda\,x \bullet x$.

The fixpoints of interest for this discussion will be fixpoints of high-level functionals, taking functions as arguments. (As elsewhere in this book, the word "functional" only applies to total functions.) Consider for example the functional

[8.3]
$$\phi: (\mathbf{N}\rightarrow\!\!\!\!\rightarrow \mathbf{N}) \longrightarrow (\mathbf{N}\rightarrow\!\!\!\!\rightarrow \mathbf{N})$$

$$\phi \triangleq \lambda\,f: (\mathbf{N}\rightarrow\!\!\!\!\rightarrow \mathbf{N}) \bullet \lambda\,n: \mathbf{N} \bullet \textbf{if } n = 0 \textbf{ then } 1 \textbf{ else } n*f\,(n{-}1) \textbf{ end}$$

Then a fixpoint of ϕ is a function $f: \mathbf{N}\rightarrow\!\!\!\!\rightarrow \mathbf{N}$ such that

[8.4]
$$f = \phi\,(f)$$

that is to say:

$$f = \lambda\,n: \mathbf{N} \bullet \textbf{if } n = 0 \textbf{ then } 1 \textbf{ else } n*f\,(n{-}1) \textbf{ end}$$

which means that for any $n \in \mathbf{N}$:

$$f\,(n) = \textbf{if } n = 0 \textbf{ then } 1 \textbf{ else } n*f\,(n{-}1) \textbf{ end}$$

We are a priori looking for possibly partial functions; since two possibly partial functions are equal if and only if they have the same domain and coincide on that domain, an equation of the form [8.4] means "$\phi\,(f)$ and f are defined for the same arguments and, for any such argument, yield the same value".

Clearly, the factorial function (total on N) is a fixpoint of ϕ. It is not difficult in this case to show that no other total function is a fixpoint: if f is a fixpoint of ϕ and is total, then, by induction on i, $h(i) = i!$ for any $i : N$. Here no partial function is a fixpoint of ϕ either, but for lack of proper notations to deal with partial functions we are not yet in a position to prove this.

8.3.2 Recursive definitions as fixpoint equations

This example shows the way towards giving unquestionable interpretations of arbitrary recursive definitions: interpret such definitions as **fixpoint equations**. Consider a recursive "definition" of an object h, of the form

$$h \triangleq \tau(h)$$

As already discussed, the standard interpretation of the $\triangleq$ symbol is not acceptable here. By relying on the notion of fixpoint, however, we may re-interpret the "definition" in an legitimate way. Assuming that τ is a member of some appropriate set of functionals, we should view the above as a fixpoint equation of the form

$$h = \tau(h)$$

and take it to mean: **Let h be one of the fixpoints of τ.**

So the examples given in [8.1] should be construed as meaning: Let f, g, d, and e be fixpoints of the functionals ϕ, γ, δ and ε, respectively, where the new functionals, all in $(N \rightarrowtail N) \rightarrow (N \rightarrowtail N)$, are defined as follows:

[8.5]

$\phi \triangleq \lambda f \bullet \lambda n \bullet$ **if** $n = 0$ **then** 1
$\qquad\qquad$ **else** $n * f(n-1)$ **end**

$\gamma \triangleq \lambda g \bullet \lambda n \bullet$ **if** $n = 0$ **then** 1
$\qquad\qquad$ **else** $\dfrac{g(n+1)}{n+1}$ **end**

$\delta \triangleq \lambda d \bullet \lambda n \bullet$ **if** $n = 0$ **then** 1
$\qquad\qquad$ **elsif** $n = 1$ **then** $d(3)$
$\qquad\qquad$ **else** $d(n-2)$ **end**

$\varepsilon \triangleq \lambda e \bullet \lambda n \bullet$ **if** $n = 1$ **then** 1
$\qquad\qquad$ **elsif** $even(n)$ **then** $e(\dfrac{n}{2})$
$\qquad\qquad$ **else** $e(3*n+1)$ **end**

Here the use of the definition symbol $\triangleq$ is correct: the above define the functionals ϕ, γ, δ and ϵ unambiguously and of course non-recursively. To facilitate reference to the original definitions ([8.1], page 228), the dummy λ-bound variables have received different names f, g, d and e.

The corresponding fixpoint equations are

$$f = \phi\ (f)$$
$$g = \gamma\ (g)$$
$$d = \delta\ (d)$$
$$e = \epsilon\ (e)$$

In each case, a solution must be a function in $\mathbf{N} \nrightarrow \mathbf{N}$. Recall that the functions considered may be partial.

8.3.3 Aims for a theory of recursive definitions

We have obtained a way to interpret a recursive "definition": consider it as a fixpoint equation $h = \tau\ (h)$.

But of course this will only be acceptable as a definition of h if τ has a fixpoint and, in case it has more than one, we have a criterion to choose between them. So the rest of this chapter is essentially devoted to three tasks:

- Defining sufficient conditions under which functionals are guaranteed to have fixpoints.
- Defining which ones of these fixpoints are actually "interesting" as solutions to the kind of fixpoint equations that arise in abstract syntax and denotational semantics.
- Showing how to compute the fixpoints when they exist.

8.4 ITERATIVE METHODS

It is convenient to start with the third task listed: how to compute a fixpoint, assuming there exists one. The discussion of when fixpoints exist and when they do not will come later; the immediate aim is not to be entirely rigorous but to give you an idea of the important notion of iterative method.

The discussion will use as example the definition of the ϕ functional, whose fixpoint should be the factorial function:

$$\phi \triangleq \lambda f: (\mathbf{N} \nrightarrow \mathbf{N}) \bullet \lambda n: \mathbf{N} \bullet \mathbf{if}\ n = 0\ \mathbf{then}\ 1\ \mathbf{else}\ n * f\ (n-1)\ \mathbf{end}$$

8.4.1 Fixpoints in real analysis

How do we compute a fixpoint of ϕ? In ordinary real analysis, fixpoint equations are often solved using an **iterative method**. That is, to find x such that $x = \tau(x)$, where τ is a continuous function, you consider the following sequence:

$$x_0 \triangleq \text{Some initial value}$$
$$x_i \triangleq \tau(x_{i-1}) \qquad \text{for } i \geq 1$$

If this sequence has a limit x, it is easily shown that under the conditions of standard real analysis x is a fixpoint of τ; whether the limit exists depends on the function τ and the initial value chosen.

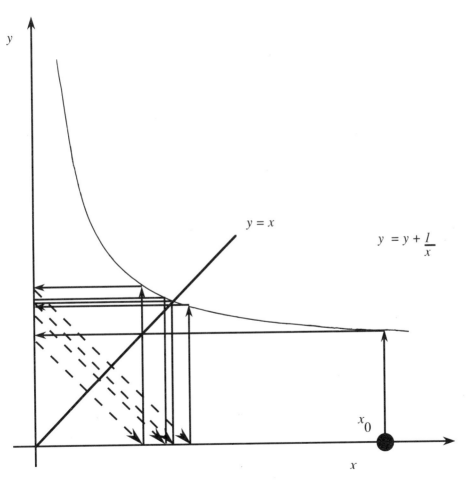

Figure 8.1: Computing a fixpoint

The above figure shows this process applied to computing the positive fixpoint of the function on reals

$$\tau \triangleq \lambda\, x : \mathbf{R} \bullet 1 + \frac{1}{x}$$

Starting with the initial value $x_0 \triangleq 5$, the sequence takes on the values 1.2, 1.833333, 1.545455, 1.647059, 1.607143, 1.622222, 1.616438, 1.618644, 1.617801, 1.618123, 1.618, ... and converges towards the limit 1.6180341 (known as the golden ratio, $\frac{1 + \sqrt{5}}{2}$), which is the abscissa of the intersection between the line $y = x$ and the curve $y = 1 + \frac{1}{x}$.

8.4.2 Functions as limits of sequences

This method may be imitated to compute fixpoints of functionals such as ϕ; here is how. The presentation here is not entirely formal; the next sections will provide a rigorous basis for the derivation.

> A reminder on terminology: recall (2.6.2) that "function" without qualification means a possibly partial function, that is to say a member of $X \nrightarrow Y$ for some X and Y. "Partial function" means a function which is not total, and so is undefined for at least one member of X; in other words, **dom** $f \subset X$ where the inclusion is strict.

We will look for a fixpoint as the "limit", in a sense yet to be defined rigorously, of a sequence of functions in $X \nrightarrow Y$, for some sets X and Y. First we need an element to start the iteration. Since no function seems to emerge as a better candidate than others, we might just as well begin with the least committing of all possible functions: the nowhere defined function

$$\varnothing_{X \nrightarrow Y}$$

This is the function whose domain is the empty subset of X, and which therefore never yields any value in Y. Its fundamental property is that for any subset A of X:

$$\varnothing_{X \nrightarrow Y} (\! A \!) \;=\; \varnothing$$

where, for any function f, $f(\!A\!)$ denotes the image of A by f (2.5.3, 2.7.7). The $\varnothing$ symbol on the right-hand side denotes the empty subset of Y.

The notation $\varnothing$ will be used for $\varnothing_{X \nrightarrow Y}$ when there is no possible confusion. Note (2.6.1) that a function is a special case of a relation, hence of a set of pairs, so that $\varnothing_{X \nrightarrow Y}$ is indeed correctly described as an empty set (a relation with no pairs in it).

The iterative method will attempt to compute the solution of a fixpoint equation such as $f = \phi\,(f)$ as the "limit" of the sequence of functions $f_0, f_1, ..., f_n, ...,$ defined inductively by

[8.6]

$$f_0 \triangleq \varnothing_{N \nrightarrow N}$$
$$f_i \triangleq \phi\,(f_{i-1}) \qquad \text{for } i \geq 1$$

What does this mean? Let us look at the first elements in the sequence. Function f_0 is $\varnothing$. Next we compute f_1:

$$f_1 \triangleq \phi\,(f_0)$$
$$= \phi\,(\varnothing)$$

So from the definition of ϕ:

[8.7]

$$f_1 = \lambda\, n \bullet \text{if } n = 0 \text{ then } 1 \text{ else } n * \varnothing\,(n-1) \text{ end}$$

$\varnothing$ never yields a result, however, so that $f_{1,}\,(n)$ is a *very* partial function, defined only for $n = 0$, for which it yields 1 – indeed the factorial of 0. Viewed as a set of pairs, f_1 is $\{<0, 1>\}$.

Not much progress yet towards the factorial function – but at least there is one correct value! Do not despair but look at f_2:

$$f_2 \triangleq \phi\,(f_1)$$

Hence:

[8.8]

$$f_2 = \lambda\, n \bullet \text{if } n = 0 \text{ then } 1 \text{ else } n * f_1\,(n-1) \text{ end}$$

Since f_1 is only defined for $n = 0$, the expression in the **else** clause is only defined for $n = 1$, and then yields 1. So f_2 is the function

$$\{<0, 1>, <1, 1>\}$$

In other words f_2 is defined only for $n = 0$ and $n = 1$, and agrees with the factorial function for these two values.

The general pattern emerges: for every i, the domain of f_i is the interval $1 .. \ i-1$ and $f_i\,(n)$ is $n!$ for any n in this interval. This may be expressed more formally as

[8.9]

$$f_i = factorial \setminus 0 .. \ i-1$$

where *factorial* is the factorial function and $\setminus$ is the restriction operator (2.7.3). You may wish to prove property [8.9] by induction (exercise 8.1).

The f_i may be viewed as successive approximations to the true solution of the fixpoint equation (the factorial function). Each brings a little more information on that solution than its predecessor f_{i-1}: it is defined for one more value, and yields the same result for any value for which they are both defined.

The factorial function was characterized above as the "limit" of the sequence of f_i. But this is a very simple notion of limit: factorial is simply the **union** of all sequence elements, each of which (viewed once again as a set of pairs) is a subset of the next. The union may not be computed by a finite number of iterations of φ; however, for any natural integer n, there exists a function in the sequence (namely f_{n+1}) attainable through a finite number of iterations of φ, which is defined for n, and yields the result (namely $n!$) which would be returned by the union.

This construction is representative of a general technique for solving fixpoint equations of the form $h = \tau(h)$ for some functional τ: start with the "least defined" function $\varnothing$ and iterate with τ. The union of all the functions obtained as successive sequence elements is the desired fixpoint.

Such an iteration strategy, outlined here (not yet in full rigor) in the specific context of computing a recursively defined function as fixpoint of a functional, is indeed fruitful for understanding recursive definitions in the most general case. It serves as the basis for the theory of recursive definitions developed in the rest of this chapter.

8.4.3 Bottom-up and top-down recursive computations

The just outlined interpretation of recursive definitions highlights the important difference between "top-down" and "bottom-up" views of recursive computation.

When you write a recursive definition – of a routine, a grammar, a meaning function – you take a top-down view of the computation: you define a certain mechanism in terms of the same mechanism applied to other, normally simpler, elements. For example, you define *factorial* as applied to n in terms of *factorial* applied to $n-1$. The act of faith – the leap into the unknown – involved in using the mechanism itself in the definition is justified by the intuitive understanding that the computation will go "down" (be applied to simpler and simpler elements) until it reaches cases for which the computation produces a result without any further use of recursion.

The fixpoint interpretation is the bottom-up view of the same computation. The process starts from the simplest components of the fixpoint and accumulates new ones through successively higher levels. To produce each level, it applies the definition's functional to the elements of the preceding level. For example, to compute factorial as a fixpoint, you start at level 0 with the empty function, then apply φ once to get a function with just one pair (level 1), then apply φ again to this function and so on.

Viewed in this way, a recursive definition covers all objects which may be obtained through a finite, although unbounded, number of iterations of the definition's functional. Here no act of faith is required: we simply have a very pragmatic method for defining a set by a recurrence equation, and using that equation to build the set from the ground up.

8.5 SOLVING RECURSIVE EQUATIONS

It is time now to provide a correct mathematical framework for interpreting recursive definitions in the above spirit.

8.5.1 Finding a fixpoint: stability

Not much is needed, in fact, to ensure that the above method yields a fixpoint. We are trying to solve

$$h = \tau(h)$$

where τ is a total function whose possible arguments are (possibly partial) functions. Since functions are a special case of sets, let us generalize the problem to τ having arbitrary sets as arguments. In the scheme illustrated by the above informal example derivation, the candidate fixpoint is

$$\tau_\infty \triangleq \varnothing \cup \tau(\varnothing) \cup \tau(\tau(\varnothing)) \cup \dots$$

which may be defined more precisely and concisely as

$$\tau_\infty \triangleq \bigcup_{i\,:\,N} t_i$$

with the sequence t being defined inductively as

[8.10]
$$t_0 \triangleq \varnothing$$
$$t_{i+1} \triangleq t_i \cup \tau(t_i) \qquad \text{for any } i \in N$$

Defining t_{i+1} (in the last line) as just $\tau(t_i)$ would in the end yield the same τ_∞; the form given has the advantage of yielding a sequence t which is a **subset chain**, that is to say a sequence of subsets such that each element is a subset of the next. A subset chain whose elements are functions may be called a **function chain**.

It is easily seen by induction that for any i:

[8.11]
$$t_{i+1} = \bigcup_{j\,:\,0..\,i} \tau(t_j)$$

Under what conditions is τ_∞ indeed a fixpoint of τ? In other words, what is required to ensure that $\tau(\tau_\infty) = \tau_\infty$? The sought property means:

$$\tau\left(\bigcup_{i\,:\,N} t_i\right) = \bigcup_{i\,:\,N} t_i$$

We can omit t_0, the empty set, from the right-hand side (in fact, since t is a subset chain, we could remove any finite number of elements without changing the union). Using the set $N^{\bullet}$ of positive integers, this means rewriting the right-hand side as

$$\bigcup_{i\,:\,N^{\bullet}} t_i$$

or equivalently

$$\bigcup_{i\,:\,N} t_{i+1}$$

which, from [8.11], means:

$$\bigcup_{i\,:\,N} \tau\,(t_i)$$

In other words, τ_∞ is a fixpoint of τ if and only if the following property holds:

[8.12]

$$\tau\,(\bigcup_{i\,:\,N} t_i)\ =\ \bigcup_{i\,:\,N} \tau\,(t_i)$$

A total function τ which satisfies this property for any subset chain t_i (not just for the sequence t_i as defined in [8.10]) will be called "chain-stable", or just **stable** for short.[1]

For a total function τ to have a fixpoint, then, it suffices that τ be stable. Although not necessary, this is a very general condition, and it seems appropriate to limit our attention to those fixpoint equations whose functionals are stable.

This gives us a clear interpretation for recursive "definitions": we will only accept those which can be written in the form $h = \tau\,(h)$, for some stable τ. Then such a definition will be understood to stand for τ_∞.

What remains to be done, after making the above definitions more formal (next section) is to show that the total functions of interest, especially for abstract syntax and denotational semantics, are stable.

8.5.2 Precise definitions

The following are precise definitions of the previous notions.

The discussion uses infinite sequences. An infinite sequence s over a set X may be formally defined as a total function from N to X. The i-th **element** of the sequence, is $s\,(i)$ – the result of applying the function to i. The i-th element may also be written s_i.

---

[1] Stability is a special case of "continuity" studied later in this chapter (8.8.15). The term "stable" is used here for the set-theoretical property, to avoid any confusion with the more general notion, applicable to total functions in ordered sets.

This definition is a generalization of finite sequences (as introduced in 2.4 and formalized in 3.9.3, with the corresponding operators definitions in 3.4.3). Several of the operators on finite sequences apply to infinite sequences as well (exercise 3.13).[2] The following figure (generalized from its correspondent for finite sequences, figure 3.4, page 77) illustrates the idea.

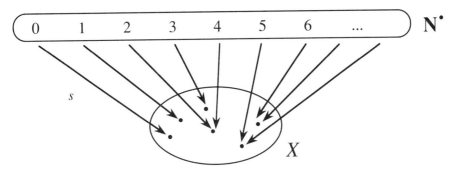

Figure 8.2: An infinite sequence as function

Let s be a sequence over X and τ a total function in $X \longrightarrow Y$ for some Y. Function $s ; \tau$, the composition of s and τ, is a sequence over Y. As illustrated below, this is the sequence obtained by applying τ to the successive elements of s. (The notation $\tau(s)$, which might at first suggest itself, would not be correct mathematically.)

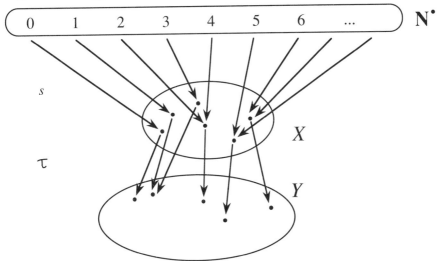

Figure 8.3: Composition of a sequence and a total function

---

[2] For finite sequences, the domain is an interval of the form $1..n$ for some n. For the discussion in this chapter, it is more convenient to start legal indices at 0.

The only sequences of interest for this discussion have elements which are subsets of a given set. As a special case, this includes sequences of functions since a function in $A \nrightarrow B$ is a subset of $A \times B$. In the rest of this chapter, "sequence" without further qualification means "infinite sequence of subsets"; "set" without further qualification means "set of subsets". X and Y in the following definitions and theorems denote such (arbitrary) sets. Because all objects involved are subsets, we can freely subject them to subset operations such as $\cup$ and $\subseteq$.

The **union** of a sequence s over an arbitrary X is defined as the following subset of X:

$$\text{union } s \triangleq \bigcup_{i\,:\,\mathbf{N}} s_i$$

In other words, a member of X belongs to **union** s if and only if it belongs to s_i for at least one integer i.

A subset chain is simply a sequence of subsets such that each element is included in the next, functions being again a special case:

Definition (Subset Chain, Function Chain): A subset chain in X is an infinite sequence s over X such that, for any $i : \mathbf{N}$,

$$s_i \subseteq s_{i+1}$$

A subset chain whose elements are functions is also called a function chain.

Function chains are particularly interesting. In a function chain, each element is a subset of the next element. This means that each successive element may bring a little more information – a few more *<argument, result>* pairs – than the previous one. An example was the sequence of functions f_i used in 8.4.2, each of which extended the partial factorial function to one more possible argument.

For chains, **union** s has a simple interpretation:

[8.13]

Theorem (Chain Union): If s is a chain of subsets of X, then
$$\text{union } s = \{x : X \mid \exists\, n : \mathbf{N} \bullet \forall\, m \in \mathbf{N} \bullet$$
$$(m \geq n) \supset x \in s_m \}$$

Proof: x is a member of **union** s if and only if $x \in s_n$ for some n; since s is a chain, this is the same as saying that $x \in s_m$ for all $m \geq n$. $\square$

The next notion is strictness:

> **Definition** (Strictness): A total function
>
> $$\tau : X \rightarrow Y$$
>
> is strict if and only if, for any a, $b : X$ such that $a \subseteq b$,
>
> $$\tau \, (a) \subseteq \tau \, (b)$$

This may be generalized to total functions of two or more arguments. A total function τ of signature

$$\tau : \ldots \times X \times \ldots \rightarrow Y$$

is strict on its i-th argument, corresponding to X, iff for any a, $b : X$ such that $a \subseteq b$:

$$\tau \, (\ldots, a, \ldots) \subseteq \tau \, (\ldots, b, \ldots)$$

all the arguments not shown being the same on both sides.

Saying that a function is strict, without specifying on what arguments, will mean that it is strict on all arguments. This is justified by the following result:

[8.14]

> **Theorem** (Separate Argument Strictness): A total function is strict on every argument if and only if it is strict on all of its arguments taken together.

Proof: Consider a function of two arguments (the generalization to more than two is immediate). Assume for clarity that it is of the form **infix** "§", used in infix form. Being "strict on all arguments taken together" means that, whenever $a \times b \subseteq c \times d$, then $a \, \S \, c \subseteq b \, \S \, d$. The theorem follows from the observation that $a \times b \subseteq c \times d$ is the same as $(a \subseteq d) \wedge (b \subseteq d)$.   □

Strictness is an important requirement on the functionals involved in fixpoint equations. Let τ be such a (total) functional, acting on possibly partial functions. For τ to be strict means that, for any f, $\tau \, (f)$ is defined wherever f is defined, and yields the same value. In other words, applying τ to f does not "lose" any of the values of f; it may only add new values, at points where f was not defined.

As a counter-example, the following functional is clearly not strict:

$$bizarre : (\mathbf{N} \twoheadrightarrow \mathbf{N}) \rightarrow (\mathbf{N} \twoheadrightarrow \mathbf{N})$$

$$bizarre \triangleq \lambda f \bullet \{ <n, 0> \in \mathbf{N} \times \mathbf{N} \mid n \notin \mathbf{dom} \, f \}$$

Function *bizarre* (f) is defined (and yields value 0) only for those arguments for which f is not defined. A recursive definition specifying the values of f in terms of the values of *bizarre* (f) would be meaningless.

Strict functions have a direct connection with chains:

[8.15]

> **Theorem** (Chain Transformation): Let s be a chain over X and τ be a total function in $X \rightarrow Y$. Then $s \, ; \, \tau$ is a chain over Y.

Proof: Let $t \triangleq \tau \, ; \, s$. For any i, t_i is $\tau \, (s_i)$ and t_{i+1} is $\tau \, (s_{i+1})$. Because s is a chain, $s_i \subseteq s_{i+1}$. Because τ is strict, this implies that $t_i \subseteq t_{i+1}$. □

The last needed notion is stability:

[8.16]

> **Definition** (Stable Function): A total function $\tau : X \rightarrow Y$ is stable if and only if:
>
> 1   • τ is strict.
>
> 2   • For any chain s over X, $\tau \, (\textbf{union } s) \subseteq \textbf{union } (s \, ; \, \tau)$

The previous theorem indicates that the right-hand side is a chain since τ is strict.

At first sight, this definition of stability seems different from the one given in the earlier less formal discussion ([8.12], page 240). The apparent contradiction is resolved by the following theorem:

> **Theorem** (Stability and Strictness): A total function $\tau : X \rightarrow Y$ is stable if and only if, for any chain s over X,
>
> $$\tau \, (\textbf{union } s) = \textbf{union } (s \, ; \, \tau)$$

Proof: Call *equal* the condition on chains given in the theorem (where the two sides are equal), and *subset_strict* the condition given by the definition of stability [8.16]. We must prove that a chain s which satisfies one of these conditions satisfies the other.

Assume first that s satisfies *equal*. We must prove that s is strict. Let x and y be such that $x \subseteq y$. Then the sequence s such that $s_0 = x$ and $s_i = y$ for any $i \geq 1$ is a chain. Property *equal* applied to that chain means that

$$\tau \, (\bigcup_{i \, : \, \textbf{N}} s_i) = \bigcup_{i \, : \, \textbf{N}} \tau \, (s_i)$$

The left-hand side is simply $\tau \, (y)$; the right-hand side is $\tau \, (x) \cup \tau \, (y)$. It is a simple set-theoretical property that, for any two subsets a and b, $a = (b \cup a)$ implies $b \subseteq a$. Therefore $\tau \, (x) \subseteq \tau \, (y)$ and τ is strict.

Conversely, assume s satisfies *subset_strict*. We must prove that for any chain s

$$\bigcup_{i:\mathbf{N}} \tau(s_i) \subseteq \tau(\bigcup_{i:\mathbf{N}} s_i)$$

since *subset_strict* already guarantees the reverse inclusion. For every i, the following property holds:

$$s_i \subseteq \bigcup_{j:\mathbf{N}} s_j$$

Since τ is strict, this implies:

$$\tau(s_i) \subseteq \tau(\bigcup_{j:\mathbf{N}} s_j)$$

Since this inclusion is true for all i, every component of the union

$$\bigcup_{i:\mathbf{N}} \tau(s_i)$$

is a subset of the right-hand side. The entire union, then, is also a subset, proving the desired property.   □

To prove that a certain function is stable, you may find, depending on the circumstances, one of the two forms of the property (*subset_strict*, which treats strictness separately, and *equal*, which relies on a single property) more convenient than the other. Both forms will be used below.

To understand stability better, it is useful, as always, to see a counter-example. Even simple functions may not be stable! Consider

> *unstable* : $\mathbf{P}(\mathbf{N}) \rightarrow \mathbf{P}(\mathbf{N})$
>
> *unstable* (X) ≜ **if finite** X **then** X **else** $X \cup \{0\}$

This function is strict since if $X \subseteq Y$ and X is infinite then Y must be infinite too. Let us prove, however, that *unstable* is not stable. Let s be the sequence over $\mathbf{P}(\mathbf{N})$ such that, for any i, s_i is the interval $1 .. i+1$. Then **union** s is $N^{\bullet}$, the set of positive integers. This is an infinite set, so

> *unstable* (**union** s) = $\mathbf{N}^{\bullet} \cup \{0\}$
>
>   = $\mathbf{N}$

Since every s_i is finite, the sequence s ; *unstable* is the same as s, so that

> **union** $(s$; *unstable*$)$ = $\mathbf{N}^{\bullet}$

meaning that *unstable* (**union** s) is not a subset of **union** $(s$; *unstable*).   □

As with strictness, we can extend the definition of stability to the notion of a multi-argument function being stable on one of these arguments. "Stable" without qualification will mean stable on all arguments. This is justified by the following result:

[8.17]

> **Theorem** (Separate Argument Stability): A total function is stable on every argument if and only if it is stable on all of its arguments taken together.

Proof: The strictness part has already been taken care of ([8.14], page 243). What remains to prove is that if a strict function **infix** "§" (assumed for simplicity to be of two arguments) is separately stable on each argument, in other words such that for any subsets x, y and subset chains a, b:

$$(\bigcup_{i:N} a_i) \ § \ y \ \subseteq \ \bigcup_{i:N} (a_i \ § \ y) \qquad\qquad \text{-- "§" is left-stable}$$

$$x \ § \ (\bigcup_{j:N} b_j) \subseteq \bigcup_{j:N} (x \ § \ b_j) \qquad\qquad \text{-- "§" is right-stable}$$

then, also for any x, y, a, b:

[8.18]
$$(\bigcup_{i:N} a_i) \ § \ (\bigcup_{j:N} b_j) \ \subseteq \ \bigcup_{i:N} (a_i \ § \ b_i) \qquad\qquad \text{-- "§" is stable}$$

Note that [8.18] may be expressed more concisely as (using the "&" dispatching function introduced in 2.8.1) as:

union a § **union** b $\subseteq$ **union** $((a$ & $b)$; "§")

Developing the left-hand side of [8.18] (under the first form given), we get:

$$(\bigcup_{i:N} a_i) \ § \ (\bigcup_{j:N} b_j) \ \subseteq \ \bigcup_{i:N} (a_i \ § \ (\bigcup_{j:N} b_j))$$

-- By applying the left-stability of "§"

$$\subseteq \ \bigcup_{i:N} (\bigcup_{j:N} a_i \ § \ b_j)$$

-- By applying the right-stability of "§"

-- to each element of the union

$$\subseteq \ \bigcup_{i,j:N \times N} a_i \ § \ b_j$$

The desired right-hand side is $\bigcup\limits_{i\,:\,N} a_i \,\S\, b_i$; the last union expression obtained contains many more terms and so appears to denote a larger set. But this is not the case: for every pair of integers i, j, there exists an integer q such that $a_i \,\S\, b_j \subseteq a_q \,\S\, b_q$; that q is simply max (i, j). This property follows from the observation that our sequences are chains, and from the strictness of "§". As a result, each element of the union in the last expression obtained is a subset of $a_q \,\S\, b_q$ for some q, which implies that the whole expression is a subset of

$$\bigcup\limits_{i\,:\,N} a_i \,\S\, b_i$$

□

The next result is the main theorem of this chapter:

Theorem (Fixpoints of Stable Functions): Let $\tau : X \longrightarrow X$ be a stable total function. Let t be the sequence defined inductively by

- $t_0 \triangleq \varnothing$

- $t_{i+1} \triangleq \tau\,(t_i)$ for any $i : N$

This sequence is a chain.

Let $\tau_\infty \triangleq$ **union** t. Then τ_∞ is a fixpoint of τ.

The proof was given earlier (8.5.1) but may now be rephrased more concisely. First the strictness of τ implies that sequence t is a chain. (In other words, the sequence is the same as defined in [8.10].) Applying the definition of stability to the chain t yields

$$\tau\,(\tau_\infty) = \textbf{union} \;\; (t \;;\; \tau)$$

But $t \;;\; \tau$ is simply t deprived of its first element; since every chain element is a subset of the next, removing the first element does not change the **union**, so that the above means

$$\tau\,(\tau_\infty) = \tau_\infty$$

□

8.5.3 The smallest fixpoint

For any stable function τ, we now have a fixpoint, τ_∞ (and even a computational technique to obtain it, although in finite time the technique will only yield part of the answer).

Of course there may be more than one fixpoint for a given function. How "good" a fixpoint is τ_∞ in this case?

The following theorem gives the answer:

[8.19]

> **Theorem** (Smallest Fixpoint): Let τ be a stable functional and fp be a fixpoint of τ. Then $\tau_\infty \subseteq fp$.

Proof: Let us prove by induction that $t_i \subseteq fp$ for every integer i. Since τ_∞ is the union of all subsets t_i, this will yield the result.

The base step is trivial: t_0 is ∅, and ∅ $\subseteq A$ for any A. For the induction step, assume that $t_i \subseteq fp$. Then t_{i+1} is $\tau (t_i)$. Since τ is strict:

$$t_{i+1} \subseteq \tau (fp)$$

But $\tau (fp) = fp$ since fp is a fixpoint of τ. This proves the induction step.   □

8.5.4 Why choose the smallest?

The last theorem provides insight into the nature of τ_∞. Being the smallest fixpoint of τ makes τ_∞ the "least committing" one. This is the set containing objects that must be members of every fixpoint – but those objects only. Set τ_∞ is restricted to objects which can be strictly deduced from the recursive definition $f = \tau (f)$, without any "personal initiative" from whomever (human or automaton) is entrusted with the task of solving the corresponding recursive equation.

For fixpoints of functionals, "smallest" means "most partial": τ_∞ will be the function which is defined for the fewest possible argument values compatible with the recursive definition.

One of the recursively defined integer functions, as introduced above, provides an immediate illustration. (We must accept that the corresponding functional is stable, although this has not been proved yet.) For the functional

   δ ≜ λ d • λ n • **if** $n = 0$ **then** 1
                      elsif $n = 1$ **then** d (3)
                      else d ($n-2$) **end**

you can see immediately (by building the chain of successive functions d_i, as was done for the f_i in 8.4.2) that δ_∞ is the constant partial function defined only for even integers, with value 1:

   δ_∞ ≜ {<n, 1> | n ∈ EVEN }

(*EVEN* and *ODD* are the odd and even subsets of **N**.)

Function δ_∞ is not, however, the only fixpoint of δ: as noted (page 229), there are indeed an infinity of fixpoints, all of the form

$$\delta_\infty \uplus odd_{ov}$$

where odd_{ov}, for an arbitrary integer ov, is also a constant partial function, this one defined only for odd integers and yielding value ov:

$$odd_{ov} \triangleq \{<n, ov> \mid n \in ODD\}$$

Using any fixpoint other than δ_∞, however, requires that we try to get more out of the recursive definition $d = \delta(d)$ than what it really says. By sticking to δ_∞ and not choosing any particular ov, we refuse to take any initiative not implied by the definition.

The choice of the smallest fixpoint is particularly significant for the functionals involved in semantic specifications. If the definition of a meaning function is recursive, we want to interpret the definition as denoting the function which expresses the essential semantics of the language.

If τ is the functional used in the recursive definition of a meaning function and τ_∞ is not defined for a certain argument c, this means that the computation represented by c may not terminate, at least on some hardware, in some implementations or under some circumstances. If there are other fixpoints, the above theorem tells us that they must be more defined (less partial) than τ_∞, although they must agree with (yield the same results as) τ_∞ wherever τ_∞ is defined, this being a formal version of the **portability** requirement of language implementations.

What τ_∞ gives us is the semantic properties that must be satisfied by **all** hardware, with all implementations and under all circumstances. What any other fixpoint gives us is a property of computations which only holds for some hardware, implementations or circumstances. This would not be appropriate as semantic specification for the language: if a computation *may* not terminate, its denotation *must* not be defined.

This discussion completes the theoretical treatment of recursive definitions. What remains to be seen is that the functions involved in previously encountered definitions do satisfy the stability requirement. This is the object of the following section.

8.6 STABLE FUNCTIONS

For some of the total functions used in recursive definitions of syntactic domains and meaning functions, the arguments are arbitrary subsets; in other cases, the arguments are functions. The corresponding stability properties will be studied in turn.

8.6.1 Stable subset operations

The first results cover the basic total functions on sets:

> **Theorem (Stable Subset Operations)**: For any set X, the following total functions on subsets of X are stable:
>
> 1. • Constant function: $\lambda\, a \bullet m$, where m is a subset of X.
> 2. • Identity: $\lambda\, a \bullet a$
> 3. • Union: $\lambda\, a, b \bullet a \cup b$
> 4. • Intersection: $\lambda\, a, b \bullet a \cap b$
> 5. • Composition of stable functions: $\lambda\, a \bullet \psi\,(\tau\,(a))$, where τ and ψ are stable.
> 6. • First projection: $\lambda\, a, b \bullet a$, as well as second projection and the generalization to more arguments.

In the lambda expressions of the theorem, a and b range over $\mathbf{P}\,(X)$.

Proof: Clauses 1, 2 and 6 are trivial. Clause 5 expresses that if for any chains s and t

$$\tau\,(\mathbf{union}\; s\,) = \mathbf{union}\;(s\; ;\; \tau)$$

$$\psi\,(\mathbf{union}\; t\,) = \mathbf{union}\;(t\; ;\; \psi)$$

then for any chain u

$$\psi\,(\tau\,(\mathbf{union}\; u\,)) = \mathbf{union}\;(u\; ;\; \tau\; ;\; \psi)$$

The conclusion follows directly from the premises if we take first $s \triangleq u$ and then $t \triangleq (u\; ;\; \tau)$.

Clauses 3 and 4 are a consequence of the following simple set-theoretical properties, true of any sequences h and k of subsets of a given set X:

$$\bigcup_{i\,:\,\mathbf{N}} (h_i \cup k_i) = \left(\bigcup_{i\,:\,\mathbf{N}} h_i\right) \cup \left(\bigcup_{i\,:\,\mathbf{N}} k_i\right)$$

$$\bigcup_{i\,:\,\mathbf{N}} (h_i \cap k_i) \subseteq \left(\bigcup_{i\,:\,\mathbf{N}} h_i\right) \cap \left(\bigcup_{i\,:\,\mathbf{N}} k_i\right)$$

          □

The last property is only an inclusion, as written, if h and k are arbitrary subsets of X. In the case of subset chains, however, it is an equality. (This is another way of expressing that $\cap$ is strict.)

Lest you conclude hastily that *all* subset operations of interest are stable, you may wish to check two counter-examples: set difference and complement.

8.6.2 Stable predicates and fixpoint induction

An important group of total functions is predicates, whose target set is **B**. At first, the preceding theory seems not to apply, since it requires functions whose targets, as well as their sources, are sets of subsets. We can easily correct this, however, by identifying **B** with

$$\{\varnothing, E\}$$

where E is some (arbitrary but fixed) non-empty set. In this way, **B** is viewed as a member of **P** (E), with *true* being identified with $\varnothing$, the empty subset, and *false* with E, the full subset. (Not the reverse! See exercise 8.2.)

The interpretation extends immediately to boolean operations: we may interpret $\wedge$ as $\cup$, $\vee$ as $\cap$, $\supset$ (implies) as $\subseteq$, $\neg$ (negation) as complement.

With **B** defined in this way, the stability of a predicate π means that, if π is true of all elements of a sequence, π will also be true of the sequence's **union**. Note that the stability of π does not tell us anything if π is *false* for all sequence elements. To prove that π is *false* for the **union** in this case, we must prove separately that the predicate **not** p is stable.

The basic result on predicates is the following:

[8.20]

> **Theorem** (Stable Predicates): The following predicates are stable:
>
> 1 • Equality: $\lambda\, x, y \bullet x = y$.
>
> 2 • Inclusion: $\lambda\, x, y \bullet x \subseteq y$
>
> 3 • Boolean combinators: $\lambda\, x, y \bullet \psi\,(x)\, \S\, \xi\,(y)$ where ψ and ξ are stable predicates and $\S$ is any of the boolean operators $\wedge$ (and), $\vee$ (or) and $\supset$ (implies).

Proof: Clause 1 will follow from 2 and 3 since $x = y$ for subsets may be expressed as $x \subseteq y \,\wedge\, y \subseteq x$. For clause 2, let us prove that $\subseteq$ is stable on its first argument. This means that for any chain s, if for some b

$$\forall\, i : \mathbf{N} \bullet s_i \subseteq b$$

then

$$\bigcup_{i\,:\,\mathbf{N}} s_i \subseteq b$$

which is certainly a correct deduction. Similar reasoning proves stability on the second argument.

With the chosen interpretation of the boolean operators, the stability of $\wedge$ and $\vee$ (clause 3) is simply a special case of the stability of $\cup$ and $\cap$ given by the Stable Subset Operations theorem, and the stability of $\supset$ is a restatement of clause 2. $\square$

Since the Stable Subset Operations theorem allowed composition of stable functions, the clauses given yield many other properties, for example (from clause 1) that for any stable functions ψ and ξ the following predicate is stable:

$$\lambda\, x, y \bullet \psi\,(x)\ =\ \xi\,(y)$$

Here too, you should not conclude that all interesting predicates are stable. For example (as you are invited to check by devising a counter-example), applying the negation operator to a stable predicate may not yield a stable predicate. Another non-stable predicate is:

[8.21]
$$partial\ \triangleq\ \lambda\, f : X \nrightarrow Y \bullet \mathbf{dom}\ f \neq X$$

This predicate yields *true* if and only if its argument is a partial function. To see that this is not stable, just look at a chain of function such as the f_i: every f_i is partial, but their fixpoint, the factorial function, is total.

A stable predicate, if satisfied by all elements of a chain, will also be satisfied by the chain's smallest fixpoint (its **union**). This is what make this notion important as one of the major tools for proving properties of recursively defined objects (sets or functions). The resulting general method, which extends standard induction on integers, is called **fixpoint induction**[3] and is captured by the following theorem.

[8.22]

> **Theorem**: Let $\tau \colon X \longrightarrow X$ be a stable total function and π a stable predicate on X. If the following two properties hold:
>
> - $\pi\ (\varnothing_X \rightarrow x)$
> - $\forall\, h : X \longrightarrow X \bullet \pi\ (h) \supset \pi\ (\tau\ (h))$
>
> Then $\pi\ (\tau_\infty)$ holds, where τ_∞ is the smallest fixpoint of τ.

Proof: The theorem's two premises imply, by ordinary induction, that $\pi\ (t_i)$ is true for every element t_i in the sequence that serves to define τ_∞. The conclusion then follows from the stability of π. $\square$

---

[3] The generalization to "continuous" predicates (8.8.15 below) is also known as **Scott's induction**. Continuous predicates are also called "admissible".

As an example of using fixpoint induction, consider the functional ϕ used in the recursive "definition" of the factorial function ([8.3], page 232). Although the stability of ϕ itself will only be proved later, let us accept that ϕ is indeed stable. Then it has a smallest fixpoint ϕ_∞.

Function ϕ_∞ is what the recursive "definition" of factorial yields when interpreted rigorously according to the results of this chapter. Let us prove that ϕ_∞ is indeed what the informal interpretation of recursive definitions suggests it should be: *factorial*, the factorial function. Consider the predicate:

is_factorial_approximation: $((\mathbf{N} \nrightarrow \mathbf{N}) \rightarrow \mathbf{B})$

is_factorial_approximation $\triangleq \lambda\, h \bullet h \subseteq factorial$

The stability of *is_factorial_approximation* follows from the Stable Subset Operations theorem since this predicate is obtained by composition of total functions shown to be stable: the constant functional $\lambda\, h \bullet factorial$ and the " $\subseteq$ " operation. It is easy to prove that both of the following hold:

is_factorial_approximation $(\varnothing)$

is_factorial_approximation $(h) \supset$ is_factorial_approximation $(\phi\,(h))$

By fixpoint induction, this yields

is_factorial_approximation (ϕ_∞)

In other words, $\phi_\infty \subseteq factorial$ holds.

We must prove that ϕ_∞ is the factorial function, not just a subset. To deduce $\phi_\infty = factorial$, it suffices to prove that ϕ_∞ is total; if both h and k are total functions with the same source set, $h \subseteq k$ is the same as $h = k$. For this part of the proof, however, fixpoint induction is of no use. In fact, every f_i is partial, so fixpoint induction, assuming it were applicable, would enable us to prove that ϕ_∞ is *not* total! But we precisely saw that the *partial* predicate [8.21] is not stable, excluding any use of fixpoint induction here. So we must use other means to prove that ϕ_∞ is total.

The proof is easy. If ϕ_∞ were partial, some integer n would not be a member of **dom** ϕ_∞. But it is easily seen ([8.9] and exercise 8.1) that the domain of f_{n+1} is $0 .. n$. This yields a contradiction.   □

The stable predicates used in fixpoint induction bear a close relationship to the loop invariants which we will encounter in axiomatic semantics in the next chapter (see 9.7.6). The pattern seen in the last example, where the proofs require two separate parts -- a proof that the fixpoint enjoys certain properties, using fixpoint induction, and a different proof to show that the fixpoint is a total function – anticipates the separate proofs of invariance and termination used in the "partial correctness" approach (which will be studied in 9.4.3 and 9.7.7). Chapter 10 explores the relationship formally.

8.6.3 Stable functionals

The Stable Subset Operations theorem applies to the special case of functionals (total functions on sets of functions), since their arguments, functions, are also subsets. In this case, however, further properties are applicable, as given by the following theorem.

> **Theorem** (Stable Functionals): The following total functions, admitting functions as arguments, are stable:
>
> 1 • Dispatching: **infix** "&"
>
> 2 • Parallel application: **infix** "#"
>
> 3 • Restriction: $\lambda f \bullet f \backslash A$, for any subset A of the source set of f.
>
> 4 • Overriding union: **infix** "⩊", when applied to operands with disjoint domains.
>
> 5 • Composition: **infix** ";"

To avoid any confusion, remember that stability is only meaningful for total functions, and that by definition a functional is such a total function, although its arguments, themselves functions, may be partial. The functionals "&" and "#" were introduced in 2.8.1.

The theorem is generic, applying to functionals over any appropriate sets of functions. More precisely, for any U, V, X, Y, Z, the signatures of the functionals involved are:

"&": $(U \nrightarrow X) \times (U \nrightarrow Y) \longrightarrow (U \nrightarrow (X \times Y))$

"#": $(U \nrightarrow X) \times (V \nrightarrow U) \longrightarrow ((U \times X) \nrightarrow (V \times Y))$

Restriction: $(X \nrightarrow Y) \longrightarrow (X \nrightarrow Y)$ (for a given A).

"⩊": $(X \nrightarrow Y) \times (X \nrightarrow Y) \longrightarrow (X \nrightarrow Y)$

";": $(X \nrightarrow Y) \times (Y \nrightarrow Z) \longrightarrow (X \nrightarrow Z)$

Do not confuse the stability of the ";" functional operator (clause 5 of this theorem) with the earlier result that the composition of two stable functions is stable (clause 5 of the Stable Subset Operations theorem, page 250).

Proof: Clauses 1 and 2 are immediate: simply express the definition of stability and apply it to "&" and "#"; this can be done for each argument separately thanks to the Separate Argument theorem ([8.17], page 246). For restriction (clause 3), we must prove that for any function chain s:

$$\bigcup_{i\,:\,\mathbf{N}} (s_i \backslash A) = (\bigcup_{i\,:\,\mathbf{N}} s_i) \backslash A$$

But (see 2.7.3) for any function h in $X \nrightarrow Y$, $h \setminus A$ is simply $h \cap (A \times Y)$. Then the property follows from the distributivity of $\cap$ with respect to $\cup$.

In clause 4, the overriding union is not overriding any more since it is restricted to functions with disjoint domains. Then we simply have a special case of the stability of the "$\cup$" operation. Non-disjoint domains would still be acceptable for functions which agree on their domains. Without this hypothesis, however, "$\uplus$" is not strict (and hence not stable), as shown by the following counter-example. Take

$$h \triangleq \{<0, a>\}, \quad k \triangleq \emptyset$$
$$h' \triangleq \{<0, a>\}, \quad k' \triangleq \{<0, b>\}$$

Then $h \subseteq h'$ and $k \subseteq k'$, but:

$$h \uplus k = \{<0, a>\}$$
$$h' \uplus k' = \{<0, b>\}$$

and the first of these functions is not a subset of the second.

For clause 5, the proof is greatly facilitated by the Separate Argument theorem [8.17], which allows us to prove left-stability and right-stability separately. Right stability means that, for any function a and any function chain b with the appropriate signatures,

$$a \; ; \bigcup_{i:N} b_i = \bigcup_{i:N} (a \; ; b_i)$$

Let us develop the left-hand side (omitting the declarations of x, y, z, which range over the source, middle and target sets of the functions, and of i, which ranges over $\mathbf{N}$):

$$a \; ; \bigcup_{i:N} b_i = \{<x, z> \mid \exists \, y \bullet <x, y> \in a \, \wedge \, <y, z> \in \bigcup_{i:N} b_i\}$$

-- By the definition of composition

$$= \{<x, z> \mid \exists \, y \bullet \exists \, i \bullet <x, y> \in a \, \wedge \, <y, z> \in b_i\}$$

$$= \{<x, z> \mid \exists \, i \bullet \exists \, y \bullet <x, y> \in a \, \wedge \, <y, z> \in b_i\}$$

-- By reversing the $\exists$

$$= \{<x, z> \mid \exists \, i \bullet <x, z> \in (a \cdot \; ; b_i)\}$$

$$= \bigcup_{i:N} (a \; ; b_i)$$

Left stability is proved similarly.   □

This proof of the Stable Functionals theorem completes the major aim of this chapter: showing that the recursively defined meaning functions of denotational semantics make sense. The definition of $M_{Instruction}$ and auxiliary functions (6.5) only involves the following kinds of operations on functions:

- Functionals covered in the Stable Functionals theorem.
- Composition of functionals.
- Reasoning by case analysis on specimens of choice constructs, which may be interpreted as overriding union on arguments with disjoint domains (see below).

All these operations are stable; this guarantees that the recursive equations have fixpoints.

> You may have noted that some definitions (for example the definition of $M_{Conditional}$ in 6.5.5) use non-stable functionals such as set difference. This is of no consequence, however, since these functionals only serve to define sets such as *Where_true*, *Where_false*, used as operands to the restriction operator (itself stable). They do not otherwise participate in defining the functionals of the recursive definitions.

What the fixpoints mean in practice corresponds to the intuitive interpretation of recursive definitions. Taking as example one of the most interesting recursive definitions, M_{Loop} $[l]$ was defined (6.5.6) as

$$(Id \setminus Where\_false) \;\underline{\cup}$$

$$((M_{Instruction} \; [l.body]; M_{Loop} \; [l]) \setminus Where\_true)$$

Now we know how to interpret this definition: M_{Loop} is the infinite union

$$ML_0 \cup ML_1 \cup ML_2...$$

Starting with $\varnothing$ as argument, ML_i is the i-th iteration of the functional

$$loop\_functional \;\triangleq\; \lambda \, m \, \bullet$$

$$(Id \setminus Where\_false) \;\underline{\cup}$$

$$((M_{Instruction} \; [l.body]; m \; [l]) \setminus Where\_true)$$

and $M_{instruction}$ is the fixpoint of *loop_functional*. Applying the functional to $\varnothing$, we only get a contribution from the first operand of the "$\underline{\cup}$" since the composition of any function with $\varnothing$ (in the second operand) yields $\varnothing$:

$$ML_0 \;\triangleq\; Id \setminus Where\_false$$

ML_0 defines the semantics of all computations for which the loop body is executed zero times because the initial state belongs to $Id \setminus Where\_false$ – meaning that the loop test is initially false. Then:

$$ML_1 \;\triangleq\; ML_0 \cup loop\_functional \, (ML_0)$$

$$= (Id \setminus Where\_false) \;\underline{\cup}\; ((M_{Instruction} \; [l.body]; ML_0 \; [l]) \setminus Where\_true)$$

$$= (Id \setminus Where\_false) \;\underline{\cup}$$

$$((M_{Instruction} \; [l.body]; Id \setminus Where\_false) \setminus Where\_true)$$

The first operand of the "$\lor$" is the same as ML_0; the second describes the computations for which the loop body is executed once, producing a state in which the loop test is false. In other words, ML_1 defines the semantics of computations for which the loop body is executed at most once. In general, ML_i describes the semantics of computations for which the loop body is executed at most i times.

> For some i, of course, ML_i may be the same as ML_{i-1} if the program is such that the loop cannot be executed exactly i times, or it may be the empty function if the program is such that the loop is always executed at least $i + 1$ times.

ML_{Loop}, the union of all ML_i, describes the full semantics of the loop – for any possible number of executions of the body.

8.6.4 Abstract syntax constructors

We are now in a position to justify the recursive definitions of constructs in abstract syntax (chapter 3). It suffices to check that the operators involved in defining constructs are stable. There are three such constructors, corresponding to the three kinds of production: aggregate, choice, sequence.

A mathematical model for these operators was introduced in 3.9.3. Referring to the results of that section, we may consider that the following total functions are involved, for all possible positive integers n, and all possible members x of the set of tags T used in defining aggregates:

[8.23]

$$choice_n \triangleq \lambda x \bullet x \times \{n\}$$

$$aggregate_z \triangleq \lambda x \bullet \{f : T \underset{f}{\nrightarrow} x \mid \textbf{dom } f = \{z\}\}$$

$$list \triangleq \bigcup_{n\,:\,\textbf{N}} \lambda x \bullet (1 \mathrel{..} n \to x)$$

Complemented by $\cup$ and $\lor$, these total functions suffice to build all useful syntactic domains. For example, the choice expression $Apple \mid Orange$, the aggregate expression $v: Variable \ ; \ t: Type$ and the list expression $List^*$ are expressed as

$$choice_1\,(Apple) \cup choice_2\,(Orange)$$

$$aggregate_v\,(Variable) \lor aggregate_t\,(Type)$$

$$list\,(Instruction)$$

The overriding union "$\lor$" must only be applied (as here) to operands obtained from $aggregate_z$ functions, all for different z. This corresponds to the obvious requirement that the tags used in a given aggregate production must all be different. Similarly, the union "$\cup$" must only be applied to operands obtained from $choice_i$ functions with the values of i forming an interval of the form $1 \mathrel{..} n$.

Recursive construct definitions may be interpreted as fixpoint equations involving (for all possible integers n and tags t), the functions $choice_n$, $aggregate_z$, $list$, "$\cup$" and "ψ". The last two must only be applied under the restrictions mentioned. These fixpoint equations are to be solved over the set **C** of constructs, which is the image of **BC**, the set of basic constructs, through any number of applications of these functions. **BC** is the disjoint union of basic constructs on which the grammar is based:

$$\textbf{BC} \triangleq \textbf{N} \mid \textbf{B} \mid \textbf{S} \mid \dots$$

These basic constructs are assumed to be predefined, representing well-known mathematical sets.

> **Theorem** (Stable Abstract Syntax Constructors): Functions $choice_n$, $aggregate_z$ and $list$ are stable for any choice of n and z.

Proof: Functions $choice_n$ and $aggregate_z$ merely "plunge" x into a bigger set, preserving all subset relationships.

The case of $list$ is a little more subtle. We may note that $list = \bigcup_{n\,:\,\textbf{N}} list_n$, where for all integers n:

$$list_n \triangleq \lambda x \bullet (1 \mathrel{..} n \rightarrow x)$$

This sequence is not a chain since a member of $1 \mathrel{..} i \rightarrow x$ is not necessarily a member of $1 \mathrel{..} i+1 \rightarrow x$. (See exercise 8.3.)

The following general property will be useful, however: for any sequence of stable functions τ_n over any set X, the function

$$\tau \triangleq \lambda x : X \bullet \bigcup_{n\,:\,\textbf{N}} \tau_n (x)$$

is stable. This property comes from the following equalities (for any chain x):

$$\tau \left(\bigcup_{i\,:\,\textbf{N}} x_i \right) = \bigcup_{n\,:\,\textbf{N}} \tau_n \left(\bigcup_{i\,:\,\textbf{N}} x_i \right)$$

$$= \bigcup_{n\,:\,\textbf{N}} \left(\bigcup_{i\,:\,\textbf{N}} \tau_n (x_i) \right)$$

-- Because of the stability of each τ_n

$$= \bigcup_{i\,:\,\textbf{N}} \left(\bigcup_{n\,:\,\textbf{N}} \tau_n (x_i) \right)$$

$$= \bigcup_{i\,:\,\textbf{N}} \tau (x_i)$$

All we have to do, then, is to show that every $list_n$ function is stable. Strictness follows from the property that if $x \subseteq y$ then, for any a, $(a \rightarrow x) \subseteq (a \rightarrow y)$. (The situation would be reversed if we considered subset relations on domains rather than ranges.) Then, for a chain x:

$$list_n \; (\textbf{union} \; x_i) \quad = \; (1..n \rightarrow \bigcup_{i:N} x_i)$$

$$\textbf{union} \; (x \; ; \; list_n) = \bigcup_{j:N} (1..n \rightarrow x_j)$$

Call A and B the right-hand sides of these two equalities; we must prove that any member h of A is also a member of B. Such an h is a function which takes its arguments in $1..n$ and yields results in one or more of the x_i. In contrast, a member of B is a function all of whose values are in x_j for the same j.

What saves us, however, is that $1..n$ is finite. For every m in the interval $1..n$, let $index \; (m)$ be an integer such that $h \; (m) \in x_{index \; (m)}$. Then the set of integers $index \; (1..n)$ (the set of $index$ values for all m in $1..n$) is finite. Let j be the maximum of this set; then, because x is a chain, all pairs of h have their second element in x_j, meaning that h is a member of $1..n \rightarrow x_j$. This proves that $A \subseteq B$ and hence that $list_n$ is stable – completing the proof that $list$ is stable.   □

The other functions used in syntactic definitions are union and overriding union, both of which are stable.

So we now know that all constructors used in recursive syntactic definitions are stable, establishing the mathematical respectability of these definitions as fixpoint equations.

By now you should have seen enough examples of fixpoint interpretations of recursive definitions to understand the meaning of a grammar defined through productions which are directly or indirectly recursive. To obtain the language defined by such a grammar, we start from the productions which give us elementary language objects – specimens of terminal constructs. Then we repeatedly apply the grammar's recursive productions to obtain successive levels of more and more complex specimens. Any language specimen may be obtained through a finite number of such iterations.

8.6.5 A linear algebra analogy

To get a concrete understanding of this fixpoint view of recursion – the iterative, bottom-up view – as applied here to the "computation" of a grammar's specimens, it is interesting to express it in terms of notations borrowed from another field of mathematics – linear algebra. In contrast with the previous sections, this will not be a rigorous discussion, but merely an illustration of the concepts through mathematical analogy.

The extremely simple language Lewd ("Language Easier than your Wildest Dreams") will serve to introduce the ideas. Lewd is defined by the following abstract grammar, whose terminal constructs are *Variable* and *Constant*.

$$
\begin{array}{rcl}
Program & \triangleq & Instruction \\
Instruction & \triangleq & Write \mid Assignment \\
Write & \triangleq & v\colon Variable \\
Assignment & \triangleq & target\colon Variable;\ source\colon Expression \\
Expression & \triangleq & Variable \mid Constant \mid Sum \\
Sum & \triangleq & first\colon Variable;\ tail\colon Expression
\end{array}
$$

To simplify the discussion, this grammar only uses choice and aggregate productions; in practice, *Sum* would better be described by a list production.

Since this discussion is only an informal explanation, we may take a few poetic licenses with the above grammar. Droppping the tags of aggregate productions, we rewrite the disjoint union operator "|" as + and the concatenation operator ";" as ∗. This is justified by an informal property of distributivity of "|" with respect to ";". To simplify notations, we replace each construct name by its first initial, using upper-case for non-terminals (*I* for *Instruction*) and lower-case for terminals (*v* for *Variable*). Finally, the definitions being recursive, we should really use "=" rather than " $\triangleq$ ". The grammar's resulting form resembles standard algebraic equations:

$$
\begin{vmatrix}
P = I \\
I = W + A \\
W = v \\
A = v * E \\
E = v + c + S \\
S = v * E
\end{vmatrix}
$$

which, by expanding some "sums" and getting rid of intermediate "variables", we may rewrite as

$$
\begin{vmatrix}
P &=& I \\
I &=& v + v * E \\
E &=& v + c + v * E
\end{vmatrix}
$$

It is convenient to express the above as a single equation using matrix notation:

$$
\begin{vmatrix} P \\ I \\ E \end{vmatrix}
=
\begin{vmatrix} 0 \\ v \\ v + c \end{vmatrix}
+
\begin{vmatrix} 0 & 1 & 0 \\ 0 & 0 & v \\ 0 & 0 & v \end{vmatrix}
*
\begin{vmatrix} P \\ I \\ E \end{vmatrix}
$$

As we know from earlier discussions, "0" really means ∅, the empty function, and "1" means *Id*, the identity function. The use of "∗" follows the rules of matrix multiplication.

Written in this form, a grammar such as that of Lewd may be viewed as a matrix equation

[8.24]
$$N = T + G * N$$

where, as above, N, the unknown, is the vector of non-terminals (P, I, E for Lewd), T is a vector made only of terminals, and G is the matrix representing the productions of the grammar.

The preceding theory tells us, then, that a language defined by such a grammar is a fixpoint of the total function

$$\gamma \triangleq \lambda N \bullet \; T + G * N$$

The fixpoint is a set, whose members are vectors of construct specimens. The addition of semantic constraints would restrict acceptable vectors to a subset of that fixpoint.

If [8.24] were an equation on a set equipped with both a subtraction and a division (inverse operations of "+" and "$*$"), we could rewrite it as

$$N = \frac{T}{1 - G}$$

which under the appropriate conditions would admit the solution

[8.25]
$$N_\infty = T * (1 + G + G^2 + ...)$$
$$= T + T * G + T * G^2 + ...$$

Here the infinite sum denotes the limit (if it exists) of the sequence defined by

$$N_i \triangleq \sum_{j=0}^{i} M_i \qquad \qquad \text{-- For any } i : \mathbf{N}$$

with

$$M_0 \triangleq T$$
$$M_{i+1} \triangleq G * M_i \qquad \qquad \text{-- For any } i : \mathbf{N}$$

Sequence N_i is indeed used to compute approximate solutions to matrix equations on real numbers when the matrix G has suitable properties – even though no division operation is defined on such matrices.

For a language-defining equation, N_i is the chain whose "limit" (disjoint union) is the language that the grammar, as given by T and G, defines. Even though the last derivation was informal, it is essentially correct since the stability of all operators involved implies that a fixpoint does exist.

Continuing on the informal interpretation, we may see more clearly what the fixpoint means. Remember that + stands for disjoint union; in other words, every successive element of the sequence M_i brings a new set of possible specimens for the language's terminal constructs. The first element, M_0, yields the simplest specimens of Lewd:

$$\begin{vmatrix} P_0 \\ I_0 \\ E_0 \end{vmatrix} = \begin{vmatrix} 0 \\ v \\ v+c \end{vmatrix}$$

These are the language specimens obtained directly from terminals: no programs yet; instructions which are limited to *Write*; and expressions limited to variables and constants. The first iteration of γ (the total function whose fixpoint is Lewd) defines M_1, adding specimens at the next level of complexity:

$$\begin{vmatrix} P_1 \\ I_1 \\ E_1 \end{vmatrix} = \begin{vmatrix} 0 & 1 & 0 \\ 0 & 0 & v \\ 0 & 0 & v \end{vmatrix} * \begin{vmatrix} P_0 \\ I_0 \\ E_0 \end{vmatrix}$$

$$= \begin{vmatrix} v \\ v*v + v*c \\ v*v + v*c \end{vmatrix}$$

Here we get the programs consisting of a single *Write*, the *Assignment* instructions whose right-hand side is a variable or a constant, and the *Sum* expressions having just two operands, of which the second is a variable or constant. (The grammar of Lewd restricts the first operand of a *Sum* to be a variable in all cases.)

By applying successive iterations of γ, we get more and more of the Lewd construct specimens. Any given specimen is obtained after a finite number of iterations of γ. But no finite number of iterations will cover the entire language.

The grammar of Lewd was contrived so that matrix G would contain terminals only, making equation [8.24] "linear". In all but trivial cases, this will not be the case. But the pattern shown above remains applicable: obtain all language constructs through the iterative process which starts with the terminals and repeatedly applies the productions.

8.7 DEALING WITH PARTIAL FUNCTIONS

The preceding discussion has developed a theory which covers all the recursive definitions encountered in syntactic and semantic specifications of previous chapters.

The functionals involved in those specifications did not use lambda expressions[4]. Instead, they were entirely defined in terms of a powerful group of stable higher-level functionals, also called **combinators** – overriding union, restriction, dispatching, parallel application, identity and others – defined so as to accept possibly partial functions as arguments.

In contrast, some of the definitions used earlier in this chapter to illustrate the basic issues, such as the recursive definition of the factorial function, involved lambda expression. As introduced in chapter 5, however, lambda notation was only applicable to total functions, whereas most of our fixpoint computations involve partial functions, such as the f_i in the computation of factorial as a fixpoint. To clear up any remaining question on the meaning of recursive definitions, then, we must provide a clear interpretation of lambda expressions involving possibly partial functions.

The discussion will lead us to a closer look at the notion of strictness. We encountered strictness as part of the stability requirement, which any recursive definition must satisfy if it is to be tractable. Beyond this theoretical role, however, strictness has important practical implications in such diverse areas of computer science as concurrent computation, functional programming and compiler construction.

8.7.1 Undefinedness in lambda expressions

Consider a functional defined by a lambda expression, such as

$$\phi \triangleq \lambda f: (\mathbf{N} \nrightarrow \mathbf{N}) \bullet \lambda n: \mathbf{N} \bullet \text{ if } n = 0 \text{ then } 1 \text{ else } n * f \ (n-1) \text{ end}$$

We proved above (see page 253) that, assuming ϕ is stable, its smallest fixpoint is indeed the factorial function. We still have to prove that ϕ is stable.

How do we interpret the application of ϕ to partial functions, such as those which arise in the computation of its fixpoint? For example, the second element of the chain is defined [8.7] as:

$$f_1 = \lambda n \bullet \text{ if } n = 0 \text{ then } 1 \text{ else } n * \varnothing \ (n-1) \text{ end}$$

However since $\varnothing \ (n-1)$ is not defined for any n the meaning of the product in the **else** clause is not clear. So far the discussion has relied on the intuitive interpretation that $a * b$ is "undefined" if a or b is undefined, so that the **else** clause does not bring any useful contribution to the definition of f_1. On the other hand, the expression $n * f_1 \ (n-1)$, occurring in the definition of f_2 ([8.8]), should contribute one value since f_1 is defined for $n = 1$.

Such extensions of operators to handle possibly undefined arguments are called **strict extensions**. We need a consistent and rigorous definition of these extensions.

---

[4] You may have noted that $M_{Assignment}$ (6.5.3) includes a lambda expression which, however, appears in a non-recursive part and so does not impact the stability of the definition's functional (it may be viewed as a constant functional).

8.7.2 Combinators

As noted, the earlier discussions were able to avoid the undefinedness problem thanks to the use of combinators, defined so as to handle partial functions properly.

Rather than develop a new theory, it is simplest to show lambda expressions may be interpreted in terms of these combinators. Then the results of the previous sections may be applied directly.

Carrying out a full proof of correspondence would require that we list all the basic mathematical operations that may be used in our lambda expressions. Rather than attempting exhaustivity, we will consider a few examples, which should suffice to show that all practically useful lambda expressions may be interpreted in terms of combinators.

Any successive application of two functions to the same argument may be understood in terms of the composition combinator. For example, defining l as

$$l \triangleq \lambda x \bullet k \ (h \ (x)),$$

is equivalent to defining it as

$$l \triangleq h \ ; k$$

The dispatching combinator "&" (2.8.1) is useful whenever you need to refer twice to the same object in an expression. For example,

$$square \triangleq \lambda x \bullet x * x$$

may be restated, using the identity function Id, as

$$square \triangleq (Id \ \& \ Id) \ ; \ "*"$$

The parallel application combinator "#" (2.8.1) serves to apply two different functions to two different arguments. For example (using the functions $plus1$ and $minus1$ which add and subtract 1) you may restate

$$w \triangleq \lambda a , b \bullet (a + 1) * (b - 1)$$

as

$$w \triangleq (plus \ 1 \ \# \ minus1) \ ; \ "*"$$

The approach may be pursued by introducing other appropriate combinators; each must have suitable rules defining the domain of its result. For functions with more than two arguments, you may need combinators such as &3, &4, ..., #3, #4, ...

To deal with predicates, the following four combinators are useful; they correspond to boolean operations (not, and, or, implies). All are generic; when applied to a set X, they have signatures

$not: (X \rightarrow \mathbf{B}) \rightarrow (X \rightarrow \mathbf{B})$

$and, or, implies: (X \rightarrow \mathbf{B}) \times (X \rightarrow \mathbf{B}) \rightarrow (X \rightarrow \mathbf{B})$

and are defined by:

[8.26]

$$not \quad \triangleq \quad \lambda\, p \bullet \lambda\, x \bullet \quad \neg\, p\ (x)$$

$$and \quad \triangleq \quad \lambda\, p, q \bullet \lambda\, x \bullet \quad p\ (x) \wedge q\ (x)$$

$$or \quad \triangleq \quad \lambda\, p, q \bullet \lambda\, x \bullet \quad p\ (x) \vee q\ (x)$$

$$implies \triangleq \lambda\, p, q \bullet \lambda\, x \bullet \quad p\ (x) \supset q\ (x)$$

Finally, to deal with the conditional expressions used in the definition of ϕ and many other functionals, we need a generic "if-then-else" combinator, the **conditional combinator**. This may be called "?" and defined (for generic sets X and Y) as

[8.27]

$$?: (X \rightarrow \mathbf{B}) \times (X \rightarrow Y) \times (X \rightarrow Y) \ \rightarrow\ (X \rightarrow Y)$$

$$? \quad \triangleq \lambda\, p, h, k \bullet \lambda\, x \bullet \quad \textbf{if}\ p\ (x)\ \textbf{then}\ h\ (x)\ \textbf{else}\ k\ (x)\ \textbf{end}$$

Note that p must be of signature $X \rightarrow \mathbf{B}$, that is to say a predicate on X.

Instead of [8.27], the conditional combinator may be defined in terms of the other combinators:

[8.28]

$$? \quad \triangleq \lambda\, p, h, k \bullet h \backslash (X / p) \ \underline{\vee}\ k \backslash (X / not\ (p\,))$$

This is the style of definition used in chapter 6 for $M_{Conditional}$ and M_{Loop}, by distinguishing between two disjoint subsets of a function's source set. As will be seen below, this last definition yields a conditional combinator which differs in a subtle way from the result of the preceding definition [8.27].

The combinators defined so far are sufficient to cover many practical instances of function definitions, provided they are complemented by an appropriate set of basic functions (such as *plus1*, "$*$", and constant functions to represent constants such as 0 or *true*). For example, the function ϕ as defined ([8.5], page 233) yields for any function $f : \mathbf{N} \rightarrow \mathbf{N}$:

[8.29]

$$\phi\ (f) \triangleq \lambda\, n \bullet \textbf{if}\ n = 0\ \textbf{then}\ 1\ \textbf{else}\ n * f\ (n-1)\ \textbf{end}$$

which may be rewritten as

[8.30]

$$\phi\ (f) \triangleq\ ?\,(Iszero,\, One,\, ((Id\ \&\ (minus1\ ;\, f))\,;\, "*"))$$

Here *Iszero* is the obvious predicate on $\mathbf{N}$; *One* is assumed to be the constant function $\lambda\, n : \mathbf{N} \bullet 1$.

With this approach, many fixpoint equations may be expressed as $h = \tau\,(h)$ with a τ defined by purely through combinators.

There is of course no need to carry out the transformation explicitly if you prefer to manipulate expressions in lambda form or equivalent. What is important is to know that the transformation is theoretically possible, so that the results obtained using functionals may be directly transposed to lambda expressions.

8.7.3 Strictness and lambda expressions

For lambda expressions involving possibly partial functions, strictness has a natural intepretation. Consider a lambda expression of the form

[8.31]
$$\lambda\,x,\,y,\,\ldots\,\bullet\,EXP\,,$$

where EXP is an expression obtained by applying some possibly partial functions to the formal arguments $x, y, \ldots$. Then [8.31] also denotes a possibly partial function. Informally, the strict interpretation means that this function, when applied to well-defined arguments, will yield a result.

This indeed reflects the earlier rigorous definition of strictness (page 243), which stated that a functional τ is strict on its i-th argument if and only if, for $f \subseteq g$, $\tau\,(\ldots, f, \ldots)$ $\subseteq \tau\,(\ldots, g, \ldots)$, with f and g at the i-th position and all arguments not shown being the same on both sides. Since " $\subseteq$ ", on functions, means "less or as defined, but equal where defined", this corresponds to the informal property stated above.

For example, under its strict interpretation, the function

$$\lambda\,n\,\bullet\,n*\emptyset\,(n-1)$$

(appearing in the **else** clause of the definition of the first element of the factorial sequence, f_1) is defined for all n such that:

- n defined, which is always the case.
- $n - 1$ is defined, that is to say (since only natural integers are considered) $n > 0$.
- This being given, $n - 1 \in$ **dom** $\emptyset$.
- Finally, $<n, \emptyset\,(n - 1)> \in$ **dom** "$*$", which (assuming the previous condition is satisfied) is not a problem since "$*$" is total.

Of course, the third condition is always false since $\emptyset$ is nowhere defined, so that the domain of the function is $\mathbf{N} \times \emptyset$ (where $\emptyset$ here denotes the empty subset of $\mathbf{N}$), that is to say empty.

Applying the same reasoning to the second element of the factorial sequence:

[8.8]
$$f_2 = \lambda\,n\,\bullet\,\textbf{if } n = 0 \ \textbf{ then } 1 \ \textbf{ else } n*f_1\,(n-1) \ \textbf{ end}$$

we may interpret the **else** part as denoting z (n), where z is the partial function

$$\lambda\, n \bullet \; n * f_1\, (n-1)$$

and the domain of z is the intersection of the domains of the arguments: $\mathbf{N} \cap \mathbf{dom}\ (minus1\ ; f_1)$.

The domain of *minus1* is the set of positive integers; let us accept (although this has not been proved yet) that the domain of f_1 is the single-element set $\{0\}$. Then the domain of their composition is $\{1\}$; so the domain of z under the strict interpretation is $\mathbf{N} \cap \{1\}$, or just $\{1\}$.

This, then, is the practical meaning of strictness: accepting only the components of a complex expression that "make sense" both by themselves and as components of the expression.

Since all basic combinators have been shown to be strict, this seems to close the discussion.

In spite of appearances, however, we need to devote a little more of our attention to strictness. The remaining issues involve the boolean combinators ([8.26], page 265) and the conditional combinator "?" ([8.28], page 265).

Although *not*, defined in terms of negation, is not strict (which is not a problem in our uses of recursion since it only serves to define subsets on which to apply restrictions "\"), the other combinators under consideration, *and, or, implies* and "?" are immediately seen to be strict from their definitions in terms of basic combinators.

This is misleading: the strictness of these combinators is actually less obvious than at first sight. This is the last major issue we must settle in this chapter.

8.7.4 Semi-strict interpretations of the conditional combinator

Consider the first element of the factorial chain:

$$f_1 \;\triangleq\; ?\, (Iszero\, ,\, One\, ,\, ((Id \;\&\; (minus1\ ;\ \varnothing))\ ;\ "*"))$$

If we use the straightforward strict interpretation of "?", deriving from [8.27], we note that in the right-hand side of this definition the first two operands of ? have $\mathbf{N}$ as their domain, but the last one involves $\varnothing$ and so has an empty domain: the most significant consequence of the strict interpretations is that a single $\varnothing$ in a functional expression corrupts the whole expression, giving it an empty domain.

So the domain of f_1, as defined by this expression, appears to be

$$\mathbf{N} \cap \mathbf{N} \cap \varnothing_{\mathbf{N}}$$

that is to say $\varnothing_{\mathbf{N}}$. So f_1 turns out to be, like f_0, an empty function, whereas we would like it to be the one-element restriction of the factorial, $\{<0, 1>\}$.

What went wrong? The problem is an overly strict interpretation of "?". To be able to make sense of the expression

   $?\,(p\,,h\,,k\,)\,(x\,)$

that is to say

   if $p\ (x)$ **then** $h\ (x)$ **else** $k\ (x)$ **end**

we certainly want that x belong to the domain of p (otherwise we cannot even perform the test), but not, as the strict interpretation would have us believe, that x belong to the domains of both h and k. Two further cases in which the expression should have a perfectly valid meaning are when either:

- x belongs to the domain of h and $p\ (x)$ is true.
- x belongs to the domain of k and $p\ (x)$ is false.

It does not matter whether x is outside the domain of k in the first case or h in the second, since by the very nature of conditional expressions only the other function will be used to evaluate the result of the expression.

These extensions of the strict interpretation are not just for the sake of completeness. Being able to describe a value through a set of alternative formulae, each of which may not be defined in the cases where it is not needed, is one of the main reasons for using conditional expressions. For example when you write (using a real value x)

   if $x \geq 0$ **then** $\sqrt{x}$ **else** $\sqrt{-x}$ **end**

the purpose of the conditional expression is precisely to provide an acceptable answer when the expression of the **then** branch is not defined. Were it always defined, you probably would not need a conditional.

So it appears that for the conditional combinator the fully strict interpretation is not the appropriate one. The problem disappears, however, if instead of the lambda form we use the definition based on combinators ([8.28], page 265):

   $?\quad \triangleq\ \lambda\, p\,,h\,,k \bullet h\backslash(X\,/p\,)\ \underset{\sim}{\cup}\ k\backslash(X\,/\,not\ (p\,))$

In this definition, the first argument p, representing the test, may itself be a partial function. The definition assumes the appropriate interpretation of *not* and the quotient combinator "/":

- Function *not* (p) has the same domain as p (and yields the inverse value). This is the only reasonable convention: *not* (p) is defined where and only where p is defined.
- $X\,/p$ is the subset of $X \cap$ **dom** p on which p is defined and yields value *true*. Again, this is the only acceptable choice consistent with the intuitive understanding of the quotient operator: if $X\,/p$ is the subset of X where p yields *true*, this can only include values to which p is applicable.

With this **semi-strict** definition of the conditional combinator, the domain of "?" applied to given arguments is:

$$\mathbf{dom}\ (?\ (p, h, k))\ =\ (X\ /\ p\ \cap\ \mathbf{dom}\ h)\ \cup\ (X\ /\ not\ (p)\ \cap\ \mathbf{dom}\ k)$$

This interpretation of "?" is needed in most non-trivial uses of the conditional combinator and will be assumed for the remainder of this discussion.

8.7.5 Semi-strict interpretations of predicate combinators

Semi-strict interpretations are also useful for the boolean combinators on predicates ([8.26], page 265).

Under a strict interpretation, combinators *and*, *or* and *implies* are only defined when both of their operands are defined. As with the conditional combinator, this may be too restrictive. The following observations justify the need for semi-strict variants of these combinators:

- The result of *and* $(p\ (x), q\ (x))$, if defined, is *false* whenever $p\ (x)$ is *false* or $q\ (x)$ is *false*.
- The result of *or* $(p\ (x), q\ (x))$, if defined, is *true* whenever $p\ (x)$ is *true* or $q\ (x)$ is *true*.
- The result of *implies* $(p\ (x), q\ (x))$, if defined, is *true* whenever $p\ (x)$ is *false* or $q\ (x)$ is *true*.

This suggests that it is not unreasonable to define semi-strict versions which will yield a result even if one of the operands is undefined, provided the other is sufficient to determine the result according to the above rules.

These versions will be called *ss_and, ss_or, ss_implies*; they have the following values (defined using the constant predicates $F \triangleq \lambda\ x \bullet false$ and $T \triangleq \lambda\ x \bullet false$):

[8.32]

     ss_and $\triangleq \lambda\ p, q\ \bullet$
                $(F \setminus ((X\ /\ not\ (p)) \cup (X\ /\ not\ (q))))\ \ \underline{\cup}\ \ (T \setminus ((X\ /\ p) \cap (X\ /\ q)))$

     ss_or $\triangleq \lambda\ p, q\ \bullet$
                $(T \setminus ((X\ /\ p) \cup (X\ /\ q)))\ \ \underline{\cup}\ \ (F \setminus ((X\ /\ not\ (p)) \cap (X\ /\ not\ (q))))$

     $ss\_implies \triangleq \lambda\ p, q\ \bullet$
                $(T \setminus ((X\ /\ not\ (p)) \cup (X\ /\ q)))\ \ \underline{\cup}\ \ (F \setminus ((X\ /\ p) \cap (X\ /\ not\ (q))))$

(All overriding unions apply in fact to functions with disjoint domains.)

These definitions yield the domains of the functions obtained through the application of the combinators, which may be expressed as follows:

[8.33]
$$\textbf{dom } \textit{ss\_and} \ (p, q) \quad = \ (X \ / \ not \ (p)) \cup (X \ / \ not \ (q)) \cup (\textbf{dom } \ p \cap \textbf{dom } \ q)$$
$$\textbf{dom } \textit{ss\_or} \ (p, q) \quad = \ (X \ / \ p) \cup (X \ / \ q) \cup (\textbf{dom } \ p \cap \textbf{dom } \ q)$$
$$\textbf{dom } \textit{ss\_implies} \ (p, q) = \ (X \ / \ not \ (p)) \cup (X \ / \ q) \cup (\textbf{dom } \ p \cap \textbf{dom } \ q)$$

The values of the semi-strict boolean combinators may also be expressed using ? in its semi-strict version; for example:

$$ss\_and \ = \ \lambda \, p, q \bullet ? \ (not \ (p), F, ? \ (not \ (q), F, and \ (p, q)))$$

This form is unfortunately non-symmetric in p and q, whereas the combinators are symmetric with respect to their operands. (Non-symmetric versions of the combinators, suitable for sequential execution, will be seen below.)

To use the vocabulary of computer manufacturers, the semi-strict combinators are "**upward-compatible**" with the strict combinators *and*, *or*, *implies*: using conjunction as example, $ss\_and \ (p, q)$ will always yield the same result as *and* (p, q) when applied to a value x for which the *and* form was defined; this value is *true* if and only if both $p \ (x)$ and $q \ (x)$ have value *true*. But the predicates obtained with the non-strict combinators may also yield results in cases for which the strict combinators do not. For example, $ss\_and \ (p, q) \ (x)$ is defined if $p \ (x)$ is defined and false, even though $q \ (x)$ is not defined; in such a case, *and* $(p, q) \ (x)$ is simply not defined.

8.7.6 The importance of being strict – or not

Strictness is a pervasive issue which appears under various disguises in many practical programming situations. Let us examine a few.

The first issue is argument passing in routine calls. The technique known as "call by value", where actual arguments are copied into local variables representing formal arguments at call time, is the strictest possible: if just one of the actual arguments is not defined, the routine will not be able to perform its computations. If you wish to think of an undefined program entity as of one whose computation does not terminate, the routine would wait indefinitely for its argument to be available.

Why would anyone want a convention other than total strictness as implied by call by value? We have already seen a good reason in the case of the conditional combinator: some computations may be able to proceed with an undefined argument if that argument is not needed in certain cases.

The utmost in non-strictness is the technique which evaluates each argument not at the time of the call, but at the latest possible time within the routine body, when the value of the argument is actually needed. This is known as **call by need** or **lazy evaluation**. In this approach, as with the semi-strict interpretation of ?, an undefined actual argument will not hamper execution of any particular routine call if its value is not needed in that call.

Algol 60's *call by name* repeatedly evaluates an argument whenever it is needed. Call by need is different: like call by value, it evaluates the argument only once, storing its value in a local variable; but it only does so if and when the routine absolutely needs the argument's value.

When does a routine "absolutely" need the value of an argument? The answer lies in the previous discussion: when it must pass on that value as actual argument to a routine which, for some reason, is strict on the corresponding formal argument. An example is a print routine: clearly, to print the value of an expression, you must evaluate it.

In recent years, researchers have explored approaches to programming which try to be as little strict as possible. Two areas of application are particularly worth mentioning:

- In concurrent programming, a non-strict operation is one which does not prevent other parts of the computation from proceeding in parallel. This is particularly interesting in connection with ideas from object-oriented programming, as discussed below for Eiffel.

- In functional programming, non-strictness enables programmers to deal with infinite data structures: although such data structures may not be represented in a computer, with a non-strict interpretation they are fine as long as you only evaluate finite parts.

The next two sections sketch these two applications.

8.7.7 Strictness in an object-oriented concurrency mechanism

An example of a design where the strictness issue played a major role was the design of the concurrency mechanism in Eiffel. Assume a sequence of operations of the form

$$t.proc\ (x,\ y,\ \ldots);\ \ldots\ ;\ a := t.attr$$

The first operation is a call to a procedure *proc* on an object accessible through the name *t* (in Eiffel's object-oriented style of programming, every operation is relative to a certain target object, here *t*). After other operations, the last line accesses an attribute *attr* of that object. For example, the object could be a record in a database; *proc* would change some part of the information associated with the record, and *attr* would access some part (the same or another) of that information.

Using the Eiffel mechanisms for parallelism, *t* may be declared as **separate**, meaning that all computations on this object are handled by a processor which is different from the processor used to perform the above operations. (The "processors" in question are virtual: they may be physically different computers, or time slices on a time-shared computer.)

When the processor *P* in charge of the above code executes the call *t.proc*, it may proceed with the following operations without waiting: not having to wait is indeed the aim of making *t* **separate**, and the central benefit of parallel computation. In most cases, however, *P* will eventually need to use some of the results produced by *proc*; at that stage it should wait if the processor in charge of *t* has not finished executing *proc* or is busy with some other computation.

One of the important ideas underlying Eiffel concurrency is that in such a situation programmers should not have to write an explicit re-synchronization instruction to request waiting; instead, the wait, if needed, should occur automatically whenever P needs access to the value of t. In light of the previous discussion, we know exactly what "needs" means in this case: P will wait for t to be available when (but only when) it must perform a strict operation on t.

Here, strict operations on an object include the following cases:

- Arithmetic operations such as addition.

- External operations such as *print*.

- Use as target of a routine or attribute application. (In the above case, $t.attr$ requires t to be ready and so will make P wait if the server processor is not ready.)

On the other hand, some operations are not strict in Eiffel and will not make P wait. These operations include in particular:

- Use of t as right-hand side of an assignment instruction $u := t$, at least for the most common case in which the values of t and u are references to objects, not the objects themselves. (Then it does not matter that the object's processor is not available as long as we have a reference to that object.)

- Use of t as argument to a routine, for arguments passed by reference.

The resulting mechanism, which yields a very simple and general method for programming concurrent applications, may be called **lazy wait**.

8.7.8 A lazy functional language

As an example of how it can be useful to relax strictness requirements in a programming language, let us design a non-strict Lisp-like language, to be called Grunts (for Generally Recognized by Users as Not Too Strict).

To manipulate lists of integers, Grunts provides the following primitives:

- The empty list is written *empty*.

- The first element of a non-empty list l is written $l.first$ and the remaining list $l.tail$.

- If x is an integer and l a list, *cons* (x, l) is the list with x as its *first* and l as its *tail*.

- If x is an integer and l is a list, $l + n$ is the list obtained by adding the integer n to every element of the list l.

As an example of a function definition in Grunts, the following defines the function which yields the i-th element of a list:

$$element \triangleq \lambda\, l: LIST, i: \mathbf{N} \bullet \mathbf{if}\ i = 1\ \mathbf{then}\ l.first\ \mathbf{else}\ element\ (l.tail, i-1)\ \mathbf{end}$$

All calls to this function must be assumed to satisfy $1 \le i \le l.length$.

These notations may be applied to infinite lists as well as finite ones. For example the list of all natural numbers greater than or equal to 2 may be defined as

$allnat2 \triangleq cons\ (2,\ allnat2 + 1)$

If you try to evaluate *allnat2*, you will have a hard (and long) time. However the computation of, say, *element* (*allnat2*, 3) will terminate and yield 4 if the arguments are evaluated on a lazy basis. You are invited to perform the computation step by step.

This requires *cons* itself to be lazy. This function, which plays a basic role in Lisp, is indeed a ideal candidate for lazy evaluation. ("CONS should not evaluate its arguments" is the title of one of the first articles on this approach [Friedman 1976].) In a way, the above definition of *allnat2* is pure bluff; but *allnat2* will be safe as long as the other players (that is, the other functions) only call that bluff on finite arguments.

The list of all multiples of a given integer may be similarly defined:

$multiples \triangleq \lambda\ n: \mathbf{N} \bullet cons\ (n,\ multiples\ (n) + n)$

where "+" is interpreted as defined above. Again, the computation of *element* (*multiples* (*i*), *j*) is finite for given *i* and *j* if lazy evaluation is used, although the computation of *multiples* (*i*) would not terminate.

Another example is the function *diff* that handles two (possibly infinite) non-decreasing lists of integers and yields their difference (the non-decreasing list containing the elements of the first not appearing in the second):

$diff \triangleq \lambda\ l, l' \bullet$

      if *l* = *empty* **then** *empty*

      elsif *l'* = *empty* **then** *l*

      elsif *l*. *first* > *l'*. *first* **then** *diff* (*l*, *l'* .*tail*)

      elsif *l*. *first* < *l'*. *first* **then** *cons* (*l*. *first*, *diff* (*l*.*tail*, *l'*)) **end**

      else *diff* (*l*.*tail*, *l'*)

This may be used for example to define the prime numbers:

$primes \triangleq sieve\ (allnat2)$, with:

$sieve \triangleq \lambda\ l \bullet cons\ (l.first,\ sieve\ (diff\ (l,\ multiples\ (l.first))))$

This formulation corresponds directly to the well-known mathematical definition of the sieve of Eratosthenes. What is remarkable is that, with lazy evaluation, the computation of, say, *element* (*primes*, 4) will terminate and yield the desired result (7, the fourth prime number if 1 is excluded).

Languages which (under various syntactic forms) allow this kind of definition are Miranda and Lucid (see the bibliographical notes) as well as several modern versions of Lisp.

8.7.9 Non-commutative boolean combinators

To conclude this tour of strictness it is useful to survey some important practical applications of the semi-strict predicate combinators.

The need often arises to test for a pair of conditions such that the second is meaningless unless the first is satisfied. A frequent case involves arrays: you may want to precede a condition on an array element, say c $(t$ $[i])$, with a guard expressing that the element exists. Assuming an array of bounds 1 and n a variable i about which we know for sure (to simplify the discussion) that its value is positive, a typical boolean expression on i, for some condition c, is

$i \leq n$ **and** c $(t$ $[i])$

In this case you clearly do not want the second condition to be tested if the first is false, as t $[i]$ is undefined and the result of the **and** should be considered as *false* anyhow. Perhaps the most common example is the search for a value x in t:

$i := 1$;

while $i \leq n$ **and** t $[i] \neq x$ **do**
    $i := i + 1$
end;

if $i \leq n$ **then**
    "x appears in the array at position i"
else
    "x does not appear in the array"
end

The strict interpretation of **and** is dangerous here, as it carries the risk of an out-of-bounds memory reference (to the undefined value t $[n+1]$) when x is not present in the array – all the more regrettable since the second condition need not be tested in this case, as the first one yields *false*.

To address this problem, several languages have introduced non-strict boolean operators.

In some of these languages, there is only one set of operators, and they have the non-strict semantics. This is the case in Algol W, Lisp and C.

In Ada and Eiffel, programmers have a choice between the standard **and** and **or**, whose implementation may be strict (although it does not have to be), and the operators **and then** and **or else**, which are non-strict. (These are the Ada notations; in Eiffel & and I are the strict operators, ?& and ?I the non-strict ones.) Programmers are warned not to use **and** and **or** whenever the second argument might be undefined, since these operators may evaluate both arguments. On the other hand, **and then** and **or else** are guaranteed not to evaluate the second argument when the first has value *false* or *true* respectively.

The operators **and then** and **or else** are not identical to our *ss_and* and *ss_or*. The mathematical (*ss_*) operators are symmetric on their arguments; the programming language operators (of Algol W, Lisp, C, Ada, Eiffel), being designed for sequential evaluation on a classical computer, treat their arguments in a non-symetric fashion. As combinators, these operators may be defined, using the semi-strict interpretation of ? , as

$$and\_then \quad \triangleq \quad \lambda\, p, q \bullet ? \ (p, q, F)$$
$$or\_else \quad \triangleq \quad \lambda\, p, q \bullet ? \ (p, T, q)$$

which shows their domains to be, respectively:

$$(X \,/\, not \ (p)) \cup (\mathbf{dom}\ p \cap \mathbf{dom}\ q)$$
$$(X \,/\, p) \cup (\mathbf{dom}\ p \cap \mathbf{dom}\ q)$$

(Compare to [8.33], page 270.) These operators will be used in expressions involving partial functions in chapter 10.

A corresponding non-strict version of the implication operator may be defined as

$$implies\_if\_defined \quad \triangleq \quad \lambda\, p, q \bullet or\_else \ (not \ (p), q)$$

or equivalently

$$implies\_if\_defined \quad \triangleq \quad \lambda\, p, q \bullet ? \ (not \ (p), T, q)$$

Mention was made above of the "upward compatibility" of semi-strict operators with strict ones. The practical meaning of this property is visible here: from a compiler writer's viewpoint, any correct implementation of the non-commutative operators is a correct implementation of the corresponding commutative operators. You may execute all **and**s as **and then**s if you wish, and similarly for **or**.[5] But the reverse is not true: a correct implementation of **and** is only required to return a result when both operands are defined. When either is undefined, it may do what it pleases – it may return a result, but it does not have to. So it may or may not be a correct implementation of **and then**.

In other words an Ada or Eiffel compiler (these languages are good examples because they have both sets of operators) *must* use sequential semantics for **and then**: it is not permitted to generate code that will attempt to evaluate the second argument if the first has value false. For **and**, on the other hand, the compiler may either use the **and then** implementation, or evaluate both operands followed by "and-ing" of the results.

This efficiency concern explains why both sets of operators were retained in Ada and Eiffel, even though the semi-strict operators are in principle sufficient since they may be

---

[5] The results could be different if expressions were permitted to produce side-effects; for example *f* (*x*) **and** *g* (*x*), where *f* and *g* are function subprograms which modify their argument, will yield a different result depending on the implementation of **and**. But the denotation of function calls with side-effects is ambiguous anyway.

used as implementations of the strict ones in a sequential context. Another reason is that **and** and **or** correspond more closely to the standard mathematical operators, which are commutative.

The need for both sets of operators is particularly clear in Eiffel because of the presence of a concurrency mechanism based on a theory which treats strictness, or the absence thereof, as one of the key semantic differences between sequential and parallel computation. After reading the above discussion of this mechanism (8.7.7), you should not have difficulty accepting that, if x and y are declared as **separate**, the expression

$$x.f\ (\ldots)\ \textbf{and}\ y.g\ (\ldots)$$

will not be evaluated in the same way as the comparable expression using **and then**. With the strict operator, both operands may be executed concurrently, taking advantage of any available hardware parallelism. With the semi-strict operator, evaluation of the second operand may not proceed until after the evaluation of the first has been completed.

8.8 A MORE GENERAL THEORY

[The rest of this chapter, excluding the exercises, may safely be skipped on first reading.]

The above discussion concludes the presentation of a mathematical theory which may serve as a basis for all practical uses of recursion. Mathematically, the discussion has relied entirely on simple properties of elementary set theory.

The theory found in most of the published literature on denotational semantics is more general, relying on somewhat more advanced mathematical notions; it includes the above theory as a special case. Its extra generality is not needed, however, for the applications to modeling programming languages studied in this book.

This last section, which should be treated as supplementary material, sketches the more general theory. Its aim is mostly to help you feel at home when you go from this book to the rest of the literature. None of the concepts it introduces is used in subsequent chapters.

8.8.1 Definition

The more general theory is based on "closed orders". (Even this is in fact a variant of the most commonly used approach; the last section of this chapter will explain the differences.)

The first step is to recall the standard notion of order relation:

[8.34]

> **Definition** (Order Relation): Let $\leqslant$ be a relation on a set X. This relation is an order relation if and only if the following three conditions are met for all $x, y, z \in X$:
>
> (Reflexivity)   • $x \leqslant x$
>
> (Transitivity)   • if $x \leqslant y$ and $y \leqslant z$, then $x \leqslant z$
>
> (Antisymmetry) • if $x \leqslant y$ and $y \leqslant x$, then $x = y$.

If $\leqslant$ is an order relation on X, X is said to be an ordered set under $\leqslant$. When $x \leqslant y$, x is said to be "less than or equal to" y, and y is "greater than or equal to" x.

The order relations considered here may be partial in the sense that, for arbitrary members x and y of X, three cases are possible:

• $x \leqslant y$.

• $y \leqslant x$ (exclusive of the first case if $x \neq y$).

• None of the above.

The objects x and y are said to be **comparable** for relation $\leqslant$ if and only if one of the first two cases holds. An order relation such that any two members of X are comparable is called a **total order** relation. An order relation which is not total (that is to say which includes at least one incomparable pair) is said to be **partial**.

A note on terminology: "Order" denotes a relation which may be either a partial order or a total order. Some authors use "partial order" for "order"; however it is more consistent to use "order" for the general case and qualify with "total" or "partial" as needed in specific cases. This is similar to the convention used in this book for "function" and "partial function".

8.8.2 Simple examples

The following are examples of ordered sets. In some cases, the order is total, as indicated.

[R]   • **R** under $\leq$ (total)

[Q]   • **Q** (the set of rationals) under $\leq$ (total)

[N]   • **N** under $\leq$ (total)

[PS]   • **P** (S) under $\subseteq$, S being an arbitrary set

[RI]   • A closed interval of **R**, $a \mathinner{.\,.} b$, under $\leq$ (total)

[QI]   • A closed interval of **Q** (the set of rational numbers) under ≤ (total)

[PC]   • Propositional calculus under implication.

A name in square brackets has been associated with each example. This name will be used below to refer to the corresponding set equipped with the corresponding order relation.

You are invited to check that the axioms of order relations are indeed satisfied in each case.

8.8.3 Approximating real numbers

The following example is more relevant to our present purposes. Let SRI, for "sets of real intervals", be the set whose members are sets of non-empty, pairwise disjoint, closed intervals of **R**; for example, the following set of intervals, pictured on the figure below, is a member of SRI:

$$r1 \triangleq \{[-7, -2], [1, 2], [4, 6]\}$$

A few notations will be useful to discuss real intervals: $[a, b]$ is the closed interval between a and b, that is to say the set of real numbers x such that $a \leq x \leq b$; $]a, b[$ is the open interval, that is to say the set of x such that $a < x < b$; the semi-open intervals are written $[a, b[$ and $]a, b]$.

0

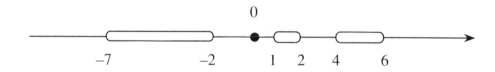

−7   −2   1   2   4   6

Figure 8.4: Approximating real numbers by intervals

If $CLOSED$ is the set of closed intervals of R, defined as

[8.35]
$$CLOSED \triangleq \{Interval : \mathbf{P}\,(\mathbf{R}) - \{\varnothing\} \mid$$
$$\exists\, a, b : \mathbf{R} \bullet Interval = \{x : \mathbf{R} \mid a \leq x \wedge x \leq b\}$$

then SRI may be defined as

[8.36]
$$SRI \triangleq \{Interval\_set : \mathbf{P}(CLOSED) \mid \forall\, a, b : Interval\_set.xi.xmSRI \bullet a = b \vee a \cap b = \varnothing\}$$

The definition of *CLOSED* excludes empty intervals (for which $a > b$) to avoid cluttering members of *SRI* with useless values.

One way to look at *SRI* is to consider that a member of *SRI* (a set of intervals) gives us information, usually partial, on some real number. For example, $r1$ above may be seen as a partial characterization of some number, say x, which lies in one of the three intervals that constitute $r1$: $[-7, -2]$, $[1, 2]$ and $[4, 6]$. To obtain perfect information on that number, we would need the member of SRI consisting of the single one-value interval $[x, x]$.

An interesting order relation on *SRI* is the following: $r \leqslant s$ if and only if every interval of s is a subset of an interval of r. Note the order of the inclusion. Formally, for $r, s \in SRI$:

$$r \leqslant s \text{ iff } \quad \forall is: s \bullet \exists\, ir: r \bullet is \subseteq ir$$

For example, $r1 \leqslant r2$, where $r2 \triangleq \{[-5, -3], [5, 6]\}$.

According to the interpretation given, you may view $r \leqslant s$ as meaning "r is **less informative than** or equal to s": if they are not equal, s gives a more precise characterization of some sought real number.

If, for example, you look at both $r1$ and $r2$ as partial characterizations of a real number r, then $r1 \leqslant r2$ means that $r2$ gives more information than $r1$ about r. Assume you knew that r is in $r1$ and somehow you learn that it is in $r2$ as well: then you may rule out the middle interval $[1, 2]$ of $r1$ and restrict the other two.

Let us prove that this indeed defines an order relation. The relation is obviously reflexive and transitive; to show that it is antisymmetric, assume that $r \leqslant s$ and $s \leqslant r$. Consider an arbitrary interval *is* in s. Because $r \leqslant s$, there is an interval *ir* in r such that $is \subseteq ir$; because $s \leqslant r$, there is an interval *is'* in s such that $ir \subseteq is'$. Hence $is \subseteq is'$; since the intervals of s are pairwise disjoint, *is'* must be the same as *is* and so $ir = is$. Thus every interval in s is also in r. By symmetry the converse is true, yielding $r = s$.   □

This example will be denoted by [SRI] below.

8.8.4 Flat orders

The most trivial example of order relation on any set X is the **flat order**, defined as the identity relation:

$$Id_X \triangleq \{<x, x>: X \times X\}$$

That is to say, relation *Id* (introduced as a total function in 5.2) holds only between every element and itself. *Id* trivially satisfies the axioms of order relations ([8.34]).

Flat ordering makes it possible to consider every set as an ordered set, albeit in a trivial sense.

8.8.5 Order induced on cartesian products

[8.37]

Definition (Cartesian Product Order): Let X and Y be sets with respective order relations $\leqslant_X$ and $\leqslant_Y$. Then $X \times Y$ is an ordered set under the relation $\leqslant_{X \times Y}$, called the **cartesian product order** and defined by:

$$\langle x, y \rangle \; \leqslant_{X \times Y} \; \langle x', y' \rangle \quad \text{iff} \quad (x \leqslant_X x') \wedge (y \leqslant_Y y')$$

The proof is immediate. In practice the notation will be just $\leqslant$ for $\leqslant_X, \leqslant_{X \times Y}$ etc. when there is no possible confusion.

8.8.6 Function order

A simple order relation is defined on any function space $X \nrightarrow Y$. This fundamental relation has a straightforward definition:

[8.38]

Definition (Function Order): Let X and Y be arbitrary sets. Then $X \nrightarrow Y$ is an ordered set under the relation $\leqslant_{X \nrightarrow Y}$, called the **function order** on $X \nrightarrow Y$, defined by:

$$h \; \leqslant_{X \nrightarrow Y} \; k \qquad \text{iff} \qquad h \subseteq k$$

The function order is nothing else, then, than the order of subset inclusion [PS] as seen earlier; here the subsets considered are functions, that is to say sets of pairs (subsets of $X \times Y$).

The function order is the only one which is really useful for the study of abstract syntax and denotational semantics. This is why all of the preceding discussion in this chapter simply used the $\subseteq$ operator, without explicitly introducing it as an order relation. The current discussion will simply generalize the concepts to other kinds of order.

The following theorem characterizes the function order from a function (rather than subset) perspective.

[8.39]

> **Theorem**: For any two functions h and k in $X \nrightarrow Y$,
>
> 1   • If $h \leqslant_{X \nrightarrow Y} k$,   then **dom** $h \subseteq$ **dom** k.
>
> 2   • $h \leqslant_{X \nrightarrow Y} k$ if and only if $k \setminus$ **dom** $h = h$

The two properties follow immediately from the definition.

Unlike the induced order on cartesian products, the function order on $X \nrightarrow Y$ exists independently of whether X and Y are ordered or not, and (if any of them is) does not depend on their respective order relations.

8.8.7 Minimum members

> **Definition** (Minimum Member): Let X be a set with an order relation relation written $\leqslant$. A minimum member of X is an object $m \in X$ such that:
>
> $$\forall x : X \bullet m \leqslant x$$

A minimum member is also called a minimum element.

[8.40]

> **Theorem**: An ordered set has at most one minimum member.

Proof: If m_1 and m_2 are minimum members of A, then $m_1 \leqslant m_2$ and $m_2 \leqslant m_1$; so $m_1 = m_2$ since $\leqslant$ is antisymmetric.   □

So we may talk (when it exists) of "the" minimum member. Some of the previous examples indeed have a minimum member:

- [N] (**N** with the standard order relation): 0
- [PC] (propositional calculus under implication): *false*;
- [RI], [QI] (some closed interval in **R** or **Q**): the smallest number in the interval;
- [PS] (subsets of a set S, under inclusion): the empty set; this property extends to the function order on $X \nrightarrow Y$, where the minimum is the empty function $\varnothing_{X \nrightarrow Y}$.

Clearly, if X and Y have minimum members ω_X and ω_Y, then $X \times Y$, under the induced order [8.37], has minimum member $<\omega_X, \omega_Y>$.

On the other hand, [R] and [Q], for example, do not have a minimum member. Nor does [SRI] (sets of real intervals); if set *CLOSED* ([8.35]) is extended to include **R** as one of its members, then {**R**} is the minimum member for the resulting relation.

8.8.8 Upper bounds

[8.41]

> **Definition** (Upper Bound): Let X be a set with an order relation written ⩽. Let A be a subset of X. An upper bound of A in X is an object $l \in X$ such that:
>
> $$\forall a : A \bullet a ⩽ l$$

Thus an upper bound of A is greater than or equal to all members of A. In contrast with a minimum member, an upper bound of A may or may not be in A. In the [R] example, any real number in $[5, +\infty[$ is an upper bound of both the closed interval $[3, 5]$ and the right-open interval $[3, 5[$ (the latter subset has no upper bound belonging to the subset itself). The subset **N** of **R** has no upper bound in **R**. Nor has **R**, viewed as its own subset.

In [SRI], an arbitrary subset A does not necessarily have an upper bound. Consider for example

$$A \triangleq \{a_1, a_2\}$$

with

$$a_1 \triangleq \{[0, 1]\}$$
$$a_2 \triangleq \{[3, 4]\}$$

Here A contains two members, each of which is a set consisting of a single real interval. But the two members have no common upper bound: to be greater than or equal to a_1, a member l of *SRI* would have to consist of sub-intervals of $[0, 1]$; but to be greater than or equal to a_2, l would have to consist of sub-intervals of $[3, 4]$.

Only subsets of *SRI* consisting of pairwise not entirely disjoint intervals have upper bounds. Chains, to be defined soon for arbitrary partial orders, are an important example of such subsets.

In [PS] (subsets of a given set), an upper bound of a set A of subsets is a subset h such that $u \subseteq h$ for all $u \in A$. In the case of a function space $X \nrightarrow Y$ with the function order, this means that the following two conditions are satisfied:

[8.42]

$$\bigcup_{u\,:\,A} \mathbf{dom}\ x \subseteq \mathbf{dom}\ h$$

$$\forall u : A \bullet \forall x : \mathbf{dom}\ h \bullet u\ (x) = h\ (x)$$

In other words, the function u must be defined wherever any function u in A is defined, and then yield the same value as u. This is only possible for very special sets A of functions: any two members in A must yield the same value wherever both are defined.

8.8.9 Least upper bound

[8.43]

> **Definition** (Least Upper Bound): Let X be a set with an order relation written $\leqslant$. Let A be a subset of X. A least upper bound of A in X is an object $l \in X$ such that:
>
> - l is an upper bound of A in X.
>
> - For any upper bound l' of A in X, $l \leqslant l'$.

In [R], both intervals [3, 5] and [3, 5[have least upper bound 5.

A subset A of an ordered set X may have upper bounds but no least upper bound: for example, in [Q] (rationals), the set of all members less than or equal to the (non-rational) number $\sqrt{2}$ has an infinity of upper bounds but no least upper bound. As another example, take $\mathbf{R} - \{1\}$ for X and the set of all numbers less than 1 for A.

[8.44]

> **Theorem**: A subset of an ordered set has at most one least upper bound.

As a consequence, we may talk about "the" least upper bound of a subset. The proof is as for uniqueness of the minimum member ([8.40]).

In the rest of this discussion the least upper bound of a subset A, when it exists, is written **lub** A.

Here are a few more examples of least upper bounds. In [PC], the least upper bound of a set A of propositions is their "or":

$$\mathbf{lub}\ A = \mathbf{or}_{u\,:\,A}\ u$$

Similarly, in [PS] (subsets of a given set S, under inclusion), a subset A is a set of subsets of S (thus a member of $\mathbf{P}\,(\mathbf{P}\,(S\,))$; such an A always has a least upper bound as follows:

[8.45]

$$\mathbf{lub}\ A\ =\ \bigcup_{u\,:\,A} u$$

That this indeed defines a least upper bound is easily seen by noting that the right-hand side contains every member of A and is thus an upper bound of A, and that any other upper bound must contain all members of A and thus their union.

This is precisely the notion of least upper bound used to build the theory of recursion throughout the earlier part of this chapter. The same is applicable for the special case of the function order, provided the set of functions satisfies condition [8.42], which guarantees the existence of upper bounds.

8.8.10 Chains

[8.46]

> **Definition** (Chain): In an ordered set with relation $\leqq$, a chain is an infinite sequence $x\ =\ <x_0, x_1, x_2, x_3, \dots >$ such that, for all $i \in \mathbf{N}$,
> $$x_i \leqq x_{i+1}$$

In the special cases of [PS] and the function order, this coincides with subset chains and function chains as defined on page 242, where each element is a subset of the next. For a function chain, the notation **union** f is equivalent to **lub** f.

A sequence x given by the formula for its elements will be written $<x_i>_{i=0}^{\infty}$, or just $<x_i>$ if there is no ambiguity. For example, $<i^2>$ is the sequence $<0, 1, 4, 9, 16, 25, \dots>$.

A chain as defined above is a non-decreasing sequence. As a special case, a sequence which is initially increasing and then takes a constant value, for example the integer sequence $<1, 3, 46, 100, 100, 100, 100, 100\dots>$, is a chain; such a chain is said to be **stationary**.

In [SRI], a chain is a sequence of interval sets such that every interval of an element of the sequence is contained in an interval of the previous element – meaning, in our informal interpretation, that each element includes at least as much information as its predecessor.

The discussion below considers least upper bounds of chains and uses the notation **lub** x where x is a chain. Note that this is a slight abuse of language; what is really meant is the least upper bound of the *set of values* of the elements of x, that is to say (remembering that x is formally a function) **lub** (**ran** x).

The following properties of least upper bounds of chains may be noted at the outset:

- A stationary chain always has a least upper bound, its infinitely repeated value.
- The least upper bound of a chain, if it exists, does not occur in the chain unless the chain is stationary. This is because if **lub** x is equal to some x_i, then for any $j > i$ it is both true that $x_i \leqslant x_j$ since x is a chain and that $x_j \leqslant x_i$ since x_i is an upper bound.
- If X is finite, or its order is flat (as defined on page 279), all chains are stationary and so have least upper bounds.
- In the function order, a chain is a sequence of functions such that, for all i, h_{i+1} is identical to h_i on the domain of h_i (but may have a larger domain); such a chain always has a least upper bound, defined earlier in this chapter as **union** h.

8.8.11 Closed orders

[8.47]

> **Definition** (Closed Order): Let X be an ordered set and A a subset of X. A is said to be lub-closed (or just closed for short) if and only if every chain with all its values in A has a least upper bound in A.

An important special case is when A is the whole set X. Since the rest of this chapter only considers ordered sets, the expression "a closed set" will stand for "an ordered set which is closed".

From the properties mentioned earlier, any ordered set which is finite or flatly ordered is closed.

Among the preceding examples, [R], [Q] and [N] are clearly not closed; note however that **N** becomes closed if, instead of $\leq$, the inverse relation $\geq$ is chosen as order relation, in which case all chains are stationary. In the [PS] and [PC] cases (subsets and propositions), it has already been seen that any subset has a least upper bound, so these examples are closed. A non-empty interval of **Q** is not closed under $\leq$. A non-empty interval of **R** is closed under $\leq$ if and only if it is right-closed; in this case the least upper bound of a chain is what is commonly called the limit of the chain.

Whether [SRI] is closed is the subject of exercise 8.7.

If X is closed and A is a subset of X, any chain of A has a least upper bound in X; if this least upper bound always belongs to A, A is a closed subset of X. As a counter-example, [3, 5[is not a closed subset in [3, 5] for $\leq$.

8.8.12 Induced closed sets

[8.48]

> **Theorem**: Let X and Y be closed sets. Then $X \times Y$ is closed under the induced order.

Proof: Consider a chain in $X \times Y$. This chain is a sequence of pairs

$$\ll x_i, y_i \gg_{i=0}^{\infty}$$

where, because of the definition of the induced order, both x and y are chains, in X and Y respectively; thus the chain in $X \times Y$ admits as least upper bound the pair $<x, y>$ of their two least upper bounds. □

For function spaces:

[8.49]

> **Theorem**: Let X and Y be sets. Then $X \rightarrowtail Y$ is closed under the function order.

The remarkable feature of this theorem is that X and Y need not be closed nor even ordered themselves. The proof is immediate, since the least upper bound of a function chain is simply its **union**.

8.8.13 Intersection and union

[8.50]

> **Theorem** (Intersection): Let X be an ordered set; let A and B be two closed subsets of X. Then $A \cap B$ is closed. Note that X itself does not need to closed.

Proof: Any chain of $A \cap B$ is both a chain of A and a chain of B, so it has a least upper bound which belongs to both A and B, and hence to their intersection. □

If, however, we replaced $A \cap B$ by $A \cup B$, the corresponding property would not be a theorem. The problem is that a chain in $A \cup B$ could "oscillate" between A and B.

Consider the example illustrated by the figure below: $\mathbf{R} \times \mathbf{R}$ (set of pairs of real numbers) with the order relation $\leqslant$ defined as follows:

$$<a, b> \leqslant <a', b'> \quad \text{iff} \quad b < b' \vee (a = a' \wedge b = b')$$

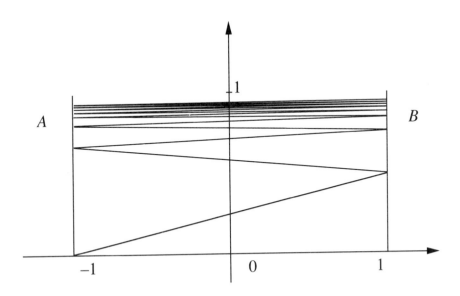

Figure 8.5: The union of two closed subsets is not always closed

In other words, $p \leqslant p'$ if and only if p (as a point in a two-dimensional space) is strictly "below" p' or equal to p'. Your are invited to check that this is indeed an order relation (the restriction to $b < b'$ in the first case is needed to ensure antisymmetry). Next consider the subsets represented by the vertical segments on the figure:

$$A \triangleq \{-1\} \times [0, 1]$$
$$B \triangleq \{1\} \times [0, 1]$$

Both of these subsets are closed, but their union is not, since (among others) the following chain in $A \cup B$, represented on the figure by the vertices of the saw-like line, has no least upper bound:

$$x_i \triangleq <-1, 1 - \frac{1}{i + 1}> \quad (i \text{ even})$$

$$x_i \triangleq <1, 1 - \frac{1}{i + 1}> \quad (i \text{ odd})$$

Theorem [8.50] does not require X to be closed. If X is closed then the theorem becomes true for $\cup$ as well as $\cap$:

[8.51]

> **Theorem** (Union): Let X be a closed set; let A and B be two
> closed subsets of X. Then $A \cup B$ is closed.

In the above example, no subset of $\mathbf{R} \times \mathbf{R}$ containing both A and B is closed for the
order given, so the theorem does not apply.

Proof: Let x be a chain in $A \cup B$. Since X is closed, the chain has a least upper
bound in X, say xab. The property to prove is $xab \in A \cup B$. If x_i is a member of B
(respectively, A) for only a finite number of indices i, then xab is in A (respectively B)
and the theorem trivially holds.

Otherwise there are infinitely many values of i for which x_i is in A, and also
infinitely many for which x_i is in B. (This does not preclude the sequence from having
only a finite number of different values in A or B or both.) So we may construct two
chains, one in A, the other in B, each consisting of the x_i values belonging to the
corresponding subset, taken in their original order. Since A and B are closed, these
chains have least upper bounds $xa \in A$ and $xb \in B$. Let us show that $xa = xb = xab$,
which will prove the theorem in this case.

First, since xab is an upper bound of both chains, $xa \circleddash xab$ and $xb \circleddash xab$. Since
the two chains are infinite subsequences of the whole chain, for any i such that $x_i \in A$
there are integers j and k such that $i < j < k$, $x_j \in B$ and $x_k \in A$; so xa is an upper
bound of the B chain, impying that $xb \circleddash xa$. By symmetry, $xa \circleddash xb$; so $xa = xb$. It has
been shown in passing that xa is an upper bound of the original chain, so $xab \circleddash xa$. This
means that $xa = xb = xab$.   □

As a consequence of this result, it has also been proved that if A and B are disjoint,
any chain in $A \cup B$ has a finite number of elements in either A or B (for if this was not
the case the least upper bound $xab = xa = xb$ would belong to both A and B).

8.8.14 Monotonic functions

[8.52]

> **Definition** (Monotonicity): Let F and G be ordered sets. A total
> function $\tau : F \longrightarrow G$ is **monotonic** if and only if
>
> $$\forall h_1, h_2 : F \bullet \quad h_1 \circleddash h_2 \Longrightarrow \tau(h_1) \circleddash \tau(h_2)$$

For sets and functions, monotonicity is identical to strictness (as defined on page
243).

For the customary order relations, this property corresponds to the usual notion of monotonicity. Its meaning goes further, however, if you consider the function order or the order defined in [SRI] ("less informative than or equal to"). For such orders, a monotonic function is one which does not lose any information, in the sense that if h_1 is less informative than or equal to h_2, then the same will hold between $\tau(h_1)$ and $\tau(h_2)$.

8.8.15 Continuous functions

> **Definition** (Continuous Function): Let F and G be closed sets. A total function $\tau: F \longrightarrow G$ is **continuous** if and only if:
>
> 1   • τ is monotonic.
>
> 2   • For any chain h, $\tau(\textbf{lub } h) = \textbf{lub } \tau(h)$

A continuous function is a monotonic function which is consistent with least upper bounds. In the [RI] example, namely some real interval $[a, b]$ with $\leq$, this notion of continuity is indeed consistent with the usual notion of continuity in real analysis: if $\phi: \mathbf{R} \longrightarrow \mathbf{R}$ is continuous on $[a, b]$, and x_i is an increasing sequence of elements in $[a, b]$, then

$$\text{limit}_{i \,\rightarrow\, \infty} \, \phi(x_i) = \phi(\text{limit}_{i \,\rightarrow\, \infty}(x_i))$$

For sets and functions, continuity is identical to stability as defined on page 244.

In the case of predicates (total functions with $\mathbf{B}$ as their target set), a continuous predicate is also called *admissible*. The method of **fixpoint induction**, introduced for stable predicates (page 252) applies more generally to continuous predicates on any closed set. The proof of the generalized theorem ([8.22] with the word "continuous" substituted for "stable") is immediate.

8.8.16 Least fixpoint

Let F be a set. As seen previously, a **fixpoint** of a total function $\tau: F \longrightarrow F$ is an object $h \in F$ such that $h = \tau(h)$. In the case when F is ordered, a **least fixpoint** of τ is a fixpoint h of τ such that, for any other fixpoint h',

$$h \lessapprox h'$$

Note that a total function may have no fixpoint, or it may have one or more fixpoints but no least fixpoint. Clearly, a least fixpoint, if it exists, is unique.

[8.53]

> **Theorem** (Least Fixpoint): Let F be a closed set with a minimum
> ·member. Any continuous function $\tau: F \to F$ has a least fixpoint.

A closed set with a minimum member is usually called a complete partial order or **cpo**.

The corollary of most practical interest is relative to the function order; this was theorem [8.19] (page 248).

The proof of theorem [8.53] is constructive (it considers a particular chain and proves that its least upper bound is the fixpoint sought); it generalizes the corresponding proof for function fixpoints.

Let ω be the minimum member of F. Consider the sequence h defined as follows:

$h_0 \triangleq \omega$

$h_i \triangleq \tau\,(h_{i-1})$ (for $i > 0$)

By induction, this sequence is a chain:

- $h_0 = \omega \circledcirc h_1$

- Assuming that $h_{i-1} \circledcirc h_i$ for some $i > 0$, then since τ is continuous, and consequently monotonic, $\tau\,(h_{i-1}) \circledcirc \tau\,(h_i)$, that is to say, $h_i \circledcirc h_{i+1}$.

Then h has a least upper bound, which we call τ_∞. Let us prove that τ_∞ is the least fixpoint of τ. First τ_∞ is a fixpoint:

$\tau\,(\tau_\infty) = \tau\,(h\,)$

$\qquad = \textbf{lub}\ \tau\,(h\,)$ -- since τ is continuous

$\qquad = \textbf{lub}\ <h_i>_{i=1}^{\infty}$

$\qquad = \tau_\infty$

The last equality comes from the trivial property that removing a finite number of elements from a chain (here just the first one) does not change its least upper bound.

It remains to see that τ_∞ is not just one possible fixpoint but the least. First a lemma:

[8.54]

> **Lemma**: let h and k be two chains in a closed ordered set, such that
>
> $\qquad \forall i : \mathbf{N} \bullet\ h_i \circledcirc k_i$
>
> Then:
>
> $\qquad \textbf{lub}\ <h_i> \circledcirc \textbf{lub}\ <k_i>$

Proof: Let $lh \triangleq$ **lub** h and $lk \triangleq$ **lub** k. For all $i \in \mathbf{N}$, $h_i \leqslant k_i \leqslant lk$. Hence lk is an upper bound for h. Since lh is the least upper bound of h, this implies $lh \leqslant lk$.　□

Coming back to the proof of the fixpoint theorem, let fp be a fixpoint of τ. We must prove that $\tau_\infty \leqslant fp$. Consider the constant chain k such that $k_i = fp$ for all i. Since τ is strict, it is easy to prove by induction that for all i:

$$h_i \leqslant k_i$$

So the chains h and k satisfy the conditions of lemma [8.54]; by considering their least upper bounds, we see that $lh \leqslant lh'$. This completes the proof of theorem [8.53].　□

8.8.17 Other approaches

As an introduction to the bibliographical notes that follow, a word of warning is appropriate for the reader who will go from this discussion to other presentations of the theoretical basis for denotational semantics.

Using partial functions is not the standard technique. Most authors insist that all functions be **total**, using a mathematical device: extending every domain X with a special element, usually written $\perp_X$, or just $\perp$ if there is no ambiguity; the symbol is pronounced "bottom". A bottom must be present in every domain, including extensions of basic sets such as $\mathbf{N}$ etc.

The flat order relation (8.8.4) is then defined on basic sets by

$$x \leqslant y \quad \text{iff} \quad x = \perp \lor x = y$$

The function order on $X \rightarrow Y$ (note that only total functions are considered in this framework) is not any more a universal relation defined for any X and Y but an induced order, like the cartesian product order [8.37], which depends on Y being ordered; for $h, k : X \rightarrow Y$:

$$h \leqslant_{X \rightarrow Y} k \quad \text{iff} \quad \forall x : X \bullet f(x) \leqslant_Y k(x)$$

where each order relation is indexed by the domain to which it applies. The minimum member of this function order (corresponding to the partial function $\varnothing_{X \nrightarrow Y}$ used in the preceding discussion) is the constant function

$$\perp_{X \rightarrow Y} \triangleq \lambda x : X \bullet \perp_Y$$

In this theory, all the domains considered are complete partial orders (closed, with a minimum member); in the approach of this book, only function spaces need to have a minimum member.

This framework has one advantage: it makes the notion of strictness more tangible. Here a function

$$f: X_1 \times X_2 \times \ldots \rightarrow Y$$

is strict if and only if it yields $\perp_Y$ whenever at least one of its arguments is $\perp_{X_i}$; it is not necessary to use combinators as done previously (8.7.2) or to extend lambda notation to deal with partial functions (as in exercise 8.6).

The price to pay, however, is to see the specifications and the discussions polluted throughout by the special bottom elements. Whenever you look at a member of a function's domain, you must ask yourself whether it is "normal" or "special", since the treatment will almost always different. This is all the more annoying that the supplementary elements do not have a clear intuitive interpretation, except in the case of function spaces where they denote non-terminating computations; but then in this case the partial function model is just as adequate. Bottom elements of the basic sets, such as $\perp_N$ of $\perp_B$, appear rather artificial.

In contrast, we have seen in this chapter how the use of partial functions makes it possible to build the entire theory on elementary set-theoretical properties, the only order relation of interest being subset inclusion.

We will encounter further benefits of partial functions in chapter 10, which uses the denotational model to derive proof techniques for programs. The discussion will show how to express properties of a program construct as relationships between assertions (predicates on the state) satisfied before and after execution of each construct. If we identify an assertion a with a subset of *State* and consider the denotation of a construct to be a partial function f, then the assertion satisfied after execution of the construct will essentially be $f (\cdot a \cdot)$ if a was satisfied before. This use of the image operator is made possible by partial functions, and enables much of the discussion to rely on simple properties of sets. With $\perp$-extended total functions, the same device is much more cumbersome to apply (you must make specific provisions for bottom arguments and bottom results); standard properties of image, union, intersection etc. are no longer directly relevant.

8.9 BIBLIOGRAPHICAL NOTES

The basic references for the material covered in this chapter form a subset of the general references on denotational semantics listed in the bibliographical notes to chapter 6. Particularly relevant among these are [Scott 1970], [Scott 1971], [Scott 1972], [Manna 1974], [Livercy 1978], [Stoy 1977]; see also, among chapter 10 references, [De Bakker 1982] and [Loeckx 1984].

The notion of bottom-up computation of recursive programs (page 238) comes from [Berry 1976].

Semantic specifications of call by need, which forms the basis for lazy evaluation (studied starting on page 270) may be found in [Cadiou 1972] and [Vuillemin 1976]. Lazy evaluation (non-strict functions) as a programming technique is described in [Friedman 1976]; it plays a central role in the functional language Miranda [Turner 1985] and in the dataflow language Lucid [Ashcroft 1985]. The use of strictness for object-oriented concurrent programming is described in [Meyer 1990]. On lazy wait (or "wait by necessity"), see also [Caromel 1989].

The functional language FP [Backus 1978] includes a number of high-level function combinators similar to those of section 8.7.2.

EXERCISES

8.1 Factorial as limit

Prove by induction that for any $i \in \mathbf{N}$

$$f_i = factorial \setminus 0 .. i-1$$

where f_i is defined inductively by [8.6].

8.2 Modeling booleans for stability

The definition of predicate stability (page 251) models **B** in such a way that *true* is the empty set, $\wedge$ is union, $\vee$ is intersection etc. Explain why this convention is used rather than the reverse. (**Hint**: Consider the definition of stability.)

8.3 A chain for list productions

The function *list* used in interpreting the list productions of abstract syntax specifications (8.6.4) was defined (page 258) as the union of a sequence which is not a function chain. Show that *list* can also be defined as the union of a function chain.

8.4 Structural induction

Justify structural induction and structural induction proofs (2.9) on the basis of the theory developed in this chapter.

8.5 Stability of image operations

Let X and Y be arbitrary sets, C and D arbitrary subsets of X and Y respectively. Prove that the following functionals are stable:

1   • $image_C : (X \nrightarrow Y) \rightarrow \mathbf{P}(Y)$, where $image_C \triangleq \lambda f \cdot f \, (\! C \!)$

2   • $inverse\_image_D : (X \nrightarrow Y) \rightarrow \mathbf{P}(X)$, where $inverse\_image_D \triangleq \lambda f \cdot f^{-1} \, (\! D \!)$

3   • $from\_to_{C,D} : (X \nrightarrow Y) \rightarrow \mathbf{B}$, where $from\_to_{C,D} \triangleq \lambda f \cdot f \, (\! C \!) \subseteq D$

4   • $to\_from_{D,C} : (X \nrightarrow Y) \rightarrow \mathbf{B}$, where $to\_from_{D,C} \triangleq \lambda f \cdot f^{-1} \, (\! D \!) \subseteq C$

8.6 Strictness

Define the strict interpretation of basic functions (8.7) in the framework of lambda calculus rather than combinators. Use the abstract syntax of lambda notation (5.4), appropriately extended for types (see exercise 6.1), conditional expressions and basic operators (such as predicate combinators).

8.7 Sets of real intervals

Is the ordered set SRI ([8.36], page 278) closed?

8.8 Examples of closed sets

For every ordered set X from the examples of 8.8.2, limiting the selection to those X which are closed, give examples of

  • A closed proper subset of X.
  • A subset of X which is not closed.
  • A function in $X \rightarrow X$ which is not monotonic.
  • A function in $X \rightarrow X$ which is monotonic but not continous.

8.9 Park's induction principle

Prove that if τ is a continuous function on a closed set X with a minimum member (cpo), and h is a member of X such that $\tau(h) \leqslant h$, then $\mu\tau \leqslant h$, where $\mu\tau$ is the least fixpoint of τ.

9

Axiomatic semantics

9.1 OVERVIEW

As introduced in chapter 4, the axiomatic method expresses the semantics of a programming language by associating with the language a mathematical theory for proving properties of programs written in that language.

The contrast with denotational semantics is interesting. The denotational method, as studied in previous chapters, associates a denotation with every programming language construct. In other words, it provides a **model** for the language.

This model, a collection of mathematical objects, is very abstract; but it is a model. As with all explicit specifications, there is a risk of *overspecification*: when you choose one among several possible models of a system, you risk including irrelevant details.

Some of the specifications of chapters 6 and 7 indeed appear as just one possibility among others. For example, the technique used to model block structure (chapter 7) looks very much like the corresponding implementation techniques (stack-based allocation). This was intended to make the model clear and realistic; but we may suspect that other, equally acceptable models could have been selected, and that the denotational model is more an abstract implementation than a pure specification.

The axiomatic method is immune from such criticism. It does not attempt to provide an explicit model of a programming language by attaching an explicit meaning to every construct. Instead, it defines **proof rules** which make it possible to reason about the properties of programs.

In a way, of course, the proof rules are meanings, but very abstract ones. More importantly, they are ways of reasoning *about* programs.

Particularly revealing of this difference of spirit between the axiomatic and denotational approaches is their treatment of erroneous computations:

- A denotational specification must associate a denotation with every valid language construct. As noted in 6.1, a valid construct is structurally well-formed but may still fail to produce a result (by entering into an infinite computation); or it may produce an error result. For non-terminating computations, modeling by partial functions has enabled us to avoid being over-specific; but for erroneous computations, a denotational model must spill the beans and say explicitly what special "error" values, such as *unknown* in 6.4.2, the program will yield for expressions whose value it cannot properly compute. (See also the discussion in 6.4.4.)

- In axiomatic semantics, we may often deal with erroneous cases just by making sure that no proof rule applies to them; no special treatment is required. This may be called the unobtrusive approach to erroneous cases and undefinedness.

You may want to think of two shopkeepers with different customer policies: Billy's Denotational Emporium serves all valid requests ("No construct too big or too small" is its slogan), although the service may end up producing an error report, or fail to terminate; in contrast, a customer with an erroneous or overly difficult request will be politely but firmly informed that the management and staff of Ye Olde Axiomatic Shoppe regret their inability to prove anything useful about the request.

Because of its very abstractness, axiomatic semantics is of little direct use for some of the applications of formal language specifications mentioned in chapter 1, such as writing compilers and other language systems. The applications to which it is particularly relevant are program verification, understanding and standardizing languages, and, perhaps most importantly, providing help in the construction of correct programs.

9.2 THE NOTION OF THEORY

An axiomatic description of a language, it was said above, is a theory for that language. A theory about a particular set of objects is a set of rules to express statements about those objects and to determine whether any such statement is true or false.

As always in this book, the word "statement" is used here in its ordinary sense of a property that may be true or false – not in its programming sense of command, for which this book always uses the word "instruction".

9.2.1 Form of theories

A theory may be viewed as a formal language, or more properly a **metalanguage**, defined by syntactic and semantic rules. (Chapter 1 discussed the distinction between language and metalanguage. Here the metalanguage of an axiomatic theory is the formalism used to reason about languages.)

The syntactic rules for the metalanguage, or **grammar**, define the meaningful statements of the theory, called **well-formed formulae**: those that are worth talking about. "Well-formed formula" will be abbreviated to "formula" when there is no doubt about well-formedness.

The semantic rules of the theory (*axioms* and *inference rules*), which only apply to well-formed formulae, determine which formulae are *theorems* and which ones are not.

9.2.2 Grammar of a theory

The grammar of a theory may be expressed using standard techniques such as BNF or abstract syntax, both of which apply to metalanguages just as well as to languages.

An example will illustrate the general form of a grammar. Consider a simple theory of natural integers. Its grammar might be defined by the following rules (based on a vocabulary comprising letters, the digit 0 and the symbols =, <, $\supset$, $\neg$ and '):

1   • The formulae of the metalanguage are **boolean expressions**.
2   • A boolean expression is of one of the four forms

$$\alpha = \beta$$
$$\alpha < \beta$$
$$\neg \gamma$$
$$\gamma \supset \delta$$

where α and β are **integer expressions** and γ and δ are boolean expressions.

3   • An integer expression is of one of the three forms

$$0$$
$$n$$
$$\alpha'$$

where n is any lower-case letter from the roman alphabet and α is any integer expression.

In the absence of parentheses, the grammar is ambiguous, which is of no consequence for this discussion. (For a fully formal presentation, abstract syntax, which eliminates ambiguity, would be more appropriate.)

According to the above definition, the following are well-formed formulae:

$0 = 0$

$0 \neq 0$

$m''' < 0''$

$0 = 0 \supset 0 \neq 0$

The following, however, are not well-formed formulae (do not belong to the metalanguage of the theory):

$0 < 1$ -- Uses a symbol which is not in the vocabulary of the theory.

$0 < 'n'$ -- Does not conform to the grammar.

9.2.3 Theorems and derivation

Given a grammar for a theory, which defines its well-formed formulae, we need a set of rules for **deriving** certain formulae, called **theorems** and representing true properties of the theory's objects.

The following notation expresses that a formula f is a theorem:

$\vdash f$

Only well-formed formulae may be theorems: there cannot be anything interesting to say, within the theory, about an expression which does not belong to its metalanguage. Within the miniature theory of integers, for example, it is meaningless to ask whether $0 < 1$ may be derived as a theorem since that expression simply does not belong to the metalanguage. Here as with programming languages, we never attempt to attach any meaning to a structurally invalid element. The rest of the discussion assumes all formulae to be well-formed.

> The restriction to well-formed formulae is similar, at the metalanguage level, to the conventions enforced in the specification of programming languages: as noted in 6.1, semantic descriptions apply only to statically valid constructs.

To derive theorems, a theory usually provides two kinds of rules: **axioms** and **inference rules**, together called "rules".

9.2.4 Axioms

An axiom is a rule which states that a certain formula is a theorem. The example theory might contain the axiom

A_0

$$\vdash \; 0 < 0'$$

This axiom reflects the intended meaning of ' as the successor operation on integers: it expresses that zero is less than the next integer (one).

9.2.5 Rule schemata

To characterize completely the meaning of ' as "successor", we need another axiom complementing A_0:

$A_{successor}$
      For any integer expressions m and n:

$$\vdash \;\;\; m < n \;\; \supset \;\; m' < n'$$

This expresses that if m is less than n, the same relation applies to their successors.

$A_{successor}$ is not exactly an axiom but what is called an axiom **schema** because it refers to arbitrary integer expressions m and n. We may view it as denoting an infinity of actual axioms, each of which is obtained from the axiom schema by choosing actual integer expressions for m and n. For example, choosing $0''$ and 0 for m and n yields the following axiom:

$$\vdash \;\;\; 0'' < 0 \;\; \supset \;\; 0''' < 0'$$

In more ordinary terms, this says: "2 less than 0 implies 3 less than 1" (which happens to be a true statement, although not a very insightful one).

In practice, most interesting axioms are in fact axiom schemata.

The following discussion will simply use the term "axiom", omitting "schema" when there is no ambiguity. As a further convention, single letters such as m and n will stand for arbitrary integer expressions in a rule schema: in other words, we may omit the phrase "For any integer expressions m and n".

9.2.6 Inference rules

Inference rules are mechanisms for deriving new theorems from others. An inference rule is written in the form

$$\frac{f_1, f_2, \; ..... \; , f_n}{f_0}$$

and means the following:

> If $f_1, f_2, \ldots, f_n$ are theorems, then f_0 is a theorem.

The formulae above the horizontal bar are called the **antecedents** of the rule; the formula below it is called its **consequent**.

As with axioms, many inference rules are in fact inference rule schemata, involving parameterization. "Inference rule" will be used to cover inference rule schemata as well.

The mini-theory of integers needs an inference rule, useful in fact for many other theories. The rule is known as **modus ponens** and makes it possible to use implication in inferences. It may be expressed as follows for arbitrary boolean expressions p and q:

MP

$$\frac{p, \quad p \supset q}{q}$$

This rule brings out clearly the distinction between logical implication ($\supset$) and inference: the $\supset$ sign belongs to the metalanguage of the theory: as an element of its vocabulary, it is similar to $<$, $'$, 0 etc. Although this symbol is usually read aloud as "implies", it does not by itself provide a proof mechanism, as does an inference rule. The role of modus ponens is precisely to make $\supset$ useful in proofs by enabling q to be derived as a theorem whenever both p and $p \supset q$ have been established as theorems.

Another inference rule, essential for proofs of properties of integers, is the rule of induction, of which a simple form may be stated as:

IND

$$\frac{\phi\,(0), \quad \phi\,(n) \supset \phi\,(n')}{\phi\,(n)}$$

9.2.7 Proofs

The notions of axiom and inference rule lead to a precise definition of theorems:

> **Definition** (Theorem): A theorem t in a theory is a well-formed formula of the theory, such that t may be derived from the axioms by zero or more applications of the inference rules.

The mechanism for deriving a theorem, called a **proof,** follows a precise format, already outlined in 4.6.3 (see figure 4.10). If the proof rigorously adheres to this format, no human insight is required to determine whether the proof is correct or not; indeed the task of checking the proof can be handed over to a computer program. *Discovering* the proof requires insight, of course, but not checking it if it is expressed in all rigor.

The format of a proof is governed by the following rules:

1   • The proof is a sequence of lines.

2   • Each line is numbered.

3   • Each line contains a formula, which the line asserts to be a theorem. (So you may consider that the formula on each line is preceded by an implicit $\vdash$.)

4   • Each line also contains an argument showing unambiguously that the formula of the line is indeed a theorem. This is called the **justification** of the line.

The justification (rule 4) must be one of the following:

A   • The name of an axiom or axiom schema of the theory, in which case the formula must be the axiom itself or an instance of the axiom schema.

B   • A list of references to previous lines, followed by a semicolon and the name of an inference rule or inference rule schema of the theory.

In case B, the formulae on the lines referenced must coincide with the antecedents of the inference rule, and the formula on the current line must coincide with the consequent of the rule. (In the case of a rule schema, the coincidence must be with the antecedents and consequents of an instance of the rule.)

As an example, the following is a proof of the theorem

$$\vdash \; i < i'$$

(that is to say, every number is less than its successor) in the the above mini-theory.

[9.1]

Number	Formula	Justification
M.1	$0 < 0'$	A_0
M.2	$i < i' \;\supset\; i' < i''$	$A_{successor}$
M.3	$i < i'$	M.1, M.2; IND

On line M.2 the axiom schema $A_{successor}$ is instantiated by taking i for m and i' for n. On line M.3 the inference rule IND is instantiated by taking $\phi\,(n)$ to be $i < i'$. Note that for the correctness of the proof to be mechanically checkable, as claimed above, the justification field should include, when appropriate, a description of how a rule or axiom schema is instantiated.

The strict format described here may be somewhat loosened in practice when there is no ambiguity; it is common, for example, to merge the application of more than one rule on a single line for brevity (as with the proof of figure 4.10). The present discussion, however, is devoted to a precise analysis of the axiomatic method, and it needs at least initially to be a little pedantic about the details of proof mechanisms.

9.2.8 Conditional proofs and proofs by contradiction

[This section may be skipped on first reading.]

Practical proofs in theories which support implication and negation ften rely on two useful mechanisms: conditional proofs and proofs by contradiction.

A conditional proof works as follows:

[9.2]

> **Definition** (Conditional Proof): To prove $P \supset Q$ by conditional proof, prove that Q may be derived under the assumption that P is a theorem.

A conditional proof, usually embedded in a larger proof, will be written in the form illustrated below.

Number	Formula	Justification
$i-1$	...	...
$i.1$	P	Assumption
$i.2$	...	...
...		
$i.n$	Q	...
i	$P \supset Q$	Conditional Proof
$i+1$	...	...

Figure 9.1: A conditional sub-proof

The goal of the proof is a property of the form P **implies** Q, appearing on a line numbered i. The proof appears on a sequence of lines, called the **scope** of the proof and numbered $i.1, i.2, ..., i.n$ (for some $n \geq 1$). These lines appear just before line i. The formula stated on the first line of the scope, $i.1$, must be P; the justification field of this line, instead of following the usual requirements given on page 301, simply indicates "Assumption". The formula proved on the last line of the scope, $i.j$, must be Q. The justification field of line i simply indicates "Conditional Proof".

Conditional proofs may be nested; lines in internal scopes will be numbered $i.j.k$, $i.j.k.l$ etc.

The proof of the conclusion Q in lines $i.2$ to $i.n$ may use P, from line $i.1$, as a premise. It may also use any property established on a line preceding $i.1$, if the line is not part of the scope of another conditional proof. (For a nested conditional proof, lines established as part of enclosing scopes are applicable.)

P is stated on line $i.1$ only as assumption for the conditional proof; it and any formula deduced from it and may not be used as justifications outside the scope of that proof.

Proofs by contradiction apply to theories which support negation:

Definition (Proof by Contradiction): To prove P by contradiction, prove that *false* may be derived under the assumption that $\neg P$ is a theorem.

The general form of the proof is the same as above; here the goal on line i is P, with "Contradiction", instead of "Conditional Proof", in its justification field. The property proved on the last line of the scope, $i.j$, must be *false*.

9.2.9 Interpretations and models

As presented so far, a theory is a purely formal mechanism to derive certain formulae as theorems. No commitment has been made as to what the formulae actually represent, except for the example, which was interpreted as referring to integers.

In practice, theories are developed not just for pleasure but also for profit: to deduce useful properties of actual mathematical entities. To do so requires providing **interpretations** of the theory. Informally, you obtain an interpretation by associating a member of some mathematical domain with every element of the theory's vocabulary, in such a way that a boolean property of the domain is associated with every well-formed formula. A **model** is an interpretation which associates a true property with every theorem of the theory. The only theories of interest are those which have at least one model.

When a theory has a model, it often has more than one. The example theory used above has a model in which the integer zero is associated with the symbol 0, the successor operation on integers with the symbol ', the integer equality relation with = and so on. But other models are also possible; for example, the set of all persons past and present (assumed to be infinite), with 0 interpreted as modeling some specific person (say the reader), x' interpreted as the mother of x, $x < y$ interpreted as "y is a maternal ancestor of x" and so on, would provide another model.

Often, a theory is developed with one particular model in mind. This was the case for the example theory, which referred to the integer model, so much so that the vocabulary of its metalanguage was directly borrowed from the language of integers. Similarly, the theories developed in the sequel are developed for a specific application such as the semantics of programs or, in the example of the next section, lambda expressions. But when we study axiomatic semantics we must forget about the models and concentrate on the mechanisms for deriving theorems through purely logical rules.

9.2.10 Discussion

As a conclusion of this quick review of the notion of theory and proof, some qualifications are appropriate. As defined by logicians, theories are purely formal objects, and proof is a purely formal game. The aim pursued by such rigor (where, in the words of [Copi 1973], "a system has rigor when no formula is asserted to be a theorem unless it is logically entailed by the axioms") is to spell out the intellectual mechanisms that underlie mathematical reasoning.

It is well known that ordinary mathematical discourse is not entirely formal, as this would be unbearably tedious; the proof process leaves some details unspecified and skips some steps when it appears that they do not carry any conceptual difficulty.

The need for a delicate balance between rigor and informality is well accepted in ordinary mathematics, and in most cases this works to the satisfaction of everyone concerned – although "accidents" do occur, of which the most famous historically is the very first proof of Euclid's *Elements*, where the author relied at one point on geometrical intuition, instead of restricting himself to his explicitly stated axioms. Formal logic, of course, is more demanding.

Although purely formal in principle, theories are subject to some plausibility tests. Two important properties are:

- Soundness: a theory is sound if for no well-formed formula f the rules allow deriving both f and $\neg f$.

- Completeness: a theory is complete if for any well-formed formula f the rules allow the derivation of f or $\neg f$.

Both definitions assume that the metalanguage of the theory includes a symbol $\neg$ (not) corresponding to denial.

Soundness is also called "non-contradiction" or "consistency". It can be shown that a theory is sound if and only if it has a model, and that it is complete if and only if every true property of any model may be derived as a theorem.

An unsound theory is of little interest; any proposed theory should be checked for its soundness. One would also expect all "good" theories to be complete, but this is not the case: among the most importants results of mathematical logic are the incompleteness of such theories as predicate calculus or arithmetic. The study of completeness and soundness, however, falls beyond the scope of this book.

9.3 AN EXAMPLE: TYPED LAMBDA CALCULUS

[This section may be skipped on first reading. It assumes an understanding of sections 5.4 to 5.10.]

Before introducing theories of actual programming languages, it is interesting to study a small and elegant theory, due to Cardelli, which shows well the spirit of the axiomatic method, free of any imperative concern.

Chapter 5 introduced the notion of typed lambda calculus and defined (5.10.3) a mechanism which, when applied to a lambda expression, yields its type. The theory introduced below makes it possible to prove that a certain formula has a certain type – which is of course the same one as what the typing mechanism of chapter 5 would compute.

The theory's formulae are all of the form

$$b \mid e : t$$

where e is a typed lambda expression, t is a type and b is a binding (defined below). The informal meaning of such a formula is:

"Under b, e has type t."

Recall that a type of the lambda calculus is either:

1   • One among a set of basic predefined types (such as **N** or **B**).
2   • Of the form $\alpha \rightarrow \beta$, where α and β are types.

In case of ambiguity in multi-arrow type formulae, parentheses may be used; by default, arrows associate to the right.

A binding is a possibly empty sequence of <*identifier, type*> pairs. Such a sequence will be written under the form

$$x : \alpha + y : \beta + z : \gamma$$

and may be informally interpreted as the binding under which x has type α and so on. The notation also uses the symbol + for concatenation of bindings, as in $b + x : \alpha$ where b is a binding. The same identifier may appear twice in a binding; in this case the rightmost occurrence will take precedence, so that under the binding

$$x : \alpha + y : \beta + x : \gamma$$

x has type γ. One of the axioms below will express this property formally.

In typed lambda calculus, we declare every dummy identifier with a type (as in $\lambda x : \alpha \bullet e$). This means that the types of all bound identifier occurrences in a typed lambda expression are given in the expression itself. As for the free identifiers, their types will be determined by the environment of the expression when it appears as a sub-expression of a larger expression. So if an expression contains containing free identifier occurrences we can only define its type relative to the possible bindings of these identifiers.

To derive the type of an expression e, then, is to prove a property of the form

$$b \quad | \quad e : \alpha$$

for some type α. The binding b may only contain information on identifiers occurring free in e (any other information would be irrelevant). If no identifier occurs free in e, b will be empty.

Let us see how a system of axioms and inference rules may capture the type properties of lambda calculus. In the following rule schemata, e and f will denote arbitrary lambda expressions, x an arbitrary identifier and b an arbitrary binding.

The first axiom schema gives the basic semantics of bindings and the "rightmost strongest" convention mentioned above:

Right

$$b + x : \alpha \quad | \quad x : \alpha$$

In words: "Under binding b extended with type α for x, x has type α" – even if b gave another type for x.

Deducing types of identifiers other than the rightmost in a binding requires a simple axiom schema:

Perm

$$b + x : \alpha + y : \beta \quad | \quad x : \alpha \qquad \text{if } x \text{ and } y \text{ are different identifiers}$$

To obtain the rules for typing the various forms of lambda expressions, we must remember that a lambda expression is one of atom, abstraction or application.

Atoms (identifiers) are already covered by Right: their types will be whatever the binding says about them. We do not need to introduce the notion of predefined identifier explicitly since the theory will yield a lambda expression's type relative to a certain binding, which expresses the types of the expression's free identifiers. If a formula is incorrect for some reason (as a lambda expression involving an identifier to which no type has been assigned), the axiomatic specification will not reject it; instead, it simply makes it impossible to prove any useful type property for this expression.

Abstractions describe functions and are covered by the following rule:

$I_{Abstraction}$

$$\frac{b \,+\, x: \alpha \quad | \quad e: \beta}{b \quad | \quad \{\lambda\, x: \alpha \bullet e\}: \alpha \rightarrow \beta}$$

This rule captures the type semantics of lambda abstractions: if assigning type α to x makes it possible to assign type β to e, then the abstraction $\lambda\, x: \alpha \bullet e$ describes a function of type $\alpha \rightarrow \beta$.

In a form of the lambda calculus that would support generic functions with implicit typing (inferred from the context rather than specified in the text of the expression), this rule could be adapted to:

$I_{Generic\_abstraction}$

$$\frac{b \,+\, x: \alpha \quad | \quad e: \beta}{b \quad | \quad \{\lambda\, x \bullet e\}: \alpha \rightarrow \beta}$$

making it possible, for example, to derive $\alpha \rightarrow \alpha$, for **any** α, as type of the function:

$Id \triangleq \lambda\, x \bullet x$

and similarly for other generic functions. But we shall not pursue this path any further.

In an axiomatic theory covering programming languages rather than lambda calculus, a pair of rules similar to Right and $I_{Abstraction}$ could be written to account for typing in block-structured languages, where innermost declarations have precedence.

Finally we need an inference rule for application expressions:

$I_{Application}$

$$\frac{b \quad | \quad f: \alpha \rightarrow \beta \qquad b \quad | \quad e: \alpha}{b \quad | \quad f\,(e): \beta}$$

In other words, if a function of type $\alpha \rightarrow \beta$ is applied to an argument, which must be of type α, the result is of type β. This completes the theory.

This theory is powerful enough to derive types for lambda expressions. It is interesting to compare the deduction process in this theory with the "computations" of types made possible by the techniques introduced in 5.10. That section used the following expression as example:

$\lambda\, x: \mathbf{N} \rightarrow \mathbf{N} \bullet \lambda\, y: \mathbf{N} \rightarrow \mathbf{N} \bullet \lambda\, z: \mathbf{N} \bullet x \,(\, \{\lambda\, x: \mathbf{N} \bullet y \,(x)\} \,(z)\,)$

E.1 $x: \mathbf{N} \rightarrow \mathbf{N} + y: \mathbf{N} \rightarrow \mathbf{N} + z: \mathbf{N} \mid x: \quad \mathbf{N} \rightarrow \mathbf{N}$

                                                                                            Right, Perm

E.2 $x: \mathbf{N} \rightarrow \mathbf{N} + y: \mathbf{N} \rightarrow \mathbf{N} + z: \mathbf{N} + x: \mathbf{N} \mid z: \quad \mathbf{N}$

                                                                                            Right, Perm

E.3 $x: \mathbf{N} \rightarrow \mathbf{N} + y: \mathbf{N} \rightarrow \mathbf{N} + z: \mathbf{N} + x: \mathbf{N} \mid x: \quad \mathbf{N}$

                                                                                            Right

E.4 $x: \mathbf{N} \rightarrow \mathbf{N} + y: \mathbf{N} \rightarrow \mathbf{N} + z: \mathbf{N} + x: \mathbf{N} \mid y: \quad \mathbf{N} \rightarrow \mathbf{N}$

                                                                                            Right, Perm

E.5 $x: \mathbf{N} \rightarrow \mathbf{N} + y: \mathbf{N} \rightarrow \mathbf{N} + z: \mathbf{N} + x: \mathbf{N} \mid y \ (x): \quad \mathbf{N}$

                                                                                            E.3, E.4; I_{App}

E.6 $x: \mathbf{N} \rightarrow \mathbf{N} + y: \mathbf{N} \rightarrow \mathbf{N} + z: \mathbf{N} \mid \lambda x: \mathbf{N} \bullet y \ (x): \quad \mathbf{N} \rightarrow \mathbf{N}$

                                                                                            E.5; I_{Abst}

E.7 $x: \mathbf{N} \rightarrow \mathbf{N} + y: \mathbf{N} \rightarrow \mathbf{N} + z: \mathbf{N} \mid \{\lambda x: \mathbf{N} \bullet y \ (x)\} \ (z): \quad \mathbf{N}$

                                                                                            E.2, E.6; I_{App}

E.8 $x: \mathbf{N} \rightarrow \mathbf{N} + y: \mathbf{N} \rightarrow \mathbf{N} + z: \mathbf{N} \mid x \ (\{\lambda x: \mathbf{N} \bullet y \ (x)\} \ (z)): \quad \mathbf{N}$

                                                                                            E.1, E.7; I_{App}

E.9 $x: \mathbf{N} \rightarrow \mathbf{N} + y: \mathbf{N} \rightarrow \mathbf{N} \mid \lambda z: \mathbf{N} \bullet x \ (\{\lambda x: \mathbf{N} \bullet y \ (x)\} \ (z)):$

                                                                                            $\mathbf{N} \rightarrow \mathbf{N}$

                                                                                            E.8; I_{Abst}

E.10 $x: \mathbf{N} \rightarrow \mathbf{N} \mid \lambda y: \mathbf{N} \rightarrow \mathbf{N} \bullet \lambda z: \mathbf{N} \bullet x \ (\{\lambda x: \mathbf{N} \bullet y \ (x)\} \ (z)):$

                                                                                            $(\mathbf{N} \rightarrow \mathbf{N}) \rightarrow (\mathbf{N} \rightarrow \mathbf{N})$

                                                                                            E.9; I_{Abst}

E.11 $\mid \lambda x: \mathbf{N} \bullet \lambda y: \mathbf{N} \rightarrow \mathbf{N} \bullet \lambda z: \mathbf{N} \bullet x \ (\{\lambda x: \mathbf{N} \bullet y \ (x)\} \ (z)):$

                                                                                            $(\mathbf{N} \rightarrow \mathbf{N}) \rightarrow ((\mathbf{N} \rightarrow \mathbf{N}) \rightarrow (\mathbf{N} \rightarrow \mathbf{N}))$

                                                                                            E.10; I_{Abst}

Figure 9.2: A type inference in lambda calculus

The figure on the adjacent page shows how to derive the type of this expression in the theory exposed above. You are invited to compare it with the type computation of figure 5.4, which it closely parallels. (The subscripts in $I_{Application}$ and $I_{Abstraction}$ have been abbreviated as *App* and *Abst* respectively on the figure.)

The rest of this chapter investigates axiomatic theories of programming languages, which mostly address dynamic semantics: the meaning of expressions and instructions. This example just outlined, which could be transposed to programming languages, shows that the axiomatic method may be applied to static semantics as well.

9.4 AXIOMATIZING PROGRAMMING LANGUAGES

9.4.1 Assertions

The theories of most interest for this discussion apply to programming languages; the formulae should express relevant properties of programs.

For the most common class of programming languages, such properties are conveniently expressed through **assertions**. An assertion is a property of the program's objects, such as

$$x + y > 3$$

which may or may not be satisfied by a state of the program during execution. Here, for example, a state in which variables x and y have values 5 and 6 satisfies the assertion; one in which they both have value 0 does not.

For the time being, an assertion will simply be expressed as a boolean expression in concrete syntax, as in this example; this represents an assertion satisfied by all states in which the boolean expression has value true. A more precise definition of assertions in the Graal context will be given below (9.5.2).

9.4.2 Preconditions and postconditions

The formulae of an axiomatic theory for a programming languages are not the assertions themselves, but expressions involving both assertions and program fragments. More precisely, the theory expresses the properties of a program fragment with respect to the assertions that are satisfied before and after execution of the fragment. Two kinds of assertion must be considered:

- **Preconditions**, assumed to be satisfied before the fragment is executed.

- **Postconditions**, guaranteed to be satisfied after the fragment has been executed.

A program or program fragment will be said to be correct with respect to a certain precondition P and a certain postcondition Q if and only if, when executed in a state in which P is satisfied, it yields a state in which Q is satisfied.

The difference of words – *assumed* vs. *ensured* – is significant: we treat preconditions and postconditions differently. Most significant program fragments are only applicable under certain input assumptions: for example, a Fortran compiler will not produce interesting results if presented with the data for the company's payroll program, and conversely. The precondition should of course be as broad as possible (for example, the behavior of the compiler for texts which differ from correct Fortran texts by a small number of common mistakes should be predictable); but the specification of any realistic program can only predict the complete behavior of the program for a subset of all possible cases.

It is the responsibility of the environment to invoke the program or program fragment only for cases that fall within the precondition; the postcondition binds the program, but only in cases when the precondition is satisfied.

So a pre-post specification is like a contract between the environment and the program: the precondition obligates the environment, and the postcondition obligates the program. If the environment does not observe its part of the deal, the program may do what it likes; but if the precondition is satisfied and the program fails to ensure the postcondition, the program is incorrect. These ideas lie at the basis of a theory of software construction which has been termed **programming by contract** (see the bibliographical notes).

Defined in this way, program correctness is only a *relative* concept: there is no such thing as an intrinsically correct or intrinsically incorrect program. We may only talk about a program being correct or incorrect with respect to a certain specification, given by a precondition and a postcondition.

9.4.3 Partial and total correctness

The above discussion is vague on whose responsibility it is to ensure that the program terminates. Two different approaches exist: *partial* and *total* correctness.

The following definitions characterize these approaches; they express the correctness, total or partial, of a program fragment a with respect to a precondition P and a postcondition Q.

> **Definition** (Total Correctness). A program fragment a *is* totally correct for P and Q if and only if the following holds: Whenever a is executed in any state in which P is satisfied, the execution terminates and the resulting state satisfies Q.

> **Definition** (Partial Correctness). A program fragment a is partially
> correct for P and Q if and only if the following holds: Whenever a
> is executed in any state in which P is satisfied and this execution
> terminates, the resulting state satisfies Q.

Partial correctness may also be called conditional correctness: to prove it, you are
only required to prove that the program achieves the postcondition **if** it terminates. In
contrast, proving total correctness means proving that it achieves the postcondition **and**
that it terminates.

You might wonder why anybody should be interested in partial correctness. How
good is the knowledge that a program *would* be correct if it only were so kind as to
terminate? In fact, any non-terminating program is partially correct with respect to any
specification. For example, the following loop

> **while** $0 = 0$ **do**
>   *print* (*"We try harder!"*)
> **end**;
> *print* (*"We have proved Fermat's last theorem"*)

is partially correct with respect to the precondition *true* and a postcondition left for the
reader to complete (actually, any will do).

The reason for studying partial correctness is pragmatic: methods for proving
termination are often different in nature from methods for proving other program
properties. This encourages proving separately that the program is partially correct and that
it terminates. If you follow this approach, you must never forget that partial correctness is
a useless property until you have proved termination.

9.4.4 Varieties of axiomatic semantics

The work on axiomatic semantics was initiated by Floyd in a 1967 article (see the
bibliographical notes). Floyd's techniques, however, relied on programs expressed by
flowcharts.

The current frame of reference for this field is the subsequent work of Hoare, which
proposes a logical system for proving properties of program fragments. The well-formed
formulae in such a system will be called **pre-post formulae**. They are of the form

> $\{P\}\ a\ \{Q\}$

where P is the precondition, a is the program fragment, and Q is the postcondition.
(Hoare's original notation was $P\ \{a\}\ Q$, but this discussion will use braces according to
the convention of Pascal and other languages which treat them as comment delimiters.)

The notation expresses **partial correctness** of a with respect to P and Q: in this method, termination must be proved separately.

So a Hoare theory of a programming language consists of axioms and inference rules for deriving certain pre-post formulae. This approach may be called **pre-post semantics**.

Another approach was developed by Dijkstra. Its aim is to develop, rather than a logical theory, a **calculus** of programs, which makes it possible to reason on program fragments and the associated assertions in a manner similar to the way we reason on arithmetic and other expressions in calculus: through the application of well-formalized transformation rules. Another difference with pre-post semantics is that this theory handles total correctness. This approach may be called **wp-semantics**, where wp stands for "weakest precondition"; the reason for this name will become clear later (9.8).

We will look at these two approaches in turn. Of the two, only the pre-post method fits exactly in the axiomatic framework as defined above. But the spirit of wp-semantics is close.

9.5 A CLOSER LOOK AT ASSERTIONS

The theory of axiomatic semantics, in either its "pre-post" or "wp" flavor, applies to formulae whose basic constituents are assertions. To define the metalanguage of the theory properly, we must first give a precise definition of assertions and of the operators applicable to them.

Because assertions are properties involving program objects (variables, constants, arrays etc.), the assertion metalanguage may only be defined formally within the context of a particular programming language. For the discussion which follows that language will be Graal.

9.5.1 Assertions and boolean expressions

An assertion has been defined as a property of program objects, which a given state of program execution may or may not satisfy.

Graal, in common with all usual programming languages, includes a construct which seems very close to this notion: the boolean expression. A boolean expression also involves program objects, and has a value which is true or false depending on the values of these objects. For example, the boolean expression $x + y > 3$ has value true in a state if and only if the sums of the values that the program variables x and y have in this state is greater than three.

Such a boolean expression may be taken as representing an assertion as well – the assertion satisfied by those states in which the boolean expression has value true.

Does this indicate a one-to-one correspondence between assertions and boolean expressions? This is actually two questions:

1   • Given an arbitrary boolean expression of the programming language, can we
     always associate an assertion with it, as in the case of $x + y > 3$?

2   • Can any assertion of interest for the axiomatic theory of a programming language
     be expressed as a boolean expression?

For the axiomatic theory of Graal given below, the answer to these questions turns
out to be yes. But this should not lead us confuse assertions with boolean expressions;
there are both theoretical and practical reasons for keeping the two notions distinct.

On the theoretical side, assertions and boolean expressions belong to different worlds:

• Boolean expressions appear *in* programs: they belong to the programming
  language.

• Assertions express properties *about* programs: they belong to the formulae of the
  axiomatic theory.

On the practical side, languages with more powerful forms of expressions than Graal,
including all common programming languages, may yield a negative answer to both
questions 1 and 2 above. To express the assertions of interest in such languages, the
formalism of boolean expressions is at the same time too powerful (not all boolean
expressions can be interpreted as assertions) and not powerful enough (some assertions are
not expressible as boolean expressions).

Examples of negative answers to question 1 may arise from functions with side-
effects: in most languages you can write a boolean expression such as

$$f (x) > 0$$

where f is a function with side-effects. Such boolean expressions are clearly inadequate to
represent assertions, which should be purely descriptive ("applicative") statements about
program states.

As an example of why the answer to question 2 could be negative (not all assertions
of interest are expressible as boolean expressions), consider an axiomatic theory for any
language offering arrays. We may want to use an axiomatic theory to prove that any state
immediately following the execution of a sorting routine satisfies the assertion

$$\forall i: 1 .. n-1 \bullet t [i] \leq t [i+1]$$

where t is an array of bounds 1 and n. But this cannot be expressed as a boolean
expression in ordinary languages, which do not support quantifiers such as $\forall$.

Commonly supported boolean expressions are just as unable to express a requirement
such as "the values of t are a permutation of the original values" – another part of the
sorting routine's specification.

To be sure, confusing assertions and boolean expressions in the specification of a
language as simple as Graal would not cause any serious trouble. It is indeed often
convenient to express assertions in boolean expression notation, as with $x + y > 3$ above.
But to preserve the theory's general applicability to more advanced languages we should
resist any temptation to identify the two notions.

9.5.2 Abstract syntax for assertions

To keep assertions conceptually separate from boolean expressions, we need a specific abstract syntactic type for assertions. For Graal it may be defined as:

> *Assertion* $\triangleq$ *exp: Expression*

with a static validity function expressing that the acceptable expressions for *exp* must be of type boolean:

[9.3]

> $V_{Assertion}$ [*a* : *Assertion* , *tm* : *Type_map*] $\triangleq$
>
> $V_{Expression}$ [*a. exp*, *tm*] $\wedge$ *expression_type* (*a. exp*, *tm*) = *bt*

This yields the following complete (if rather pedantic) form for the assertion used earlier as example under the form $x + y > 3$:

[9.4]

> *Assertion*
>> (*exp: Expression* (*Binary*
>>> (*term1: Expression* (*binary*
>>>> (*term1: Variable* (*id:* "x");
>>>> *term2: Variable* (*id:* "y");
>>>> *op: Operator* (*Arithmetic_op* (*Plus*))));
>>> *term2: Constant* (*Integer_constant* (3));
>>> *op: Operator* (*Relational_op* (*Gt*)))))

or if we just use plain concrete syntax for expressions:

> *Assertion* (*exp:* $x + y > 3$)

For simplicity, the rest of this chapter will use concrete syntax for simple assertions and their constituent expressions; furthermore, it will not explicitly distinguish between an assertion an the associated expression when no confusion is possible. So the above assertion will continue to be written $x + y > 3$ without the enclosing *Assertion* (*exp:* ...).

In the same spirit, the discussion will freely apply boolean operators such as **and**, **or** and **not** to assertions; for example, P **and** Q will be used instead of

> *Assertion* (*exp: Expression* (*Binary*
>> (*term1: P.exp*;
>> *term2: Q.exp*;
>> *op: Operator* (*Boolean_op* (*And*)))))

It is important, however, to bear in mind that these are only notational facilities.

The next chapter shows how to give assertions a precise semantic interpretation in the context of denotational semantics.

9.5.3 Implication

In stating the rules of axiomatic semantics for any language, we will need to express properties of the form: "Any state that satisfies P satisfies Q". This will be written using the infix **implies** operator as

$\quad$ P **implies** Q

When such a property holds and the reverse, Q **implies** P, does not, P will be said said to be **stronger** than Q, and Q **weaker** than P.

The **implies** operator takes two assertions as its operands; its result, however, is not an assertion but simply a boolean value that depends on P and Q. This value is true if and only if Q is satisfied whenever P is satisfied. P **implies** Q is a well-formed formula of the metalanguage of axiomatic semantics, not a programming language construct.

9.6 FUNDAMENTALS OF PRE-POST SEMANTICS

The basic concepts are now in place to introduce axiomatic theories for programming languages such as Graal, beginning with the pre-post approach.

This section examines general rules applicable to any programming language; the next section will discuss specific language constructs in the Graal context.

9.6.1 Formulae of interest in pre-post semantics

The formulae of pre-post semantics are pre-post formulae of the form $\{P\}$ a $\{Q\}$. The purpose of pre-post semantics is to to derive certain such formulae as theorems. The intuitive meaning of a pre-post formula is the following:

[9.5]

> **Interpretation of pre-post formulae**: A pre-post formula $\{P\}$ a $\{Q\}$ expresses that a is partially correct with respect to precondition P and postcondition Q.

From the definition of partial correctness (page 310), this means that the computation of a, started in any state satisfying P, will (if it terminates) yield a state satisfying Q. The next chapter will interpret this notion in terms of the denotational model.

9.6.2 The rule of consequence

The first inference rule (in fact, as the subsequent rules, a rule schema) is the language-independent rule of consequence, first introduced in 4.6.2. It states that "less informative" formulae may be deduced from ones that carry more information. This concept may now be expressed more rigorously using the **implies** operator on assertions:

CONS

$$\frac{\{P\}\ a\ \{Q\}, \quad P'\ \textbf{implies}\ P, \quad Q\ \textbf{implies}\ Q'}{\{P'\}\ a\ \{Q'\}}$$

9.6.3 Facts from elementary mathematics

The axiomatic theory of a programming language is not developed in a vacuum. Programs manipulate objects which represent integers, real numbers, characters and the like. When we attempt to prove properties of these programs, we may have to rely on properties of these objects. This means that our axiomatic theories for programming languages may have to embed other, non-programming-language-specific theories.

Assume that in a program manipulating integer variables only, we are able (as will indeed be the case with the axiomatic theory of Graal) to prove

[9.6]

$$\vdash \{x + x > 2\}\ y := x + x\ \{y > 1\},$$

but what we really want to prove is

[9.7]

$$\vdash \{x > 1\}\ y := x + x\ \{y > 1\}$$

> Before going any further you should make sure that you understand the different notations involved. The formulae in braces {...} represent assertions, each defined, as we have seen, by the associated Graal boolean expression. Occurrences of arithmetic operators such as + or > in these expressions denote Graal operators – not the corresponding mathematical functions, which would be out of place here. If programming language constructs (such as the Graal operator for addition) were confused with their denotations (such as mathematical addition), there would be no use or sense for formal semantic definitions.

How can we prove [9.7] assuming we know how to prove [9.6]? The rule of consequence is the normal mechanism: from the antecedents

[9.6]

$$\{x + x > 2\}\ y := x + x\ \{y > 1\}$$

[9.8]
    $\{x > 1\}$ **implies** $\{x + x > 2\}$

direct application of the rule of consequence will yield [9.7].

This assumes that we can rely on the second antecedent, [9.8]. But we cannot simply accept [9.8] as a trivial property from elementary arithmetic. Actually, its formula does not even *belong* to the language of elementary arithmetic; as just recalled, it is not a mathematical property but a well-formed formula of the Graal assertion language. Deductions involving such formulae require an appropriate theory, transposing to programming language objects the properties of the corresponding objects in mathematics – integers, boolean values, real numbers.

When applied to actual programs, written in an actual programming languages and meant to be executed on an actual computer, this theory cannot be a blind copy of standard mathematics. For integers, it needs to take size limitations and overflow into account; this is the object of exercise 9.1. For "real" numbers, it needs to describe the properties of their floating-point approximations.

For the study of Graal, which only has integers, we will accept arithmetic at face value, taking for granted all the usual properties of integers and booleans. The rest of this discussion assumes that the theory of Graal is built on top of another axiomatic theory, called EM for elementary mathematics. EM is assumed to include axioms and inference rules applicable to basic Graal operators (+, –, <, >, **and** etc.) and reflecting the properties of the corresponding mathematical operators. Whenever a proof needs a property such as [9.8] above, the justification will simply be the mention "EM".

EM also includes properties of the mathematical implication operation, transposed to the **implies** operation on assertions. An example of such a property is the transitivity of implication: for any assertions P, Q, R,

    $\vdash$ $((P$ **implies** $Q)$ **and** $(Q$ **implies** $R))$ **implies** $(P$ **implies** $R)$

Chapter 10 will use the denotational model to define the semantics of assertions in a formal way, laying the basis for a rigorously established EM theory, although this theory will not be spelled out.

Using EM, the proof that [9.7] follows from [9.6] may be written as:

1	[9.6] $\{x > 1\}$ $y := x + x$ $\{y > 1\}$	(proved separately)
2	$x > 1$ **implies** $x + x > 2$	EM
3	[9.7] $\{x > 1\}$ $x := x + x$ $\{y > 1\}$	T1, T2; CONS

The EM rules used in this chapter are all straightforward. In proofs of actual programs, you will find that axiomatizing the various object domains may be a major part of the task. One of the proofs below (the "tower of Hanoi" recursive routine, 9.10.9), as well as exercises 9.25 and 9.26, provide examples of building theories adapted to specific problems. But some object domains are hard to axiomatize. For example, producing a good theory for floating-point numbers and the associated operations, as implemented by computers, is a difficult task. Such problems are among the major practical obstacles that arise in efforts to prove full-scale programs.

9.6.4 The rule of conjunction

A language-independent inference rule similar in scope to the rule of consequence is useful in some proofs. This rule states that if you can derive two postconditions you may also derive their logical conjunction:

CONJ

$$\frac{\{P\}\ a\ \{Q\}, \quad \{P\}\ a\ \{R\}}{\{P\}\ a\ \{Q\ \textbf{and}\ R\}}$$

Note that conversely if you have established $\vdash \{P\}\ a\ \{Q\ \textbf{and}\ R\}$, then you may derive both $\vdash \{P\}\ a\ \{Q\}$ and $\vdash \{P\}\ a\ \{Q\}$. This property does not need to be introduced as a rule of the theory but follows from the rule of consequence, since the following are EM theorems:

$(Q\ \textbf{and}\ R)\ \textbf{implies}\ Q$

$(Q\ \textbf{and}\ R)\ \textbf{implies}\ R$

Wp-semantics, as studied later in this chapter, will enable us to determine whether there is a corresponding "rule of disjunction" for the **or** operator (see 9.9.4).

9.7 PRE-POST SEMANTICS OF GRAAL

We now have all the necessary background for the axiomatic theory of Graal instructions.

9.7.1 Skip

The first instruction to consider is *Skip*. The pre-post axiom schema is predictably neither hard nor remarkable.

A_{Skip}

$\quad \vdash \quad \{P\}\ Skip\ \{P\}$

Skip does not do anything, so what the user of this instruction may be guaranteed on exit is no more and no less than what he is prepared to guarantee on entry.

9.7.2 Assignment

The axiom schema for assignment uses the notion of **substitution**. For any assertion Q:

$A_{Assignment}$

$\vdash$ $\{Q \,[x \leftarrow e\,]\}$ *Assignment (target: x; source: e)* $\{Q\}$

This rule introduces a new notation: $Q \,[x \leftarrow e\,]$, read as "Q with x replaced by e", is the substitution of e for all occurrences of x in Q. This notation is applicable when Q and e are expressions and x is a variable; it immediately extends to the case when Q is an assertion.

Substitution is a purely textual operation, involving no computation of the expression: to obtain $Q \,[x \leftarrow e\,]$, you take Q and replace occurrences of x by e throughout. We need to define this notion formally, of course, but let us first look at a few examples of substitution. As mentioned above, the expressions apply arithmetic and relational operations in standard concrete syntax.

1     $\vdash$ $3 \,[x \leftarrow y + 1] \;=\; 3$

2     $\vdash$ $(z * 7) \,[x \leftarrow y + 1] \;=\; z * 7$

3     $\vdash$ $x \,[x \leftarrow y + 1] \;=\; y + 1$

4     $\vdash$ $(x^2 - x^3) \,[x \leftarrow y + 1] \;=\; (y+1)^2 - (y+1)^3$

5     $\vdash$ $(x + y) \,[x \leftarrow y + 1] \;=\; (y+1) + y$

6     $\vdash$ $(x + y) \,[x \leftarrow x + y + 1] \;=\; (x + y + 1) + y$

In the first two examples, x does not occur in Q, so that $Q \,[x \leftarrow e\,]$ is identical to Q (a constant in the first case, a binary expression not involving x in the second). In example 3, Q is just the target x of the substitution, so that the result is e, here $y + 1$. In example 4, x appears more than once in Q and all occurrences are substituted. Example 5 shows a case when a variable, here y, appears in both Q and e; note that rules of ordinary arithmetic would allow replacement of the right-hand side by $2*y + 1$, but this is outside the substitution mechanism. Finally, example 6 shows the important case in which x, the variable being substituted for, appears in e, the replacement.

We need a way to define substitution formally. Let

$Q \,[x \leftarrow e\,] \;\triangleq\; subst \,(Q, e, x \,.\, id\,)$

where function *subst*, a simplified version of the substitution function introduced in 5.7 for lambda calculus (see figure 5.2), is defined by structural induction on expressions:

[9.9]

> *subst* (*Q*: *Expression*, *e*: *Expression*, *x*: *Identifier*) $\triangleq$
>
> > **case** *Q* **of**
> >
> > > *Constant* $\Rightarrow$ *Q* |
> > >
> > > *Variable* $\Rightarrow$ **if** *Q*.*id* = *x* **then** *e* **else** *Q* **end** |
> > >
> > > *Binary* $\Rightarrow$
> > > > *Expression* (*Binary* (
> > > > > *term1*: *subst* (*Q*.*term1*, *e*, *x*);
> > > > > *term2*: *subst* (*Q*.*term2*, *e*, *x*);
> > > > > *op*: *Q*.*op*))
> >
> > **end**

We may need to compose substitutions. The following property will apply:

[9.10]

$$(Q \ [a \leftarrow f]) \ [b \leftarrow g] = Q \ [a \leftarrow (f \ [b \leftarrow g])]$$

This rule applies both when *a* and *b* are the same and when they are different variables. Its proof by structural induction, using the definition of function *subst*, is the subject of exercise 9.20.

In the pre-post theory, *subst* will only be applied to boolean expressions (associated with assertions); but as these may be relational expressions involving sub-expressions of any type, we need *subst* to be defined for general expressions.

The pre-post axiom schema for assignment ($A_{Assignment}$) uses substitution to describe the result of an assignment. The idea is quite simple: whatever is true of *x* after the assignment *x* := *e* must have been true of *e* before.

The following are simple examples of the use of the axiom schema. Carry out the substitutions by yourself to see the mechanism at work.

1	$\vdash$	$\{y > z - 2\}$ $x := x + 1$ $\{y > z - 2\}$
2	$\vdash$	$\{2 + 2 = 5\}$ $x := x + 1$ $\{2 + 2 = 5\}$
3	$\vdash$	$\{y > 0\}$ $x := y$ $\{x > 0\}$
4	$\vdash$	$\{x + 1 > 0\}$ $x := x + 1$ $\{x > 0\}$

Example 1 shows that an assertion involving only variables other than the target of an assignment is preserved by the assignment. The assertion of the second example only involves constants and is similarly maintained. Note that the rule says nothing about the precondition and postcondition being "true" or "false": all that example 2 says is that if two plus two equaled five before the assignment this will still be the case afterwards – a theorem, although a useless one since its assumption does not hold.

Examples 3 and 4 result from straightforward application of substitution. For the latter, the assignment rule does not by itself yield a proof of

$$\{x > -1\} \quad x := x + 1 \quad \{x > 0\}$$

For this, EM and the rule of consequence are needed. The proof may be written as follows:

A1	$\{x + 1 > 0\}$ $x := x + 1$ $\{x > 0\}$	$A_{Assignment}$
A2	$x > -1$ **implies** $x + 1 > 0$	EM
A3	$\{x > -1\}$ $x := x + 1$ $\{x > 0\}$	A1, A2; CONS

Three important comments apply to the assignment rule.

First, the rule as given works **"backwards"**: it makes it possible to deduce a precondition Q $[v \leftarrow e]$ from the postcondition Q rather than the reverse. A forward rule is possible (see exercise 9.9), but it turns out to be less easy to apply. The observation that proofs involving assignments naturally work by sifting the postcondition back through the program to obtain the precondition has important consequences on the structure and organization of these proofs.

In a simple case, however, the backward rule yields an immediate forward property, If the source expression e for an assignment is a plain variable, rather than a constant or a composite expression, then for any assertion P:

[9.11]
$$\vdash \quad \{P\} \quad Assignment \text{ } (target: x \text{ ; } source: e) \text{ } \{P \text{ } [x \leftarrow e]\}$$

This is easily derived from $A_{Assignment}$ by taking P $[x \leftarrow e]$ for Q and noting that, by the rule for composition of substitutions ([9.10], page 320), Q $[e \leftarrow x]$ is P.

The second comment reflects on the nature of assignment. This instruction is one of the most imperative among the features that distinguish programming from the "applicative" tradition of mathematics (1.3). An assignment is a command, not a mathematical formula; it specifies an operation to be performed at a certain time during the execution of a program, not a relation that holds between mathematical entities. As a consequence, it may be difficult to predict the exact result of an assignment instruction in a program, especially since repeated assignments to the same variable will cancel each other's effect.

Axiom $A_{Assignment}$ establishes the mathematical respectability of assignment by enabling us to interpret this most unabashedly imperative of programming language constructs in terms of a "pure" – that is to say, applicative – mathematical concept: substitution.

The third comment limits the applicability of the rule. As given above, this rule only applies to languages (such as Graal) which draw a clear distinction between the notions of expression and instruction. In such languages, expressions produce values, with no effect on the run-time state of the program; in contrast, instructions may change the state, but do not return a value. This separation is violated if an expression may produce **side-effects**, usually through function calls. Consider for example a function

> *asking_for_trouble* (*x*: **in out** *INTEGER*): *INTEGER* **is**
> > **do**
>
> > > *x* := *x* + 1;
> > > *global* := *global* + 1;
> > > *Result* := 0
> > > > -- The function's returns as result the final value of
> > > > -- the predefined variable *Result* (Eiffel convention)
> > **end** -- *asking_for_trouble*

where *global* is a variable external to to *asking_for_trouble* in some fashion but declared outside of the scope of *asking_for_trouble*; for example *global* may be external in C, part of a *COMMON* in Fortran, declared in an enclosing block in Pascal, in the enclosing package in Ada or in the enclosing class in Eiffel. The following pre-post formulae are false in this case even though they would directly result from applying $A_{Assignment}$ (with a proper rule for functions):

> {*global* = 0} *global* := *asking_for_trouble* (*a*) {*global* = 0}
>
> {*a* = 0} *u* := *asking_for_trouble* (*a*) {*a* = 0}

It is possible to adapt $A_{assignment}$ to account for possible side-effect in expressions, but this makes the theory significantly more complex. Since, however, most programming languages allow functions to produce side-effects, we need a way to describe the semantics of the corresponding calls. A solution, already suggested in the discussion of denotational semantics (7.7.2), is to limit the application of $A_{Assignment}$ to assignments whose source expression does **not** include any function call. Then to deal with an assignment whose right-hand side is a function call, such as

[9.12]
> *y* := *asking_for_trouble* (*x*)

we consider that, in abstract syntax, this is not an assignment but a routine call; the abstract syntax for such an instruction includes an input argument, here *x*, and an output result, here *y*. The instruction then falls under the scope of the inference rule for such routine calls, given later in this chapter (9.10.2).

Only for the purposes of a proof do you actually need to translate an assignment of the [9.12] form into a routine call; the translation, done in abstract syntax, leaves the original concrete program unchanged. (As noted in chapter 7, this is an example of the "two-tiered specifications" discussed in 4.3.4.)

Of course, functions which produce arbitrary side-effects are bad programming practice, they damaging referential transparency. We should certainly not condone a function such as *asking_for_trouble*. But in practice many functions will need to change the state in some perfectly legitimate ways. For example any function that creates and returns a new object does perform a side-effect (by allocating memory), although from the caller's viewpoint it simply computes a result (the object) and is referentially transparent.

Because it is difficult to define useful universal rules for distinguishing between "good" and "bad" side-effects, most programming languages, even the few whose designers worried about the provability of programs, allow side-effects in functions, with few or no restrictions. To prove properties of assignments involving functions, then, you should treat them as routine calls using the transformation outlined above.

The existence of such a formal mechanism is not an excuse for undisciplined use of side-effects in expressions, especially those which do not even involve a function call, as with the infamous value-modifying C expressions of the form $x{+}{+}$ or $-{-}x$.

9.7.3 Dealing with arrays and records

The assignment axiom, as given above, is directly applicable to simple variables. How can we deal with assignments involving array elements or record fields?

Plain substitution will not work. Take for example the Pascal array assignment

$$t \ [i] := t \ [j] + 1$$

Then by naive application of axiom $A_{Assignment}$ we could prove a property such as:

[9.13]
$$\{t \ [j] = 0\} \quad t \ [i] \ := \ t \ [j] + 1 \quad \{t \ [j] = 0\}$$

Here the substitution appears trivial since the assignment's target, $t \ [i]$, does not occur in the postcondition.

Unfortunately, the above is not a theorem since the assignment will fail to ensure the postcondition if $i = j$. The problem here is a fundamental property of arrays, dynamic indexing: when you see a reference to an array element, $t \ [i]$, the program text does not tell you which array element it denotes. So it is only at run time that you will find out whether $t \ [i]$ and $t \ [j]$ denote the same array elements or different ones. Such a situation, where two different program entities may at run time happen to denote the same object, is known as **dynamic aliasing**.

One solution is to consider an assignment to an array element as an assignment to the whole array. More precisely, we may treat this operation as a separate instruction, with abstract syntax

$$Array\_assign \ \triangleq \ target: Variable \ ; \quad index: Expression \ ; \quad source: Expression$$

The associated rule is a variant of $A_{Assignment}$:

A_{Array_assign}

$\vdash$ $\{Q\ [t \leftarrow t\ (i : e)]\}$ *Array_assign (target : t ; index : i ; source : e)* $\{Q\}$

The new notation introduced, $t\ (i : e)$, denotes an array which is identical to t except that its value at index i is e. This property may be described by two axioms:

A_{Array}

$\vdash$ $i \neq j$ **implies** $t\ (i : e)\ [j] = t\ [i]$

$\vdash$ $i = j$ **implies** $t\ (i : e)\ [j] = e$

These rules yield the following two theorems (replacing [9.13]):

[9.14]

$\vdash$ $\{i \neq j$ **and** $t\ [j] = 0\}$ $t\ [i] := t\ [j] + 1$ $\{t\ [j] = 0\}$

$\vdash$ $\{i = j$ **and** $t\ [j] = 0\}$ $t\ [i] := t\ [j] + 1$ $\{t\ [j] = 1\}$

The proof is left as an exercise (9.10)

We may use a similar method to deal with objects of record types. (See also the denotational model in 7.2.) If x is such an object, and a is one of the component tags, we should treat the assignment $x.a := e$ as an assignment to x as a whole. In line with the technique used for arrays, $x\ (a : e)$ is defined as denoting an object identical to x except that its a component is equal to v. The axioms schemata for this operation are simpler with records than with arrays, as here there is no dynamic aliasing: an array index may only be known at run-time, but the tag of a reference to a record field is known statically[1].

A_{Record}

$\vdash$ $(x\ (a : e)).b = x.b$

$\vdash$ $(x\ (a : e)).a = e$

where: x is an object of a record type; a and b are different component tags of this type; dot notation $x.t$ denotes access to the component of x with tag t.

To obtain a variant of the assignment axiom applicable to record components, just imitate A_{Array_assign} after introducing the suitable abstract syntax.

---

[1] In object-oriented languages such as Eiffel or Smalltalk, the technique known as **dynamic binding** means that in some cases the actual tag must be computed at run-time.

9.7.4 Conditional

The remaining instructions are not primitive commands, but control structures used to construct complex instructions from simpler ones; as a consequence, their semantics is specified through inference rules (actually rule schemata) rather than axioms.

Here is the inference rule for conditionals:

$I_{Conditional}$

$$\{P \text{ and } c\} \ a \ \{Q\}, \qquad \{P \text{ and not } c\} \ b \ \{Q\}$$
$$\overline{\{P\} \ Conditional \ (test: c; \ thenbranch: a; \ elsebranch: b) \ \{Q\}}$$

Let us see what this means. Assume you are requested to prove the correctness, with respect to P and Q, of the instruction given in abstract syntax at the bottom of the rule, which in more casual notation would appear as

if c **then** a **else** b **end**

Since the result of executing this instruction is to execute either a or b, you may proceed by proving separately that both a and b are correct with respect to P and Q; however in the case of a you may "and" the precondition with c, since this branch will only be executed when c is initially satisfied; and similarly with **not** c for the other branch.

As an example of using this rule, consider the proof of the following program fragment, which you may recognize as an extract from Euclid's algorithm, in its variant using subtraction rather than division. (The proof of the extract will be used later as part of the proof of the complete algorithm.)

[9.15]
$$\{m, n, x, y > 0 \text{ and } x \neq y \text{ and } gcd \ (x, y) = gcd \ (m, n)\}$$

if $x > y$ **then**

$x := x - y$

else

$y := y - x$

end

$$\{m, n, x, y > 0 \text{ and } gcd \ (x, y) = gcd \ (m, n)\}$$

where all variables are of type *INTEGER*, *gcd* (u, v) denotes the greatest common divisor of two positive integers u and v and the notation $u, v, w, \ldots > 0$ is used as a shorthand for

$u > 0$ **and** $v > 0$ **and** $w > 0$ **and** $\ldots$

C1 $\{m, n, x - y, y > 0$ **and** $gcd\ (x - y, y) = gcd\ (m, n)\}$

$x := x - y$

$\{m, n, x, y > 0$ **and** $gcd\ (x, y) = gcd\ (m, n)\}$ $A_{Assignment}$

C2 $m, n, x, y > 0$ **and** $x \neq y$ **and**

$\qquad\qquad gcd\ (x, y) = gcd\ (m, n)$ **and** $x > y$

implies

$\qquad m, n, x - y, y > 0$ **and** $gcd\ (x - y, y) = gcd\ (m, n)$ EM

C3 $\{m, n, x, y > 0$ **and** $x \neq y$ **and**

$\qquad\qquad gcd\ (x, y) = gcd\ (m, n)$ **and** $x > y\}$

$x := x - y$

$\{m, n, x, y > 0$ **and** $gcd\ (x, y) = gcd\ (m, n)\}$ C1, C2; CONS

C4 $\{m, n, x, y - x > 0$ **and** $gcd\ (x, y - x) = gcd\ (m, n)\}$

$y := y - x$

$\{m, n, x, y > 0$ **and** $gcd\ (x, y) = gcd\ (m, n)\}$ $A_{Assignment}$

C5 $m, n, x, y > 0$ **and** $x \neq y$ **and**

$\qquad\qquad gcd\ (x, y) = gcd\ (m, n)$ **and not** $x > y$

implies

$\qquad m, n, y - x, y > 0$ **and** $gcd\ (x, y - x) = gcd\ (m, n)$ EM

C6 $\{m, n, x, y > 0$ **and** $x \neq y$ **and**

$\qquad\qquad gcd\ (x, y) = gcd\ (m, n)$ **and not** $x > y\}$

$y := y - x$

$\{m, n, x, y > 0$ **and** $gcd\ (x, y) = gcd\ (m, n)\}$ C4, C5; CONS

C7 $\{m, n, x, y > 0$ **and** $x \neq y$ **and**

$\qquad\qquad gcd\ (x, y) = gcd\ (m, n)\}$

CONDIT

$\{m, n, x, y > 0$ **and** $gcd\ (x, y) = gcd\ (m, n)\}$ C3, C6; $I_{Conditional}$

Figure 9.3: Proof involving a conditional instruction

The proof of [9.15] is given in full detail on the adjacent page. *CONDIT* denotes the conditional instruction under scrutiny. *P* and *Q* being the precondition and postcondition, the proof proceeds by establishing two properties separately:

$\vdash \{P \text{ and } x > y\}\ x := x - y\ \{Q\}$ (Line C3)

$\vdash \{P \text{ and } y > x\}\ y := y - x\ \{Q\}$ (Line C7)

Both cases are direct applications of the EM property that

[9.16]
$\vdash u > v > 0 \text{ implies } gcd\ (u, v) = gcd\ (u{-}v, v)$

[9.16] as well as the precondition and postcondition of [9.15] illustrate the "unobtrusive approach" to undefinedness mentioned at the beginning of this chapter. The greatest common divisor of two integers is only defined if both are positive. To deal with this problem, the assertions of [9.15] include clauses, **and**ed with the rest of these assertions, stating that the elements whose gcd is needed are positive; the formula in [9.16] uses a similar condition as the left-hand side of an **implies**.

Rather than introducing explicit rules stating when an expression's value is defined and when it is not, it is usually simpler, as here, to permit the writing of potentially undefined expressions, but to ensure through the axioms and inference rules of the theory that one can never prove anything of interest about their values.

9.7.5 Compound

Two rules are needed to deal with compound instructions. The first, an axiom schema, expresses that a zero-element compound is equivalent to a *Skip*:

$A0_{Compound}$

$$\vdash \ \{P\}\ Compound\ (<>)\ \{P\}$$

The second rule enables us to to combine the properties of more than one compound. It assumes *c* is a compound and *a* is an instruction.

$I_{Compound}$

$$\frac{\{P\}\ c\ \{Q\}, \qquad \{Q\}\ a\ \{R\}}{\{P\}\quad c\ ++ <a>\quad \{R\}}$$

The derivation shown below illustrates the technique for proving properties of compounds, based on these two rules. The property to prove is

$\{m, n > 0\}\ x := m;\ y := n\ \{m, n, x, y > 0 \text{ and } gcd\ (x, y) = gcd\ (m, n)\}$

S1 $\{m, n > 0\}$
      implies
      $\{m, n, m, n > 0 \text{ and } gcd\ (m, n) = gcd\ (m, n)\}$ EM

S2 $\{m, n, m, n > 0 \text{ and } gcd\ (m, n) = gcd\ (m, n)\}$
      $x := m$
      $\{m, n, x, n > 0 \text{ and } gcd\ (x, n) = gcd\ (m, n)\}$ $A_{Assignment}$

S3 $\{m, n > 0\}$
      $x := m$
      $\{m, n, x, n > 0 \text{ and } gcd\ (x, n) = gcd\ (m, n)\}$ S1, S2; CONS

S4 $\{m, n, x, n > 0 \text{ and } gcd\ (x, n) = gcd\ (m, n)\}$
      $y := n$
      $\{m, n, x, y > 0 \text{ and } gcd\ (x, y) = gcd\ (m, n)\}$ $A_{Assignment}$

S5 $\{m, n > 0\}$
      $x := m; y := n$
      $\{m, n, x, y > 0 \text{ and } gcd\ (x, y) = gcd\ (m, n)\}$ S3, S4; $I_{Compound}$

Figure 9.4: Proof involving a compound instruction

9.7.6 Loop

The last construct to study is the loop, for which the rule is predictably more delicate. It
is an inference rule, as follows:

I_{Loop}

$$\frac{\{I \text{ and } c\}\ b\ \{I\}}{\{I\}\ Loop\ (test: c;\ body: b)\ \{I \text{ and not } c\}}$$

This rule embodies two properties of loops. In concrete syntax, the loop considered is

   while c **do** b **end**

First, the postcondition includes **not** c because the continuation condition c will not
hold upon loop exit (otherwise the loop would have continued). Note that I_{Loop} is a
partial correctness rule, which is of little interest if the loop does not terminate. You must
prove termination separately, using techniques explained below.

The second property relates to an assertion I, called a loop **invariant**, which is assumed to be such that:

$\{I \textbf{ and } c\} \, b \, \{I\}$

In other words, if I is satisfied before an execution of b, I will still be satisfied after that execution – hence the name "invariant". The actual precondition in this hypothesis is actually not just I but I **and** c since executions of b are of interest only when they occur as part of loop iterations, that is to say when c is satisfied. The rule expresses that if the truth of I is maintained by one execution of b (under c), then it will also be maintained by any number of executions of b, and hence by a loop having b as body.

> The expressions I **and** c and I **and not** c appearing in I_{Loop} are a slight abuse of language since **and** and **not** as defined (page 314) take assertions as operands, whereas c is just a Graal boolean expression. The correct notations would use *Assertion* (*exp*: c) rather than c.

What is a loop invariant? The consequent of the rule gives a hint. Its postcondition represents what the loop is supposed to achieve, its "goal". This goal is

I **and not** c

which makes the invariant I appear as a weakened form of the goal. But I is also the precondition of the consequent. This means that I is weak enough to be satisfied in the state preceding execution of the loop, but strong enough to yield the desired goal on exit when combined with the exit condition.

As an example, take Euclid's algorithm for computing the greatest common divisor of two positive integers a and b:

$x := m; \; y := n;$

  while $x \neq y$ **loop**

      if $x > y$ **then**

          $x := x - y$

      else

          $y := y - x$

      end

  end;

  $g := x$

The proofs of the previous examples show that that this loop admits the following property as invariant:

[INV]
    $x > 0$ **and** $y > 0$ **and** $gcd \, (x, y) = gcd \, (m, n)$

The invariant is satisfied before the loop begins, since by straightforward application of $A_{Assignment}$, $I_{Compound}$ and EM:

$\vdash$ $\{m > 0 \text{ and } n > 0\}$

　　　$x := m \; ; \; y := n$

　　　$\{x > 0 \text{ and } y > 0 \text{ and } gcd \; (x, y) = gcd \; (m, n)\}$

So on loop exit we may infer both the invariant, hence $gcd \; (x, y) = gcd \; (m, n)$, and the loop exit condition $x = y$; the conjunction of these assertions implies $x = y = gcd \; (m, n)$.

Note how INV corresponds to the informal notion of a "weakened form of the goal":

- INV yields $x = gcd \; (m, n)$, that is to say essentially the goal, when $x = y$.
- But INV is also is weaker (more general) than this goal. In fact it is weak enough to be satisfied trivially by taking $x = a, y = b$.

You may consider an execution of the loop, then, as a process designed to maintain INV, making it a little stronger (closer to the goal) on each iteration. The last part of this chapter (9.11) shows how this view leads to a systematic approach for building correct software.

Below is the formal proof. It uses a few abbreviations: *LOOP* for the loop, *CONDIT* for the loop body (which is the conditional instruction studied previously), and *EUCLID* for the whole program fragment.

L1	$\{m, n > 0\}$	
	$x := m; \; y := n$	
	$\{m, n, x, y > 0 \text{ and } gcd \; (x, y) = gcd \; (m, n)\}$	S5 (see page 328)
L2	$\{m, n > 0\} \; x := m; \; y := n \; \{INV\}$	L1, definition of INV
L3	$\{INV \text{ and } x \neq y\} \; CONDIT \; \{INV\}$	C9 (see page 328)
L4	$\{INV\} \; LOOP \; \{INV \text{ and } x = y\}$	I_{Loop}
L5	$\{m, n > 0\} \; x := m; \; y := n; \; LOOP \; \{INV \text{ and } \; x = y\}$	L2, L4; $I_{Compound}$
L6	$\{x, y > 0 \text{ and } x = y \; \textbf{implies} \; gcd \; (x, y) = x$	EM
L7	$INV \text{ and } x = y \; \textbf{implies} \; gcd \; (m, n) = x$	L6, definition of INV
L8	$\{INV \text{ and } x = y\} \; g := x \; \{g = gcd \; (m, n)\}$	L7; CONS
L9	$\{m, n > 0\} \; EUCLID \; \{g = gcd \; (m, n)\}$	L5, L8; CONS

Figure 9.5: Proof involving a loop

9.7.7 Termination

The previous rules are partial correctness rules; this leaves open the termination problem. As programmers know all too well, loops may fail to terminate; they are the only construct studied so far which introduces that possibility, although of a course a compound or conditional may also not terminate if one of its constituent instructions does not.

The inference rule for loops, I_{Loop}, is clearly applicable to terminating constructs only. Otherwise the problem of automatic programming would be easy: to solve any computing problem characterized by an output condition Q, use a program of the form

while not Q **loop** *Skip* **end**

Using any assertion as invariant, rule I_{Loop} makes it possible to infer Q upon exit. The problem, of course, is that usually will be no exit at all. The above loop rule is of no help here.

To prove termination, you may attempt to find a suitable **loop variant**, according to the following definition.

> **Definition** (Variant): A variant for a loop is an expression V of type integer, involving some of the program's variables, and whose possible run-time values may be proved to satisfy the following two properties:
>
> • The value of V is non-negative before the execution of the loop.
>
> • If the value of V is non-negative and the loop continuation condition is satisfied, an execution of the loop body will decrease the value of V by at least one while keeping it non-negative.

If these two conditions are satisfied, execution of the loop will clearly terminate, since you cannot go on indefinitely decreasing the value of an integer expression which never becomes negative.

As an example, the expression

$V \triangleq \max(x, y)$

is an appropriate variant for the loop in the *EUCLID* program fragment.

More general variants may be used: rather than integer, the type of the variant expression could be any well-founded set, that is to say any set in which every decreasing sequence is finite. An example of well-founded set other than **N** is the set of nodes of a possibly infinite tree, where $m \le n$ is defined as "m is an ancestor of n or n itself". However the use of integer variants entails no loss of generality: if v is a variant in any well-founded set, then there is also an integer variant $|v|$, defined for any value n of v as the longest length of a decreasing sequence starting at n.

A variant may be viewed as an expression of the program's variables which, prior to each iteration of the loop, provides an upper bound on the number of remaining iterations. To prove that the loop terminates, you must exhibit such a bound. If your sole purpose is to prove termination, you are not required to guarantee that the bound is close to the actual number of remaining iterations, but a close enough bound will help you estimate the program's efficiency.

This informal description of the method for proving termination may now be made more precise. Consider a pre-post formula of the form

$\{P\}$ *Loop* (*test*: c ; *body*: b) $\{Q\}$

To prove rigorously that the loop terminates when started with precondition P satisfied, you must find an appropriate variant expression V and prove the following properties:

[9.17]

    P **implies** $(V \geq 0)$

[9.18]

    $\{(V \geq 0)$ **and** $c\}$ $z := V; b$ $\{0 \leq V < z\}$

Here z is assumed to be a fresh variable of type integer, not appearing in the loop or the rest of the program. This variable is used to record the value of the variant before execution of the loop body b, to express that b decreases V strictly. The concrete form $z := V; b$ has been used as an abbreviation for

Compound (<*Instruction* (*Assignment* (*source*: V ; *target*: z)), b>)

Using this method, you are invited to carry out formally the proof that *EUCLID* terminates.

> Note: it seems useless to have the condition $V \geq 0$, rather than just $V > 0$, in the precondition of [9.18]. Since the postcondition shows that V is decreased by at least one, V could not possibly have had value 0 before the execution of b. Can you see why it is in reality essential to use $\geq$ rather than $>$? (For an answer, see exercise 9.17).

The termination rule may be merged with I_{Loop} to yield a total correctness rule:

IT_{Loop} -- T for termination: total correctness rule

$$\frac{(I \textbf{ and } c) \textbf{ implies } V > 0,\qquad \{I \textbf{ and } c\}\ z := V; b\ \{I \textbf{ and } (V < z)\}}{\{I\}\ Loop\ (test: c; body: b)\ \{I \textbf{ and not } c\}}$$

Recall that I (the invariant) must be an assertion, treated here as a boolean expression, V (the variant) is an integer expression, and z is a fresh integer variable not appearing elsewhere in the program fragment considered.

The new rule handles both partial correctness and termination. As compared to [9.18], the second antecedent of the rule has a simpler postcondition: $0 \leq V$ is not needed there any more, since (because of the first antecedent):

I **and** $(V \leq 0)$ **implies** (**not** c)

so that the loop stops whenever V becomes non-positive. In essence, the condition c **implies** $(V > 0)$ has been integrated into the invariant.

This rule completes the pre-post theory of basic Graal. The treatment of other language features in this framework (arrays, pointers and procedures) will be outlined below (9.10).

9.8 THE CALCULUS OF WEAKEST PRECONDITIONS

The previous section has given the pre-post semantics of the Graal constructs. It is interesting to consider these constructs again from a complementary viewpoint: weakest precondition semantics.

9.8.1 Overview and definitions

In pre-post semantics, the assertions used to characterize an instruction are not necessarily the most "interesting" ones. For a formula of pre-post semantics:

[9.19]
$$\vdash \; \{P\} \, a \, \{Q\}$$

the rule of consequence will also yield

[9.20]
$$\vdash \; \{P'\} \, a \, \{Q'\}$$

for any P' stronger than P and Q' weaker than Q ("stronger" and "weaker" were defined on page 315). Thus [9.19] may be said to be more interesting than [9.20], as the latter may be derived from the former and so is less informative. More generally, we may define "more interesting than" as an order relation between formulae: the weaker the precondition, and the stronger the postcondition, the more interesting (informative) the formula.

When the aim is to prove specific properties of a given program, we often need to derive formulae which are not the most interesting among all possible ones. But when we define the semantics of a language we should look for the most interesting statements about the instructions of that language. All axioms and inference rules given in the preceding section, except for the properties of loops, are indeed "most interesting" specifications of instructions, in the sense that the given Q is the strongest possible postcondition for the given P, and P is the weakest possible precondition for Q.

Even so, we have many possible choices of pre-post pairs to characterize any particular instruction. It is legitimate to restrict the potential for arbitrary choice by fixing one of the two assertions. For example any instruction a may be characterized by the answer to either of the following questions:

- For an arbitrary assertion P, what is the strongest assertion Q such that $\{P\}\ a\ \{Q\}$?

- For an arbitrary assertion Q, what is the weakest assertion P such that $\{P\}\ a\ \{Q\}$?

In both cases, we view an instruction as an **assertion transformer**, that is to say, a mechanism that associates with a given precondition or postcondition the most interesting postcondition or precondition (respectively) which corresponds to it through the instruction.

The method to be described now, due to Dijkstra, follows this approach. Of the two questions asked, the more fruitful turns out to be the second: given an instruction and a postcondition, find the weakest precondition. This is due to both a technical and a conceptual reasons.

- The technical reason, already apparent in the above presentation of pre-post semantics, is that for common languages it is easier to express preconditions as functions of postconditions than the reverse.

- The conceptual reason has to do with the use of axiomatic techniques for program construction. A program is built to satisfy a certain goal, expressed as a property of the output results – that is to say, a certain postcondition. It is natural to construct the program by working backwards from the postcondition, choosing preconditions as the weakest possible (least committing on the input data).

The weakest precondition approach is based on these observations: it defines the semantics of a programming language through a set of rules which associate with every construct an assertion transformer, yielding for any postcondition the weakest corresponding precondition.

Three other features distinguish the theory given below from the above pre-post theory: it does not require, at least in principle, the invention of a variant and invariant; it directly handles total correctness; finally, it deals with non-deterministic constructs (which, however, could also be specified with pre-post semantics).

9.8.2 Basic definitions

The basic objects of the theory are **wp-formulae** (wp for weakest precondition) written under the general form

[9.21]

$$a \ \textbf{wp} \ Q$$

where a is an instruction and Q an assertion. Such a formula denotes, not a property which is either true or false (as was the case with a pre-post formula), but an **assertion**, defined as follows:

[9.22]

> **Definition** (Weakest Precondition): The wp-formula $a \ \textbf{wp} \ Q$, where a is an instruction and Q an assertion, denotes the weakest assertion P such that a is totally correct with respect to precondition P and postcondition Q

The expression "calculus of weakest preconditions" indicates the ambition of the theory: to provide a set of rules for manipulating programs and their associated assertions in a purely formal way, similar to how mathematical formulae are manipulated in ordinary arithmetic or algebra. To compute an expression such as $(x^2 - y^3)^2$, you merely apply well-defined transformation rules; these rules are defined by structural induction on the structure of expressions. Similarly, the calculus of weakest preconditions provides rules for computing $a \ \textbf{wp} \ Q$ for a class of instructions a and assertions Q; the rules defined inductively on the structure of a and Q if a and Q are complex program objects.

Unfortunately, the calculus of programs and assertions is not as easy as elementary arithmetic; computing $a \ \textbf{wp} \ Q$ remains a difficult or impossible endeavor as soon as a contains a loop. The theory nevertheless yields important insights and is particularly useful in connection with the constructive approach to program correctness, discussed below in 9.11.

9.8.3 True and false as postconditions

The theory relies on a set of simple axioms. The first one, called the "Law of the excluded miracle" by Dijkstra, states that no instruction can ever produce the postcondition *False*:

[9.23]

$$\vdash \quad a \ \textbf{wp} \ False \ = \ False$$

This is an axiom schema, applicable to any instruction a. In words: The weakest precondition that ensures satisfaction of *False* after execution of a is *False* itself. Since it is impossible to find an initial state for which *False* is satisfied, there is no state from which a will ensure *False*.

Having seen that, for consistency, a **wp** *False* must be *False* for any instruction a, you may legitimately ask what a **wp** *True* is. *True* is the assertion that all states satisfy. But do not conclude hastily that a **wp** *True* is *True* for any a. If an instruction is started in a state satisfying *True*, that is to say in any state, the final state will indeed satisfy *True* – provided there is a final state; in other words, provided a terminates. So a **wp** *True* is precisely the weakest precondition that will ensure termination of a.

This property is the first step towards establishing the calculus of weakest preconditions as a theory not just of correctness but of total correctness.

9.8.4 The rule of consequence

It is interesting to see how the rule of consequence (CONS, page 316) appears in this framework:

[9.24]

$$\frac{Q \text{ implies } Q'}{(a \ \textbf{wp} \ Q) \text{ implies } (a \ \textbf{wp} \ Q')}$$

In words: if Q is stronger than Q', then any initial condition which guarantees that instruction a will terminate in a state satisfying Q also guarantees that a will terminate in a state satisfying Q'. That is to say, one may derive new properties from "more interesting" ones.

9.8.5 The rule of conjunction

The rule of conjunction has a similarly simple wp-equivalent:

[9.25]
$$\vdash \quad a \ \textbf{wp} \ (Q \ \textbf{and} \ Q') = (a \ \textbf{wp} \ Q) \ \textbf{and} \ (a \ \textbf{wp} \ Q')$$

You are invited to study by yourself the practical meaning of this rule.

9.8.6 The rule of disjunction

The corresponding rule for boolean "or" may be written as:

[9.26]
$$\vdash \quad a \ \textbf{wp} \ (Q \ \textbf{or} \ Q') = (a \ \textbf{wp} \ Q) \ \textbf{or} \ (a \ \textbf{wp} \ Q')$$

This rule requires more careful examination; as will turn out, it is satisfied for Graal and ordinary languages, but not for more advanced cases. At this point you are invited to ponder the meaning of this rule and decide for yourself whether it is a theorem or not. (For an answer, see 9.9.4 below.)

9.8.7 *Skip* **and** *Abort*

We are now ready to start studying the wp-rules for language constructs. The axiom schema for the *Skip* instruction is predictably trivial:

$$\vdash \quad Skip \textbf{ wp } Q = Q$$

for any assertion Q.

An instruction (not present in Graal) that would do even less than *Skip* is *Abort*, characterized by the following axiom schema:

$$\vdash \quad Abort \textbf{ wp } Q = False$$

In other words, *Abort* cannot achieve *any* postcondition Q – not even *True*, the least committing of all. Quoting from [Dijkstra 1976]:

This one cannot even "do nothing" in the sense of "leaving things as they are"; it really cannot do a thing.

"Leaving things as they are" is a reference to the effect of *Skip*.

You may picture *Abort* as a non-terminating loop: by failing to yield a final state, it fails to ensure any postcondition at all. But this view, although not necessarily wrong, is overspecifying: all the rule expresses is the impossibility of proving anything of interest about *Abort*. This is another example of the already noted unobtrusiveness of the axiomatic method, where the "meaning" of a program consists solely of what you may prove about it. What *Abort* "does" practically, like looping forever or crashing the system, is irrelevant to the theory. To paraphrase Wittgenstein's famous quote: What one cannot prove about, one must not talk about.

9.8.8 **Assignment**

The wp-rule for assignments is:

[9.27]
$$\vdash \quad Assignment\,(target\colon x \;;\; source\colon e\,) \textbf{ wp } \quad \{Q\} \;=\; \{Q\;[x \leftarrow e\,]\}$$

This is the same as the corresponding pre-post rule ($A_{Assignment}$, page 319), with the supplementary information that $Q\;[x \leftarrow e]$ is not just one possible precondition but the most interesting – weakest.

9.8.9 Conditional

The the wp-rule for conditional instructions is also close to the pre-post rule ($I_{Conditional}$, page 325):

[9.28]

$\vdash$ *Conditional (test: c ; thenbranch: a ; elsebranch: b)* **wp** Q =

   $((a$ **wp** $Q)$ **and** $c)$ **or** $((a$ **wp** $Q)$ **and not** $c)$

In words: for the instruction **if** c **then** a **else** b **end** to terminate in a state where Q is satisfied, a necessary and sufficient condition is that one of the following combinations hold in the initial state:

- c and the necessary and sufficient condition for a to terminate in a state where Q is satisfied.

- **not** c and the necessary and sufficient condition for b to terminate in a state where Q is satisfied.

As before, this wp-rule expresses that the precondition of the pre-post rule was weakest. Yet here it also includes something else: a termination property. The rule implies that a conditional instruction will terminate if and only if every branch terminates whenever its guard is true. Here the "guard" of a branch is the condition under which it is executed (c for the *thenbranch* and **not** c for the *elsebranch*).

9.8.10 Compound

For compounds too the wp-rules directly reflect the pre-post rules (page 327):

[9.29]

$\vdash$ *Compound (<>)* **wp** Q = Q

[9.30]

$\vdash$ $(c ++ <a>)$ **wp** Q = c **wp** $(a$ **wp** $Q)$

In the second rule, c is an arbitrary compound and a an arbitrary instruction.

9.8.11 Loop

We may expect the rule for loops to be more difficult; also, it is interesting to see how the theory handles total correctness.

The basic wp-rule for loops is:

[9.31]

$\vdash$

    given

        $l \triangleq Loop\ (test: c\ ;\ body: b)$ -- i.e. **while** c **do** b **end**

        $G_0 \triangleq$ **not** c **and** Q ;

        $G_i \triangleq c$ **and** $(b\ \mathbf{wp}\ G_{i-1})$ -- for $i > 0$

    then

        $l\ \mathbf{wp}\ Q\ =\ \exists\ n: \mathbf{N} \bullet G_n$

    end

The rule may be explained as follows. For the loop to terminate in a state satisfying Q, it must do so after a finite number of iterations. So the weakest precondition is of the form

G_0 **or** G_1 **or** G_2 **or** ...

where, for $i \geq 0$, G_i is the weakest precondition for the loop to terminate after exactly i iterations in a state satisfying Q. A loop started in an initial state σ terminates after i iterations in a state satisfying Q if and only if:

- For $i = 0$:

    – No iteration is performed, so σ satisfies **not** c.

    – σ satisfies Q.

- For $i > 0$:

    – One iteration is performed, so σ satisfies c.

    – This iteration brings the computation to a state from which the loop performs exactly $i-1$ further iterations and then terminates in a state satisfying Q: in other words, σ satisfies $b\ \mathbf{wp}\ G_{i-1}$.

By combining these cases, we obtain the above inductive definition of G_i.

Rather than G_i, it is sometimes more convenient to use H_i, the condition for l to yield Q after **at most** i iterations (see exercise 9.17).

Rule [9.31] addresses total correctness. But it is not directly useful in practice: to check whether $l\ \mathbf{wp}\ Q$ is satisfied it would require you to check a potentially infinite number of conditions. This can only be done through a proof by induction, which in fact amounts to using an invariant and variant, as with the pre-post approach. The connection between the wp-rule and the pre-post rules is expressed by the following theorem, which reintroduces the invariant I and the variant V:

[9.32]

> **Theorem** (Invariant and variant in wp-semantics): Let I be a loop
> with body b and test c, I an assertion and V an integer-valued
> function of the state. If for any value $z \in \mathbf{N}$
>
> $\qquad$ (I **and** c **and** $V = z$) **implies**
>
> $\qquad\qquad$ (($z > 0$) **and** (b **wp** (I **and** ($0 < V < z$))))
>
> then:
>
> $\qquad$ I **implies** (I **wp** (I **and not** c))

This theorem is equivalent to the inference rule IT_{Loop} (page 332). Its proof requires
an appropriate model of the axiomatic theory, which will be introduced in the next
chapter.

9.8.12 A concrete notation for loops

In a systematic approach to program construction, you should think of loop variants and
invariants not just as "decoration" to be attached to a loop if a proof is required, but as
components of the loop, conceptually as important as the body or the exit condition.
Abstract and concrete syntax should reflect this role.

$\qquad$ Whenever the rest of this chapter needs to express loops in concrete syntax, it will
use the Eiffel notation for loops, which is a direct consequence of the above discussion
and looks as follows:

```
from
        Compound                - - Initialization
invariant
        Assertion
variant
        Integer_expression
until
        Boolean_expression      - - Exit condition
loop
        Compound                - - Loop body
end
```

Like other uses of assertions in Eiffel, the **invariant** and **variant** clauses are optional.

$\qquad$ The execution of such a loop consists of two parts, which we may call A and B.
Part A simply executes the initialization *Compound*. Part B does nothing if the exit
condition is satisfied; otherwise it proceeds with the loop body, and starts part B again.

In other words this is like a Pascal or Graal "while" loop, with its initialization included (**from** clause), and an exit test rather than a continuation test.

The reason for including the initialization follows from the axiomatic semantics of loops as studied above: every loop must have an initialization, whose aim is to ensure the initial validity of the invariant. (In some infrequent cases where the context of the loop guarantees the invariant the initialization *Compound* is empty.)

The reason for using an exit condition (**until** rather than **while**) is to make immediately visible what the outcome of the loop will be. By looking at the loop, you see right away the postcondition that will hold on loop exit:

$$G \triangleq I \textbf{ and } E$$

where I is the invariant and E the exit condition.

In the constructive approach, as discussed below (9.11), we will design loop algorithms by starting from G, the **goal** of the algorithm, and deriving I and E through various heuristics.

9.9 NON-DETERMINISM

A class of constructs enjoys a particularly simple characterization by wp-rules (although pre-post formulae would work too): non-deterministic instructions. A non-deterministic instruction is one whose effect is not entirely characterized by the state in which it is executed.

Simple examples of non-deterministic instructions are the guarded conditional and the guarded loop.

9.9.1 The guarded conditional

In concrete syntax (see exercise 9.2 for abstract syntax), the guarded conditional may be written as follows:

[9.33]
> **if**
> > $c_1 \implies a_1$ $\square$
> > $c_2 \implies a_2$ $\square$
> > $\cdots$ $\square$
> > $c_n \implies a_n$
> **end**

where there are n branches ($n \geq 0$). The c_i, called guards, are boolean expressions, and the a_i are instructions.

Informally, the semantics of this construct is the following: the effect of the instruction is undefined if it is executed in a state in which none of the guards is true; otherwise, execution of the instruction is equivalent to execution of one a_i such that the corresponding guard c_i is true.

The standard **if** c **then** a **else** b **end** of Graal and most common languages may be expressed as a special case of this construct:

[9.34]

> **if**
>
> $\qquad c \implies a \; \square$
>
> $\qquad$ **not** $c \implies b$
>
> **end**

The guarded conditional has three distinctive features: first, it treats the various possible cases in a more symmetric way than the **if...then... else...** conditional; second, it is non-deterministic; third, it may fail – produce an undefined result.

The first property, symmetry, follows directly from the above informal specification. The non-determinism comes from the absence in that specification of any prescription as to which of all possible branches is selected when more than one guard is true. So the instruction

[9.35]

> **if**
>
> $\qquad x \geq 0 \implies x := x + 1 \; \square$
>
> $\qquad x \leq 0 \implies x := x - 1$
>
> **end**

could yield $x = -1$ as well as $x = +1$ when started with $x = 0$.

This suggests the following axiom schema, which is both a generalization and a simplification of the wp-rule for the standard conditional ([9.28], page 338); *guarded_if* denotes the above construct [9.33].

[9.36]

> $\vdash$
>
> $\qquad$ *guarded_if* **wp** $Q \quad = $
>
> $\qquad\qquad ((a_1 \; \textbf{wp} \; Q) \; \textbf{and} \; c_1) \; \textbf{or}$
>
> $\qquad\qquad ((a_2 \; \textbf{wp} \; Q) \; \textbf{and} \; c_2) \; \textbf{or}$
>
> $\qquad\qquad \ldots \; \textbf{or}$
>
> $\qquad\qquad ((a_n \; \textbf{wp} \; Q) \; \textbf{and} \; c_n)$

Note how simply this axiom expresses the non-determinism of the construct's informal semantics. For *guarded_if* to ensure satisfaction of Q, there must be a branch whose guard c_i is true and whose action a_i ensures Q. There may be more than one such branch; if so, it does not matter which one is selected, as only the result, Q, counts. The axiom describes this precisely through the **or** operator.

The axiom also captures the last of the construct's three key properties listed above: regardless of Q, the weakest precondition is *False* – that is to say, non-satisfiable by any state – if none of the c_i is true. This means that *guarded_if* is informally equivalent in this case to *Abort*, since we may not prove anything about it.

Many people are shocked by this convention when they first encounter the symmetric **if**: should *guarded_if* not behave like *Skip*, not *Abort*, when no guard is satisfied?

There are serious arguments, however, for the interpretation implied by [9.36]. One of the dangers of the **if** ... **then** ... **else** construct is that it lumps the last case with all unforeseen cases in the **else** branch. More precisely, assume a programmer has identified n cases for which a different treatment is required. The usual way to write the corresponding instruction is the following (using the Algol 68-Ada-Eiffel abbreviation **elsif** to avoid useless nesting of conditionals):

> **if** c_1 **then** a_1
>
> **elsif** c_2 **then** a_2
>
> ...
>
> **elsif** c_{n-1} **then** a_{n-1}
>
> **else** a_n **end**
>
>   -- No need to specify that the last branch corresponds to the case
>   -- c_n true, c_j false $(1 \leq j \leq n-1)$

The risk is to forget a case. When all of the c_i, including c_n, are false, the instruction executes a_n, which is almost certainly wrong; but the error may be hard to catch.

In the guarded conditional, on the other hand, every branch is explicitly preceded by its guard and executed only if the guard is true. If no guard is satisfied, a good implementation will produce an error message and stop execution, or raise an exception, or loop forever; this is better than proceeding silently with a wrong computation.

9.9.2 The guarded loop

The other basic non-deterministic construct is the guarded loop, which may be written as:

[9.37]
    loop

$$c_1 \Rightarrow a_1 \; \square$$
$$c_2 \Rightarrow a_2 \; \square$$
$$\ldots \; \square$$
$$c_n \Rightarrow a_n$$

    end

with the following informal semantics: if no c_i is true, the instruction does nothing; otherwise it executes one of the a_i such that c_i is true, and the process starts anew. The formal wp-rule for this construct is left for your pleasure (work from [9.31], page 338, and [9.36], page 342). The rule should make it clear, as [9.36], that it does not matter which branch is chosen when several are possible.

Here the case in which no c_i is satisfied is not an error but normal loop termination. In particular, for $n = 0$, the guarded loop is equivalent to *Skip*, not to *Abort* as with the guarded conditional.

9.9.3 Discussion

Why should one want to specify non-deterministic behavior? There are two main reasons.

The first reason is that non-deterministic programs may be useful to model non-deterministic behavior of the real world, as in real-time systems. (The non-determinism is not necessarily in the events themselves, but sometimes only in our perception of them; however the end result is the same.)

The second reason has to do with the desire not to overspecify, mentioned at the beginning of this chapter: if it does not matter which branch of (say) a conditional is selected in a certain case, as both branches will lead to equally acceptable results, then the programmer need not choose explicitly. The principle here is abstraction: when a feature of the implementation is irrelevant to the specification, you should be able to leave it implicit.

How can we implement a non-deterministic construct such as the guarded conditional or loop? You must not think that such an implementation needs to use some kind of random mechanism for choosing between possible alternatives. All that the rules say is that whenever more than one c_i is satisfied, every corresponding a_i must yield the desired postcondition, and then any of the corresponding branches may be selected. Any implementation which observes this specification is correct.

Examples of correct implementations include: one that test the guards in the order in which they are written, and takes the first branch whose guard is true (as with the **if** ... **then** ... **elsif** ...); one that starts from the other end; one that behaves like the first on even-numbered days and like the second on odd-numbered days; one that uses a random number generator to find the order in which it will evaluate the guards; one that starts n

parallel processes to evaluate the guards (or asks *n* different nodes on a network), and chooses the branch whose guard is first (or last) computed as true; and many others.

No proof of properties of the construct is correct if it relies on knowledge about the actual policy used for choosing between competitive true guards. But as long as the proof is only based on the official, policy-independent rules, any implementation that abides by these rules is acceptable.

> One way to picture the situation is to imagine that a **demon** is in charge of choosing between acceptable branches when more than one guard is true. The demon does not have to be erratic, although he may well be; some demons are bureaucrats who always follow the same routine, others take pleasure in constantly changing their policies to defeat any attempt at second-guessing. But regardless of the individual psychology of the demon that has been assigned to us by the Central Office of Demon Services, he is in another room, and *we are not allowed to look.*

9.9.4 The rule of disjunction

The above remarks are the key to the pending issue of the rule of disjunction ([9.26], page 336). The (so far tentative) rule may be written as

[9.38]
> **given**
>> *lhs* $\triangleq$ *a* **wp** (*Q* **or** *Q'*) ;
>>
>> *rhs* $\triangleq$ (*a* **wp** *Q*) **or** (*A* **wp** *Q'*)
>
> **then**
>> *lhs* = *rhs*
>
> **end**

The rule expresses an equality between two assertions, that is to say a two-way implication: according to this rule, whenever a state satisfies *lhs*, it satisfies *rhs*, and conversely.

Look first at *rhs*. This assertion is true of states *s* such that one or both of the following holds:

- *a*, started in *s*, is guaranteed to terminate in a state satisfying *Q*.
- *a*, started in *s*, is guaranteed to terminate in a state satisfying *Q'*.

Each of these conditions implies that *a*, started in *s*, is guaranteed to terminate in a state satisfying *Q* **or** *Q'*; in other words, it implies that state *s* satisfies *lhs*. So *rhs* implies *lhs*.

Assume, conversely, that s satisfies lhs. Instruction a, started in s, is guaranteed to terminate in a state satisfying Q or satisfying Q'. Does this imply that s is either guaranteed to terminate in a state satisfying Q or guaranteed to terminate in a state satisfying Q'? The answer is yes in the absence of non-deterministic constructs: since a, started in in s, is always executed in the same fashion, a guarantee that it ensures Q or Q' means either a guarantee that it ensures Q or a guarantee that it ensures Q'.

This is no longer true, however, if we introduce non-deterministic constructs. Assume for example that a is "toss a coin", Q is the property of getting heads and Q' of getting tails. Before tossing the coin you are guaranteed to get heads or tails: so a **wp** $(Q$ **or** $Q')$ is true. But you are not guaranteed to get heads: thus a **wp** Q is false; so is a **wp** Q' and hence their **or**. Tossing a coin may be viewed as an implementation of the following program:

> **if**
>> $true \;\rightarrow\; produce\_heads$ $\Box$
>> $true \;\rightarrow\; produce\_tails$
> **end**

where

$$produce\_heads \; \textbf{wp} \; (result = heads) = True$$
$$produce\_heads \; \textbf{wp} \; (result = tails) \; = False$$
$$produce\_tails \; \textbf{wp} \; (result = heads) \; = False$$
$$produce\_tails \; \textbf{wp} \; (result = tails) \; = True$$

This discussion assumes a non-deterministic coin-tossing process, with unpredictable result: the coin is tossed by a demon, who does not reveal his tossing policies.

9.10 ROUTINES AND RECURSION

The presentation of language features in denotational semantics summarized the role of routines in software development (7.8.1). Now we must see what axiomatic semantics has to say about them.

This section will shows how to derive properties of software elements containing routine calls, including recursive ones.

9.10.1 Routines without arguments

Consider first routines with no arguments and no results. The abstract syntax of a routine declaration is then just:

Routine ≙ *name*: *Identifier*; *body*: *Instruction*

and a routine call (new branch for the abstract syntax production describing instructions) just involves the name of the routine:

Call ≙ *called*: *Identifier*

Then a call instruction simply stands for the insertion of the corresponding routine body at the point of call. This is readily translated into an inference rule (for any routine declaration r):

$10_{Routine}$

$$\frac{\{P\}\ r.body\ \{Q\}}{\{P\}\ Call\ (called:\ r.name)\ \{Q\}}$$

The rule expresses that any property of the body yields a similar property of the call.

9.10.2 Introducing arguments

Routines without arguments are not very exciting; let us see how arguments affect the picture. The discussion will first introduce arguments; then, as was done in 7.7 for the denotational specification, it will show how we can avoid complicating the specification by treating argument and result passing as assignment.

In many languages, the arguments to a routine may be of three kinds: "in" arguments, passed to the routine; results, also called "out" arguments, computed by the routine; and "in-out" arguments, which are both consumed and updated. In some language such as Algol W or Ada, routine declarations qualify each argument with one of these modes.

As in 7.7.5, it is convenient to restrict the discussion to in arguments and out arguments, from now on respectively called arguments and results. Callers may still obtain the effect of in-out arguments by including variables in both the argument and result actual lists, subject to limitations given below.

A further simplification is to write every routine with exactly one (in) formal argument and one result, both being lists (finite sequences). This is not a restriction in practice since lists may have any number of elements. Proof examples given below in concrete syntax will follow the standard style, with individually identified arguments and result; but grouping arguments and results into two lists makes the theoretical presentation clearer.

Routines are commonly divided into functions, which return a result, and procedures, which do not. A procedure call stands for an instruction; a function call stands for an expression. Our routines cover both functions and procedures, but for consistency it will be preferable to treat all calls as instructions. A routine which represents a procedure will have an empty result list; a routine representing a procedure or function with no arguments will have an empty argument list.

The call instruction now has the following abstract syntax, generalized from the form without arguments given page 347:

$$Call \triangleq called: Identifier; input: Expression^*; output: Variable^*$$

The elements of the actual *input* list may be arbitrary expressions, whose value will be passed to the routine; the actual *output* elements will have their value computed by the routine, so they must be variables (or, more generally, elements whose value may be changed at execution time, such as arrays or records).

For a routine *f* representing a function, a call using *i* as actual arguments and *o* as actual results, described in abstract syntax as

$$Call (called: f; input: i; output: o)$$

corresponds to what is commonly thought of as an assignment instruction with a function call on the right-hand side:

$$o := r (i)$$

so that the discussion below will allow us to derive an axiomatic semantics for such assignments, which the earlier discussion (see page 322) had specifically excluded from the scope of the assignment axiom.

Because every routine has exactly one argument list and one result list, there is no need to make the formal argument and result explicit. We may simply keep the abstract syntax

$$Routine \triangleq name: Identifier; body: Instruction$$

with the convention that every *body* accesses its argument and result lists through predefined names: *argument* and *result*. (Eiffel uses this convention for results, as seen below.) We do not allow nesting of routine texts, so any use of these names unambiguously refers to the enclosing routine. We must of course make sure that no "normal" variable is called *argument* or *result*.

With these conventions, we may derive a first rule for for routines with arguments by interpreting a call instruction

$$Call (called: f; input: i; output: o)$$

as the sequence of instructions (in mixed abstract-concrete syntax)

$$argument := i;$$

$$called.body;$$

$$o := result$$

(Section 7.7.6 gave a more precise equivalence, taking into account possible name clashes in block structure. The above equivalence suffices for this discussion.)

Taking this interpretation literally, assume that we know the axiomatics of the body in the form of a theorem or theorem schema

$$\{P\}\ called.body\ \{Q\}$$

Then we can use the assignment axiom to include the first instruction above, the initialization of *argument*:

$$\{P\ [argument \leftarrow i]\}\ argument := i;\ called.body;\ \{Q\}$$

It appears at first more difficult to include the final instruction, the assignment to o. But here *result* includes only variables, as opposed to composite expressions or constants; so the forward rule for assignment ([9.11], page 321) applies. It yields for the whole instruction sequence the pre-post formula

$$\{P\ [argument \leftarrow i]\}$$

$$argument := i;\ called;\ called.body;\ o := result$$

$$\{Q\ [result \leftarrow o]\}$$

In other words, taking the instruction sequence to represent the call: if the body is characterized by a precondition P and a postcondition Q, which may involve the local variables *argument* and *result* representing the arguments, then any call will be characterized by precondition P applied to the actual inputs i instead of *argument*, and postcondition Q applied to the actual results o instead of the formal *result*.

This yields the first version of the rule for routines with arguments, applicable to a non-recursive routine r. Some restrictions, given below, apply.

$\text{I1}_{Routine}$

$$\{P\ \}\ r.body\ \{Q\}$$

$$\{P\ [argument \leftarrow i]\}\ Call\ (called:\ r.name;\ input:\ i;\ output:\ o)\ \{Q\ [result \leftarrow o]\}$$

This rule admits a simple weakest precondition version:

> **given**
> $$c \triangleq Call\ (called:\ r.name;\ input:\ i;\ output:\ o)$$
> **then**
> $$c\ \textbf{wp}\ Q' = (r.body\ \textbf{wp}\ (Q'\ [o \leftarrow result\,]))\ [argument \leftarrow i]$$
> **end**

Here Q', an arbitrary assertion subject to the restrictions below, corresponds to $Q\ [result \leftarrow o]$ in the pre-post rule.

9.10.3 Simultaneous substitution

In rule $11_{Routine}$ and it weakest precondition counterpart, the source and targets of substitutions are list variables, representing lists of formal and actual arguments and results. Since the original definition of substitution applied to atomic variables, we must clarify what the notation means for lists.

The generalization is straightforward: if vl is a list of variables and el a list of expressions, take

$$Q \; [vl \leftarrow el]$$

to be the result of replacing simultaneously in Q every occurrence of vl (1) with el (1), every occurrence of vl (2) with el (2) etc. For example:

$$(x + y) \; [<x, y> \leftarrow <3, 7>] = (3 + 7)$$

$$(x + y) \; [<x, y> \leftarrow <y, x>] = (y + x)$$

The simultaneity of substitutions is essential. In the second example, if the substitutions were executed in two steps in the order given, the first step would yield $(y + y)$, which the second would transform into $(x + x)$ – not the desired result. A formal definition of simultaneous substitution, generalizing the *subst* function for single substitutions ([9.9], page 320), is the subject of exercise 9.21.

The simultaneity requirement only makes sense if all the elements in the variable list vl are different: if x appeared as both vl (j) and vl (k) with $j \neq k$, the result would be ambiguous since you would not know whether to substitute el (j) or el (k) for x. The absence of duplicate variables is one of the constraints listed below on the application of $11_{Routine}$.

The example proofs that follow list arguments individually, rather than collectively as list elements. To avoid introducing lists in such a case, it is convenient to use the notation

$$Q \; [x_1 \leftarrow a_1, \; ..., \; x_n \leftarrow a_n]$$

as a synonym for

$$Q \; [<x_1, \; ..., \; x_n> \leftarrow <a_1, \; ..., \; a_n>]$$

9.10.4 Conditions on arguments and results

The application of rule $11_{Routine}$ assumes that the call satisfies some constraints. One, already noted, is absence of recursion; we shall see below how to make the rule useful for recursive routines. Let us first study the other seven constraints, which could be expressed as static semantic validity functions (exercise 9.19). The constraints are the following:

1　• No identifier may occur twice in the formal argument list.

2　• No identifier may occur twice in the formal result list.

3　• No identifier may occur in both the formal argument list and the formal result list.

4　• In any particular call, no variable may occur twice in the actual *output* result list.

5　• No variable local to the body of the routine may have the same name as a variable accessible to the calling program unit, unless it occurs in neither the precondition P nor the postcondition Q.

6　• No element of the *result* list may appear in P.

7　• If the postcondition Q involves any element of the *argument* list, then the corresponding element of the actual *input* list may not occur in the *output* list (that is to say, it may not be used as an in-out argument).

We already encountered the first four constraints in the denotational specification (7.7.4 and 7.7.7).

Constraints 1 and 2 follow directly from the consistency condition for simultaneous substitutions, as given above. From a more practical point of view, a duplicate identifier in the argument or result formal list would amount to a duplicate declaration; occurrences of the identifier in the routine body would then be ambiguous.

The latter observation also applies to an identifier appearing in both formal lists, justifying constraint 3.

Constraint 4 precludes any call which uses the same variable twice as actual result. Assume this constraint is violated and consider a routine

s (**out** x, y: *INTEGER*) **is**
　　　　do　　　　　-- *BODY*
　　　　　　　$x := 0; \ y := 1$
　　　　end -- s

whose body makes the following pre-post formula hold:

$$\vdash \quad \{true\} \ BODY \ \{x = 0 \ \textbf{and} \ y = 1\}$$

Then rule $\text{I1}_{Routine}$ could be used to deduce the contradictory result

$$\{true\} \ \textbf{call} \ s \ (a, a) \ \{a = 0 \ \textbf{and} \ a = 1\}$$

From a programmer's viewpoint, this means that the outcome would depend on the order in which the final values of the formal results (here x and y) are copied into the corresponding actual arguments on return from a call – a decision best left to the compiler writers and kept out of the language manual. Many programming language specifications indeed include constraint 4.

Nothing in constraints 1 to 4 precludes an expression from occurring more than once in the actual *input* list, or a variable from occurring in both the actual *input* and *output* lists. The latter case achieves the effect of in-out arguments.

Constraint 5 precludes sharing of local variable names between the routine and any of its callers. Such "puns" would cause incorrect application of the rule: if a local variable of r occurs in P or Q, then it will also occur in P $[i \leftarrow argument]$ or Q $[o \leftarrow result]$, and may yield an incorrect property of its namesake in the calling program. Lambda calculus raised similar problems (5.7).

A name clash of this kind, resulting from the independent choice of the same identifier in different program units, may be removed by manual renaming; more conveniently, compilers and formal proof systems can disambiguate the names statically. The denotational specification of block structure described one way of doing this in a formal system (see 7.2, especially 7.2.3). The same techniques could be applied here, removing the need for constraint 5. (This constraint had no equivalent in the denotational discussion of routines, which could afford to be more tolerant precisely because it assumed a block structure mechanism as a basis.)

Constraint 5 is not, however, a serious impediment for programmers or program provers:

- It does not prevent routines from accessing global variables, as long as there is no name conflicts with locally declared variables. It is important to let routines access externally declared variables, especially if they use globals in the disciplined style enforced by object-oriented programming.

- If the local variable is used in neither the precondition nor the postcondition, no harm will result. In this case the computation performed by the routine uses the variable for internal purposes, but its properties do not transpire beyond the routine's boundaries. This means that constraint 5 is essentially harmless in practice, since meaningful pre-post assertions for a routine have no business referring to anything else than *argument*, *result* and global variables.

You may then interpret constraint 5 as a requirement on language implementers, specifying that each routine which uses a certain variable name must allocate a different variable for that name (and in the case of recursive routines, studied below, that every *call* to a routine must allocate a new instance of the variable).

Constraints 6 and 7 are in fact special cases of constraint 5, applying to the variable lists *argument* and *result*, implicitly declared in every routine, and hence raising many apparent cases of possible name clashes between routines and their callers.

To avoid any harm from such clashes, we must first exclude any element of *result* from the precondition P; since *result* is to be computed by the routine, its presence in the precondition would be meaningless anyway. This is constraint 6.

The presence of *input* (or any of its elements) in Q is a problem only if the calling routine uses its own *input* (or the corresponding element of its *input*) as *result* (or part of it). Assume for example a routine with a single integer argument and a single integer argument, whose body computes

$result := argument + 1$

Then with *true* as precondition P we may deduce

$$result = argument + 1$$

as postcondition Q. Now assume a call in which the caller's *argument* is used as both actual argument and actual result; this is expressly permitted, to allow the effect of in-out arguments. But then blind application of $I1_{Routine}$, without constraint 7, would allow us to infer, as postcondition for the call, that

$$argument = argument + 1$$

which is absurd. Constraint 7 specifically prevents this. It does not prohibit the presence of *argument* in Q if *argument* is not used as actual result for the call. As you are invited to check, this case does not raise any particular problem; nor does the possible presence of *argument* in P or *result* in Q.

9.10.5 A concrete notation for routines

Like invariants and variants for loops, routine preconditions and postconditions play such a key role in building, understanding and using software that they deserve to be part of the abstract and concrete syntax for routines, on a par with the argument list or the body.

When they need a concrete syntax, subsequent examples of routines will use the Eiffel notation, which results from the preceding discussion and rule $I1_{routine}$. (It also supports the extended rule for recursive routines, given below.) An Eiffel routine is of the form

> *routine_name* (*argument*: *TYPE*; *argument*: *TYPE*; ...): *RESULT_TYPE* **is**
>> -- Header comment (non-formal)
>
>> **require**
>>> *Precondition*
>> **do**
>>> *Compound*
>> **ensure**
>>
>>> *Postconditions*
>>
>> **end** -- *routine_name*

expressing the precondition and the postcondition as part of the routine text, through the **require** and **ensure** clauses. These clauses, like other uses of assertions, are of course optional.

A call to the routine is correct if and only if it satisfies the *Precondition*; if the routine body is correct, the caller may then rely on the *postcondition* on routine return. This is the idea, already mentioned above (page 310), of **programming by contract**. A routine call is a contract to perform a certain task. The caller is the "client", the called routine is the "supplier". As in every good contract, there are advantages and obligations for both parties:

- The precondition is an obligation for the client; for the supplier, it is a benefit, since, as expressed by $11_{Routine}$, it relieves the routine body from having to care about cases not covered by the precondition.
- For the postcondition the situation is reversed.

An Eiffel routine, as given by the above form, is a function, returning a result. That result is a single element rather than a list. This is sufficient for the examples below; generalization to a list of results would be immediate. The examples below will use the Eiffel convention for computing the result of a function: any function has an implicitly declared variable called *Result*, of type *RESULT_TYPE*, to which values may be assigned in the body; its final value is the result returned to the caller.

The notation also supports procedures, which do not return a result. A routine is a procedure if its header does not include the part

   $: RESULT\_TYPE$

9.10.6 Recursion

Rule $11_{Routine}$, it was said above, is not applicable to recursive routines. This is not because it is wrong in this case, but rather because it becomes useless.

The problem is that the rule only enables you to prove a formula of the form

   $\vdash \{P\}$ **call** $s\ (...)\ \{Q\}$

if you can prove the corresponding property of the body b of s, with appropriate actual-formal argument substitutions. If s is recursive, however, its body will contain at least one call to s, so that proving properties of b will require proving properties of calls to s, which because of the inference rule will require proving properties of.... The proof process itself becomes infinitely recursive.

If, as with loops, we take a partial correctness approach, accepting the necessity to prove termination separately, we need not change much to $11_{Routine}$ to make it work for recursive routines. The idea is that you should be allowed to use inductively, when trying to prove a property of b, the corresponding property of **calls** to s.

To understand this, look again at the application of the non-recursive rule. As noted, the goal is to prove

[9.39]
   $\{P'\}$ **call** $s\ (...)\ \{Q'\}$

by proving

[9.40]
   $\{P\}$ *BODY* $\{Q\}$

where P' and Q' differ from P and Q by substitutions only. So the proof of [9.39] includes two steps: first prove [9.40], the corresponding property on the body; then, using $I1_{Routine}$, derive [9.39] by carrying out the appropriate substitutions.

If the same approach is applied to recursive routines, the first step in this process – the proof relative to the body – must be allowed to assume the property of the call, the very one which is the ultimate goal of the proof.

The more general rule for routine calls follows from this observation. (It is applicable to non-recursive routines as well, although in this case the former rule suffices). The restrictions of 9.10.4 apply as before.

$I2_{Routine}$

   $\{P \ [argument \leftarrow i]\}\ Call\ (called:\ r.name;\ input:\ i;\ output:\ o)\ \{Q \ [result \leftarrow o]\}$

$$\supset$$

   $\{P \ \}\ r.body\ \{Q\}$

   $\{P \ [argument \leftarrow i]\}\ Call\ (called:\ r.name;\ input:\ i;\ output:\ o)\ \{Q \ [result \leftarrow o]\}$

The premise of this rule is of the form $F \supset G$, and its conclusion of the form H, where F, G, H are pre-post formulae. The rule means: "If you can prove that F implies G, then you may deduce H". The antecedent being an implication, its proof will often be a conditional proof. What is remarkable, of course, is that H is in fact the same as G.

With the Eiffel concrete notation for preconditions and postconditions, as introduced above, rule $I2_{Routine}$ indicates that the instructions leading to any recursive call in the body (**do** clause) must guarantee the precondition (**require** clause) before that call, and may be assumed to guarantee the postcondition (**ensure** clause) on return, with appropriate actual-formal substitutions in both cases. The rule also indicates that if you try to check the first property (precondition satisfied on call), you may recursively assume that property on routine entry.

You will have noted the use of the terms "may assume" and "must guarantee" in the preceding discussion. They reflect the client-supplier relationship as derived from the contract theory of software construction. Here the routine is its own client and supplier, and the alternating interpretations of the assertions' meaning reflect this dual role.

The article that first introduced the axiomatics of recursive routines [Hoare 1971] stressed the elegance of the recursive routine rule in particularly apt terms:

> *The solution of the infinite regress is simple and dramatic: to permit the use of the desired conclusion as a hypothesis in the proof of the body itself. Thus we are permitted to prove that the procedure body possesses a property, on the assumption that every recursive call possesses that property, and then to assert categorically that every call, recursive or otherwise, has that property. This assumption of what we want to prove before embarking on the proof explains well the aura of magic which attends a programmer's first introduction to recursive programming.*

9.10.7 Termination

In any practical call, the regress had better be finite if you hope to see the result in your lifetime. (This was apparent in the last chapter's denotational study of recursion: even though in non-trivial cases no finite number of iterations of a function chain f will yield its fixpoint f_∞, once you choose a given x you know there is a finite i such that $f(x)$ is $f_i(x)$.)

To prove termination, it suffices, as with loops, to exhibit a variant, which here is an integer expression of which you can prove that:

- Its value is non-negative for the first (outermost) call.

- If the variant's value is non-negative on entry to the routine's body, it will be at least one less, but still non-negative, for any recursive call.

9.10.8 Recursion invariants

Like loops, recursive routines have variants. Not unpredictably, they also share with loops the notion of invariant.

A *recursion invariant* is an assertion I such that the recursive routine rule, $I2_{Routine}$, will apply if you use I both as precondition (P in the rule as given above) and postcondition (Q).

Here the rule means that if you are able to prove, under the assumption that any call preserves I, that the body preserves I as well, then you may deduce that any call indeed preserves I. The proof and deduction must of course be made under the appropriate actual-formal argument substitutions.

As an example of use of a recursion invariant in a semi-formal proof, consider a procedure for printing the contents of a binary search tree:

print_sorted (*t*: *BINARY_TREE*) **is**

    -- Print node values in order

 require

    -- *t* is a binary search tree, in other words:

  given

    left_nodes $\triangleq$ *subtree* (*t*.*left*);

    right_nodes $\triangleq$ *subtree* (*t*.*right*)

      -- where *subtree* (*x*) is the set of nodes

      -- in the subtree of root *x*

  then

    $\forall l$: *left_nodes*, *r* : *right_nodes* • *l*.*value* $\leq$ *t*.*value* $\leq$ *r*.*value*

  end

 do

  if not *t*.*Void* **then**

    print_contents (*t*.*left*);

    print (*t*.*value*);

    print_contents (*t*.*right*)

  end

 ensure

    "All values in *subtree* (*t*) have been printed in order."

 end -- *print_sorted*

This assumes primitives *left*, *right*, *empty* and *value* applicable to any tree node, and a predefined procedure *print* to print a value. The variant "height of subtree of root *t*" ensures termination.

Here the informal recursion invariant is "If any value in *subtree* (*t*) has been printed, then all values of *subtree* (*t*) have been printed in order". The invariant is trivially satisfied before the call since no node value has been printed yet. If *t* is a void tree, then *subtree* (*t*) is an empty set and the procedure preserves the invariant since it prints nothing at all. If *t* is not void, then the the procedure calls itself recursively on *t*.*left*, then prints the value attached to the root *t*, then calls itself recursively on *t*.*right*. Since *t* is a binary search tree (see the precondition), this preserves the invariant. Furthermore, we know that in this case at least one value, *t*.*value*, has been printed, so the invariant gives the desired postcondition – "All values in *subtree* (*t*) have been printed in order".

Transforming this semi-formal proof into a fully formal one requires developing a small axiomatic theory describing the target domain – binary trees. This is the subject of exercise 9.26; the following section, which builds such a mini-theory for another target domain, may serve as a guideline.

Since loops share the notion of invariant with recursive routines, it is natural to ask whether the the two kinds of invariant are related at all, especially for recursive routines which have a simple loop equivalent. The most common examples are "tail-recursive" routines, such as a recursive routine for computing a factorial, which may be written

factorial (*n*: *INTEGER*): *INTEGER* **is**
             -- Factorial of *n*
     require
         $n \geq 0$
     do
         if $n = 0$ **then**
             Result := 1
         else
             Result := *n* ∗ *factorial* (*n* − 1)
         end
     ensure
         Result = *n*!
     end -- *factorial*

To simplify the proof, let us rely on the convention that *Result*, before explicitly receiving a value through assignment, has the default initialization value 0. If we prove that the property

    Result = 0 **or** *Result* = *n*!

is invariant, and complement this by the trivial proof that *Result* cannot be 0 on exit, we obtain the desired postcondition *Result* = *n*!.

This recursive algorithm has a simple loop counterpart with an obvious invariant:

    i: *INTEGER*;
   from
       i := 0; *Result* := 1
   variant
       n − *i*
   invariant
       Result = *i* !
   until *i* = *n* **loop**
       i := *i* + 1; *Result* := *Result* ∗ *i*
   end

As this example indicates, although there may be a relation between a recursion invariant and the corresponding loop invariants, the relation is not immediate.

The underlying reason was pointed out in the analysis of recursive methods in the previous chapter: although a recursive computation will be executed, as its loop counterpart, as a "bottom-up" computation, the recursive formulation of the algorithm describes it in top-down format (see 8.4.3). The loop and recursion invariants reflect these different views of the same computation.

9.10.9 Proving a recursive routine

To understand the recursive routine rule in detail, it is useful to write a complete proof. The object of this proof will be what is perhaps the archetypal recursive routine: the solution to the Tower of Hanoi puzzle [Lucas 1883].

In this well-known example, the aim is to transfer n disks initially stacked on a peg A to a peg B, using a third peg C as intermediate storage. The argument n is a non-negative integer. Only one operation is available, written

   move (x, y)

Its effect is to transfer the disk on top of x to the top of y (x and y must each be one of A, B, C). The operation may be applied if and only if pegs x and y satisfy the following constraints:

- There is at least one disk on x; let d be the top disk.

- If there is at least one disk on y, then d was above the top disk on y in the original stack.

Another way to phrase the second constraint is to assume that the disks, all of different sizes, are originally stacked on A in order of decreasing size, and to require that *move* never transfers a disk on top of a smaller disk.

The proof will apply to the following procedure for solving this problem:

```
Hanoi (n: INTEGER; x, y, z: PEG) is
            -- Transfer n disks from peg x to peg y, using z as intermediate storage.
      do
         if n > 0 then
               Hanoi (n – 1, x, z, y);
               move (x, y);
               Hanoi (n – 1, z, y, x)
         -- else do nothing
         end
      end -- Hanoi
```

Although based on a toy example, this is an interesting routine because it is "really" recursive: in contrast with simpler examples of recursive computations (such as the recursive definition of the factorial function) it does not admit a trivial non-recursive equivalent. In addition, its structure closely resembles that of many useful practical recursive algorithms such as Quicksort or binary tree traversal (see exercises 9.25 and 9.26).

The proof of termination is trivial: n is a recursion variant. What remains to prove is that if there are n disks on A and none on B or C, the call *Hanoi* (n, A, B, C) transfers the n disks on top of B, leaving no disks on A or C. The proof that disk order does not change will be sketched later.

It turns out to be easier to prove a more general property: if there are n or more disks on A, the call will transfer them on top of those of B if any, leaving C in its original state.

Much of the proof work will be preparatory: building the right model for the objects whose properties we are trying to prove. This is a general feature of proofs: often the task of **specifying** what needs to be proved is as hard as the proof proper, or harder.

Here we must find a formal way to specify piles of disks and their properties. As a simple model, consider "generalized stacks" whose elements may be pushed or popped by whole chunks, rather than just one by one as with ordinary stacks. The following operations are defined on any generalized stacks s, t, for any non-negative integer i:

$|s|$

-- Size: an integer, the number of disks on s.

s^i

-- Top: the generalized stack consisting of the n top elements of s,
-- in the same order as on s. Empty if $i = 0$.
-- Defined only if $0 \le n \le |s|$.

$s - i$

-- Pop: the generalized stack consisting of the elements of s
-- except for the n top ones.
-- Defined only if $0 \le i \le |s|$.

$s + t$

-- Push: the generalized stack consisting of the elements
-- of t on top of those of s.

These operations satisfy a number of properties, given by the box on the adjacent page.

The rest of this discussion accepts these properties as the axioms of the theory of generalized stacks (also known as the specification of the corresponding "abstract data type"). Alternatively, you may wish to prove them using a *model* for generalized stacks, such as finite sequences; chapter 10 gives a more complete example of building a model for an axiomatic theory.

The axioms apply to any generalized stacks s, t, u and any integers i, j. Axioms G3.b, G5.b, G7 and G10 use "+" and "−" also as ordinary integer operators.

The associativity of "+" (property G1) will make it possible to write expressions such as $s + t + u$ without ambiguity.

[9.41]

Definition (Axioms for generalized stacks):

G1	$\vdash$	$s + (t + u) = (s + t) + u$	
G2	$\vdash$	$s - 0 = s$	
G3.a	$\vdash$	$0 \leq i \leq |t|$	$\supset (s + t)^i = t^i$
G3.b	$\vdash$	$|t| < i \leq |s| + |t|$	$\supset (s + t)^i = s^{i-|t|} + t$
G4	$\vdash$	$0 \leq j \leq i \leq |s|$	$\supset (s^i)^j = s^j$
G5.a	$\vdash$	$0 \leq i \leq |t|$	$\supset (s + t) - i = s + (t - i)$
G5.b	$\vdash$	$|t| \leq i \leq |s| + |t|$	$\supset (s + t) - i = s - (i - |t|)$
G6	$\vdash$	$i \leq |s|$	$\supset (s - i) + s^i = s$
G7	$\vdash$	$0 \leq i + j \leq |s|$	$\supset (s - i) - j = s - (i + j)$
G8	$\vdash$	$0 \leq i \leq |s|$	$\supset |s^i| = i$
G9	$\vdash$	$0 \leq i \leq |s|$	$\supset |s - i| = |s| - i$
G10	$\vdash$	$|s + t| = |s| + |t|$	

The following axiom schema (for any assertion Q and any generalized stacks s and t) expresses the properties of the *move* operation:

[9.42]
$$\vdash \{|s| > 0 \text{ and } Q [s \leftarrow s - 1, \ t \leftarrow t + s^1]\} \ move \ (s, \ t) \ \{Q\}$$

In words: the effect of *move* (s, t) is to replace s by $s - 1$ (s with its top element removed) and t by $t + s^1$ (t with the top element of s added on top). The first clause of the precondition expresses that s must contain at least one disk.

To state this axiom is to interpret *move* as two assignments: the axiom rephrases $A_{Assignment}$ (page 319) applied to the generalized stack assignments

$$t := t + s^1;$$

$$s := s - 1$$

where the assignments should really be carried out in parallel, although they will work in the order given (but not in the reverse order).

We must prove that the call $Hanoi$ (n, x, y, z) transfers the top n elements of x onto the top of y, leaving z unchanged. Expressed as a pre-post theorem schema, for any assertion Q, any integer i and any generalized stacks s, t, u, the property to prove is

[9.43]
$$\{|s| \geq i \text{ and } Q \ [s \leftarrow s - i, \ t \leftarrow t + s^i]\} \ Hanoi \ (i, s, t, u) \ \{Q\}$$

Let $BODY$ be the body of routine $Hanoi$ as given above. To establish [9.43], rule $12_{Routine}$ tells us that it suffices to prove the same property applied to $BODY$ with the appropriate argument substitutions:

[9.44]
$$\{||x| \geq n \text{ and } Q \ [x \leftarrow x - n, \ y \leftarrow y + x^n]\} \ BODY \ \{Q\}$$

and that the proof is permitted to rely on [9.43] itself. This is the goal for the remainder of this section.

Thanks to $I_{Conditional}$ (page 325) we can dispense with the trivial case $n = 0$; for positive n, $BODY$ reduces to the following (with assertions added as comments):

[9.45]

$$\text{-- } \{Q_1\}$$

$Hanoi$ $(n - 1, x, z, y)$;

$$\text{-- } \{Q_2\}$$

$move$ (x, y);

$$\text{-- } \{Q_3\}$$

$Hanoi$ $(n - 1, z, y, x)$

$$\text{-- } \{Q_4\}$$

We must prove that the above is a correct pre-post formula if Q_4 is Q and Q_1 is the precondition given in [9.44]. Since we are dealing with a compound and generalized assignments, the appropriate technique is to work from the end, starting with the postcondition Q as Q_4, and derive successive intermediate assertions Q_3, Q_2 and Q_1, such that Q_1 is the desired precondition.

To obtain Q_3, we apply [9.43] to the second recursive call; this requires substituting the actual arguments $n-1, z, y, x$ for i, s, t, u, v respectively. Then:

$$Q_3 \triangleq |z| \geq n-1 \text{ and } Q \ [z \leftarrow z - (n-1), \ y \leftarrow y + z^{n-1}]$$

Moving up one instruction, application of the $move$ axiom [9.42] to Q_3, with actual arguments x and y substituted for s and t respectively, yields:

$$Q_2 \triangleq |x| > 0 \text{ and } Q_3 \ [x \leftarrow x - 1, \ y \leftarrow y + x^1]$$

$$= |x| > 0 \text{ and } |z| \geq n-1 \text{ and }$$

$$Q \ [x \leftarrow x - 1, \ y \leftarrow y + x^1 + z^{n-1}, \ z \leftarrow z - (n-1)]$$

The only delicate part in obtaining Q_2 is the substitution for y, derived by combining two successive substitutions; this uses the rule for composition of substitutions ([9.10], page 320).

Finally, applying [9.43] again to the first recursive call with actual arguments $n-1, x, z, y$ yields Q_1:

$$Q_1 \triangleq |x| \geq n-1 \text{ and } Q_2 \; [x \leftarrow x - (n-1), \; z \leftarrow z + x^{n-1}]$$

so that, composing substitutions again:

[9.46]
$$Q_1 = |x| \geq n-1 \text{ and } |x - (n-1)| > 0 \text{ and } |z + x^{n-1}| \geq n-1 \text{ and}$$
$$Q \; [x \leftarrow (x-1) - (n-1),$$
$$y \leftarrow y + (x - (n-1))^1 + (z + x^{n-1})^{n-1}$$
$$z \leftarrow (z + x^{n-1}) - (n-1)]$$

There remains to simplify Q_1, using the various axioms for generalized stacks [9.41]. Consider the first part of Q_1 (the conditions on sizes). From axiom G9, the clause $|x - (n-1)| > 0$ is equivalent to $|x| \geq n$. From axioms G10 and G8,

$$|z + x^{n-1}| = |z| + |x^{n-1}|$$
$$= |z| + n - 1$$
$$\geq n - 1$$

so that the first line of the expression for Q_1 [9.46] is equivalent to just $|x| \geq n$

Now call x_{new}, y_{new} and z_{new} the replacements for x, y and z in the substitutions on Q on the next three lines. Then:

$$x_{new} \triangleq (x - 1) - (n - 1)$$
$$= x - n$$
$$\text{-- From G7}$$

$$y_{new} \triangleq y + (x - (n-1))^1 + (z + x^{n-1})^{n-1}$$
$$= y + (x - (n-1))^1 + x^{n-1}$$
$$\text{-- From G10 and G3.a}$$
$$= y + (x - (n-1) + x^{n-1})^n$$
$$\text{-- This comes from G3.b, used from right to left}$$
$$\text{-- for } i \triangleq n, s \triangleq x - (n-1) \text{ and } t \triangleq x^{n-1};$$
$$\text{-- applicability of G3.b is deduced from G8, G9 and G10.}$$
$$= y + x^n$$
$$\text{-- From G6, with } s \triangleq x \text{ and } i \triangleq n-1$$

$$z_{new} \;\triangleq\; (z + x^{n-1}) - (n-1)$$

$$= z$$

-- From G5.b, justified by G8, and G2

As a result of these simplifications, the overall precondition Q_1 obtained in [9.46] is in fact

$$Q_1 = |x| \geq n \textbf{ and } Q \; [x \leftarrow x - n, \; y \leftarrow y + x^n]$$

which is the desired precondition [9.44].   □

The proof does not take into account disk ordering constraints, as represented by rules on disk sizes. Here is one way to refine the above discussion so as to remove this limitation. (The method will only be sketched; you are invited to fill in the details.) Add to the specification of generalized stacks an operation written s_i, so that s_i, an integer, is the size of the i-th disk in s from the top. Define a boolean-valued function on generalized stacks, written $s!$ and expressing that s is sorted, as:

$$s! \;\triangleq\; \forall i: 2..|s| \bullet s_{i-1} < s_i$$

To adapt the specification so that it will only describe sorted stacks, add to all axioms involving a subexpression of the form $s + t$ a guard (condition to the left of the $\supset$ sign) of the form

$$|s| \geq 1 \;\wedge\; |t| \geq 1 \;\supset\; t_{|t|} < s_1$$

and add to the precondition of *move* (s, t) a similar clause stating that if t is not empty its top disk is bigger than the top disk of s.

Then you need to prove that the property

$$x! \textbf{ and } y! \textbf{ and } z!$$

is a recursion invariant, by adding it to the postcondition Q and moving it up until it yields the precondition.

9.11 ASSERTION-GUIDED PROGRAM CONSTRUCTION

Among the uses of formal specifications listed in chapter 1, the most obvious applications of the axiomatic techniques developed in this chapter seem to be program verification and language standardization.

Perhaps less immediately apparent but equally important is the application of axiomatic techniques to the construction of reliable software. Here the goal is not to prove an existing program, but to integrate the proof with the program construction process so as to ensure the correctness of programs from the start. This may be called the **constructive approach** to software correctness.

There are several reasons why this approach deserves careful consideration:

- Unless you make the concern for correctness an integral part of program building, it is unlikely that you will be able to produce provably correct programs. Were you able to prove anything at all, the most likely outcome is a proof of *in*correctness.

- With the methods of this chapter, proofs require that the program be stuffed with assertions. The best time to write these assertions is program design time. Many of them will in fact come from the preceding phases of analysis.

- In many practical cases, you will not be able to carry out complete proofs of correctness, if only because of technical limitations such as the lack of a complete axiom system for a given programming language. But the techniques of this chapter can still go a long way toward ensuring correctness by helping you to write programs so as to pave the way for a hypothetical proof.

The rest of this chapter expands on these ideas by showing examples of how axiomatic techniques can help make the correctness concern an integral part of the software design.

A warning is in order: the techniques developed below are neither fail-safe nor universal. Formal proofs are the only way to guarantee correctness (and even they are meaningful only to the extent that you can trust the compiler, the operating system and the hardware). But an imperfect solution is better than the standard approach to program construction, where correctness concerns play a very minor role, if any role at all.

9.11.1 Assertions in programming languages

Because assertions are such a help in designing correct software, and such a good trace of the specification and design process that led to a particular software element, it seems a pity not to include them in the final software text.

Of course, you may always include assertions as comments. This is indeed highly recommended if you are using a programming language that offers no better deal. Having more formal support for assertions as part of the programming language proper offers a number of advantages:

1   • The path from specification to design and implementation becomes smoother: the first phase produces the assertions; the next ones yield instructions which satisfy the corresponding pre-post formulae.

2   • If the language includes a formal assertion sublanguage, software tools can extract the assertions from a software element automatically to produce high-level documentation about the element. This is a better approach than having programmers write software documentation as a separate effort.

3   • Even in the absence of a program proving mechanism, a compiler may have an option which will generate code for checking assertions at run-time (the next best thing to a proof). This turns out to be a remarkable debugging aid, since many bugs will manifest themselves as violations of the consistency conditions expressed by assertions.

4   • Assertions also have a direct connection with the important issue of exception handling, which, however, falls beyond the scope of the present discussion.

A number of programming languages have included some support for assertions. The first was probably Algol W, which has an instruction of the form

   ASSERT (*b*)

where *b* is a boolean instruction. Depending on a compilation option, the instruction either evaluates *b* or is equivalent to a *Skip*. In the first case, program execution will terminate with an informative message if the value of *b* is false. The C language offers a similar mechanism.

Such constructs, however, are mostly debugging aids – application 3 above. They are insufficient to support the full role of assertions in the software construction process, especially applications 1 and 2.

Some languages take the notion of assertion more seriously. An example is the Anna design language (see bibliographical notes). Another is Eiffel.

Eiffel's mechanism, used for the examples of assertion-guided software construction in the rest of this discussion, directly supports all four applications above. Two aspects of the mechanism have already been described:

   • The syntactic inclusion of invariant, variant and initialization clauses in loops (page 340).

   • The **require** and **ensure** clauses in routines, supporting the principle of "programming by contract", as discussed on page 353.

Eiffel assertions appear in two other important contexts:

   • A class may (and often does) have a **class invariant**, which expresses global properties of the class's instances. Class invariants are theoretically equivalent to clauses added to both the precondition and postcondition of every exported routine of a class, but they are better factored out at the class level.

   • A check instruction, of the form **check** *Assertion* **end**, may be used at any point where you want to assert that a certain property will hold, outside of the constructs just discussed.

In the programming examples which follow, the notation **check** *Assertion* **end** will replace the Metanot braces used earlier in this chapter, as in {*Assertion*}.

More generally, the examples will rely on the Eiffel notation, slightly adapted for the circumstance: first, some assertions will include quantified expressions ($\forall$ ... and $\exists$ ...), currently not supported by the Eiffel assertion sublanguage, which is based on boolean expressions; second, the examples do not take advantage of some specific Eiffel structures and mechanisms (the class construct, deferred routines for specification without implementation, genericity, the treatment of arrays as abstractly defined data structures and others) which have not been described in this book.

It is often necessary, in a routine postcondition, to refer to the value an expression had on routine entry. The discussion will use the Eiffel **old** notation, of which an example is given by the following routine specification:[2]

> *enter* (*x*: *T*; *t*: **table of** *T*): *BOOLEAN* **is**
>
> > -- Insert *x* into *t* ; increment *count*.
>
> **require**
>
> > **not** *full* -- There should be room in the table
>
> **do**
>
> > . . .
>
> **ensure**
>
> > . . .
> >
> > *count* = **old** *count* + 1
>
> **end** -- *enter*

9.11.2 Embedding strategies

Among the control structures studied in this chapter, the most interesting ones, requiring invention on the part of the programmer, are routines (especially recursive ones) and loops. This discussion will focus on loops.

The inference rules for loops express the postcondition – goal – of a loop as

> $G \triangleq I$ **and** E

where I is the invariant and E is the exit condition.

This suggests that the invariant is a **weakened version of the goal**: weak enough that you can ensure its validity on loop initialization; but strong enough to yield the desired goal when combined with the exit condition.

---

2 Here *count* has to be externally available to the routine. In Eiffel it would usually be an attribute of the class. Also, the argument *t* would normally be implicit, routine *enter* being part of a class describing tables.

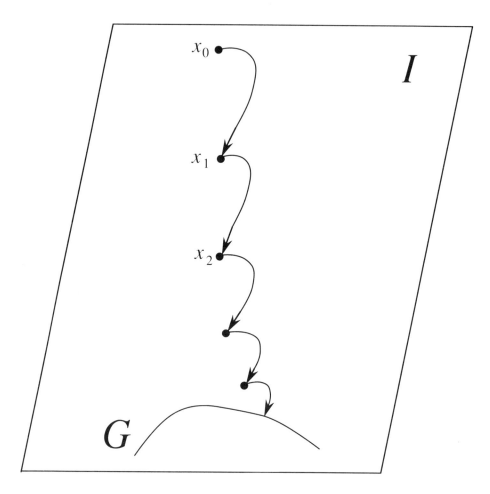

Figure 9.6: Embedding

Loop construction strategies, then, may be viewed as various ways to weaken the goal.

The above figure illustrates the underlying view of loops. When looking for a solution to a programming problem, you are trying to find one or more objects satisfying the goal in a certain solution space – the curve G on the figure. G corresponds to the goal. The aim is to find an element x in G. If you do not see any obvious way to hit G directly, you may try a loop solution, which is an iterative strategy working as follows:

- Embed G into a larger space, I. I represents the set of states satisfying the invariant.

- Define E so that G is the intersection of I and E. E corresponds to the exit condition.

- Choose as starting value for x some point x_0 in I. Because I is a superset of G, it will be easier in general to find this element than it would be to find an element of G right away. Element x_0 corresponds to the loop's initialization.
- At each step let V be the "distance" from x to G. V corresponds to the loop's variant.
- Apply an iterative mechanism which, at each step, determines if x in G, in which case the iteration terminates (you have reached a solution), and otherwise computes the next element by applying to x a transformation B which must keep x in I but will decrease V. B corresponds to the loop body.

The loop is of the form

from
  $x := x_0$
invariant
  I
variant
  V
until $x \in G$ **loop**
  B
end

check I **and** $s \in G$ **end** -- (i.e. G)

We may now view loop construction as the problem of finding the best way to embed goal spaces such as G into larger "invariant" spaces I, with the associated choices for the starting point s_0, the variant V, and the body B.

The following sections study two particular embedding strategies:

- Constant relaxation.
- Uncoupling.

9.11.3 Constant relaxation

With the constant relaxation strategy, you obtain the invariant I from the goal G by substituting a variable for a constant value. The initialization will assign some trivial value to the variable to ensure I; each loop iteration gets the variable's value closer to that of the constant, while maintaining the invariant.

The simple example of linear search in a non-sorted list provides a good illustration of the idea.

Assume you have an array of elements of any type T, and an element x of the same type, and you want to determine whether x is equal to any of the elements in t.

You can write the routine as a function *has* returning a boolean value, with the postcondition

[9.47]
$$Result = (\exists\ k : 1 .. n \bullet x = t\ [k])$$

In other words, the result is true if and only if the array contains an element equal to x.

The function may be specified as follows (assuming n is a non-negative constant):[3]

> *has* (*x: T; t:* **array** *[1..n]* **of** *T*): *BOOLEAN* **is**
>   -- Does x appear in t?
>   **require**
>   **true** -- No precondition
>   **do**
>
>   ...
>
>   **ensure**
> $Result = (\exists\ k : 1 .. n \bullet x = t\ [k])$ -- [9.47]
> **end** -- *has*

In assertion-guided program construction, we examine the specification (the postcondition) and look for a refinement which will yield a solution (the routine body). For a loop solution, the refinement is an embedding as defined above.

To find such an embedding, we may note that any difficulty in obtaining the goal G, as given by [9.47], is the presence of the interval $1 .. n$. The smaller the n, the easier; with a value such as 1 or better yet 0 the answer is trivial. For 0, it suffices to use *false* for *Result*.

This yields an embedding based on the constant relaxation method: introduce a fresh variable i which will take its values in the interval $0 .. n$ and rewrite the goal [9.47] as

$$Result = (\exists\ k : 1 .. i \bullet x = t\ [k])\qquad -- I$$
$$\textbf{and}\ \ i = n$$

which is trivially equivalent to the original. Call I the condition on the first line. I has all the qualifications of an invariant:

- I is easy to ensure initially (take **false** for *Result* and 0 for *j*).
- I is a weakened form of the goal, since it coincides with it for $j = n$.
- Maintaining I while bringing j a little closer to n will not be too difficult (see next).

This prompts us to look for a solution of the form

---

[3] In normal Eiffel usage this function would appear in a class describing some variant of the array data structure; as a consequence, the argument *t* would be implicit.

from
    $i := 0$; *Result* := **false**;
invariant
    I
variant
    $n - i$
until
    $i = n$
loop
    "Get i closer to n, maintaining the validity of I"
end

        check [9.47] **end**

The loop body ("Get i...") is easy to obtain. It must be an instruction *LB* which makes the following pre-post formula correct:

    check *I* **and** $i < n$ **end**

LB

    check *I* **and** $0 \leq n - i < $ **old** $(n - i)$ **end**

The **old** notation makes it possible to refer to the value of the variant, $n - i$, before the loop body (although **old** usually applies to routines).

The simplest way to "Get i closer to n" is to increase it by 1. This suggests looking for an instruction *LB'* such that the following is correct:

    check
        $Result = (\exists\ k : 1 .. i \bullet x = t\ [k])$

            and $i < n$
    end

  $i := i + 1$; *LB'*

    check $Result = (\exists\ k : 1 .. i \bullet x = t\ [k])$ **end**

The postcondition is very close to the precondition; more precisely, the precondition implies that after execution of the instruction $j := i + 1$ the following holds:

    $Result = (\exists\ k : 1 .. i{-}1 \bullet x = t\ [k])$

so that the specification for *LB'* is:

    check $Result = (\exists\ k : 1 .. i{-}1 \bullet x = t\ [k])$ **end**

LB'

    check $Result = (\exists\ k : 1 .. i \bullet x = t\ [k])$ **end**

An obvious solution is to take for *LB'* the instruction

$Result := Result$ **or else** $(t \ [i] = x)$

which application of the assignment rule ($A_{Assignment}$, page 319) easily shows to satisfy the specification. The **or else** could be an **or**, but we do not need to perform the test on $t \ [i]$ if $Result$ is already true.

This gives a correct implementation of has:

```
has (x: T; t: array [1..n] of T): BOOLEAN is
             -- Does x appear in t?
        require
             true -- No precondition
        local
             i: INTEGER
        do
             from
                   i := 0; Result := false
             invariant
                   Result = ( ∃ k : 1.. i • x = t [k])
             variant
                   n − i
             until
                   i = n
             loop
                   i := i + 1;
                   Result := Result or else (t [i] = x)
             end
        ensure
             Result = ( ∃ k : 1.. n • x = t [k])
        end
end -- has
```

You are invited to investigate for yourself how to carry out the obvious improvement – stopping the loop as soon as $Result$ is found to be true – in the same systematic framework.

This example is typical of the constant relaxation method, applicable when the postcondition contains a constant such as n above and you can obtain an invariant by substituting a variable such as i. The variant is the difference between the constant and the variable; the loop body gets the variable closer to the constant and re-establishes the invariant.

"For" loops of common languages support this strategy.

9.11.4 Uncoupling

Another embedding strategy, related to constant relaxation but different, is "uncoupling". It applies when the postcondition is of the form

p (i) **and** q (i)

for some variable i. In other words, the postcondition introduces a "coupling" between two clauses p and q. You may then find it fruitful to introduce a fresh variable j, rewrite the postcondition as

p (i) **and** q (j) -- I

   and $i = j$

and use the first line as candidate loop invariant I, the variant being $|j-i|$. Because you have "uncoupled" the variables in the two conditions p and q, it may be much easier to ensure the initial validity of I. The loop body is then of the form

"Bring i and j closer, maintaining I"

which will often be done in two steps:

"Bring i and j closer";

"Re-establish I if needed"

As an example of this strategy, consider a variation on the preceding searching problem, with the extra hypothesis that T has an order relation, written $\leq$, and the array t is sorted. This assumption may be expressed as a precondition:[4]

[9.48]
$$\forall k : 2 .. n \bullet t \ [k-1] \leq t \ [k]$$

The previous version of *has* would still work, of course, but we may want to rewrite it to take advantage of t being sorted. One possibility is to write the body of the new *has* under the form

[9.49]
$position := index \ (t, x);$

$Result \ := \ position \in 1 .. n \ \textbf{and then} \ x = t \ [position]$

where the auxiliary function *index* returns a position such that x either appears at that position or does not appear in the array at all.

---

4 In Eiffel's object-oriented software decomposition, such a property would normally be expressed not as the precondition of an individual routine, but as a **class invariant** for the enclosing class.

The precise specification of *index*'s postcondition turns out to be perhaps the most delicate part of this problem (which you are invited to try out by yourself first):

A • The specification must be satisfiable in all cases: whatever the value of x is relative to the array values, there must be at least one *Result* satisfying the postcondition.

B • To make the above algorithm [9.49] a correct implementation of *has*, the *Result* must be the index of an array position where x appears, or otherwise must enable us to determine that x does not occur at all.

The following postcondition satisfies these requirements:

[9.50]
$$Result \in 0 .. n$$
$$(\text{and } \forall k : 1 .. Result \bullet t \, [k] \leq x) \qquad \text{-- } p \, (Result)$$
$$(\text{and } \forall k : Result+1 .. n \bullet t \, [k] \geq x) \qquad \text{-- } q \, (Result)$$

To check for condition A above, note that 0 will do for *Result* if x is smaller than all array values, and n if it is larger than all array values. (Remember once again that $\forall x : E \bullet P$ is always true if E is empty.) For condition B, [9.50] implies that x appears in t if and only if

$$i > 0 \text{ and then } t \, [Result] = x$$

Specification [9.50] is non-deterministic: if two or more (necessarily consecutive) array entries have value x, any of the corresponding indices will be an acceptable *Result*. There are several ways to change the postcondition so that it defines just one *Result* in all cases; we may for example change the last clause to read

$$(\forall k : Result+1 .. n \bullet t \, [k] > x)$$

so that, in case of multiple equal values, *Result* will be the highest adequate index. It is preferable, however, to keep the more symmetric version [9.50].

The problem, then, is to write the body for

```
index (x: T; t: array [1..n] of T): INTEGER is
            -- Does x appear in t?
      require
            [9.48] -- t is sorted
      do
            ...
      ensure
            [9.50]
      end -- has
```

How do we ensure the postcondition [9.50]? For more clarity let us use variable i instead of *Result*; the **do** clause may then end with *Result* := i. The postcondition is of the form

   $i \in 0 .. n$ **and** p (i) **and** q (i)

which the uncoupling strategy suggests rewriting as

   $i, j \in 0 .. n$ **and** p (i) **and** q (j) -- *I*

   and $i = j$

leading to a loop solution of the form

   from

   $i := i_0;$ $j := j_0$

   invariant

   p (i) **and** q (j)

   variant

   distance (i, j)

   until

   $i = j$

   loop

   "Bring i and j closer"

   end

This solution will be correct if and only if i_0 satisfies p, j_0 satisfies q, the refinement of "Bring i and j closer" conserves the invariant $p(i)$ **and** $q(j)$, and *distance* (i, j) is an integer variant.

The initialization is trivial: we choose i_0 to be 0 and j_0 to be n; p (0) and q (n) are true since they are $\forall$ properties on empty sets.

With these initializations it appears reasonable to maintain j no greater than i throughout the loop. This suggests a reinforced invariant:

   p (i) **and** q (j) **and** $0 \le i \le j \le n$

The most obvious way to "Bring i and j closer" is to increment i by 1, or alternatively decrement j by 1, and see what it takes to keep the invariant true. Since the problem is symmetric in i and j, we should treat both possibilities equally.

Assuming the invariant is satisfied and $i < j$ (the exit condition is not met yet), under what conditions may we increment i or decrement j?

Clearly, the instruction

$$i := i + 1$$

will preserve the invariant if and only if $p\ (i + 1)$ is true, and

$$j := i - 1$$

if and only if $q\ (j - 1)$ is true.

Look first at the i part. By definition,

$$p\ (i) = (\forall k : 1 .. i \bullet t\ [k] \leq x)$$

so that if $t\ [i + 1]$ is defined (in other words, for $i < n$):

$$p\ (i + 1) = p\ (i)\ \textbf{and}\ t\ [i + 1] \leq x$$

Starting from a state where $p\ (i)$ is satisfied, then, incrementing i by 1 will preserve the invariant if and only if

$$i < n \textbf{ and then } t\ [i + 1] \leq x$$

With respect to the j part

$$q\ (j) = (\forall k : j+1 .. n \bullet t\ [k] \geq x)$$

we may decrease j by 1 if and only if

$$j > 0 \textbf{ and then } t\ [j] \geq x$$

In spite of appearances, the symmetry between the conditions on i and j is perfect; simply, because in the original postcondition [9.50] p involves *Result* and q involves *Result* + 1, it is in fact a symmetry between i and $j + 1$.

The guards $i < n$ and $j > 0$ are in fact superfluous: the invariant includes $0 \leq i \leq j \leq n$, and $i > j$ will hold as long as the exit condition is not satisfied; so whenever the loop body is executed $i+1$ and j belong to the interval $1 .. n$. So we may try as loop body:

if

      $t\ [i + 1] \leq x \rightarrow i := i + 1$ ☐

      $t\ [j] \geq x \rightarrow j := j - 1$

end

Because symmetry is so strong is this problem, the solution uses the guarded conditional (see [9.33], page 341). We must be careful, however: a guarded conditional will only execute properly if, in all possible cases, at least one of the guards is true. Fortunately, here this is the case: because the array is sorted and $i < j$ is a precondition for the loop body, if the first guard is false, that is to say $t\ [i + 1] > x$, then the second guard, $t\ [j] \geq x$, is true.

The guarded conditional yields a non-deterministic instruction: if $t\,[i + 1] \leq x \leq$ $t\,[j\,]$, then the instruction may execute either of its two branches. Using the standard conditional instruction removes the non-determinism:

[9.51]
> **if** $t\,[i + 1] \leq x$ **then**
>
> > $i := i + 1$
>
> **else**
>
> > $j := j - 1$
>
> **end**

Either form yields a simple and correct version of *index:*

> *index* (x: T; t: **array** [1..n] **of** T): *INTEGER* **is**
>
> > -- Does x appear in t?
> >
> > **require**
> >
> > > [9.48] -- t is sorted
> >
> > **local**
> >
> > > i, j: *INTEGER*
> >
> > **do**
> >
> > > **from**
> > >
> > > > $i := 0; j := n$
> > >
> > > **invariant**
> > >
> > > > $p\,(i)$ **and** $q\,(j)$ **and** $0 \leq i \leq j \leq n$
> > >
> > > **variant**
> > >
> > > > $j - i$
> > >
> > > **until**
> > >
> > > > $i = j$
> > >
> > > **loop**
> > >
> > > > -- This could use the **if** ... **then** ... **else** form instead
> > > >
> > > > **if**
> > > >
> > > > > $t\,[i + 1] \leq x \;\rightarrow\; i := i + 1 \;\;\square$
> > > > >
> > > > > $t\,[j\,] \geq x \;\rightarrow\; j := j - 1$
> > > >
> > > > **end**
> > >
> > > **end**
> >
> > **ensure**
> >
> > > [9.50] -- (cf. page 374)
> >
> > **end** -- *has*

As you will have noted, this is not the way most people usually write sequential search. The standard form will follow from an efficiency improvement that we should carry out as systematically as the above development. The price to pay for this improvement is the removal of the esthetically pleasant symmetry. Whenever the first guard is false, in other words $t[i + 1] > x$, then assigning to j the value of i (rather than just $j - 1$) will still preserve the invariant. This suggests rewriting the conditional as

if $t[i + 1] \leq x$ **then**
     $i := i + 1$
else
     $j := i$
end

(Of course, the symmetric change would also work.) As a result we may dispense with variable j altogether by noting that loop termination occurs when either $i = n$ or $t[i + 1] > x$, yielding the more usual form for sequential search:

from
     $i := 0$
invariant ... **variant** ...
until $i = n$ **or else** $t[i+1] > x$ **loop**
     $i := i+1$
end

You should complete the **invariant** and **variant** clauses of this loop.

9.11.5 Binary search

Removing the symmetry between i and $j-1$ at best yielded a marginal efficiency improvement. A more promising avenue for improving the performance of sorted table searching is based on the property that t is an array, meaning constant-time access to any element whose index is known. This suggests "Bringing i and j closer" faster than by increments of $+1$ or -1.

The idea of **binary search** is to aim for the middle of the interval $i..j$. As Knuth noted in the volume on searching of his *Art of Computer Programming* [Knuth 1973]:

> *Although the basic idea of binary search is comparatively straightforward, the details can be somewhat tricky, and many good programmers have done it wrong the first few times they tried.*

If you doubt this, it should suffice to take a look at exercise 9.12, which shows four innocent-looking versions – all wrong. For each version there is a a case in which the algorithm fails to terminate, exceeds the array bounds, or yields a wrong answer. Before you read further, it is a good idea to try to come up with a correct version of binary search by yourself.

Both binary search and the above version of function *index* belong to a more general class of solutions based on the same uncoupling of the postcondition, where the loop body finds an element m in $i..j$ and assigns the value of m (or a neighboring value) to i or j.

In the version seen above m is $i + 1$ or $j - 1$; for binary search it will be approximately $(i + j)$ **div** 2, so that we can expect a maximum number of iterations roughly equal to $\log_2 n$ rather than n. (The operator **div** denotes integer division.)

This must be done carefully, however. In the general case we aim for a loop body of the form

> $m := $ *"Some value in* $1..n$ *such that* $i < m \leq j"$;
>
> **if**
>> $t[m] \leq x \;\rightarrow\; i := m$ $[\!]$
>>
>> $t[m] \geq x \;\rightarrow\; j := m - 1$
>
> **end**

which, in ordinary programming languages, will be written deterministically:

> $m := $ *"Some value in* $1..n$ *such that* $i < m \leq j"$;
>
> **if** $t[m] \leq x$ **then**
>> $i := m$
>
> **else**
>> $j := m - 1$
>
> **end**

Whether the conditional instruction is deterministic or not, it is essential to get all the details right (and easy to get some wrong):

1. • The instruction must always decrease the variant $j - i$, by increasing i or decreasing j. If the the definition of m specified just $i \leq m$ rather than $i < m$, the first branch would not meet this goal.

2. • This does not transpose directly to j: requiring $i < m < j$ would lead to an impossibility when $j - i$ is equal to 1. So we accept $m \leq j$ but then we must take $m - 1$, not m, as the new value of j in the second branch.

3. • The conditional's guards are tests on $t[m]$, so m must always be in the interval $1..n$. This follows from the clause $0 \leq i \leq j \leq n$ which is part of the invariant.

4. • If this clause is satisfied, then $m \leq n$ and $m - 1 \geq 0$, so the conditional instruction indeed leaves this clause invariant.

5. • You are invited to check that both branches of the conditional also preserve the rest of the invariant, $p(i)$ **and** $q(j)$.

Any policy for choosing m is acceptable if it conforms to the above scheme. Two simple choices are $i + 1$ and j; they lead to variants of the above sequential search algorithm.

For binary search, m will be roughly equal to the average of i and j,

> $midpoint \triangleq (i + j)$ **div** 2

The value of *midpoint* itself is not acceptable for *m*, however, because it might not satisfy requirement 1 above. Choosing *midpoint* + 1 will, however, satisfy all the above requirements.

This yields the following new version of *index*, using binary search:

index (*x*: *T*; *t*: **array** [*1..n*] **of** *T*): *INTEGER* **is**
                      -- Does *x* appear in *t*?
    require
        [9.48] -- *t* is sorted
    local
        i, *j*, *m*: *INTEGER*
    do
        from
            $i := 0; j := n$
        invariant
            p (*i*) **and** q (*j*) **and** $0 \leq i \leq j \leq n$
        variant
            $j - i$
        until
            $i = j$
        loop
            $m := (i + j)$ **div** $2 + 1$;
            if t [*m*] $\leq x$ **then**
                $i := m$
            else
                $j := m - 1$
            end
        end
    ensure
        [9.50] -- cf. page 374
end -- *has*

We can check that the loop will be executed at most $\lfloor \log_2 n \rfloor$ times by proving that $\lfloor \log_2 (j - i) \rfloor$ is a variant. ($\lfloor x \rfloor$ is the largest integer no greater than *x*.) For any real numbers *a* and *b*, $\lfloor \log_2 (a) \rfloor < \lfloor \log_2 (b) \rfloor$ if $a \leq b / 2$. Here, $j - i$ is indeed at least divided by 2 in both possible cases in the loop, since whenever $i < j$ (*i* and *j* being integers):

$$j - ((i + j) \textbf{ div } 2 + 1) \leq (j - i) \textbf{ div } 2$$

$$i - ((i + j) \textbf{ div } 2) \leq (j - i) \textbf{ div } 2$$

(To check this, consider separately the cases $i + j$ odd and $i + j$ even).

Of course, the version of binary search obtained here is not the only possible one; you may wish to obtain others through variants of the uncoupling strategy.

9.11.6 An assessment

Although they apply to well-known and relatively simple algorithms, the above examples provide a good illustration of the constructive approach:

- The same framework served to derive two classes of algorithms (sequential and binary search). In the sorted array case, it is only at the last step (choosing how to "bring i and j closer") that different design choices lead to different computing methods.
- The heuristics used, constant relaxation and uncoupling, are quite general. One of the exercises (9.24) asks you to apply uncoupling to a completely different problem, sequence or array partitioning.
- We have built all versions so as to convince ourselves that they are correct and to know why they are.

Given the human capacity for error and self-deception, it would be absurd to characterize the methods illustrated here as sure recipes to obtain correct programs, or to claim that they make other correctness techniques (such as testing) obsolete. Perfect or universal they are not; more modestly, they constitute an important tool, among others, in the battle for software reliability. This suffices to make them one of the most valuable application of axiomatic semantics.

9.12 BIBLIOGRAPHICAL NOTES

The basis of the axiomatic method is mathematical logic, based on classical rhetoric but made considerably more rigorous in this century as an attempt to solve the crisis of mathematics that followed the development of set theory at the turn of the century. There are many good introductions to mathematical logic, such as [Kleene 1967] or [Mendelson 1964]. [Copi 1973] presents the notions of truth, validity, proof, axiom, inference etc. in a particularly clear fashion. [Manna 1985] is especially geared towards computer scientists.

Work presenting mathematical foundations for axiomatic theories is usually rooted in denotational semantics; this is the area of "complementary semantics", discussed in the next chapter. See the bibliographical notes to that chapter.

The first article on program proving using techniques based on assertions was [Floyd 1967], with a suggestive title: "Assigning Meanings to Programs". The paper also introduced the notion of loop invariant, called "inductive assertion".

Floyd's techniques were refined and improved in [Hoare 1969], which expressed them as a system of axioms and inference rules associated with programming language constructs. The approach was then applied to further language constructs such as routines [Hoare 1971] and jumps [Clint 1972], and to the specification of a large part of the Pascal language [Hoare 1973b]. A comprehensive survey of Hoare semantics is given in [Apt 1981].

The weakest precondition approach was developed by Dijkstra in an article [Dijkstra 1975] and a book [Dijkstra 1976].

These publications by Dijkstra also pioneered the "constructive approach" to software correctness (9.11). [Gries 1981] is a very readable presentation of this approach. [Alagić 1978] and [Dromey 1983] apply similar ideas to teaching program design, algorithms and data structures. [Jones 1986] also emphasizes the use of program proving techniques for software development. See also work by the author [Meyer 1978, 1980] and in collaboration [Bossavit 1981], the latter describing the systematic construction of vector algorithms for supercomputers. For an account of how the spirit of the axiomatic method may be applied to the construction and proofs of algorithms in the very difficult area of concurrent programming, see the article on "on-the-fly garbage collection" [Dijkstra 1978].

The assertion mechanism of Anna is described in [Luckham 1985]. The assertion mechanism of Eiffel and its application to the construction of reliable software components are described in [Meyer 1988a]. This book and an article [Meyer 1988b] develop the theory of "Programming by Contract".

As mentioned on page 344, Dijkstra's non-deterministic choice and loop instructions have direct applications to concurrent programming. Hoare's CSP (Communicating Sequential Processes) approach to parallelism is based in part on these ideas [Hoare 1978, 1985].

The axiomatic theory of expression typing in lambda calculus (9.3) comes from [Cardelli 1984a], where it is applied to the more general problem of inferring proper types in a language (Milner's ML) where types, instead of being declared explicitly by programmers, are determined by the system from the context and the types attached to predefined identifiers. Cardelli's system also handles genericity: in other words, some of the types may include "free type identifiers" standing for arbitrary types. For example, the type of the identity function Id will be $\alpha \rightarrow \alpha$, where α stands for an arbitrary type.

EXERCISES

9.1 Integers in mathematics and on computers

Write an axiomatic theory of integers, starting from the standard Peano axioms (see [Suppes 1972], page 121, or any other text on axiomatic set theory). Then adapt the theory to account for the size limits imposed by number representation on computers.

9.2 Symmetric if instruction

Modify the abstract syntax and the denotational semantics of Graal, as given in chapter 5, to replace the classical **if...then...else...** conditional instruction by the guarded conditional (9.9.4).

9.3 Assignment and sequencing

Prove the following pre-post formula:

$\vdash$ $\{x = a$ **and** $y = b\}$

$t := x; x := x + y; y := t$

$\{x = a + b$ **and** $y = a\}$

9.4 Non-deterministic conditional

Compute A **wp** Q, for any assertion Q, where A is the instruction

if
$$x \leq 0 \;\rightarrow\; a := -x \;\square$$
$$x \geq 0 \;\rightarrow\; a := x$$
end

9.5 Weakest precondition

Show that the value of *guarded_if* **wp** Q (page 342) may also be expressed as:

guarded_if **wp** R =

$(c_1$ **or** c_2 **or** ... **or** $c_n)$ **and**

$(c_1$ **implies** $(A_1$ **wp** $R))$ **and**
$(c_2$ **implies** $(A_2$ **wp** $R))$ **and**

...

$(c_n$ **implies** $(A_n$ **wp** $R))$

9.6 Simple proofs

Prove that the following pre-post formulae, involving integer variables only and assuming perfect integer arithmetic, are theorems.

1    $\{z * x^y = K\}\ z := z * x\ \{z * x^{y-1} = K\}$

2    $\{z * x^y = K\}\ y := y - 1; z := z * x\ \{z * x^y = K\}$

3    $\{y\ even\ \text{and}\ z * x^y = K\}\ y := y\ /\ 2; x := x^2\ \{z * x^y = K\}$

4    $\{z * x^y = K\}$

    if

            $y\ odd\ \rightarrow\ y := y - 1; z := z * x$ ▯

            $y\ even\ \rightarrow\ y := y\ /\ 2; x := x^2$

    end

    $\{z * x^y = K\}$

9.7 Proving a loop

Let a and b be integers such that $a > 0, b \geq 0$. From the answers to exercise 9.6, determine the result of the following program; prove your answer.

    $x, y, z: INTEGER;$

    from

        $x := m; y := n; z := 1$

    until $y = 0$ **loop**

        if

                $y\ odd\ \rightarrow\ y := y - 1; z := z * x$ ▯

              $y\ even\ \rightarrow\ y := y\ /\ 2; x := x^2$

        end

    end

9.8 Permutability of instructions

Applications such as parallel programming and the adaptation of programs to run on parallel or vector processors ("parallelization" or "vectorization"), often require to determine whether the order of two instructions may be reversed. This exercise investigates such permutability criteria.

Define two instructions A and B to be **equivalent**, and write

    $A \equiv B$

if and only if for any assertion Q

A **wp** $Q = B$ **wp** Q

Define that the instructions *permute*, written A **perm** B, if and only if

$A; B \equiv B; A$

1 – Consider assignment instructions A and B:

- A is $x := e$
- B is $y := f$

where e, f are expressions (none of the expressions considered in this exercise may contain function calls). Let V_e and V_f be the sets of variables occurring in e and f respectively. Give a sufficient condition on V_e and V_f for

A **perm** B

to hold. Prove the result using the rules for assignment and sequence.

2 – Assume A is of the form

$x := x \oplus e$

and B is of the form

$x := x \oplus f$

where e and f are expressions, none of which contains x, and $\oplus$ is an operation which is both commutative and associative. Prove that it is true in this case that

A **perm** B

9.9 Another assignment rule

Can you imagine a "forward rule" for assignment (see page 321) ? (**Hint**: Introduce explicitly the value that the variable being assigned to had before the assignment. The rule uses an existential quantifier.)

9.10 Array assignment

Prove theorems [9.14] (page 324). **Hint**: Remember to treat the assignment as an operation on the whole array.

9.11 Simple loop construction from invariants

Write loops to compute the following values for any n by finding first the appropriate invariants, using assertion-guided techniques (9.11).

1    $f = n!$ (factorial of n)

2   F_n, the n-th Fibonacci number, defined by

$$F_0 = 0$$
$$F_1 = 1$$
$$F_i = F_{i-1} + F_{i-2} \text{ for } i > 1$$

9.12 Binary search: failed attempts

The figure on the adjacent page shows four attempts at writing a program for binary search. Each program should set *Result* to *true* if and only if the value x appears in the real array t, assumed to be sorted in increasing order.

The programs use **div** for integer division. Variable *found*, where used, is of type *BOOLEAN*.

Show that all of these programs are erroneous; it suffices for this to show that for each purported solution there exist values of the array t and the element x that produce an incorrect solution (*Result* being set to **true** although x does not appear in t or conversely) or will result in abnormal behavior at execution (out-of-bounds memory reference or infinite loop).

9.13 Indexed loops

Most languages provide a "do" or "for" loop structure in which the iteration is controlled by an index ranging over a finite range (usually an arithmetic progression over the integers, although it could be any finite set, such as a finite, sequential data structure like a linear list). In the simplest case, looping over a contiguous integer interval, the loop will be written as something like

  for i: $a..b$ **loop** A_i **end**

where A_i is some instruction, usually dependent on the value of i.
Give a proof rule for such an instruction.

Figure 9.7: Four (wrong) programs for binary search

(P1)

from

    $i := 1; j := n$

until $i = j$ **loop**

    $m := (i + j)$ **div** 2;

    if $t\,[m] \le x$ **then**

        $i := m$

    else

        $j := m$

    end

end;

$Result := (x = t\,[i])$

(P2)

from

    $i := 1; j := n; found :=$ **false**

until $i = j$ **and not** *found* **loop**

    $m := (i + j)$ **div** 2;

    if $t\,[m] < x$ **then**

        $i := m + 1$

    elsif $t\,[m] = x$ **then**

        found := **true**

    else

        $j := m - 1$

    end

end;

$Result := found$

(P3)

from

    $i := 0; j := n$

until $i = j$ **loop**

    $m := (i + j + 1)$ **div** 2;

    if $t\,[m] \le x$ **then**

        $i := m + 1$

    else

        $j := m$

    end

end;

if $i \ge 1$ **and** $i \le n$ **then**

    $Result := (x = t\,[i])$

else

    $Result :=$ **false**

end

(P4)

from

    $i := 0; j := n + 1$

until $i = j$ **loop**

    $m := (i + j)$ **div** 2;

    if $t\,[m] \le x$ **then**

        $i := m + 1$

    else

        $j := m$

    end

end;

if $i \ge 1$ **and** $i \le n$ **then**

    $Result := (x = t\,[i])$

else

    $Result :=$ **false**

end

9.14 Repeat... until

Give a proof rule for the Pascal

   repeat ... **until** ...

instruction. You may use the observation that such a loop is readily expressed in terms of the **while** loop.

9.15 Equivalences between loops

Consider two loops of the following forms:

1.   **while** c **loop**

         while c **and** c_1 **loop** A_1 **end**; **while** c **and** c_2 **loop** A_2 **end**;

   end

2.   **while** c **loop**

         if

               $c_1 \rightarrow A_1$ ⬚
               $c_2 \rightarrow A_2$

         end

   end

Prove that any invariant of loop 2 is also an invariant of loop 1.

Can you give an intuitive reason why an invariant of loop 1 might not be invariant for loop 2?

9.16 Precise requirements on variants

Consider a loop with continuation condition c and variant V (in the sense that the antecedents of rule IT_{Loop}, page 332, are satisfied). Show that

   $\vdash \quad V = 0$ **implies not** c

(**Hint**: Proof by contradiction).

9.17 Weakest preconditions for loops

Define H_i, the necessary and sufficient condition for loop l to yield postcondition Q after at most i iterations ($i \geq 0$). You should first find independently an inductive definition of H_i in the manner of the definition of G_i ([9.31], page 338), and then prove its consistency with the definition of G_i.

9.18 Keeping track of the clock

(Due to Paul Eggert.) Consider Graal extended with two notions: clock counter and non-deterministic choice from integer intervals. This means two new instructions, with possible concrete syntax

- **clock** t
- **choose** t **by** e

In both instructions t is an integer variable; in the second, e is an integer expression.

The **clock** instruction assigns to t the current value of the machine clock. The machine clock is positive, never has the same value twice, and is always increasing.

The **choose** instruction assigns to t an integer value in the interval $0 .. |e-1|$. The implementation is free to use any value in that interval.

1 – Write axiomatic semantic definitions for these two instructions.

2 – Use your semantics to prove that the following loop always terminates:

> **from**
>> **clock** i
>
> **until** $i = 0$ **loop**
>> **clock** j;
>>
>> **if** $i < j$ **then**
>>> **choose** i **by** i
>>
>> **end**
>
> **end**

9.19 Restrictions on routines

Express the restrictions on routines for rule $Il_{Routine}$ (9.10.4) as static semantic constraints by defining a $V_{Routine}$ validity function (see 6.2).

9.20 Composition of substitutions

Prove the rule for composing substitutions ([9.10], page 320), using the definition of function *subst*. **Hint**: use structural induction on the structure of Q.

9.21 Simultaneous substitution

Define formally a function

$$simultaneous\ (Q: Expression\ ;\ el: Expression*\ ;\ il: Identifier*\ )$$

which specifies multiple simultaneous substitution (page 350) in a manner similar to function *subst* for single substitution ([9.9], page 320). **Hint**: it is not appropriate to use a list **over** ... **apply** ... expression on *el* or *il*; why?

9.22 In-out arguments

Extend rule $11_{Routine}$ (page 349) to deal explicitly with in-out arguments.

9.23 Loops as recursive procedures

A loop of the form

while c **loop** a **end**

may also be written as

call s

where s is a procedure with the following body:

if c **then** a ; s **end**

Using this definition, prove the loop rules (9.7.6) from the recursive routine rule (9.10.6).

9.24 Partitioning a sequence

Various algorithms require partitioning a sequence. This operation is used in particular for sorting arrays (next exercise) and for producing "order statistics".

Partitioning is applicable if a total order relation exists on sequence elements. Partitioning s means rearranging the order of its elements to put it in the form $t ++ <p> ++ u$, where any element of t is less than or equal to p, and any element of u is greater than or equal to p. Value p, the **pivot**, is a sequence element, chosen arbitrarily; for the purpose of this exercise the pivot will be the element that initially appeared at the leftmost position. The only two permitted operations are $swap\ (i, j)$, which exchanges the elements at positions i and j, and the test $s\ (i) \leq s\ (j)$, which compares the values of the elements at positions i and j.

A general method for partitioning is to "burn the candle from both ends", the candle being the sequence deprived of its first element (the pivot). Maintain two integer cursors, "left" and "right", initialized to the leftmost and rightmost positions. At each step, increase the left cursor until it is under an element greater than the pivot, and decrease the right cursor until it is under an element lesser than the pivot. The two elements found are out of order, so swap them; then start the next step. The process ends when the two cursors meet; then you can swap the first sequence element (the pivot) with the element at cursor position.

Starting from this informal description, derive a correct algorithm for sequence partitioning, using the constructive methods described in 9.11.

Hint: The "candle-burning" process follows from the strategy of uncoupling, as discussed in 9.11.4 and 9.11.5.

9.25 Quicksort

A well-known algorithm for sorting an array is Quicksort, for which a routine may be written (in a simplified form applicable to sequences) as:

```
sorted (s: X*): X* is
            -- Produce a sorted permutation of s.
            -- (There must be a total order relation on X.)
      local
            t, u: X*
      do
            if s.LENGTH ≤ 1 then
                  Result := s
            else
                  <t, u> := partitioned (s);
                  t := sorted (t);
                  u := sorted (u);
                  Result := t ++ u
            end
      ensure                  -- s is sorted, in other words:
            ∀ i: 2 .. s.LENGTH • s (i − 1) ≤ s (i)
      end -- sorted
```

Here *partitioned* is a routine, derived from the previous exercise, which given a sequence *s* of length 2 or more returns two non-empty sequences *t* and *u* such that $t + u$ is a permutation of *s*, and all elements of *t* are less than or equal to all elements of *u*.

After putting this routine in a form suitable for application of the recursive routine rule ($I2_{Routine}$, page 355), prove its correctness.

Hint: You may follow the example of the proof for routine *Hanoi* (9.10.9).

9.26 Inorder traversal of binary search trees

Prove rigorously the routine for printing the contents of a binary search tree in order (page 356). You will need to adapt the routine so that it produces a list of values as output.

10

The consistency of semantic definitions

The previous chapters have presented denotational and axiomatic semantics as separate language specification techniques. Although from time to time you may have experienced a feeling of *déjà vu* when rediscovering from the axiomatic perspective some of the language features that had previously been described denotationally, the precise connections have not been drawn.

This chapter fills this need by showing how to treat the two theories as complementary rather than competitive.

10.1 COMPARING THE TWO APPROACHES

The relationship is not symmetric. As already pointed out, the axiomatic approach is more abstract than its denotational counterpart. Denotational semantics is an interpretation of programming languages constructs in terms of mathematical functions. Axiomatic semantics is a theory, that is to say a set of rules for proving theorems. As any theory, it may be studied and applied independently of any particular interpretation.

To show the consistency of the two approaches is to show that the rules of axiomatic semantics hold under the denotational interpretation. Using the definitions of 9.2.8, this means showing that the denotational interpretation is a **model** of the axiomatic theory. Recall that a model associates a mathematical interpretation with every formula of the theory, under which every axiom or inference rule is correct.

The inverse effort would be meaningless: since the axiomatic rules are more general than the denotational model (in the sense that we could substitute other models which would still satisfy the axioms), there is no way to deduce the model from the axioms.

The rest of this chapter is devoted to showing that the denotational interpretation is indeed a model for the axiomatic theory of Graal. This means showing that if we give the well-formed formulae of the theory their denotational interpretations according to chapter 6, then the axioms and inference rules, introduced in chapter 9 with no justification other than intuitive, may now be **proved** as theorems about these denotations.

Chapter 6 only provided interpretations (denotations) for Graal constructs, through meaning functions. To associate an interpretation with well-formed formulae, we must also introduce meaning functions for assertions, pre-post formulae and wp-formulae. This is done in 10.2 and 10.3. It is also necessary to express what it means for an axiom or inference rule to be correct under this interpretation; this is done in 10.4 and leads to the consistency proofs in 10.5.

The exercise serves several purposes. The most important is to reassure ourselves that the two approaches studied are consistent; it would be rather unpleasant if they produced incompatible views of programming languages. Another is to clarify both approaches by shedding new light on each. Since, as discussed earlier, they are not necessarily best suited to the same goals, proving their complementarity will show that these differences of viewpoint do not imply actual incompatibilities.

10.2 INTERPRETING ASSERTIONS

To show that the rules of axiomatic semantics may be proved as theorems in the denotational model, the first step is to *express* these rules within this model. In other words, we must connect the metalanguage of the axiomatic theory with the metalanguage of denotational semantics.

The properties of interest in the axiomatic theory were properties of formulae built from assertions: pre-post formulae and wp-formulae. To reconcile the two metalanguages, we need a denotational interpretation of assertions and associated constructs. This section will successively introduce denotational interpretations for:

- The notion of assertion (for which the denotations will be sets of states).
- Formulae built using the basic operators on assertions, such as **and** (with set operations as denotations).
- Formulae built with the **implies** operator, used in the rule of consequence (whose denotations are boolean values).
- Pre-post rules of the form $\{P\}\ i\ \{Q\}$ (also modeled by boolean values).
- Wp-formulae of the form i **wp** Q (each having a set of states as denotation).

10.2.1 Modeling assertions

First, we need an interpretation for the notion of assertion.

Chapter 8 introduced assertions in close connection with boolean expressions, but the discussion made it clear that the two notions must be kept separate. The corresponding abstract syntax was:

> *Assertion* $\triangleq$ *exp*: *Expression*

Whenever there was no ambiguity, chapter 8 identified every assertion *P* with the associated boolean expression $P.e$, using concrete syntax if appropriate. An example of assertion expressed in this way is:

[10.1]
$$x + y \neq x^2$$

We may follow a similar line for denotations. Expressions were modeled (chapter 6) by meaning functions of signature

> $M_{Expression}$: *Expression* $\rightarrow$ *State* $\rightarrow$ *Value*

where *Value* $\triangleq$ **N** $\cup$ **B**; if *e* is a boolean expression, $M_{Expression}$ [*e*] is a predicate, that is to say a function whose result is always in **B**.

We could take the denotation of an assertion *P* to be $M_{Expression}$ ($P.exp$), a predicate on states. Rather than predicates, however, we will use **subsets** as denotations for assertions. The difference between "predicate semantics" and "subset semantics" is one of convenience, not substance; a later section of this chapter (10.3) will clarify the correspondence between the two views.

The meaning function for assertions will then have the following signature:

> $M_{Assertion}$: *Assertion* $\rightarrow$ **P** (*State*)

Under this interpretation, the denotation of an assertion is simply the set of states in which the assertion is satisfied. For example the denotation of assertion [10.1] above should be the set

> $\{\sigma: State \mid \sigma (x) + \sigma (y) \neq (\sigma (x))^2\}$

$M_{Assertion}$ is readily expressed in terms of $M_{Expression}$:

> $M_{Assertion}$ [*a*: *Assertion*] $\triangleq$ $\{\sigma \in State \mid M_{Expression}$ [$a.exp$] $(\sigma)\}$

10.2.2 Modeling assertion operators

Many results of axiomatic semantics involved boolean operators on assertions. As an abuse of language (see 9.5.2), these were written using the standard boolean operators **and**, **or**, **not** in infix or prefix form. (A fourth operator, **implies**, has a slightly different status and will be discussed next.) We need to interpret these operators within the above framework, in terms of operations on subsets of $State$.

Formally, these three operators are syntactical functions on assertions, each yielding assertions as output. The signatures are:

infix "and", infix "or": $Assertion \times Assertion \rightarrow Assertion$

prefix "not": $Assertion \rightarrow Assertion$

P **and** Q is the assertion satisfied by all states that satisfy both P and Q; P **or** Q is the assertion satisfied by all states that satisfy P or satisfy Q; **not** P is the assertion satisfied by all states that do not satisfy P. This may be interpreted in terms of operations on the corresponding state subsets, yielding the following meaning functions:

[10.2]

$$M_{Assertion} \ [P \ \text{and} \ Q] \ \triangleq \ M_{Assertion} \ [P] \ \cap \ M_{Assertion} \ [Q]$$

$$M_{Assertion} \ [P \ \text{or} \ Q] \ \triangleq \ M_{Assertion} \ [P] \ \cup \ M_{Assertion} \ [Q]$$

$$M_{Assertion} \ [\text{not} \ P] \ \triangleq \ State - M_{Assertion} \ [P]$$

$$\text{-- The complement of } M_{Assertion} \ [P]$$

10.2.3 Modeling the implication operator

The other operator on assertions, **implies**, is different. If P and Q are assertions, P **implies** Q is not itself an assertion but a property of P and Q, which may or may not hold. It holds if and only if any state that satisfies P also satisfies Q. (This is the property that you must establish when applying the rule of consequence, as seen in 4.6.2, 9.6.2 and 9.8.4.)

So **implies** must be understood as a semantic function, not as a syntactic one like the previous assertion operators. The appropriate model is subset inclusion, yielding the following formal definition of **implies**:

[10.3]

$$P \ \text{implies} \ Q \ \triangleq \ M_{Assertion} \ [P] \ \subseteq \ M_{Assertion} \ [Q]$$

We can informally check that this definition makes sense by considering implication in ordinary logic. In propositional or predicate calculus, the implication operator $\supset$ may be defined in terms of boolean "or", "not" and "and" by

$$p \supset q \triangleq \neg p \lor q$$

This is consistent with the interpretations given here. From the preceding definitions we can easily prove that P **implies** Q is true if and only if the assertion **not** P **or** Q holds in every state (is a tautology). This is expressed as the theorem

$$P \text{ implies } Q = (M_{Assertion} [\textbf{not } P \textbf{ or } Q] = State)$$

Proof: The right-hand side means that $(State - MP) \cup MQ = State$, where MP and MQ stand for $M_{Assertion} [P]$ and $M_{Assertion} [Q]$. Elementary set theory shows this property (where all the sets considered are subsets of $State$) to be equivalent to $MP \subseteq MQ$.   □

10.2.4 Modeling pre-post rules

Next we need a model for correctness rules. First they must be assigned a suitable abstract syntax. To describe pre-post rules of the form

$$\{P\} \ i \ \{Q\},$$

where P and Q are assertions and i is an instruction, we may use the construct

$$Pre\_post \triangleq pre, post: Assertion; inst: Instruction$$

A pre-post rule such as the above is an expression of partial correctness of i with respect to P and Q: if i, started in a state where P holds, terminates, it will yield a state in which Q holds.

The denotation of a pre-post rule must express this property. It will be a boolean value, depending only on P, i and Q – not on any particular state. The signature of the meaning function is simply:

$$M_{Pre\_post}: Pre\_post \rightarrow \textbf{B}$$

The value of this function is a formal translation of the preceding explanation. The denotation $M_{Instruction} [i]$ of an instruction i is a (possibly partial) function from state to state, or "state transformer". The above pre-post rule means that this function, wherever it is defined, maps states satisfying P into states satisfying Q. The image operator provides a convenient way of expressing this: the image of P under the denotation of i must be a subset of Q. Formally:

[10.4]

$M_{Pre\_post} \; [pp : Pre\_post] \; \triangleq$
    given

        $Preset \; \triangleq \; M_{Assertion} \; [pp \cdot pre\,];$

        $Postset \; \triangleq \; M_{Assertion} \; [pp \cdot post\,];$

        $transform \; \triangleq \; M_{Instruction} \; [pp \cdot inst\,]$

    then

        $transform \; (\!\!\;Preset\;\!\!) \; \subseteq \; Postset$

    end

This interpretation is illustrated on figure 10.1, which shows the subsets *Preset* and *Postset* associated with a precondition P and a postcondition Q and the function *transform* which is the denotation of an instruction i. The interpretation of $\{P\} \; i \; \{Q\}$, as shown by the figure, is that *transform* maps *Preset* into *Postset*.

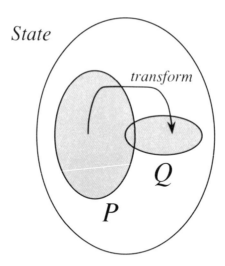

Figure 10.1: Subset interpretation of assertions and correctness rules

For example, if *transform* is the denotation of instruction i, then the denotation of $\{P\} \; i \; \{Q\}$, where Q is assertion [10.1] above, is true if and only if P is an assertion whose denotation is a subset *Preset* of *State* such that

$\forall \sigma$: *Preset* $\cap$ **dom** *transform* •

> **given**
>> $\sigma' \triangleq transform\,(\sigma)$
>
> **then**
>> $\sigma'\,(x) + \sigma'\,(y) \neq (\sigma'\,(x))^2$
>
> **end**

10.2.5 Modeling wp-rules

Finally we need an interpretation for wp-formulae of the form

i **wp** Q

It suffices to adapt the work done for pre-post formulae. We may view a wp-formula as an element of the syntactic domain

Weakest $\triangleq$ *post*: *Assertion*; *inst*: *Instruction*

A wp-formula describes a precondition, that is to say an assertion (the weakest precondition for i to yield Q). Since the model for an assertion is a set of states, the meaning function here must have the signature

$M_{Weakest}$: *Weakest* $\rightarrow$ **P** (*State*)

The denotation of a wp-formula of the above form is the set of states σ such that i, started in σ, will terminate and yield a state σ' satisfying Q – that is to say, such that $\sigma' \in Postset$, where *Postset* is the denotation of Q. Any such σ, then, must be obtainable from some element of *Postset* through the inverse of the transform associated with i. The image operator is again convenient to express this:

[10.5]
> $M_{Weakest}\,[w: Weakest\,] \triangleq$
>> **given**
>>> *Postset* $\triangleq M_{Assertion}\,[w\text{.}post\,];$
>>>
>>> *transform* $\triangleq M_{Instruction}\,[w\text{.}inst\,]$
>>
>> **then**
>>> $transform^{-1}\,(\!Postset\,)$
>>
>> **end**

For example, if *transform* is the denotation of instruction i, then the denotation of i **wp** Q, where Q is assertion [10.1] above, is the set

{σ: *State* | σ ∈ **dom** *transform* **and then**
         given
                          σ' ≜ *transform* (σ)
         then
                    σ' (x) + σ' (y) ≠ (σ' (x))²
         end }

Compare carefully definition [10.5] with the previous one ([10.4]). The difference may be narrowed down to the two properties

   Preset ⊆ *transform*⁻¹ (⟨*Postset*⟩)

which expresses that *transform* will map every element of *Preset* into an element of *Postset* (total correctness), and

   transform (⟨*Preset*⟩) ⊆ *Postset*

which expresses that *transform*, whenever it is applicable to an element of *Preset*, will map it into an element of *Postset* (partial correctness). This nicely captures the difference between the total and partial approaches to program correctness.

10.3 PREDICATE SEMANTICS

[Note: This section describes an alternative approach and its results are not used in the rest of the presentation. On first reading you should skip directly to 10.4]

An alternative to the modeling technique of the previous section uses predicates rather than sets. This approach leads to heavier notations but, as it is more commonly used in the literature, it is interesting to discuss it briefly. The denotations will use the letter P (as in $P_{Assertion}$, P_{Pre_post}) rather than M.

The difference between subset and predicate semantics affects ease of expression, not substance. The two forms may be shown to be equivalent; the proof is the subject of exercises 10.1 and 10.2.

10.3.1 Definitions

In the predicate semantics, the denotation of an assertion is a predicate on states, satisfied by any state in which the assertion holds. For example, the denotation of the example assertion [10.1] should be the predicate

   λ σ: *State* • σ (x) + σ (y) ≠ (σ (x))²

To define this semantics formally, it is convenient to introduce the semantic domain *Statepred* (*pred* for predicate):

   Statepred ≜ *State* → **B**

Then the denotation of an assertion is simply the denotation of the associated expression:

$P_{Assertion}$: *Assertion* $\rightarrow$ *Statepred*

$P_{Assertion}$ [a: *Assertion*] $\triangleq$ $M_{Expression}$ [a.*exp*]

If the static constraint $V_{Assertion}$ [a] is satisfied, a.*exp* is an expression of type boolean, so that the function $M_{Expression}$ [a.*exp*] yields boolean results and so is an element of *Statepred*.

Here is the semantics of pre-post formulae in this context:

[10.6]

P_{Pre_post}: *Pre_post* $\rightarrow$ **B**

P_{Pre_post} [pp: *Pre_post*] $\triangleq$

 given

   transform $\triangleq$ $M_{Instruction}$ [pp.*inst*];
   precond $\triangleq$ $M_{Assertion}$ [pp.*pre*];
   postcond $\triangleq$ $P_{Assertion}$ [pp.*post*]

 then

   $\forall$ σ: *State* •

     (*precond* (σ) $\wedge$ σ $\in$ **dom** *transform*)

      $\supset$ *postcond* (*transform* (σ))

 end

For wp-formulae, the definition is the following:

[10.7]

$P_{Weakest}$: *Weakest* $\rightarrow$ *Statepred*

$P_{Weakest}$ [w:*Weakest*] $\triangleq$

 given

   transform $\triangleq$ $M_{Instruction}$ [w.*inst*];
   postcond $\triangleq$ $P_{Assertion}$ [w.*post*]

 then

   λ σ: *State* •

     σ $\in$ **dom** *transform*

     and then *postcond* (*transform* (σ))

 end

For example, if Q is the example assertion [10.1] and *transform* is the denotation of an instruction i, then the denotation of i **wp** Q is the predicate

λ σ: *State* •   σ $\in$ **dom** *transform* **and then** σ (x) + σ (y) $\neq$ (σ (x))^2

10.3.2 Undefinedness

The above definitions give the values of total functions (P_{Pre_post} and $P_{Weakest}$) in terms of possibly partial ones (*transform*, that is to say $M_{Instruction}$ $[i]$ for some instruction i). To make sure that they are meaningful, we must check that the right-hand sides of the definitions are always defined.

First note that for any assertion a, $P_{Assertion}$ $[a]$ must be an element of *Statepred*, that is to say a total function in *State* $\rightarrow$ **B**. This is indeed ensured by the definition of assertions as boolean expressions: in Graal, the denotation of an expression is always a total function.

Now consider the semantics of pre-post formulae ([10.6]). The signature is

$$P_{Pre\_post}: Pre\_post \rightarrow \mathbf{B}$$

This function must be total: when you ask whether a program or program fragment is (partially) correct, which is what a pre-post formula is about, you want to hear "yes" or "no"; "undefined" is not an acceptable answer.

Since the definition of P_{Pre_post} ([10.6]) relies on a $\forall$ clause, this requirement will be met if and only if the innermost condition of this clause, namely

$$(precond(\sigma) \wedge \sigma \in \mathbf{dom} \ transform) \supset postcond \ (transform \ (\sigma))$$

is itself always defined. However this clause is of the form

$$(a \ \wedge \ b) \supset r$$

where b is $\sigma \in \mathbf{dom} \ transform$ and r is a property on $transform (\sigma)$. By the definition of the **dom** operator, $transform \ (sigma)$ is not defined if b is false; by the standard strict extensions of $\supset$ and $P_{Assertion}$, the result of the implication is undefined and the definition appears incorrect.

The problem disappears, however, if we take for $\supset$ the semi-strict interpretation *implies_if_defined* introduced in 8.7.9 through the semi-strict "or" by the identity

$$implies\_if\_defined \ \triangleq \ \lambda \ p, q \ \bullet \ or\_else \ (not \ (p), q)$$

Then *implies_if_defined* (p, q) has value true whenever p is false, even if q is undefined. For the rest of this discussion, the $\supset$ symbol denotes *implies_if_defined*. Then P_{Pre_post} as defined is total.

This interpretation reflects the intuitive meaning of "partial correctness". The property under scrutiny,

$$(precond(\sigma) \ \wedge \ \sigma \in \mathbf{dom} \ transform) \supset postcond \ (transform \ (\sigma))$$

means "if the initial state σ satisfies the precondition, and the instruction denoted by *transform* terminates, then the resulting state satisfies the postcondition". This property should be considered as true (not undefined!) if the second assumption is not satisfied, that is to say if the instruction does not terminate. This is precisely the meaning of partial correctness.

Finally we must apply the same analysis to the semantic definition of wp-rules (10.2.5). Here it is essential for any wp-formula w that $P_{Weakest}$ [w], which is a predicate on states, always be a total function: for any state σ, we must be able to determine in finite time whether σ satisfies the weakest precondition. [10.7] defined the result of $P_{Weakest}$ as the predicate

$\lambda\ \sigma:\ State\ \bullet\ \sigma \in$ **dom** *transform* **and then** *postcond* (*transform* (σ))

Here the problem was taken care of in advance thanks to the semi-strict operator **and then**.

10.3.3 Assessment

The above discussion shows why subset semantics is preferable. The image operator takes care of definedness problems in a simple fashion. Consider $f \in X \nrightarrow Y$, $x \in X$, $A \subseteq X$. The value of f (x) may or may not be defined; but f (A) is always a well-defined subset of Y. The image operator simply "forgets" any elements outside the function's domain.

Thanks to this property of images, subset semantics does not require the use of semi-strict extensions of boolean operators or any other technique that would force you constantly to worry about whether a partial function is defined.

The rest of this chapter uses subset semantics.

10.4 THE CONSISTENCY REQUIREMENT

10.4.1 Definition

With the above definitions, we may now express precisely what it means for an axiomatic rule to be correct under the denotational interpretation. A pre-post axiom of the form

$\{P\}\ i\ \{Q\}$

is correct if and only if the following holds:

M_{Pre_post} [*Pre_post* (*pre*: P ; *post*: Q ; *inst*: i)]

A pre-post inference rule of the form

$$\frac{F_1,\ F_2,\ \dots\ F_n}{F_0}$$

where every F_i is a pre-post rule or an implication, is correct if and only if the following holds:

[10.8]
$$M\ [F_1]\ \wedge\ M\ [F_2]\ \wedge\ \dots\ \wedge M\ [F_n]\ \supset\ M\ [F_0]$$

where each M stands for M_{Pre_post} or $M_{Implication}$ depending on what F_i is.

Finally, a wp-rule of the form

i **wp** $Q = P$

is correct if and only if the following holds:

[10.9]
$$M_{Weakest}\ [Weakest\ (post: Q\ ;\ inst: i)] = M_{Assertion}\ [P\,]$$

that is to say:

given

   $Preset\ \triangleq\ M_{Assertion}\ [P\,];$

   $Postset\ \triangleq\ M_{Assertion}\ [Q\,];$

   $transform\ \triangleq\ M_{Instruction}\ [i\,]$

then

   $transform^{-1}\ (\!\cdot Postset \cdot\!) = Preset$

end

In most cases, the properties to be proved are theorem schemata; in other words, they involve letters which stand for arbitrary assertions, such as Q in the pre-post axiom scheme for assignment:

$\{Q\ [x \leftarrow e\,]\}\ Assignment\ (target: x\ ;\ source: e\,)\ \{Q\}$

For such rules, the proof of correctness must be applicable to any instance of Q.

10.4.2 Two lemmas on images

Because the subset version of the semantics relies on the notion of image, the consistency proofs below will use a number of properties of the image operation. They are given here in two lemmas; the first is relative to properties of the image operator applied to a finite number of arguments, the second is its generalization to chains.

Lemma (Image Operations): Let X and Y be two arbitrary sets, r and s relations in $X \leftrightarrow Y$, f and g functions in $X \nrightarrow Y$ with disjoint domains, A and A' subsets of X, B a subset of Y. Then:

1     $r \langle\!| A \cup A' |\!\rangle = r \langle\!| A |\!\rangle \cap r \langle\!| A' |\!\rangle$

2     $f^{-1} \langle\!| B \cap B' |\!\rangle = f^{-1} \langle\!| B |\!\rangle \cap f^{-1} \langle\!| B' |\!\rangle$

3     $(r \,;\, s) \langle\!| A |\!\rangle = s \langle\!| r \langle\!| A |\!\rangle |\!\rangle$

4     $(r \cup s) \langle\!| A |\!\rangle = r \langle\!| A |\!\rangle \cup s \langle\!| A |\!\rangle$

5     $(r \cap s) \langle\!| A |\!\rangle \subseteq r \langle\!| A |\!\rangle \cap s \langle\!| A |\!\rangle$

6     $(A \subseteq A') \;\supset\; (r \langle\!| A |\!\rangle \subseteq r \langle\!| A' |\!\rangle)$

7     $(f \setminus A') \langle\!| A |\!\rangle = f \langle\!| A \cap A' |\!\rangle$

8     $(f \,\cup\kern-0.6em\cup\, g) \langle\!| A |\!\rangle = f \langle\!| A |\!\rangle \cup g \langle\!| A |\!\rangle$

9     $(f \,\cup\kern-0.6em\cup\, g)^{-1} \langle\!| B |\!\rangle = f^{-1} \langle\!| B |\!\rangle \cup g^{-1} \langle\!| A |\!\rangle$

10    $(f \setminus A)^{-1} \langle\!| B |\!\rangle = f^{-1} \langle\!| B |\!\rangle \cap A$

The proof was the subject of exercise 2.6. As an example, let us prove clause 2. We call *lhs* and *rhs* the two sides of the equality. Then *lhs* is the set of all members of X which f maps into elements of $B \cap B'$ and *rhs* is the intersection of the set of members of X which f maps into elements of B and of the set of those which f maps into elements of B'. Obviously, *lhs* $\subseteq$ *rhs*. To show the reverse inclusion, consider an object $x : rhs$. Function f maps x both into a member of B and into an member of B'. Because f is a function, these two objects must be the same, and hence belong to $B \cap B'$. $\square$

Note that clause 2 would not hold if f were an arbitrary relation. Also, the clauses involving overriding union would not hold as given without the hypothesis that the functions' domains are disjoint.

Lemma (Image Stability): Let X and Y be arbitrary sets, C and D arbitrary subsets of X and Y respectively. The following functionals are stable:

1. • $image_C : (X \nrightarrow Y) \rightarrow \mathbf{P}(Y)$

   $image_C \triangleq \lambda f \bullet f \langle C \rangle$

2. • $inverse\_image_D : (X \nrightarrow Y) \rightarrow \mathbf{P}(X)$

   $inverse\_image_D \triangleq \lambda f \bullet f^{-1} \langle D \rangle$

3. • $from\_to_{C,D} : (X \nrightarrow Y) \rightarrow \mathbf{B}$

   $from\_to_{C,D} \triangleq \lambda f \bullet f \langle C \rangle \subseteq D$

4. • $to\_from_{D,C} : (X \nrightarrow Y) \rightarrow \mathbf{B}$ $to\_from_{D,C} \triangleq \lambda f \bullet f^{-1} \langle D \rangle \subseteq C$

The proof of this lemma, which relies on simple properties of the union operator, was the subject of exercise 8.4.

The four functions defined in the lemma are total functions taking partial functions as arguments. For a function f, $image_C$ yields the image of C under f and $inverse\_image_D$ yields the image of D under f^{-1}; $from\_to$ yields true if and only if f maps every element of C into an element of D; to_from yields true if and only if every element of D is the result of applying f to some element of C.

10.4.3 The rule of conjunction

The preceding definitions and the Image Operations lemma yield our first example of consistency proof, addressing a language-independent rule: the rule of conjunction, introduced in chapter 9 without formal justification. The rule was

$$\vdash \quad a \; \mathbf{wp} \; (Q \; \mathbf{and} \; Q') = (a \; \mathbf{wp} \; Q) \; \mathbf{and} \; (a \; \mathbf{wp} \; Q')$$

According to the above interpretation [10.9], this may now be expressed as a theorem:

[10.10]
$$M_{Weakest} \, [a \; \mathbf{wp} \; (Q \; \mathbf{and} \; Q')] = M_{Weakest} \, (a \; \mathbf{wp} \; Q) \cap M_{Weakest} \, [a \; \mathbf{wp} \; Q']$$

Proof: Calling *lhs* and *rhs* the two sides of this equality, and *transform* the function $M_{Instruction} \, [a]$:

$lhs = transform^{-1} \, (\!\!\!\:M_{Assertion} \; [Q \textbf{ and } Q'\,]\!\!\!\:)$

          -- From the definition of $M_{Weakest}$, page 399

$= transform^{-1} \, (\!\!\!\:M_{Assertion} \; [Q\,] \cap M_{Assertion} \; [Q'\,]\!\!\!\:)$

          -- From the definition of **and** for assertions ([10.2], page 396).

$= transform^{-1} \, (\!\!\!\:M_{Assertion} \; [Q\,]\!\!\!\:) \cap transform^{-1} \, (\!\!\!\:M_{Assertion} \; [Q'\,]\!\!\!\:)$

          -- From the Image Operations lemma, clause 2

$= rhs$ □

10.4.4 The rule of consequence

Another important language-independent rule is the rule of consequence (4.7.2 and 9.6.2). Here too the Image Operations lemma will yield it as a theorem. The proof uses the pre-post form; the wp-form of the rule is the object of exercise 10.3.

The rule is:

CONS

$$\frac{\{P\} \; a \; \{Q\}, \quad P' \textbf{ implies } P, \quad Q \textbf{ implies } Q'}{\{P'\} \; a \; \{Q'\}}$$

From the interpretations of implication ([10.3], page 396), pre-post formulae ([10.4], page 397) and inference rules (page 403), the property to be proved is:

given

    $Preset \; \triangleq \; M_{Assertion} \; [P\,];$

    $Postset \; \triangleq \; M_{Assertion} \; [Q\,];$

    $transform \; \triangleq \; M_{Instruction} \; [i\,];$

    $Preset' \; \triangleq \; M_{Assertion} \; [P'\,];$

    $Postset' \; \triangleq \; M_{Assertion} \; [Q'\,]$

then

    $(transform \, (\!\!\!\:Preset\,)\!\!\!\:) \subseteq Postset \; \wedge \; Preset' \subseteq Preset \; \wedge \; Postset \subseteq Postset'\,)$

               $\supset (transform \, (\!\!\!\:Preset'\,)\!\!\!\:) \subseteq Postset'\,)$

end

This property follows from clause 6 of the Image Operations lemma.   □

10.5 THE CONSISTENCY PROOFS

We have now established the proper framework for proving that the denotational interpretation provides a model of the axiomatic theory.

The proof will begin with the more straightforward instructions (Skip, compound, conditional, the rule of consequence) and continue with the more delicate cases (assignment, loop). Some parts will use the pre-post form, others the wp-rules.

10.5.1 Skip

The weakest precondition rule for *Skip* is

    Skip **wp** $Q = Q$

The theorem to prove is then:

given
        Postset $\triangleq M_{Assertion}$ $[Q]$;

        transform $\triangleq M_{Instruction}$ $[Instruction\ (Skip)]$
then
        transform^{-1} $(\!\cdot Postset \cdot\!)$ = *Postset*
end

for an arbitrary assertion Q. From the semantics of *Skip* (6.5.2), *transform* is the identity function on *State*; the theorem follows since the image of any subset under identity is the subset itself.

10.5.2 Compound

The *Compound* instruction was characterized (9.8.10) by two wp-rules. The first corresponds to the empty compound:

    Compound (<>) **wp** $Q = Q$

and its proof, immediate, is similar to what has just been done for *Skip*. The more interesting rule is the second:

    $(c$ ++ $<i>)$ **wp** Q = c **wp** $(i$ **wp** $Q)$

A comparison of this rule with the definition of the denotational meaning function for compounds (6.5.4), which gives

[10.11]

$$M_{Compound}\ [c \mathbin{+\!\!+} <i>] = M_{Compound}\ [c\,]; M_{Instruction}\ [i\,]$$

shows a clear similarity; in both cases the mechanism is composition. The same observation would apply if the pre-post rule (9.7.5) had been used. The following proof establishes the correspondence rigorously.

The theorem to prove is the following, for any compound c, any instruction i and any subset *Postset* of *State* (representing the denotation of the postcondition Q in the above rule):

[10.12]

> **given**
>> $transform \triangleq M_{Compound}\ [c \mathbin{+\!\!+} <i>]\,;$
>>
>> $c\_transf \triangleq M_{Compound}\ [c\,]\,;$
>>
>> $i\_transf \triangleq M_{Instruction}\ [i\,]\,;$
>>
>> $lhs \triangleq transform^{-1}\ (\!\!(\,Postset\,)\!\!)\,;$
>>
>> $rhs \triangleq c\_transf^{-1}\ (\!\!(\,i\_transf^{-1}\ (\!\!(\,Postset\,)\!\!)\,)\!\!)$
>
> **then**
>> $lhs = rhs$
>
> **end**

The left-hand side *lhs* of the equality to be proved is the denotation of the wp-formula $(c \mathbin{+\!\!+} <i>)$ **wp** Q; the right-hand side *rhs* is the denotation of c **wp** $(i$ **wp** $Q)$. Both have been obtained by applying [10.5]. [10.11] yields:

$$lhs = (M_{Compound}\ [c\,]; M_{Instruction}\ [i\,])^{-1}\ (\!\!(\,Postset\,)\!\!)$$

that is to say, with the above definitions:

$$lhs = (c\_transf\,; i\_transf)^{-1}\ (\!\!(\,Postset\,)\!\!)$$
$$= (i\_transf^{-1}\,; c\_transf^{-1})\ (\!\!(\,Postset\,)\!\!)$$

since for any two composable relations r and s, $(r\,;s)^{-1} = (s^{-1}\,;r^{-1})$. Applying the Image Operations lemma (page 405), clause 3, gives

$$lhs = c\_transf^{-1}\ (\!\!(\,i\_transf^{-1}\ (\!\!(\,Postset\,)\!\!)\,)\!\!)$$
$$= rhs$$

which completes the proof of the wp-rule for compound instructions.   □

10.5.3 Conditional

Consider a conditional instruction

$$condinst \triangleq Conditional\ (thenbranch: tb\ ;\ elsebranch: eb\ ;\ test: c\ )$$

The weakest precondition rule for conditional instructions (9.8.11) gives:

[10.13]
$$condinst\ \textbf{wp}\ Q\ =\ ((tb\ \textbf{wp}\ Q\ )\ \textbf{and}\ c\ )\ \textbf{or}\ ((eb\ \textbf{wp}\ Q\ )\ \textbf{and not}\ c\ )$$

Let us prove that the denotations of the two sides are indeed equal. The theorem to prove, for any instructions tb and eb, any boolean expression c and any subset *Postset* of *State*, is:

> **given**
>
>> $transform \triangleq M_{Instruction}\ [condinst\ ]$;
>>
>> $lhs \triangleq transform^{-1}\ (\!\!\!\ (Postset\ )\!\!\!\ )$;
>>
>> $rhs \triangleq M_{Assertion}\ [((tb\ \textbf{wp}\ Q\ )\ \textbf{and}\ c\ )\ \textbf{or}\ ((eb\ \textbf{wp}\ Q\ )\ \textbf{and not}\ c\ )]$
>
> **then**
>
>> $lhs = rhs$
>
> **end**

As before, lhs and rhs have been obtained by direct application of [10.5]. The value of *transform* (6.5.5) is

> **given**
>
>> $where\_true \triangleq State\ /\ M_{Expression}\ [c\ ]$;
>>
>> $where\_false \triangleq State\ -\ where\_true$;
>>
>> $then\_transf \triangleq M_{Instruction}\ [tb\ ]$;
>>
>> $else\_transf \triangleq M_{Instruction}\ [eb\ ]$
>
> **then**
>
>> $(then\_transf \setminus where\_true)\ \cup\ (else\_transf \setminus where\_false)$
>
> **end**

The Image Operations lemma (page 405), clause 9, is applicable since *where_true* and *where_false* have disjoint domains; it yields

$$lhs = (then\_transf \setminus where\_true)^{-1}\ (\!\!\!\ (Postset\ )\!\!\!\ )\ \cup$$
$$(else\_transf \setminus where\_false)^{-1}\ (\!\!\!\ (Postset\ )\!\!\!\ )$$

To expand the internal expressions we may again apply the Image Operations lemma, this time clause 10, giving

$lhs = (then\_transf^{-1} (Postset) \cap where\_true) \cup$

$\qquad (else\_transf^{-1} (Postset) \cap where\_false)$

Transforming now rhs, we get:

$rhs = M_{Weakest} [(tb \textbf{ wp } Q) \textbf{ and } c] \cup M_{Weakest} [(tb \textbf{ wp } Q) \textbf{ and not } c]$

$\qquad\qquad\qquad\qquad$ -- From [10.2], page 396

$\qquad = (M_{Weakest} [tb \textbf{ wp } Q] \cap M_{Assertion} [c]) \cup$

$\qquad\quad (M_{Weakest} [eb \textbf{ wp } Q] \cap M_{Assertion} [\textbf{not } c])$

$\qquad\qquad\qquad\qquad$ -- From the rule of conjunction [10.10], page 406

The equality $lhs = rhs$ follows immediately by replacing the **not** in the last term by a complement, according to [10.2] (page 396). $\qquad\qquad\qquad\qquad\qquad\qquad\qquad\qquad$ □

10.5.4 Assignment

Next we look at assignments. For a specimen of the *Assignment* construct, of the form

$\qquad assign \triangleq Assignment \ (source: e; \ target: x)$

the wp-rule and denotation are respectively (9.8.8 and 6.5.3):

- $assign \textbf{ wp } Q = Q [x \leftarrow e]$
- $\lambda \sigma: State \cdot (\sigma \uplus \{<e, x>\})$

The theorem to prove, for any variable x, any expression e and any assertion Q, is:

given

$\qquad Postset \triangleq M_{Assertion} [Q];$

$\qquad Preset \triangleq M_{Assertion} [Q [x \leftarrow e]];$

$\qquad transform \triangleq \lambda \sigma: State \cdot \sigma \uplus \{<x, M_{Expression} [e] (\sigma)>\}$

then

$\qquad transform^{-1} (Postset) = Preset$

end

The last equality is an equality between two sets of states. A state σ belongs to the second set, *Preset*, if and only if

$\qquad \sigma \in M_{Assertion} [Q [x \leftarrow e]]$

which means that the boolean expression associated with the assertion is true in state σ, that is to say $M_{Expression}\ [Q \centerdot exp\ [x \leftarrow e\ ]]\ (\sigma)$ is true.

A state σ belongs to the second term of the equality if and only if it is mapped by *transform* into an element of *Postset*, in other words

$$\sigma \in \textbf{dom}\ transform\ \textbf{and then}\ transform\ (\sigma) \in Postset$$

Only the second operand of the **and then** matters, however, since *transform* is here a total function defined for all states.

Developing the expressions for both sides of the equality shows that the property to be proved for any state σ is:

> **given**
>
> > $QE \triangleq Q.exp;$
> >
> > $val \triangleq M_{Expression}\ [e\ ]\ (\sigma);$
> >
> > $lhs \triangleq M_{Expression}\ [QE\ ]\ (\sigma \uplus \{<x,\ val>\});$
> >
> > $rhs \triangleq M_{Expression}\ [QE\ [x \leftarrow e\ ]]\ (\sigma)$
>
> **then**
>
> > $lhs = rhs$
>
> **end**

QE is the boolean expression associated with the assertion Q. Since the notion of substitution, $QE\ [x \leftarrow e\ ]$, was defined (9.7.2) by structural induction on expressions, the proof will follow the same structure.

If QE is a boolean constant c, both lhs and rhs are equal to $c.boolean\_value$.

If QE is a variable, then

$$lhs = (\sigma \uplus \{<x,\ val>\})\ (QE\ )$$
$$= (\textbf{if}\ x = QE\ \textbf{then}\ val\ \textbf{else}\ \sigma\ (QE\ )\ \textbf{end})$$

and in this case

$$QE\ [x \leftarrow e\ ] = (\textbf{if}\ x = QE\ \textbf{then}\ e\ \textbf{else}\ QE\ \textbf{end})$$

so that rhs may be expressed as:

$$\textbf{if}\ x = QE\ \textbf{then}\ M_{Expression}\ [e\ ]\ (\sigma)\ \textbf{else}\ M_{Expression}\ [QE\ ]\ (\sigma)\ \textbf{end}$$

which is equal to lhs.

The third and last possibility is for QE to be a binary expression, with operands $t1$, $t2$ and operator *oper*. Then

lhs =
> **given**
>> $\sigma' \triangleq \sigma \cup \{<x, val>\};$
>>
>> $val1 \triangleq M_{Expression} \ [t1] \ (\sigma');$
>>
>> $val2 \triangleq M_{Expression} \ [t2] \ (\sigma')$
>
> **then**
>> *apply_binary (oper, val1, val2)*
>
> **end**

and by the definition of substitution in this case:

$$QE \ [x \leftarrow e \ ] = Expression$$
$$(Binary \ (term1: t1 \ [x \leftarrow e \ ]; t2: t2 \ [x \leftarrow e \ ]; op: oper \ ))$$

From the semantics of expressions (6.5):

$$M_{Expression} \ [QE \ [x \leftarrow e \ ]] \ (\sigma) =$$
$$apply\_binary \ (oper, M_{Expression} \ [t1 \ [x \leftarrow e \ ]] \ (\sigma), M_{Expression} \ [t2 \ [x \leftarrow e \ ]] \ (\sigma))$$

If we assume inductively that *t1* and *t2* satisfy the theorem, the equality follows in this case too.   □

10.5.5 Loops (pre-post semantics)

The last construct to examine is loops. This section studies the pre-post rule; the next section will take the weakest precondition perspective.

The pre-post rule, given in 9.7.6, reads

I_{Loop}

$$\frac{\{I \ \text{and} \ c\} \ b \ \{I\}}{\{I\} \ Loop \ (test: c; \ body: b \ ) \ \{I \ \text{and not} \ c\}}$$

To prove the correctness of this rule, we must prove (see [10.8], page 404) that

given

      premise $\triangleq$ *Pre_post* (*pre*: *I* **and** *c* ; *inst*: *bsem post*: *I*);

      loop_construct $\triangleq$ *Loop* (*test*: *c* ; *body*: *b*);

      conclusion $\triangleq$ *Pre_post* (*pre*: *I* ; *inst*: *loop_construct* ; *post*: *I* **and** **not** *c*)

then

      M_{Pre_post} [*premise*] $\supset$ M_{Pre_post} [*conclusion*]

end

Development of the *premise* and the *conclusion* shows that the property to prove is:

given

      IS $\triangleq$ $M_{Assertion}$ [*I*];   -- Invariant Set

      cS $\triangleq$ $M_{Assertion}$ [*c*];   -- *c* Set

      loop_construct $\triangleq$ *Loop* (*test*: *c* ; *body*: *b*);

      b_transf $\triangleq$ $M_{Instruction}$ [*b*];

      l_transf $\triangleq$ $M_{Instruction}$ [*loop_construct*]

then

      (*b_transf* ⟨ *IS* ∩ *cS* ⟩ ⊆ *IS*) $\supset$ (*l_transf* ⟨ *IS* ⟩ ⊆ *IS* − *cS*)

end

The ∩ and set difference come from the interpretation of boolean operators **and** and **not** on assertions ([10.2], page 396).

The property to be proved being an implication, we may use a conditional proof: we assume

[10.14]

      b_transf ⟨ *cS* ∩ *IS* ⟩ ⊆ *IS*

and must prove

[10.15]

      l_transf ⟨ *IS* ⟩ ⊆ (*IS* − *cS*)

Denotational semantics gave the following recursive equation for *l_transf* (6.5.6):

[10.16]

      l_transf = *Id* \ (*State* − *cS*) ⩊ (*b_transf* ; *l_transf*) \ *cS*

As seen in chapter 8, the solution of such a recursive equation is a fixpoint:

      l_transf $\triangleq$ **union** *l*

where l_i is the chain defined by

[10.17]

$$l_0 \triangleq \varnothing;$$

$$l_{i+1} \triangleq F\ (l_i)$$

with:

$$F \triangleq \lambda f\colon State \rightarrow State \bullet Id \setminus (State - cS) \; \underline{\cup} \; (b\_transf\ ;\ f) \setminus cS$$

We may express the goal [10.15] as p (l_transf), where p is the predicate

[10.18]

$$p \triangleq \lambda f\colon State \rightarrow State \bullet f\ (\!\!\ ^{\backprime}IS^{\backprime}\!\!\ ) \subseteq (IS - cS)$$

The form of this property, where l_transf is the "union" of a chain, suggests a proof by fixpoint induction (8.6.2). Such a proof assumes that p is a stable predicate; this is indeed the case from the Image Stability lemma (page 406), clause 3. It consists of the proofs of two separate properties:

- p ($\varnothing_{State \rightarrow State}$)   (Base step).

- $\forall f\colon State \rightarrow State \bullet\ p\ (f) \supset p\ (F\ (f))$ (Induction step).

To prove the base step, we write the property p ($\varnothing_{State} \rightarrow State$) as

$$\varnothing\ (\!\!\ ^{\backprime}IS^{\backprime}\!\!\ ) \subseteq (IS - cS)$$

This follows immediately from the definition of function $\varnothing$ (by whose image any set yields an empty subset).

For the induction step, assume that p (f) holds; we must prove that p (F (f)) holds. This means

$$F\ (f)\ (\!\!\ ^{\backprime}IS^{\backprime}\!\!\ ) \subseteq (IS - cS)$$

that is to say

$$(Id \setminus (State - cS)\ \underline{\cup}\ (b\_transf\ ;\ f) \setminus cS)\ (\!\!\ ^{\backprime}IS^{\backprime}\!\!\ ) \subseteq (IS - cS)$$

Call lhs the expression to the left of the $\subseteq$ sign. Applying the Image Operations lemma (page 405, clause 8, applicable here since the function domains are disjoint) yields

$$lhs = (Id \setminus (State - cS))\ (\!\!\ ^{\backprime}IS^{\backprime}\!\!\ ) \cup ((b\_transf\ ;\ f) \setminus cS)\ (\!\!\ ^{\backprime}IS^{\backprime}\!\!\ )$$

Clause 7 of the same lemma shows that the first operand of the $\cup$ operator is equal to $IS \cap (State - cS)$, or $IS - cS$ There remains to show that the second operand, say $lhs2$, is a subset of $(IS - cS)$. We can rewrite $lhs2$ successively as follows:

$$lhs2 = ((b\_transf\ ;\ f) \setminus cS)\ (\!\!\ ^{\backprime}IS^{\backprime}\!\!\ )$$

$$= f \, (\!\!((b\_transf \setminus cS) \, (\!\!(IS)\!\!))\!\!)$$

-- From clause 3 of the Image Operations lemma

$$= f \, (\!\!(b\_transf \, (\!\!(cS \cap IS)\!\!))\!\!)$$

-- From clause 7 of the Image Operations lemma

The premise of the theorem [10.14] was

$$btransf \, (\!\!(cS \cap IS)\!\!) \subseteq IS$$

which, with the help of clause 6 of the Image Operations lemma, yields:

$$lhs2 \subseteq f \, (\!\!(IS)\!\!)$$

but the induction hypothesis, $p \, (f)$, means precisely from the definition of p [10.18] that

$$f \, (\!\!(IS)\!\!) \subseteq f \, (\!\!(IS)\!\!)$$

which shows that $lhs2$ is a subset of $IS - cS$, and finishes the proof.   □

10.5.6 Loops (wp-semantics)

The preceding proof for loops, using the pre-post rule, only addressed partial correctness. To cover total correctness, and to provide another perspective on the relationship between denotational and axiomatic views, it is interesting to look also at the wp-rule.

Informally, the wp-rule is equivalent to the combination of the pre-post rule and the variant rule (see 9.8.11); proving the variant rule separately is the object of exercise 10.4.

The wp-rule reads as follows, for a given loop l and assertion Q:

[10.19]
   given

   $loop\_construct \triangleq Loop \ (test\!: c \ ; \ body\!: b\,);$

   $G_0 \triangleq Q$ **and not** c;

   $G_i \triangleq c$ **and** $(b \ \textbf{wp} \ G_{i-1})$ -- For $i > 0$

   then

   $l \ \textbf{wp} \ Q = (\exists \, i\!: \textbf{N} \bullet G_i)$

   end

   Define

[10.20]
   $M_i \triangleq M_{Assertion} \ (G_i)$ (for $i \in \textbf{N}$)

The notation $(\exists\; i:\mathbf{N} \bullet G_i)$ should be considered as meaning

$$\underset{i\,:\,\mathbf{N}}{\textbf{or}}\;\; G_i$$

which, by an immediate generalization of the definition of **or** for assertions ([10.2], page 396) has the following subset denotation:

$$\underset{i\,:\,\mathbf{N}}{\bigcup}\; M_i$$

So the property to be proved is the following:

[10.21]
    given

        $lhs \triangleq M_{Weakest}\; [Weakest\; (inst:Instruction\; (l)\; ;\; post:Q\,)];$

        $rhs \triangleq \underset{i\,:\,\mathbf{N}}{\bigcup}\; M_i$

    then

        $lhs = rhs$

    end

The right-hand side *rhs* is expressed as an infinite union. To prove the equality, we will rewrite the left-hand side *lhs* also as an infinite union, and show that there is a simple correspondence between terms of both infinite unions. The transformation will use the denotational interpretation of a loop as the **union** of a chain.

The value of *lhs* may be expressed as

[10.22]
    $lhs =$

        given

            $l\_transf \triangleq M_{Loop}\; [loop\_construct]$

            $Postset \triangleq M_{Assertion}\; [Q\,]$

        then

            $l\_transf^{-1}\; (\!\cdot Postset \,\cdot\!)$

        end

where, as seen in the discussion of pre-post semantics, *l_transf* is the **union** of the chain

[10.23]
    $l_0 \triangleq \varnothing$

    $l_{i+1} \triangleq Id \setminus (State - cS)\; \cup\; (b\_transf;\; l_i) \setminus cS$

giving for *lhs* the value

[10.24]

$$lhs = (\textbf{union } l)^{-1} \; (\!\!\leftarrow Postset \rightarrow\!\!)$$

Here the Image Stability lemma (page 406), clause 2, shows that the image operator may be moved inside the **union**, [10.24] being rewritten as:

[10.25]

$$lhs = \textbf{union } l^{-1} \; (\!\!\leftarrow Postset \rightarrow\!\!)$$

where l^{-1} is the chain whose i-th element, for every i, is l_i^{-1}. In other words:

[10.26]

$$lhs = \bigcup_{i\,:\,\mathbf{N}} l_i^{-1} \; (\!\!\leftarrow Postset \rightarrow\!\!)$$

The form obtained for l_i ([10.23]) yields for T_i, after applying the Image Operations lemma again:

[10.27]

$$T_0 = \varnothing;$$

$$T_{i+1} = (Postset - cS) \; \cup \; (cS \; \cap \; l_i^{-1} \; (\!\!\leftarrow b\_transf^{-1} \; (\!\!\leftarrow Postset \rightarrow\!\!) \rightarrow\!\!))$$

$$\qquad = (Postset - cS) \; \cup \; (cS \; \cap \; b\_transf^{-1} \; (\!\!\leftarrow T_i \rightarrow\!\!))$$

We now have both of the terms to be proved equal, lhs and rhs, expressed as unions:

$$lhs = \bigcup_{i\,:\,\mathbf{N}} T_i$$

$$rhs = \bigcup_{i\,:\,\mathbf{N}} M_i$$

To conclude the proof, it suffices to show that for every i:

[10.28]

$$T_i = \bigcup_{j\,:\,0\,..\,i-1} M_j$$

This will be proved by induction on i. The base step is trivial, as T_0 is empty and a union over an empty index set is empty. For the induction step, recall that M_i is given for every i by

$$M_i \triangleq M_{Assertion} \; (G_i)$$

where

$G_0 \triangleq Q$ **and not** c

$G_i \triangleq c$ **and** $(b \text{ wp } G_{i-1})$ -- For $i > 0$

Hence:

[10.29]

$M_0 = Postset - cS$

$M_{i+1} = cS \cap btransf^{-1} (\langle M_i \rangle)$

Assume that [10.28] holds for some $i \in \mathbf{N}$. Then

$$\bigcup_{j\,:\,0..i} M_j = M_0 \cup \bigcup_{j\,:\,1..i} M_j$$

$$= (Postset - cS) \cup \bigcup_{j\,:\,1..i} (cS \cap btransf^{-1} (\langle M_{j-1} \rangle))$$

-- from [10.29]

$$= (Postset - cS) \cup (cS \cap \bigcup_{j\,:\,1..i} btransf^{-1} (\langle M_{j-1} \rangle))$$

-- From the distributivity of $\cap$ with respect to $\cup$

$$= (Postset - cS) \cup (cS \cap btransf^{-1} (\langle \bigcup_{j\,:\,1..i} M_{j-1} \rangle))$$

-- From the Image Stability lemma, clause 2

$$= (Postset - cS) \cup (cS \cap btransf^{-1} (\langle T_i \rangle))$$

-- From the induction hypothesis [10.28]

$$= T_{i+1}$$

-- From the definition of T_i, [10.27]

This proves [10.28], hence the consistency of the wp-rule [10.19].   □

The last part of the proof would have been shorter if it had relied on another form of the wp-rule for loops (see 9.8.11 and exercise 9.17). Instead of G_i, that other form uses H_i, the weakest condition under which the loop will ensure the postcondition Q after **at most** i iterations. As you may have noted, T_{i+1} is precisely, for any i, the denotation of H_i.

10.6 DISCUSSION

This chapter has defined and proved the consistency of the axiomatic and denotational descriptions of Graal given in the previous chapters. The discussion only covered the fundamental language constructs; proving the consistency of the specifications given for recursive routines (see 7.6 and 9.10.3) requires more work, but may be done along the same lines.

One distinctive feature of the techniques used is their use of subset semantics, although for completeness the predicate semantics has also been sketched. The subset interpretation makes the presentation simpler; this comes from the use of possibly partial functions, as introduced in chapter 8, and the properties of the image operator.

This approach would also transpose well to an application not studied in this book in any detail: non-deterministic or parallel systems, in which the denotations M of instructions are not single-valued functions, but, in the general case, relations.

10.7 BIBLIOGRAPHICAL NOTES

The notion of complementary semantic definitions was introduced in [Hoare 1973a] and developed in [Donahue 1976]. Recent treatises that build a proof theory on the basis of a denotational specification are [De Bakker 1982] and [Loeckx 1984].

EXERCISES

10.1 Equivalence of models

Prove the equivalence between the subset-oriented and predicate-oriented definitions of the assertion semantics: that is to say, prove that the definitions of M_{Pre_post} ([10.4]) and $M_{Weakest}$ ([10.5]) are equivalent from the predicate-oriented versions ([10.6] and [10.7]). (**Hint**: Use the functions *characteristic* and the quotient operator, as introduced in 2.7.6.)

10.2 Boolean operations on assertions

Express and prove the properties of boolean operations on assertions, as in [10.2], but this time using the predicate interpretation.

10.3 The rule of consequence

Prove the wp-form of the rule of consequence (9.7.4), basing your proof on the one given for the pre-post form (10.4.4).

10.4 The rule of conjunction

Prove the rule of conjunction (9.6.4).

10.5 The variant rule

Prove the variant rule for loops (8.5.7) directly (that is to say not as a consequence of the wp-rule).

10.6 Consistency of the type theory for lambda calculus

(This exercise assumes that you have solved exercise 6.1 first.)

In 9.3, a theory was introduced for deriving the type of expressions in lambda calculus. Prove the consistency of this theory with the definition of typed lambda calculus (5.10), as formalized in exercise 6.1.

Hint: Interpret bindings as finite functions, and the "+" operation on bindings as the overriding union "⩁".

Bibliography

[Abrial 1980]
   Jean-Raymond Abrial, Stephen A. Schuman and Bertrand Meyer, "A Specification
   Language", in *On the Construction of Programs*, ed. R. McNaughten and R.C.
   McKeag, Cambridge University Press, 1980.

[Alagić 1978]
   S. Alagić and M.A. Arbib, *The Design of Well-Structured and Correct Programs*,
   Springer-Verlag, Berlin-New York, 1978.

[Apt 1981]
   Krzysztof R. Apt, "Ten Years of Hoare's Logic: A Survey – Part 1", *ACM
   Transactions on Programming Languages and Systems*, vol. 3, no. 4, pp. 431-483,
   October 1981.

[Ashcroft 1985]
   Edward A. Ashcroft and William W. Wadge, *Lucid, the Dataflow Language*,
   Academic Press, London, 1985.

[Backhouse 1979]
   Roland C. Backhouse, *Syntax of Programming Languages: Theory and Practice*,
   Prentice-Hall International, Hemel Hempstead, 1979.

[Backus 1978]
   John Backus, "Can Programming be Liberated from the Von Neumann Style? A
   Functional Style and its Algebra of Programs", *Communications of the ACM*, vol. 21,
   no. 8, pp. 613-641, August 1978.

[Barringer 1984]
H. Barringer, J. H. Cheng and Cliff B. Jones, "A Logic Covering Undefinedness in Program Proofs", *Acta Informatica*, vol. 21, no. 3, pp. 251-269, October 1984.

[Bayer 1981]
M. Bayer, B. Böhringer, J.P. Dehottay, H. Feuerhahn, J. Jasper, C.H.A. Koster and U. Schmiedecke, "Software Development in the CDL2 Laboratory", in *Software Engineering Environments*, ed. Horst Hünke, pp. 97-118, North-Holland Publishing Co., Amsterdam, 1981.

[Berg 1982]
Helmut K. Berg, William E. Boebert, William R. Franta and T.G. Moher, *Formal Methods of Program Verification and Specification*, Prentice-Hall, Englewood Cliffs, N.J., 1982.

[Berry 1976]
Gérard Berry, "Bottom-up Computation of Recursive Programs", *RAIRO (Revue française d'Automatique, Informatique et Recherche Opérationnelle), Série rouge "Informatique Théorique"*, pp. 47-82, AFCET-Dunod, March 1976.

[Bjørner 1980]
Dines Bjørner and O.N. Oest (eds), "Towards a Formal Description of Ada", Lecture Notes in Computer Science 98, Springer-Verlag, New York, 1980.

[Bjørner 1982]
Dines Bjørner and Cliff B. Jones, *Formal Specification and Software Development*, Prentice-Hall International, Hemel Hempstead, 1982.

[Bossavit 1981]
Alain Bossavit and Bertrand Meyer, "The Design of Vector Programs", in *Algorithmic Languages*, ed. Jaco de Bakker and R.P. van Vliet, pp. 99-114, North-Holland Publishing Company, Amsterdam, 1981.

[Cadiou 1972]
Jean-Marie Cadiou, "Recursive Definitions of Partial Functions and their Computations", PhD Thesis, Stanford University, 1972.

[Cardelli 1984a]
Luca Cardelli, "Basic Polymorphic Typechecking", AT&T Bell Laboratories Computing Science Technical Report, 1984.

[Cardelli1984b]
Luca Cardelli, "A Semantics of Multiple Inheritance", in *Semantics of Data Types*, ed. Gilles Kahn, David B. McQueen and Gordon Plotkin, pp. 51-67, Springer-Verlag, Berlin-New York, 1984.

[Caromel 1989]
Denis Caromel, *Service, Asynchrony and Wait-by-Necessity: A General Model for Concurrent and Distributed Object-Oriented Programming*, Journal of Object-Oriented Programming, November-December 1989.

[Church 1951]
   Alonzo Church, "The Calculi of Lambda-conversion", *Annals of Mathematical Studies*, vol. 6, Princeton University Press, Princeton (N.J.), 1951.

[Cleaveland 1977]
   J.C. Cleaveland and Robert C. Uzgalis, *Grammars for Programming Languages*, Elsevier North-Holland, New York, 1977.

[Clint 1972]
   Morris Clint and C.A.R. Hoare, "Program Proving: Jumps and Functions", *Acta Informatica*, vol. 1, pp. 214-224, 1972.

[Colmerauer 1983]
   Alain Colmerauer, Henry Kanoui and Michel van Caneghem, "Prolog, Theoretical Basis and Current Developments", *TSI (Technology and Science of Informatics)*, vol. 2, no. 4, pp. 271-311, July-August 1983.

[Copi 1973]
   Irving M. Copi, *Symbolic Logic*, Macmillan, New York, 1973. 4th Edition.

[Curry 1958]
   H.B. Curry and R. Feys, *Combinatory Logic*, 1, North-Holland Publishing Co., Amsterdam, 1958.

[Curry 1971]
   H.B. Curry, J.R. Hindley and J. Seldin, *Combinatory Logic*, 2, North-Holland Publishing Co., Amsterdam, 1971.

[Deutsch 1982]
   Michael S. Deutsch, *Software Verification and Validation: Realistic Project Approaches*, Prentice-Hall, Englewood Cliffs (N.J.), 1982.

[De Bakker 1982]
   Jaco De Bakker, *Mathematical Theory of Program Correctness*, Prentice-Hall International, Hemel Hempstead, 1982.

[Dijkstra 1975]
   Edsger W. Dijkstra, "Guarded Commands, Nondeterminacy, and Formal Derivation of Programs", *Communications of the ACM*, vol. 18, no. 8, August 1975. Also in R.T. Yeh (ed.), *Current Trends in Programming Methodology*, Volume 1, Prentice-Hall, 1976, pp. 233-242, and in D. Gries (ed.), *Programming Methodology*, Springer-Verlag, 1978, pp. 166-175.

[Dijkstra 1976]
   Edsger W. Dijkstra, *A Discipline of Programming*, Prentice-Hall, Englewood Cliffs (N.J.), 1976.

[Dijkstra 1978]

E. W. Dijkstra, L. Lamport, A.J. Martin, C.S. Scholten and E.F.M. Steffens, "On-the-Fly Garbage Collection: An Exercise in Cooperation", *Communications of the ACM*, vol. 21, no. 11, pp. 966-975, November 1978.

[Donahue 1976]

James E. Donahue, "Complementary Definitions of Programming Language Semantics", Lecture Notes in Computer Science 42, Springer-Verlag, Berlin-New York, 1976.

[Donzeau-Gouge 1980]

Véronique Donzeau-Gouge, "On the Formal Description of Ada", in *Lecture Notes on Computer Science 94: Semantics-Directed Compiler Generation*, ed. N.D. Jones , Springer-Verlag, Berlin-New York, 1980.

[Donzeau-Gouge 1984]

Véronique Donzeau-Gouge, Gérard Huet, Gilles Kahn and Bernard Lang, "Programming Environments Based on Structured Editors: The MENTOR Experience", in *Interactive Programming Environments*, ed. David R. Barstow, Howard E. Shrobe, Erik Sandewall, pp. 128-140, McGraw-Hill, New York, 1984.

[Dromey 1983]

R.W. Dromey, *How to Solve it by Computer*, Prentice-Hall International, Hemel Hempstead, 1983.

[Floyd 1967]

Robert W. Floyd, "Assigning Meanings to Programs", in *Proceedings American Mathematical Society Symposium in Applied Mathematics*, vol. 19, pp. 19-31, 1967.

[Fosdick 1976]

Lloyd D. Fosdick and Leon J. Osterweil, "Data Flow Analysis in Software Reliability", *Computing Surveys*, vol. 8, no. 3, pp. 305-330, 1976.

[Friedman 1976]

Daniel P. Friedman and D. S. Wise, "CONS should not evaluate its arguments", in *Proceedings 3rd International Colloquium on Automata, Languages and Programming*, pp. 257-284, Edinburgh University Press, 1976.

[Gehani 1986]

Narain Gehani and Andrew McGettrick (Eds.), *Software Specification Techniques*, Addison-Wesley, Wokingham (Great Britain), 1986.

[Ghezzi 1987]

Carlo Ghezzi and Mehdi Jazayeri, *Programming Language Structures, second edition*, John Wiley and Sons, New York, 1987.

[Goguen 1978]
Joseph A. Goguen, J. W. Thatcher and E. G. Wagner, "An Initial Algebra Approach to the Specification, Correctness and Implementation of Abstract Data Types", in *Current Trends in Programming Methodology,* vol. 4, ed. Raymond T. Yeh, pp. 80-149, Prentice-Hall, Englewood Cliffs (N.J.), 1978.

[Gordon 1979]
Michael Gordon, *The Denotational Description of Programming Languages, An Introduction*, Springer-Verlag, Berlin-New York, 1979.

[Gries 1981]
David Gries, *The Science of Programming*, Springer-Verlag, Berlin-New York, 1981.

[Griffiths 1974]
Michael Griffiths, "LL (1) Grammars and Analyzers", in *Compiler Construction: An Advanced Course*, ed. J. Eickel, pp. 55-84, Springer-Verlag, Berlin-New York, 1974.

[Guttag 1977]
John V. Guttag, "Abstract Data Types and the Development of Data Structures", *Communications of the ACM*, vol. 20, no. 6, pp. 396-404, June 1977.

[Guttag 1978]
John V. Guttag, Jim J. Horning and Ralph L. London, "A Proof Rule for Euclid Procedures", in *Formal Description of Programming Concepts*, ed. E. J. Neuhold, North-Holland Publishing Co., Amsterdam, 1978.

[Habermann et al. 1982]
Nico Habermann et al., *The Second Compendium of Gandalf Documentation*, Carnegie-Mellon University, Pittsburgh (Penn.), 1982. See also the special issue of *Journal of Systems and Software* (Vol. 5, no. 2, May 1985) on Gandalf.

[Hindley 1972]
J.R. Hindley, B. Lercher and J.P. Seldin, "Introduction to Combinatory Logic,", *London Mathematical Society Lecture Note Series*, vol. 7, Cambridge University Press, Cambridge (England), 1972.

[Hoare 1969]
C.A.R. Hoare, "An Axiomatic Basis for Computer Programming", *Communications of the ACM*, vol. 12, no. 10, pp. 576-580, 583, October 1969.

[Hoare 1971]
C.A.R. Hoare, "Procedures and Parameters: An Axiomatic Approach", in *Symposium on the Semantics of Programming Languages*, ed. Erwin Engeler, pp. 103-116, Springer-Verlag, Berlin-New York, 1971.

[Hoare 1973a]
C.A.R. Hoare and P.E. Lauer, "Consistent and Complementary Formal Theories of the Semantics of Programming Languages", *Acta Informatica*, vol. 3, pp. 135-153, 1973.

[Hoare1973b]

C.A.R. Hoare and Niklaus Wirth, "An Axiomatic Definition of the Programming Language Pascal", *Acta Informatica*, vol. 2, pp. 335-355, 1973.

[Hoare 1978]

C.A.R. Hoare, "Communicating Sequential Processes", *Communications of the ACM*, vol. 21, no. 8, pp. 666-677, August 1978.

[Hoare 1985]

C.A.R. Hoare, *Communicating Sequential Processes*, Prentice-Hall International, Hemel Hempstead, 1985.

[Jensen 1974]

Kathleen Jensen and Niklaus Wirth, *Pascal User Manual and Report, Second Edition*, Springer-Verlag, Berlin-New York, 1974.

[Johnson 1978]

S. C. Johnson, "Lint, a C Program Checker", Computer Science Technical Report 65, Bell Laboratories, Murray Hill (New Jersey), 1978. updated version TM 78-1273-3.

[Jones 1986]

Cliff B. Jones, *Systematic Software Development Using VDM*, Prentice-Hall, Englewood Cliffs (N.J.), 1986.

[Kahn 1983]

Gilles Kahn, Bernard Lang, Bertrand Mélèse and E. Morcos, "Metal: A Formalism to Specify Formalisms", *Science of Computer Programming*, vol. 3, no. 2, pp. 151-188, 1983.

[King 1989]

K.N. King, "The Draft Proposed Standard for Modula-2", *Journal of Pascal, Ada and Modula-2*, vol. 8, no. 6, pp. 71-75, November-December 1989.

[Kleene 1967]

Stephen C. Kleene, *Mathematical Logic*, John Wiley and Sons, New York, 1967.

[Knuth 1968]

Donald E. Knuth, "Semantics of Context-Free Languages", *Mathematical Systems Theory*, vol. 2, pp. 127-145, 1968. Correction in Vol. 5 (1971), p. 95.

[Knuth 1973]

Donald E. Knuth, *The Art of Computer Programming, Vol. 3: Sorting and Searching*, Addison-Wesley, Menlo Park (Calif.), 1973.

[Koster 1971]

C.H.A. Koster, "Affix Grammars", in *Algol 68 Implementation* (*Proceedings of IFIP Working Conference, Munich, July 20-24, 1970*), ed. J.E.L. Peck, North-Holland Publishing Co., Amsterdam, 1971.

[Lampson 1977]
   Butler W. Lampson, Jim J. Horning, Ralph L. London, J. G. Mitchell and Gerard L. Popek, "Report on the Programming Language Euclid", *SIGPLAN Notices*, vol. 12, no. 2, pp. 1-79, February 1977.

[Landin 1965]
   Peter Landin, "A Correspondence between Algol 60 and Church's Lambda Notation", *Communications of the ACM*, vol. 8, pp. 89-101, 158-165, 1965.

[Lee 1972]
   J.A.N. Lee, *Computer Semantics*, Van Nostrand Reinhold, New York, 1972.

[Livercy 1978]
   C. Livercy, *Théorie des Programmes*, Dunod, Paris, 1978.

[Loeckx 1984]
   Jacques Loeckx and Kurt Sieber, *The Foundations of Program Verification*, B.G. Teubner (Stuttgart) and John Wiley & Sons (Chichester), 1984.

[Lucas 1883]
   Edouard Lucas, *Récréations Mathématiques*, Paris, 1883. Reprint, Albert Blanchard (Paris), 1975, 5 volumes.

[Luckham 1985]
   David Luckham and Friedrich W. von Henke, "An Overview of Anna, a Specification Language for Ada", *IEEE Software*, vol. 2, no. 2, pp. 9-22, March 1985.

[Manna 1974]
   Zohar Manna, *Mathematical Theory of Computation*, McGraw-Hill, New York, 1974.

[Manna 1985]
   Zohar Manna and Richard Waldinger, *The Logical Basis for Computer Programming – Volume 1: Deductive Reasoning*, Addison-Wesley, Reading (Mass.), 1985.

[Marcotty 1976]
   Michael Marcotty, Henry F. Ledgard and Gregor V. Bochmann, "A Sampler of Formal Definitions", *Computing Surveys*, vol. 8, no. 2, pp. 191-276, 1976.

[McCarthy 1960]
   John McCarthy, "Recursive Functions of Symbolic Expressions and their Computation by machine, Part 1", *Communications of the ACM*, vol. 3, no. 4, pp. 184-195, April 1960.

[McCarthy 1963a]
   John McCarthy, "A Basis for a Mathematical Science of Computation", in *Computer Programming and Formal Systems*, ed. Braffort and Hirschberg, pp. 33-70, North-Holland Publishing Co., Amsterdam, 1963.

[McCarthy1963b]

John McCarthy, "Towards a Mathematical Science of Computation", in *IFIP 1962 Congress*, ed. C.M. Popplewell, pp. 21-28, 1963.

[Medina-Mora 1982]

Raúl Medina-Mora, David S. Notkin and Robert J. Ellison, "ALOE Users' and Implementors' Guide (Second Edition)", in *Nico Habermann et al., The Second Compendium of Gandalf Documentation*, Carnegie-Mellon University, Pittsburgh (Penn.), 1982.

[Mendelson 1964]

E. Mendelson, *Introduction to Mathematical Logic*, D. Van Nostrand, New York, 1964.

[Meyer 1978]

Bertrand Meyer and Claude Baudoin, *Méthodes de Programmation*, Eyrolles, Paris, 1978. New edition, 1984.

[Meyer 1980]

Bertrand Meyer, "A Basis for the Constructive Approach to Programming", in *Information Processing 80 (Proceedings of the IFIP World Computer Congress, Tokyo, Japan, October 6-9, 1980)*, ed. S. H. Lavington, pp. 293-298, North-Holland Publishing Company, Amsterdam, 1980.

[Meyer 1985a]

Bertrand Meyer, "On Formalism in Specifications", *IEEE Software*, vol. 3, no. 1, pp. 6-25, January 1985.

[Meyer1985b]

Bertrand Meyer, Jean-Marc Nerson and Soon Hae Ko, "Showing Programs on a Screen", *Science of Computer Programming*, vol. 5, no. 2, pp. 111-142, 1985.

[Meyer 1986a]

Bertrand Meyer, "Cépage: A Software Design Tool", *Computer Language*, vol. 3, no. 9, pp. 43-53, September 1986.

[Meyer1986b]

Bertrand Meyer, "LDL: A Language Description Language", Technical Report TR-CE-8/LD, Interactive Software Engineering Inc., Santa Barbara (Calif.), 1986.

[Meyer 1988a]

Bertrand Meyer, "Programming as Contracting", Technical Report TR-EI-12/CO, Interactive Software Engineering, Santa Barbara (Calif.), 1988.

[Meyer1988b]

Bertrand Meyer, *Object-Oriented Software Construction*, Prentice-Hall, 1988.

[Meyer 1990]
   Bertrand Meyer, "Sequential and Concurrent Object-Oriented Programming", in *TOOLS 2 (Technology of Object-Oriented Languages and Systems)*, Paris, June 1990.

[Milne 1976]
   Robert Milne and Cristopher Strachey, *A Theory of Programming Language Semantics*, Chapman and Hall Ltd., London, 1976.

[Ollongren 1974]
   A. Ollongren, *Definition of Programming Languages by Interpreting Automata*, Academic Press, London, 1974.

[Pagan 1981]
   Frank G. Pagan, *Formal Specification of Programming Languages: A Panoramic Primer*, Prentice-Hall, Englewood Cliffs (N.J.), 1981.

[Reps 1984]
   Thomas Reps, *Generating Language-Based Environments*, MIT Press, Cambridge (Mass.), May 1984.

[Schmidt 1986]
   David A. Schmidt, *Denotational Semantics – A Methodology for Language Development*, Allyn & Bacon, Boston (Mass.), 1986.

[Scott 1970]
   Dana S. Scott, "Outline of a Mathematical Theory of Computation", in *Proceedings of the Fourth Annual Princeton Conference on Information Science and Systems*, pp. 169-176, Princeton, 1970. Also Technical Monograph PRG-2, Programming Research Group, University of Oxford, 1970.

[Scott 1971]
   Dana S. Scott and Christopher Strachey, "Toward a Mathematical Semantics for Computer Languages", in *Proceedings of Symposium on Computers and Automata*, ed. J. Fox, pp. 19-46, Polytechnic Institute of Brooklyn Press, 1971. Also Technical Monograph PRG-6, Programming Research Group, University of Oxford, 1971.

[Scott 1972]
   Dana S. Scott, "Lattice Theory, Data Types and Semantics", in *New York University Symposium on Formal Semantics*, ed. Randall Rustin, pp. 64-106, Prentice-Hall, 1972.

[Spivey 1988]
   J. M. Spivey, *Understanding Z: A Specification Language and its Formal Semantics*, Cambridge University Press, 1988.

[Steel 1966]
   Tom B. (Ed.) Steel, *Formal Language Description Languages*, North-Holland Publishing Co., Amsterdam, 1966.

[Steele 1984]

Guy L. Steele, *Common Lisp*, Prentice-Hall, Englewood Cliffs (N.J.), 1984.

[Stoy 1977]

Joseph E. Stoy, *Denotational Semantics: The Scott-Strachey Approach to Programming Language Semantics*, MIT Press, Cambridge (Mass.), 1977.

[Strachey 1966]

Christopher Strachey, "Towards a Formal Semantics", in *Formal Language Description Languages for Computer Programming*, ed. Tom B. Steel Jr., pp. 198-220, North-Holland Publishing Co., Amsterdam, 1966.

[Strachey 1973]

Christopher Strachey, "The Varieties of Programming Languages", Technical Monograph PRG-10, Programming Research Group, University of Oxford, Oxford, 1973.

[Suppes 1972]

Patrick Suppes, *Axiomatic Set Theory*, Dover Publications Inc., New York, 1972.

[Suzuki 1982]

Norihisa Suzuki, "Analysis of Pointer 'Rotation'", *Communications of the ACM*, vol. 25, no. 5, pp. 330-335, May 1982.

[Tennent 1976]

Robert D. Tennent, "The Denotational Semantics of Programming Languages", *Communications of the ACM*, vol. 19, no. 8, pp. 437-453, 1976.

[Tennent 1977]

Robert D. Tennent, "Language Design Methods Based on Semantic Principles", *Acta Informatica*, vol. 8, pp. 97-112, 1977.

[Tennent 1981]

Robert D. Tennent, *Principles of Programming Languages*, Prentice-Hall International, Hemel Hempstead, 1981.

[Turner 1983]

David A. Turner, "Recursion Equations as a Programming Language", in *Functional Programming and its Applications* (eds. John Darlington, Peter Henderson and David Turner), Cambridge University Press, 1983.

[Turner 1985]

David A. Turner, "Functional Programs as Executable Specifications", in *Logic and Programming Languages,* Eds. C.A.R. Hoare and J.C. Shepherdson, pp. 29-54, Prentice-Hall International, Hemel Hempstead, 1985. (Proceedings of a meeting of the Royal Society of London.)

[van Wijngaarden 1966]

Aad van Wijngaarden, "Recursive Definition of Syntax and Semantics", in *Formal Language Description Languages for Computer Programming*, ed. Tom B. Steel Jr., pp. 13-24, North-Holland Publishing Co., Amsterdam, 1966.

[van Wijngaarden 1975]

Aad van Wijngaarden, B. J. Mailloux, J.E.L Peck, C.H.A. Koster, Michel Sintzoff, Charles H. Lindsey, Lambert G.L.T. Meertens and R.G. Fisker, "Revised Report on the Algorithmic Language Algol 68", *Acta Informatica*, vol. 5, pp. 1-236, 1975.

[Vuillemin 1976]

Jean Vuillemin, "Correct and Optimal Implementations of Recursion in a Simple Programming Language", *Journal of Computer and System Sciences*, vol. 9, pp. 332-354, 1976.

[Waite 1984]

William M. Waite and Gerhard Goos, *Compiler Construction*, Springer-Verlag, Berlin-New York, 1984.

[Wegner 1972]

Peter Wegner, "The Vienna Definition Language", *Computing Surveys*, vol. 4, no. 1, pp. 5-63, 1972.

[Welsh 1977]

Jim Welsh, W. Sneeringer and C.A.R. Hoare, "Ambiguities and Insecurities in Pascal", *Software, Practice and Experience*, vol. 7, pp. 685-696, 1977.

Index

The first few entries of this index are the special symbols of the Metanot notation, each with a brief mention of its meaning.

Program	≜	decpart: Declaration_list; body: Instruction
Declaration_list	≜	Declaration*
Declaration	≜	v: Variable; t: Type
Type	≜	Boolean_type | Integer_type
Instruction	≜	Skip | Assignment | Compound |
		Conditional | Loop
Assignment	≜	target: Variable; source: Expression
Compound	≜	Instruction*
Conditional	≜	thenbranch, elsebranch: Instruction;
		test: Expression
Loop	≜	body: Instruction; test: Expression
Expression	≜	Constant | Variable | Binary
Constant	≜	Integer_constant | Boolean_constant
Binary	≜	term1, term2: Expression; op: Operator
Operator	≜	Boolean_op | Relational_op | Arithmetic_op
Boolean_op	≜	And | Or | Nand | Nor | Xor
Relational_op	≜	Lt | Le | Eq | Ne | Ge | Gt
Arithmetic_op	≜	Plus | Minus | Times | Div
Boolean_constant	≜	value: **B**
Integer_constant	≜	value: **Z**
Variable	≜	id: **S**

The abstract grammar of Graal
(chapters 3 and 6 to 10)